ALSO BY ALVIN M. JOSEPHY, JR.

The Patriot Chiefs: A Chronicle of American Indian Resistance
The Nez Perce Indians and the Opening of the Northwest
The Indian Heritage of America
Red Power
The Long and the Short and the Tall
The Artist Was a Young Man
Black Hills—White Sky
On the Hill
Now That the Buffalo's Gone
The Civil War in the American West
America in 1492 (editor)
500 Nations: A History of North American Indians

A WALK TOWARD OREGON

A WALK
TOWARD
OREGON

A MEMOIR BY

Alvin M. Josephy, Jr.

ALFRED A. KNOPF

NEW YORK

2000

THIS IS A BORZOI BOOK
PUBLISHED BY ALFRED A. KNOPF

www.randomhouse.com

Grateful acknowledgment is made to the Estate of Richard Nixon for permission to reprint a letter from President Nixon to Alvin M. Josephy, Jr.

Knopf, Borzoi Books, and the colophon are registered
trademarks of Random House, Inc.

Library of Congress Cataloging-in-Publication Data
Josephy, Alvin M., [date]
A walk toward Oregon: a memoir / by Alvin M. Josephy, Jr. — 1st ed.
p. cm.
ISBN 0-375-40910-6
1. Josephy, Alvin M., 1915–   . 2. Journalists—United States
Biography. 3. Historians—United States Biography. 4. New York
(N.Y.)—Social life and customs—20th century. I. Title.
PN4874.J72A3 2000
070′.92—dc21
[B]   99-31384   CIP

Manufactured in the United States of America
First Edition

For Betty, Allison, Diane, Kathy, Alvin, and Joe—

all of whom helped me write this book

Eastward I go only by force; but westward I go free. The future lies that way to me, and the earth seems more unexhausted and richer on that side. . . . It is hard for me to believe that I shall find fair landscapes or sufficient wildness and freedom behind the eastern horizon. . . . I should not lay so much stress on this fact if I did not believe that something like this is the prevailing tendency of my countrymen. I must walk toward Oregon, and not toward Europe.

HENRY DAVID THOREAU
Walking, 1862

CONTENTS

FOREWORD

Several years ago, while I was attending a meeting in Washington, D.C., I received a message to call our youngest daughter, Kathy, who was living on our ranch in Oregon. Apparently something terrible had happened there. "She sounded a little hysterical," the person who gave me the message said.

I had a plane to catch back to New York, but I tried unsuccessfully to call Kathy before I left for the airport. There was no answer. On the way to the airport, my mind filled with speculation about her and about our ranch, and at the airport I tried again to call her, but again there was no answer.

On the plane, a strange thing happened. In recent months, I had been thinking about the ranch and about maybe selling it, and facing up to that prospect from time to time had got me thinking about my whole life and about the ranch as the culmination of that life. Now, my wondering during the flight to New York about what had happened to Kathy flooded my mind with memories. By the time I reached home and had finally gotten her on the phone and learned what had occurred, I had decided that I had a book to write, one that would explain the meaning of the ranch to my otherwise very full life. Beginning with as far back as my memory took me, this is that book.

A.M.J., Jr.

I ✖ THE COCOON

I   ✖   THE LITTLE RED LIGHTHOUSE

During the early 1920s, my brother, Warren, and I would sometimes be taken to play with friends around a little red lighthouse that stood (and at the present writing, still stands) on the Hudson River shore of upper Manhattan Island. It was a magical spot of sand, rocks, trees, and weeds, all bathed by the gently lapping tidal swells of the river's edge and smelling pungently of the sea and of spilled oil. The small size of the lighthouse, around whose base we raced, playing hide-and-seek and other games, gave it the scale of belonging to us as a part of our child's world, luring to our playground the gulls that wheeled and screeched above our heads and seeming to watch, with the glare of its guardian light, the occasional tankers and cargo ships that glided silently by on their way up or down the river.

At the time, we lived above the Hudson and the lighthouse in northern Manhattan's Washington Heights, having moved there into the third floor of a relatively new apartment building in the winter of 1918–19. Before that, we had lived in our own private homes in suburbs of New York City, first in Woodmere, on Long Island's southern shore, where I had been born in mid-May 1915, and then for a little more than a year completely on the other side of New York, in Westfield, New Jersey. Our new apartment home in Manhattan was on the fringe of undeveloped, rural-like parkland that descended all the way to the lighthouse and the river's edge and embraced both the site of the Revolutionary War's Fort Washington and an area in which a well-known American sculptor, George Grey Barnard, was busy helping to build a resplendent uptown museum of medieval art known as the Cloisters.

The river was the mystical border of my world, and I loved to be taken there by my mother or by a maid or a daughter of one of our neighbors whom my mother paid to look after Warren and me. From the little light-house, I could gaze westward across the water to the basalt walls of the Palisades. Like fluted ramparts protecting mysterious heights, they became compelling objects of my wonder, and I imagined that beyond the cliffs the wooded highland was inhabited by Rain-in-the-Face and other war-whooping Indians in paint and feathers, and by wolves and grizzly bears that chased people up trees, by little men in big hats who made thunder by rolling balls with Rip Van Winkle, and by all sorts of other wild and adventurous peoples and goings-on of the kind that my father made come alive in suspenseful stories that he told to my brother and me. Even my viewing site at the little lighthouse on my safe side of the Hudson River became a place of enchantment, and at night, as I lay in the darkness of our bedroom in the apartment building, waiting to fall asleep, I imagined myself miraculously crossing the river from the lighthouse to the New Jersey shore and encountering exciting perils and adventures in a wilderness of forests and mountains on top of the cliffs.

Meanwhile, my real world was one of middle-class security on Manhattan Island. The fount of the security was my mother's father, an imperious-looking man of erudition and authority named Samuel Knopf, who, despite my father's ability to provide for us, gave my mother a large monthly allowance that permitted a lot of major and minor extravagances and let us live not only comfortably but well in a seven-room apartment with tall ceilings, a playroom for Warren and me, a living room with a working fireplace, and one or two full-time servants who had their own bedroom and bath off the kitchen and slept in.

S.K., as my grandfather was known to friends, had his hands in a number of different businesses, including banking, real estate, financial consulting, and advertising. He was also the chief source of start-up and occasional cash-flow funds for the book publishing firm of his son, my mother's older brother, Alfred A. Knopf, and served as business manager of the celebrated green-covered magazine of the 1920s the *American Mercury*, which Alfred published and H. L. Mencken and George Jean Nathan edited.

I loved my grandfather very deeply and was proud of him and proud to be linked with him in front of the important people whom he knew. In the 1920s, he was in his sixties, a conservative, meticulously groomed and dressed man who carried a silver-headed cane, wore spats and a high silk hat on Sundays, and owned a top-heavy-looking Rolls-Royce sedan driven by a uniformed French chauffeur named Paul, who could scarcely speak a word of understandable English but dressed colorfully in leather puttees and a visored cap which he set at a rakish angle that made him look like a

A romp with my grandfather, S.K., whom I looked up to and who influenced me greatly during my growing-up years. This snapshot was probably made at our home in Westfield, New Jersey, about 1918, when I was three.

surviving aviation ace from the Great War.

My grandfather, in turn, looked like a squarely built, no-nonsense Prussian, although he had been born in a kicked-around part of Eastern Europe that sometimes belonged to Poland and sometimes to Russia. He had gotten out of there early, however, and as a little boy in the 1860s, he had accompanied his family first to England and then to the United States, where he was raised in New York and Texas. Somehow, he received a good education, became well read and widely traveled in the South and Midwest as a drummer, or salesman, and by the 1890s was a cultured and successful businessman in Cincinnati, where my mother was born. Soon afterward, the family moved to a house on a wooded hill above the Hudson River near 181st Street in New York City, just about where the George Washington Bridge was built in later years. My mother told me that Alfred had had a pet monkey there when she was a little girl, but she didn't know what had happened to it and didn't care to know. When I was ten, the house with a long white porch overlooking the river was still there, but it was demolished during the building of the bridge.

My grandfather doted on and spoiled my mother, his only daughter, whom he had named Sophia for some long-forgotten actress he had admired. During my mother's youth, he gave her everything she wanted, and she kind of expected it to go on forever. In her school days, she had been full of fun and had relished unabashedly her teenage reputation as a flirt. My father was eight years older than she, and on their first meeting, when they had been playing tennis on adjoining courts and she had continued to disrupt his game by running onto his court to retrieve a ball, he had raised her dander by calling her a brat. A little while later, they had a chance meeting in a restaurant, where she decided she would make him change his mind about her. She succeeded, and in April 1914 they were married in a large formal wedding at the St. Regis Hotel in New York City and went off on a honeymoon at Hot Springs, Arkansas, and then into the suburban house in Woodmere.

My mother in a hat she may have worn before I was born, because I don't remember it.

In the 1920s, my mother was still young, dark-eyed, and pretty, given to wearing sporty clothes, playing tennis, and dancing, giving and going to Jazz Age parties, and enjoying life as if she were without a care. A lot of it was deceptive, for she ran our home (and later a business) efficiently and effectively, was emotional and capable of explosions of temper, and enfolded Warren and me with motherly love and attention that, along with a wonderful comradeship with our father, reinforced our sense of security and built up our self-confidence.

As his first grandchild, I became, like my mother, adored by my grandfather. We were pals, and it came to me as a shock years later to learn that his stern and demanding looks and manner had put off a lot of people and even frightened them. Not me. He parted his hair in the middle, wore pince-nez glasses and a rich mustache with somewhat tapered ends, and it was true that at times he could look awfully fierce, especially when he clenched a long cigar between his front teeth and glowered at you. But all I saw and felt was a deep, protective love and kindness in him that stemmed from some sort of an identification with me, as if he wanted me to grow up to be like him, to adopt his enthusiasms and interests, and, in truth, be his heir, carry on, as it were, his own life after he was gone. It was his intention, he and my mother conveyed to me on numerous occasions, that when I finished college, I would join Alfred's firm and become a publisher. For as long as I could remember, I took that as a given and assumed, like a fairy-tale prince betrothed by his parents at the age of six months to some remote princess, that my career had been settled for me and that there would be nothing ever that I could do about it.

In preparation for that destiny, perhaps, my grandfather spoke to me seriously again and again, as if I were an adult and he a teacher, counsel-

S.K. with his three grandsons—my brother, Warren (right), two years younger than myself, our cousin, Alfred A. Knopf, Jr., or Pat (center), a year younger than Warren; and me, the senior of the trio.

ing me with bits of wisdom and advice that he hoped I would never forget—on such matters, for instance, as the value of a person's character ("one's most important possession—never stain it"), integrity, generosity, money ("Money should be used defensively, not offensively"), courage, the importance of the best education possible, and the ability to give leadership and make wise decisions and judgments. In later years, I would hear American Indian elders and holy people discuss some of these same values and virtues as those of their own most respected civil and spiritual leaders, and at such moments I could hear my grandfather's voice in theirs.

At the same time, though, my grandfather would occasionally come to with a start, as if realizing that I was still in knickerbockers in elementary school, more interested in major-league batting averages and in trading picture cards than in molding my character for a far-distant future, and he would take off his pince-nez glasses from the bridge of his nose and sing to me one of his favorite moralistic songs in a loud, rollicking voice, trusting that I would prefer to get the message in an entertaining way:

> *"Oh, there was an old man and he had a wooden leg;*
> *He had no tobaccy, no tobaccy could he beg;*
> *He blew in his nickels and he blew in his rocks,*
> *And he never had tobaccy in his old tobaccy box.*
> *There was another old man as sly as a fox.*
> *He saved up his nickels and he piled up his rocks,*
> *And he always had tobaccy in his old tobaccy box.*
> *Said man number one, 'Will you give me a chew?'*
> *Says man number two, 'I'll be hanged if I do.*

Go save up your money and go save up your rocks,
And you'll always have tobaccy in your old tobaccy box.' "

My grandmother took some of my grandfather's advice in her own way and did such things as maintaining a closet in her bedroom stocked "for a rainy day" with hundreds of dollars' worth of potted meats, jams, and other luxury foods from all over the world. It didn't seem to me that she needed much food, because she was a heavily built woman with tiny feet and an enormous bust that protruded so far out ahead of her that she looked as if the weight would topple her over onto her face at any moment. My grandfather spoiled her, as he did my mother, and she usually appeared in public in expensive Cartier, Tiffany, and Dreicer jewelry and fashionable lacy clothes that were wrapped so tightly around her throat and upper body that I wondered how she could breathe. She was a very sweet and kindly grandmother, who pinched my cheeks, showered me with love and little presents, and generally meant well, but she also tended at times to be a little addlepated. In fact, my father said she was the stupidest woman he had ever known, and in hindsight he wasn't far off the mark. She could get off some real doozies. During World War II, when somebody told her that my brother, Warren, had landed as an officer with the First Army at Normandy, she said, "Oh, how nice. It's so lovely in France this time of the year." In addition, she had been born and raised in Brooklyn in a family of genuine Brooklyn characters (her father, known as Harris the Hatter, had almost been killed trying to be the first man to walk across the Brooklyn Bridge by doing it on a construction catwalk long before the bridge was finished), and she had an authentic Brooklyn accent that had her pronouncing words like *oil* as "earl" and *earl* as "oil."

My father, though nothing like my grandfather, was a great guy too, a real dad and an understanding companion to Warren and me, but as I realized more fully when I was much older, life hadn't been altogether a happy journey for him, although he never showed it. He had been born on West 70th Street in New York City in 1887 and, after graduating from Cornell University in 1908, had achieved a long-held ambition and become a mechanical engineer. But that career, which he loved and which promised him the excitement of a life of travel and challenges working on skyscrapers, public buildings, and other construction projects in different parts of the world, had been suddenly aborted in 1918, a few years after I was born, when his father, a commission merchant, or broker, in the dressed-poultry business in New York, was killed by a streetcar.

At the request of my father's mother, a strong-willed, matriarchal type from Bridgeport, Connecticut, who, with her husband, had drilled a

On a Cape Cod beach with Warren (right) and our dad about 1921, when I was six and we modest men still wore bathing-suit tops.

martial-like obedience into their children, my father joined his older brother in taking over and running their father's poultry business, which was conducted from about 3 a.m. to 3 p.m., five days a week, on the noisy cobblestone streets of New York's wholesale meat and poultry market district on West 14th Street, near the New York Central's freight yards and the steamship piers on the Hudson River. It was a grueling and, to my father, a humdrum and unrewarding life of receiving daily incoming refrigerated railroad boxcars full of barrels and crates of frozen dressed turkeys, chickens, geese, and ducks from Iowan and other western shippers and transshipping them in trucks to East Coast ocean liners, hotels, fancy meat markets, and other large buyers. Although my father disliked the business, it meant income for his mother and our family, and once saddled with it, he stuck to it dutifully for the rest of his working life, only giving it up and retiring after his mother died in 1946, when he was too old to start life over again.

As a young man, he had been handsome and thin, but in his thirties he was already becoming heavyset. He still chain-smoked a collection of pipes throughout the day, a habit he had begun at Cornell, played a good game of golf with mashies, niblicks, and other clubs he had used as a member of the Cornell golf team, strummed "By the Light of the Silvery Moon" and other old tunes on a mandolin, and, along with my mother, played championship bridge with Oswald Jacoby, the Culbertsons, and other celebrated players of the day. In addition, despite his work's demanding hours and its rough physical calls on his stamina, as well as the frustrations he must have felt at not having been able to return to his profession, he possessed a tremendous reservoir of good humor and wit and was extraordinarily warm and kind to his family and friends.

To Warren and me, he was also a powerful storyteller. He would lie soaking among suds in the bathtub on weekend mornings, or at four or five o'clock on weekday afternoons after he had come home from work, and tell us wonderful stories of pirates and Indians and American heroes, of glory and valor and exploration and travel. He loved history and adventure, and he had a great gift for bringing alive in our youthful imaginations vivid and exciting scenes of patriotic deeds done by heroic men and women. We learned about Nathan Hale, the colonists' brave stand at Bunker Hill, and the taking of Fort Ticonderoga in the Revolution, about the Alamo, the Pony Express, Teddy Roosevelt's Rough Riders at San Juan Hill, and Lewis and Clark far, far out west, way beyond the Hudson River, in a strange and wonderful place called Oregon. There, my father told us, his father had once owned a piece of property that probably was a ranch with cowboys and cattle and rustlers, but that, as far as he knew, no one in the family had ever visited it. The place, he said disappointingly, had been sold after his father died.

That little piece of information intrigued me, and I kept thinking about it for several days. A ranch with cowboys and cattle rustlers. Probably Indians too. Why had they let it go, that place that could have been incredibly exciting for our own family to go to? My father told us other stories about Oregon, about the pioneer people on the Oregon Trail, and about the dramatic sixty-six-day race of the battleship *Oregon* from the West Coast around Cape Horn to help defeat the Spanish fleet in 1898. The name "Oregon," evoking images of sacrifice and romantic adventure, became planted in my head as that of some fantastic section of our country, still part of the old Wild West and offering to bold and daring people who went there plenty of thrills and excitement.

Years later, it occurred to me that my father's fabulous storytelling and love of history compensated him in a way for the absence of adventure and travel in his own life. When he was ten years old, he had gone to Europe to visit some German relatives of his father and had accompanied a group of German cousins on an adventure-packed trip to the ice fields of Spitsbergen in the Arctic Ocean north of Norway. The German cousins were quite military-minded, and my father was being schooled at an American military academy at the time, and they all got on well together. The trip apparently fueled my father's appetite for more trips to far-off, adventurous places, but I never heard that he went anyplace else exciting except to battlefields of the American Revolution and the Civil War.

I don't know what my father's feelings were when World War I broke out. Later, he told Warren and me that all five of his German cousins had been uhlans, or cavalry scouts, in the German army that invaded Belgium and that all five had been killed in the first weeks of the war, which, he assured us, had served them right for starting the war and committing atrocities in Belgium. Despite his earlier ties to his father's German relatives, they dissolved completely during the war, and Warren and I grew up only dimly aware of the existence of any relatives on the European continent. At the same time, my father, who was thirty in 1917 and was taking care of our family, never got into the war, so he didn't even get to Europe again in his life.

Both my father and mother were avid readers and kept the shelves in our hallway and in a couple of our rooms full of recently published books, as well as many that each of them had possessed since before their marriage. As I grew older, I feasted on this treasure that ranged through all the byways of literature, from Theodore Roosevelt's *The Winning of the West* and a Professor Ridpath's luridly illustrated late-nineteenth-century history of the races of mankind to the latest works of Sinclair Lewis and D. H. Lawrence. At Christmas and on other occasions, Warren and I were given our own books, ones deemed appropriate for our age. On our birthdays, for instance, our Uncle Alfred, the publisher, always sent us Knopf books. Sometimes they were great—primly proper and beautifully illustrated children's volumes written by some English author like Walter de La Mare—but sometimes Alfred or his secretary fouled up, and we would receive a copy of a thick and densely written economic treatise by a German professor or some other adult book that the Knopf firm had published in a previous year and that hadn't sold well and was eating up space in a warehouse. Inside the book would be a printed card: "With the compliments of Alfred A. Knopf. I thought you would find this book interesting."

Alfred and his wife and publishing partner, our Aunt Blanche, were always quite formal and stand-offish, even within the family. Blanche, who seemed to have an aversion to food, was bone-thin, delicate, and frail, and frequently had a warm, friendly smile on her face. But she could turn suddenly cold, tart, and contemptuous-looking, as if she was barely tolerating our presence. Nevertheless, she was admired and even beloved by many of the greatest writers in the world, who considered her a brilliant editor and publisher. Alfred, who was at least her equal as an editor and publisher, was more shy and reserved than she, but he too could kick up a violent storm, especially in arguments with Blanche, which were frequent. In addition, Alfred, who had a black mustache and was supposed to resemble King Alfonso XIII, the handsome reigning monarch of Spain, often covered his shyness and fear of someone hurting him by hurting the other person first, usually with an outrageous and unexpectedly aggressive verbal assault that insulted and stunned his victim. On many occasions, he refused to wait for dinner guests who arrived a minute or more late, and when they did arrive and were ushered into the dining room, he kept his seat and gave them a good tongue-lashing, humiliating them in front of the other guests. Such episodes, which often seemed as if Alfred was copying the ruthless example of his good friend H. L. Mencken, made him many enemies.

Alfred and Blanche had an only child, Alfred, Jr., who was three years younger than I and whom everyone called Pat. My mother said that his parents treated him formally, like an heir rather than a son. He had a French governess with big teeth and huge exposed gums that made her look like she was always grinning, but he had few, if any, friends, and he was often left alone with the governess by Alfred and Blanche. My mother felt sorry for him and said he needed the love of a family, and she had him come over and play with Warren and me and even spend nights with us. From as far back as I can remember, Warren and he didn't get on too well and used to argue and fight over all kinds of little things. At night, when we had to push our twin beds together to make room for Pat to sleep in the middle, Warren, who was two years younger than I and only a year older than Pat, would pull the beds a little apart when no one was looking, and in the night Pat would fall through. The feuding went on for years. During World War II, Pat was a flying officer with American bombers in Europe, and Warren's artillery outfit got bombed by mistake by our own planes somewhere in France. The first time Warren and I got together with Pat after the war, there was a terrible scene, in which Warren accused Pat of having been the one who flew over his outfit and deliberately dropped bombs on him.

At times, especially when he was alone with us children, Alfred could seem really friendly and outgoing, as if he knew that with us he was in complete command and could let down his guard. He was a devotee of classical music and a friend of many conductors and concert musicians, and he felt that we should be dunked in cultural waters and exposed to good music and the other arts as soon as we were old enough to behave ourselves in public. When he felt that we had at last reached that age, he began taking Pat, Warren, and me downtown on Saturday mornings to Walter Damrosch's children's concerts at Carnegie Hall on 57th Street, and during holidays to performances of *H.M.S. Pinafore* or other Gilbert and Sullivan operettas, or to a ballet or a special cultural event for children.

The Dr. Damrosch concerts were usually boring, and so like a punishment that we had to be dragooned and bribed with the promise of a post-concert ice-cream-parlor visit to agree to go to them pleasantly. But other events could be fun. At one time, one of my favorite adventure books was Hugh Lofting's *The Story of Dr. Dolittle*, and I went almost sleepless with excitement for three nights when I was told that Alfred was taking us to a small private reading for children by the man who had written the adventures of the wonderful doctor from Puddleby-on-the-Marsh and all his bird and animal friends, with whom he could converse, including Polynesia, the parrot, and the strange two-headed beast, the Pushmi-Pullyu.

The reading, an enthralling afternoon in a downtown office where about twenty of us—each one related, I suppose, to somebody in the publishing business—sat cross-legged at Mr. Lofting's feet while he entertained us and showed us drawings from his books, stamped in my mind, more firmly than ever, a vivid image of what his fictional chubby, snub-nosed doctor looked like. A few weeks later, my mother took me downtown again, and we stopped in to see my grandfather in the office he maintained at the Knopf firm. As a receptionist showed us in, my grandfather rose to greet us, and I saw another man—with a round, chubby face and what seemed to be a smallish nose and almost no neck, and who had his hair parted in the middle and slicked down against the top of his head—leaning back in one of the chairs at a long conference table in the room, puffing on a cigar and looking at us with friendly, inquiring eyes. I was suddenly stricken with fright. Before I could blurt out to my mother, "It's Doctor Dolittle!" the man rose politely, and my grandfather said, "Henry, you know my daughter—and this is my grandson." The next instant, he was introducing me to the famous editor of the *American Mercury*, H. L. Mencken.

Mencken's name meant nothing to me at the time. Later, I learned that he was also a stockholder in the firm and a deeply committed editorial and publishing consultant to Alfred and Blanche. Each month he came up by train from Baltimore, where he filled somewhat the same role as a stockholder in, and a columnist for, the *Sun* newspapers. While he was in New York, he made his headquarters in the Knopf offices, meeting authors, planning and overseeing the next issues of his magazine, and visiting with Alfred and Blanche, as well as with my grandfather, the business manager of the *Mercury*, with whose financial advice he usually disagreed and whose mild editorial proposals he spurned as suicidal. For a time after I first met Mencken, I kept thinking of him as Dr. Dolittle. But over the years, I saw him increasingly at my grandfather's office, and eventually, at a most critical moment, he would play an important role in my life.

During my growing-up years, I was rarely invited into the offices of Alfred or Blanche, but my grandfather, whose spacious quarters were as big as our living room at home and included a private tiled bathroom and a liquor closet, always welcomed our visits and introduced us to any authors or publishing people who happened to be meeting with him. One of those about whom my grandfather talked a lot in very warm terms, and whom I eventually met, was the Nebraska author Willa Cather, whom Alfred published. When she was in New York, she spent much of her time in the Knopf offices and with S.K., whom she seemed to admire and from whom she sought advice and counsel on all sorts of subjects. Mencken did not particularly like Cather, whom he called derisively "a one hundred percent American," and in 1931, while Prohibition was still in effect, he noted in his diary that she had asked S.K. to get her a bottle of gin and one of brandy because she was giving a party and didn't know any bootleggers. My grandfather, according to Mencken, sent her two bottles out of his own supply.

Our trips downtown from Washington Heights to doctors, dentists, department stores, and my grandfather's office were generally made on the open-air top deck of a Fifth Avenue bus that wended its way along Riverside Drive, with its views of the Palisades and the busy movements of tugboats, ferries, and day liners on the river, and were always wondrous adventures. Boarding in uptown Manhattan, near the start of the bus's run, Warren and I were usually able to clamber up the curving outside steps at the rear of the bus ahead of adults and rush forward to claim one of the front seats, which gave us a windswept but exciting grandstand view of all that we passed.

Sometime around 1923, to shorten my father's long daily commute to work, we left Washington Heights and moved down to another large apartment on West 92d Street between West End Avenue and Riverside Drive. In our new location, my trips to the little red lighthouse ended, but a host of new interests, including the busy routine of public school classes and weekend and afternoon play in the streets, took over my life. For a while, the New York City public school I attended on Amsterdam Avenue near our new address was coed. But after the first half of the fourth grade, we boys in that school were transferred to P.S. 166, an all-boys school on West 89th Street, and with the exception of a few women teachers, my education from then on was in an all-male setting. Discipline meant something in those days, and my memories are full of male teachers at P.S. 166 throwing blackboard erasers at us, sneaking up behind us and rapping us sharply over the head with their long wooden pointers, punishing us by making us go in the clothes closet or walk around the perimeter of the room till the dismissal bell rang and ended the class, or, if we were really a problem, ordering us to sit for a week at the rear of the room with the two or three "exiles" in the class. These students usually included the son of a newly arrived immigrant family who couldn't speak English or the class's only African-American, whom the hard-boiled teachers referred to cruelly as "the slow learners" or "the mental deficients."

The New York public schools at the time were looked on as melting pots of children from different ethnic backgrounds, and at recess time, when we played and fought in the school's outdoor courtyard, or after school, when we stopped in a candy store or wrestled out in the streets on our way home, the Irish, Italian, Jewish, Scandinavian, Polish, German, English, "Pure American," and other kids had little hesitation in flinging at each other the filthiest and most insulting ethnic names they could think of. Nobody ever seemed to feel bad or brood about it; it was just a part of life—like the Irish, Italian, Hebrew, and "coon" joke books that some kids bought at the candy store for a nickel and guffawed over. At the same time, we had a lot of fistfights, with black eyes and bloody noses, over such things as bullying and cheating or snitching on one another. The worst mess that I got into was with a nasty little guy who stole the favorite shooter I used in games of marbles and dared me to try to get it back. I took up the dare, and after he hit me in the mouth and bit my ear, I landed him on the ground and pummeled him blindly while everyone stood around and cheered. After a while, he gave up and returned my marble, and we both went home with torn clothes and bloody faces.

Despite such surface divisions, P.S. 166 did a good job on the whole of welding us all together by instilling among us a strong common bond of patriotism for America. At many times during the year, particularly before holidays, they would push back the movable walls of all the classrooms on tracks in the floor so that suddenly all of the classes were together, facing forward in a single large assembly. We would pledge allegiance to the American flag; the principal, with no thought of a constitutional church-state problem, would read us a lesson from the Bible; and the music-appreciation teacher, standing at an upright piano in the front, would lead us in singing something patriotic like "Tenting Tonight" or "When Johnny Comes Marching Home Again, Hurrah! Hurrah!" Then we would get a lecture, or some kind of a more interesting program that included turning off the lights, pulling down the large window shades, and lowering a screen for the projection of slides or even for a special movie that was relevant to the coming holiday. When the lights went back on again, some kid would always be caught in the middle of punching the kid next to him in the shoulder. The culprit would be yanked out of his seat by the teacher and stood against the teacher's desk for punishment, the program would come to an end, and the movable walls would be pushed back into place to enclose each class again.

Not all holidays gave us full days off from school. On the birthday of the recently deceased Theodore Roosevelt, who among most Americans was still right up there with Washington, Jefferson, and Lincoln as one of the four greatest presidents in our history, we had a patriotic assembly in the morning and then got the afternoon off. The same was true of Armistice Day, when we had an assembly at a quarter to eleven in the morning of November 11, and at eleven minutes after eleven (the exact time when the armistice took effect in 1918 and ended the First World War), we stood in silence for a moment while the music teacher played a recording of "Taps" on a windup Victrola. Then we went home for the rest of the day. Other so-called holidays were cheats; we never got off at all. I remember particularly Audubon Day, when we had to buy bird-identification cards and listen every year to the story of how a homing pigeon named Cher Ami carried a message that saved the Lost Battalion in the recent war in France, and Arbor Day, when we donated pennies for trees and were told how important it was for everybody to plant trees, which seemed a little stupid to us when we had no idea how to get a tree or where to plant it.

Outside of Christmas, my favorite real, full-day holiday was Decoration, or Memorial, Day, which came on May 30, a few weeks before we got out of school for summer vacation. On that day each year, New York put on what had to be the grandest, longest, and most stirring military parade in the country. Composed of veterans of all of our wars as far back as the Civil War, including British, French, Belgian, Italian, Polish, White Russian, and other veterans of our allies in World War I, as well as West Point cadets and marching units and bands of every branch of America's military service, the parade came up Riverside Drive for speeches and the laying of wreaths at the marble Grecian-style Soldiers' and Sailors' Monument at 89th Street and then proceeded on through 92d Street, right under our windows and past our apartment building, to a nearby headquarters of the Union Civil War veterans' organization, the Grand Army of the Republic.

It was a thrilling spectacle, and going downstairs to watch it more closely from the sidewalk, Warren and I stood with our father for what seemed to be hours as he brought history excitingly alive to us, describing what we were seeing. There were still long ranks of old veterans of the Civil War, proudly marching, hobbling along, or riding in open cars, waving to the cheering crowds while bands ahead and behind them played "Marching Through Georgia" and "The Battle Hymn of the Republic." A few of the old men wore the short blue jackets and red baggy pants of Zouaves, who, our father explained, had held the line at Gettysburg, and others were in jaunty little blue forage caps and bemedaled uniforms of units that had fought with General Grant at Spotsylvania and the Wilderness. Behind them were veterans of the Indian wars who had fought the Sioux and Apaches in the West, and sailors and Rough Riders from the Spanish-American War, some of the latter on prancing horses and others on foot in broad-brimmed western hats and blue, open-necked shirts and brown riding pants, with musicians playing "There'll Be a Hot Time in the Old Town Tonight," and then long columns of American Legionnaires and other veterans of the Great World War, with big brass bands playing "Over There" and battle streamers hanging from their flags, and some of them wearing their helmets and tight-fitting khaki uniforms from the war and riding atop rumbling tanks and huge, roaring, self-propelled cannons. The parade went on and on, with Allies in their own national uniforms, who had fought the German Kaiser with us in the Great War— and then the trim lines of West Point cadets in tall hats and gray and white uniforms and Marines and sailors and unit after unit of the regular army, some marching and some on horseback. It was a glorious event, and for days after it was over, it made me feel connected to it and important simply because it had come through the street on which we lived.

At the same time, the parties and presents and general excitement of the weeks around Thanksgiving and Christmas and New Year's were hard to beat as holidays. Every Thanksgiving, my parents took Warren and me to see the Cornell-Pennsylvania football game, played either in Philadelphia or New York, and bundled up in blankets to our noses against the usually freezing weather, we waved Cornell pennants and cheered for my father's alma mater and wished that the game would hurry up and be over so that we could get home to the big fat turkey dinner that was waiting for us. My father was a great fan of intercollegiate football, and almost every weekend from the end of September to December, he got box seats and, accompanied by some of his friends, took us to see Notre Dame, the Army, Stanford, and other major teams play at the Polo Grounds or the Yankee Stadium. But none of the games were as important to him as the annual Cornell-Penn "turkey day" meeting, and as if we had gone to his college ourselves, Warren and I yelled and beat each other happily when Cornell scored, and after the game was over, we stood by our father's side in the stands and grasped his hand and sang with him the Cornell anthem, "Far Above Cayuga's Waters."

Then on the next day, right after Thanksgiving, came a pre-Christmas visit to F. A. O. Schwarz's wonderland toy store on Fifth Avenue about 30th Street, and with it the joyous freedom to run loose with other kids all over the store, watching the Lionel electric trains roar out of tunnels, playing with Punch and Judy puppets and magic sets, and picking out things we hoped to get for Christmas. On Christmas Eve, my parents were up half the night, wrestling into our playroom, from hiding places in their bedroom closet, the maid's room, the dumbwaiter in the kitchen, and the building's back stairway, a ceiling-high tree that had been delivered that afternoon and boxes of toys that had come from Schwarz's and other stores during the previous weeks. When we still believed in Santa Claus, my father ensured that we would not sneak into our playroom in the middle of the night, after he and our mother had gone to sleep, by warning us earlier as we had climbed into our own beds that Santa Claus always left behind a pack of weasels to guard until morning whatever presents he delivered.

In the morning, my father then armed himself with a broom or the kitchen mop and while Warren and I waited bug-eyed and impatiently down the hall in our bathrobes, he let himself into the playroom and closed the door quickly behind him. Shouting fiercely, "Get out of here, you weasels! Go on! Scram! Beat it! Whack! There, that will teach you!" so that we could imagine a terrible battle going on, he hurriedly set in motion the electric trains and all the windup toys that moved or lit up or made a noise. Then he turned on the tree lights and a Christmas record on our Victrola, and with a triumphal "There goes the last of them!" he finally opened the door and ushered us into the magical room. In time, Warren and I got to enjoy the fearsome weasel ritual so much that for years after we knew that there was no Santa Claus, and no weasels, either, we prevailed on our father to continue chasing them out on Christmas morning before we went in to view the tree and receive our presents. In a way, it was like a desperate effort to hold on to something too precious to lose, the protections and security of our childhood, which for me continued to be linked strangely to the recurring memory of a long-ago lighthouse.

With the exception of Decoration Day, there was relatively little traffic on our 92d Street block, and it usually made a pretty safe playground. In our first years there, lots of tradesmen, including the Sheffield Farms milkman, the Knickerbocker Company iceman, and people selling potted geraniums and all kinds of other things, had horse-drawn wagons that made stops all along the block. It made it easy to hitch short rides, and one of my most vivid early memories of my adventures in the street was of hanging on to the back of an iceman's wagon that was moving slowly from one building to another; when the iceman spotted me and waved his tongs at me threateningly to get off, I jumped without looking onto another kid right behind the wagon who was hurrying along the street, carrying a bunch of newspapers and looking up at the apartment house windows and yelling, "Extra! President Harding Dead!" I didn't know anything about a President Harding and wouldn't have cared that he had died suddenly while returning from a trip to Alaska. The other kid and I went down in a tumble, but I helped him pick up his scattered papers, and instead of beating me up, all he did was rub his head, yell at me "You shit!," and continue down the street crying "Extra!"

Later that afternoon, I walked into our living room, where my mother and a lot of her friends were involved in three tables of contract bridge. I sidled over to her and in what I guess should have been a whisper in her ear, but came out as something of a loud shout to everyone in the room, asked, "Mother, what does *shit* mean?" In an age when even the word *cancer* uttered in public was shockingly impolite, my question was like a bursting bomb. Amid silence and then smothered laughs and confusion, my mother hustled me into my room and, giving me the clinical facts, told me to stay there and read a book till all of her company went home.

As I grew older, I became a real city kid, at first having the elevator man take me down on my own in the apartment house to play hopscotch and other games with the girls and younger boys on boards that we chalked outside on the sidewalks, jumping on one foot over the lines from box to box and shouting the same song the Rough Riders' band played in the Memorial Day parades:

> *"Spain! Spain! Spain!*
> *You ought to be ashamed!*
> *Why? Why? Why?*
> *For blowing up the Maine!*
> *One! Two! Three!*
> *And Cuba will be free!*
> *There'll be a hot time*
> *In the old town tonight!"*

Then as I matured, I moved from the girls' games to playing stickball and other forms of baseball out in the middle of the street with boys from the neighborhood, or throwing my Swiss army knife in games of mumblety-peg in patches of earth around trees lining the sidewalks on West End Avenue, or in winter coasting on my Flexible Flyer sled from Riverside Drive all the way down a fabulously long hill known to all the kids in the area as "the Gully," almost to the railroad tracks and the banks of the Hudson River.

Around me were unforgettable hallmarks of the city, such as immigrant Italian organ-grinders, one of them working alone with a monkey in a pill-box hat and a music box on a stick, or two of them with a big hurdy-gurdy box on baby-carriage wheels, the first man to crank out "O Sole Mio" and other melodies, the second to walk around and pick up the pennies and nickels that people threw to them out of the apartment windows. In later years, Mayor La Guardia would ban forever all organ-grinders from the streets of New York. Also doomed to future disappearance were itinerant hucksters who came into the apartment courtyards from lower Manhattan and screamed up announcements of what they were selling or buying. Among the latter were the buyers of used clothing, who appeared in courtyards wearing about three overcoats and a tower of five or six hats on their heads from purchases made earlier in the day. In voices that could reach to the top floor of the building, they hollered, "I cash clothes." Windows would go up and people would call down to them that they had something to sell and to come up to such and such an apartment.

The long summer vacations, of course, were the best holidays of all, with no school or homework and plenty of time for play and to go to the movies. When I was three years old, I had shocked my family by taking a live goldfish out of its bowl and feeding it to Warren, who was then a one-year-old baby. I later learned that my mother thought it meant that I had an overdeveloped sense of the dramatic, which she admitted ran in the Knopf family, and maybe she was right, because, first, certain movies and, later on, also radio plays and books of adventure began to appeal greatly to my imagination and to hit some mysterious chord within me that got me dreaming and wanting to tell or write my own stories.

The first movies I remember seeing were with the grown daughter of one of our neighbors in the Washington Heights apartment. She was taking care of me one day, and when it started to rain, she took me into the shelter of an elegant neighborhood theater that was showing a double bill of Jackie Coogan and Charlie Chaplin in *The Kid* and a rerun of *The Birth of a Nation.* That was about 1921, when I was six, and I don't remember much about the occasion or of what I saw, except that we sat watching the movies for about four hours, and when I finally got taken home, my mother was good and frightened and mad from worrying over where we had been.

After that, most of the pictures I was taken to, usually as a holiday or a Saturday-afternoon treat by my grandmother, were big historic epics like *The Big Parade*—which was about World War I—that cost a lot to see and showed in crowded theaters around Times Square that sold only reserved seats and had intermissions and sometimes a live orchestra instead of just an organist to accompany the movie. The movies were all black-and-white ones and without sound, but many of the epics were very realistic and made a strong impression on me because they were about the West, which my father told us about and which lay somewhere across the Hudson River and beyond the Palisades. These pictures, like *The Covered Wagon*, which was about brave settlers and pioneers on the Oregon Trail, and *The Iron Horse*, which told of the building of the first railroad across the country, and especially *The Flaming Frontier*, the story of Custer's Last Stand, which had taken place only thirty-nine years before I was born, showed romantic landscapes of plains and mountains and rivers with quicksand and really reawakened my wanting to see that exciting western part of the country for myself. Everything must still be like it looked in the movies, I thought, for after all, my father told me that the wife of General Custer was still alive and living right in New York City.

At the time, our parents had given us a subscription to *St. Nicholas*, a well-known children's magazine, and after reading an article in it about the hobby of collecting autographs, I had started my own collection. I wrote politely to Mrs. Custer for her signature and enclosed a stamped, self-addressed return envelope, but she never replied. However, I got the autographs of lots of famous people, including Thomas Edison and Governor Al Smith of New York and Queen Victoria (which I bought with birthday money from a dealer), and over the years built up a big collection. It was also the so-called Golden Age of Sports Heroes, and I managed to get the autographs of a lot of them, too, including Babe Ruth, whom I saw knock a lot of home runs in different games that I went to at Yankee Stadium and who made me into a loyal Yankee rooter; Red Grange, whom my father took me to see play professional football after he graduated from the University of Illinois; Bobby Jones, the golfer; Helen Wills and long, lanky Bill Tilden, the tennis stars; Johnny Weissmuller, the great swimming champ, and Gertrude Ederle, who swam across the English Channel; the boxers Jack Dempsey and Gene Tunney; and lots of others, most of whom I never saw in person but who had someone answer my letters and send me their signatures.

At about the same time, when I was eleven, I finally satisfied the urge to have my own say and for seven months "published" a magazine that I called *Fun and Sport*, typing out a single copy of it each month on a clattering Remington portable typewriter that my grandfather had given me for my ninth birthday and then circulating it among a number of my aunts, uncles, and other relatives who subscribed for fifteen cents a month. The magazine, brightened up by drawings that I made with colored pencils and with pasted-down pictures that I clipped from other publications, was composed mostly of superdramatic stories that I wrote about Indians, spies, and heroes of American wars and that were usually inspired by the plot and characters of one of the epic movies I had recently seen or by a gripping book I had read, like Charles Carleton Coffin's *The Boys of '76*, about four boys in the American Revolution. In addition, it included articles, pictures, cartoons, and other features on sports and different subjects that interested me, such as how to build your own crystal headphone radio set or the growth of population in the United States, which in the 1920 census had reached 105 million.

The onset of some serious illness that kept me in bed for almost a month put a sudden end to the magazine. I don't remember which sickness it was this time, but during my childhood I had at one time or another just about all of them, often passing them on to Warren, and sometimes to my mother. Starting with pneumonia, which almost deranged my then twenty-three-year-old mother with fright when I was three, and a few years later with an operation on our living room table at home for the removal of my tonsils and adenoids, which required the terrorizing use of

ether through a horn over my face, making me think I was being smothered to death, I had, among other things, diphtheria, whooping cough, the
measles, the German measles, the mumps, chicken pox, and scarlet fever.

My parents became veterans at handling these crises, and somehow
brought everybody, including themselves, safely through the onslaughts
without lasting effects. But they were a trial and left me with memories of
my parents putting embarrassing quarantine signs on our apartment door
for some of the sicknesses like scarlet fever that kept friends, delivery boys,
and others at a distance. I also remember having to lie in bed under an
opened umbrella with a sheet draped over it, and with burning mustard
plasters on my chest and the spout of a croup kettle on a Sterno can next
to the bed poking in under the sheet and filling the umbrella tent with a
fog of choking medicated steam.

At the same time, the unexpected vacation from schoolwork gave me
lots of opportunity for the kind of reading I did for pleasure. I had already
been making my way through many of the series of adventure books for
boys, like the Rover Boys, the Motor Boys, and the Boy Allies, the last of
whom managed to participate in almost every battle of World War I, as
well as books that I had inherited from my father's childhood, like *Lost in
the Rockies* by the prolific Edward S. Ellis and almost a shelfful of spell-
binding historical novels for boys, such as *With Clive in India* and *Under
Drake's Flag* by a masterful British storyteller named G. A. Henty. But
now, through articles and stories in the magazine *Boy's Life*, to which I had
recently subscribed, I began to grow interested in the Boy Scouts and
soon became immersed in a series of books about Tom Slade, Roy Blake-
ley, Peewee Harris, and some other Scouts, who seemed to live the kind of
adventure-packed lives I had frequently dreamed about. A lot of kids I
knew, many of them a little older than I was, belonged to Scout troops that
met in schools and churches along the West Side, and I went to a meeting
with one of them and borrowed a *Boy Scout Handbook* from a scoutmaster
and could hardly sleep after reading in it articles that said things like the
following:

> When you are a Scout, forests and fields, rivers and lakes are
> your playground. You are completely at home in God's great
> outdoors. You learn to notice every sound, to observe every
> track. Birds and animals become your friends. You master the
> skills of walking noiselessly through the woods, of stalking
> close to a grazing deer without being noticed, of bringing a
> bird to you by imitating its call. You learn to find your way
> cross-country by map and compass, to make a meal when you

are hungry, to take a safe swim when you are hot, to make yourself comfortable for the night in a tent or under the stars. You become a true outdoorsman.

It seemed almost as if Daniel Boone, Kit Carson, and other western heroes who had populated many of the stories my father had told us and the books that I had read were beckoning to me to come join them and learn their way of life. I soon joined a troop that met in a public school at 83d Street and West End Avenue, and I was not disappointed. I started to learn first aid and to make fires without a match, and to read a compass and tie a bowline and other kinds of knots, to blow a bugle and recognize the tracks of different animals, and to take care of and fly the American flag, which my father had already taught me to do. One great Saturday, I went with my troop across the Hudson River on the Dyckman Street ferry to a camping place along the Palisades, where we made a fire by twirling one stick into another one and seared hot dogs and marshmallows over the flames.

It was my first exciting trip to what I had thought of for so long as the beginning of the storied West, but a couple of weeks later—on a day when, unexpectedly, no one could think of anything but newspaper extras that were announcing the thrilling news that a young American aviator, Charles A. Lindbergh, had been sighted over Ireland after flying alone across the Atlantic Ocean on his way to Paris—we went on a large Hudson River day liner from its pier at 125th Street all the way upriver to the opposite shore at Bear Mountain and hiked even farther into the woods. Somehow, the buoyancy of my enthusiasm disappeared that day in the larger excitement and suspense of knowing that a great event of daring and adventure was occurring and a genuine new American hero was in the making, and besides, I now realized well enough that these woods were not Oregon, but only the start of three thousand miles of the United States that led in the direction of that state.

Yet the idea of knowing for myself what lay beyond the farthest I could see to the west, and of exploring in that direction to places where I had never been, would not die. From the time we had first moved into the city from New Jersey, my parents seemed at times to miss the country, and in most of the summers they took us away with them, sometimes for a couple of weeks at a beach and at other times for the whole summer to houses they rented in Pleasantville, a quiet village among the hills north of White Plains in New York's Westchester County, from which my father could commute to work on one of the New York Central Railroad lines. Signs at the edge of town proclaimed to approaching motorists that Pleasantville

That's Warren in the tire, and me on top in Pleasantville about 1925, when I was ten and wearing knickerbockers and neckties. From time to time through the years, we had different family cars, all the names of which no longer exist. I think this one was a Willys-Overland.

was ALL THAT THE NAME IMPLIES, but many of my memories were of unpleasant things like mosquitoes, humidity and heat, and attacks of asthma from grass and flower pollens. Relying on patent cures, like smoking Cubebs, did me no good, and occasionally severe attacks put me in bed with some of G. A. Henty's books to help me try to forget my wheezing and escape in my imagination to other lands and other centuries. My second-floor bedroom windows in Pleasantville, however, always seemed to look westward across the tops of trees to a wooded valley that rose, in turn, to a prominent ridge black with hardwood trees and underbrush and rearing toward the clouds like a wall that barred me from knowing what lay on its other side. Many times I gazed at the ridge, but, knowing that I was in America, and not in one of Henty's foreign lands, I decided that it was just as adventurous and romantic a setting for historical happenings as his locations were, and I imagined dreamily that the trees on the hill were still full of naked, war-painted Iroquois Indians who guarded access to what lay beyond the summit.

One year, our landlord in Pleasantville was the famous writer Marquis James, who twice won a Pulitzer Prize, for his biographies of Sam Houston and Andrew Jackson. Mr. James, originally a newspaperman from Missouri, had been in the army in France during World War I and after the war was on the staff of the American Legion's magazine. When I heard from my father that he was an author of historical books for adults, I wanted to meet him, but he had apparently rented his house to us so he could go abroad that summer, and I didn't meet him until many years later, in the 1950s, when I was with *Time* magazine and his daughter, whom I had gotten to know, brought us together. He was a modest, extremely likable man, but then in his early sixties and ill, and he died soon after we met. Another person my parents knew in Pleasantville was a prominent New York corporate publicist named Pendleton Dudley. He was a hearty man with a loud, friendly manner, and I learned that a year or so before I met him, DeWitt and Lila Wallace had started their new magazine, the *Reader's Digest*, in part of a building that Dudley had rented them on his property in Pleasantville.

In 1926, my parents began sending Warren and me away to a summer camp for boys known as Camp Androscoggin on an island in a lake of the same name near the little town of Wayne, Maine. Up to then, Warren and I had been very close companions. In our New York City playroom, we put on leather helmets and shoulder pads and crashed into each other, playing tackle football on the rug, and in Pleasantville we had played serious golf together, following our parents around the course at the town's sporty Nannahagan Golf Club and learning the finer points of the game from caddies who played with us. Being two years younger than I, Warren was now classified as a "midget" at Androscoggin and was thrown together with boys his age rather than mine. It was the start of our being separated from each other, and from then on we seemed increasingly to have our own circles of different interests and friends.

Androscoggin was owned by a very patriotic, military-minded man named Edward M. Healy, whom we all called "Chief," and his pretty but physically frail wife, whom we called Aunt Helen. Chief's older brother, Jeff, a U.S. Marine in World War I, had been killed at Château-Thierry, and Chief ran the camp practically as a memorial to Jeff. Because I had learned to blow the bugle in the Boy Scouts, I became the camp bugler and all day long seemed to be blowing reveille, assembly, chow, tattoo, taps, or some other call. We fell in in formation around the camp flagpole for the raising of the colors in the morning and their lowering in the evening, and both times the campers stood at attention while I blew the appropriate call. At flag-lowering, moreover, Chief gave a nightly patriotic lecture about the sacrifices of Jeff and the other men who had given their lives for our country, and a designated camper pulled a lanyard that fired a large blank cartridge in a miniature but thunderous cannon which sat on the ground. At the same time, Chief's repetitive lectures about Jeff and on the Marine Corps as the best branch of service because, like Camp Androscoggin, it placed a high priority on building character and manhood, ended up convincing me that if ever I had to go to war, I would want to do so as a marine.

Although Androscoggin was not a military camp, but actually focused during the days on athletics, intercamp rivalries, trips through the woods, rivers, and lakes of Maine, and the usual activities of a place for happy memories, with which the kids could regale their parents so that the parents would send them back the following year, Chief's patriotic sermons seemed natural and even expected in the 1920s. Most campers and their parents were even pleased and proud that among our council-lors, whom we called Uncles, were always three or four ramrod-stiff West Point cadets, including, when Warren and I were there, Uncle Frank Merrill, who in World War II would become legendary as the commander of a famed unit known as Merrill's Marauders, which fought in the jungles of the China-Burma-India theater of war.

The family trio, Pat, Warren, and I, assembled in front of my bunkhouse at Camp Androscoggin in Maine for this picture my father took during a visit to the camp in 1926 to see how we were doing. He was not the best of photographers, and here made Warren look knock-kneed and Pat and me bowlegged.

To me, the best thing about Androscoggin was the hiking and canoe trips we went off on. These were a regular part of the camp experience, and the adventures of traveling through the Maine wilderness and sleep-ing outdoors at night on the shore of a silent lake or alongside the roaring rapids of a river more than satisfied my long-held dreams. One year, his-tory was brought alive vividly for us when we hiked for several days through miles of woods inhabited by deer, bears, and woodchucks and over hills and rough country in the Dead River region of northwestern Maine, following the route taken early in the American Revolution by

Benedict Arnold's half-starved, suffering colonists on their ill-fated attempt to capture Quebec from the British.

At other times, with councillors paddling stern and the campers paddling bow or sitting in the center of the canoes among piles of knapsacks, ponchos, and trip boxes heavy with food, we traveled in fleets of canoes through chains of Maine's streams and lakes with Indian names like Chesuncook, Caucomgomoc, and Mooselookmeguntic. We carried the overturned canoes above our heads at portages, ran white-water rapids in the Allagash and other rivers, sought suitable camping spots where the ground was soft and thick with pine needles to serve as mattresses for our bedrolls, pulled the canoes well up on the sand to beach them securely when the setting sun turned the water orange, and listened to the lonely calls of loons and other sounds of the darkness as we sat around campfires before getting under our blankets at night. To me, this was living as I had long imagined it and wanted it to be.

Back in Manhattan, my elementary schooling ended at last in June 1928, in a ceremony marked by my graduation from Class 8B at P.S. 166 and by an eloquent speech by some invited city dignitary who assured us and our families in passionately inspiring words that, if we had gotten nothing else from our school, it had trained us in democracy and in how to get on in brotherhood with every other American in a country where no one was born better than anyone else. We had met and played with all kinds of kids from all kinds of backgrounds and all kinds of religions and stations in life, he said, and that was the greatest thing about our country and about schools like P.S. 166, where we had all been treated the same. Listening to the speech in the presence of our parents made us feel rather self-satisfied and proud, as if we had come through some kind of trial by fire and had achieved a victory by ending up being loved by our school and by all the teachers and the other kids, even the toughest and nastiest ones, who had been our classmates.

At the same time, ironically, we were about to separate for the future along lines of inequality, and although I took the speech to heart, the impending divisions seemed natural and expected and I didn't see any clash with what we had just listened to. A very few of us, whose parents, like mine, were fortunate enough to be able to afford the tuition, were going on to the advantages of a private high school which would prepare us for college. A small number of others, who were scholastically at the top of the class but whose families could not afford a private high school, were steered to Townsend Harris, a New York public high school for the city's brightest of the bright, or what we called "the class geniuses," who hoped to go on eventually to the public City College of New York. The great bulk of our former classmates, earmarked for high school vocational training for a job in a trade and with little or no expectation of going to college, disappeared among the huge student bodies of DeWitt Clinton, Evander Childs, Stuyvesant, and other New York City public high schools.

Five of us went from P.S. 166 far north to the third form, or high school freshman year, of the Horace Mann School for Boys, a private college preparatory school in the suburban Riverdale section of the Bronx. It was a day school, and only a small number of students, whose parents for one reason or another felt that their sons were better off full-time under the school's wing, lived at a nearby school-owned dormitory, where they seemed to engage regularly in escapades of various sorts. The two most daring and therefore secretly applauded and celebrated boarders whom I recall were the future Hollywood actor Keenan Wynn, who was the son of Ed Wynn, a famous "star of stage, screen, and radio," who billed himself as "the Perfect Fool," and Herbert Bayard Swope, Jr., the son of the well-known executive editor of the *New York World* and a nephew of the president of the General Electric Company. At one time, one of those boarders enjoyed a burst of fame as the school's hero by falling down the dormitory's fire escape and breaking his leg in an after-dark attempt to steal off to adventures in downtown Manhattan.

Of the day students, like myself, a few of the more affluent arrived each morning sunk down and half-asleep on the cavernous backseats of their parents' Packards and Pierce-Arrows, driven by uniformed chauffeurs who picked them up again at the school late in the afternoon to take them home. Others came by various means from scattered locations, those of us who lived in Manhattan taking a long daily subway ride of an hour or so to the end of one of the lines at Van Cortlandt Park, near Riverdale, and then hiking up a hill to the school. The subway ride had a compensation, for the train was crowded every morning with attractive and bright schoolgirls of our own age who were on their way to the all-girl Fieldston School, which was located close to Horace Mann, and the screeching, lurching cars were the setting for many flirtations and heavy romances.

Horace Mann had been founded as a model school in 1887 and for a long time had been associated with Teachers College of Columbia University. My father and one or two of his sisters had graduated from the school early in the century, which was why I ended up going there, and I was startled early on to discover that several of my teachers had had my father as a student a quarter of a century earlier. In the intervening years, one of them, who taught higher mathematics, had gone completely eccentric, on occasion picking up the roll-call book from some other teacher's class and marking everybody absent when no one answered, "Present," and half the time asking me questions about my family and other subjects that made it obvious that he thought that I was my father.

On the whole, however, Horace Mann had an outstanding faculty, laced with truly gifted and inspiring teachers. My favorite, a tough, fast-talking English teacher and instructor in creative writing named Alfred Baruth, had without question the greatest impact on me and my future of any teacher I ever had anywhere, not only teaching me how to write but also encouraging and strengthening my desire to become a rounded, educated person anxious to live life to the fullest. An electric personality who had previously been an actor with the Theatre Guild and a reporter for the Hearst newspapers, he would blow into a classroom like a storm, striding furiously back and forth in front of the class, challenging us, for example, to define the word *art*, then scrawling chalk marks all over the blackboard and jabbing his finger at the air to emphasize his point while asserting like a dictator that, to him, the mess on the blackboard was art, and did anybody want to argue with him, and if not, why not?

I had Mr. Baruth toward the start of his career at Horace Mann, when he was a young man. Eventually, he taught there for fifty-five years before he died in 1980 at the age of seventy-seven, and to each new generation of his students, whom he helped or inspired to become professional writers—and who over the years included Jack Kerouac, the Pulitzer Prize–winning poet Peter Viereck, the newspaper columnist Anthony Lewis, *The New Yorker* magazine's E. J. Kahn and Bruce Bliven, Jr., among many others—he was undoubtedly one of the most respected and beloved teachers at the school. "Of all the qualities of mind and character," he once wrote, "that which is paramount in the development of students is a zest for living. For them life must be a great adventure, an always setting-forth and an always discovering. . . . If the zest for living or intellectual curiosity desert a student, if it finally settles down into some unthinking and often unfelt routine, a mere mechanical set of daily procedures, life for him is really over." This was his basic lesson, and most, if not all, of us on whom he left an indelible impression never forgot it.

3   ✠   H. L. MENCKEN

During the fall of 1929, in my second year at Horace Mann, the under-pinnings of my world began to slip, although I didn't know it. One Octo-ber morning in the subway, all the papers that people were reading had big black headlines about the stock market crash on Wall Street. Although I had grown used to hearing my parents and other adults talking about Wall Street and the stock market, I knew little about it and thought of it as just a downtown business center for wealthy and powerful men like J. P. Mor-gan and John D. Rockefeller who owned the big banks and corporations. Everything, in fact, having to do with finances and the economic and political situation of the country appeared pretty irrelevant to my life and interests, and although I often heard my father and grandfather and their business and social friends talking about such subjects as the terribly hard times that American farmers had been suffering since prices had collapsed at the end of World War I, and the big risks that normally sensible people were now taking to get in on the big bull market on Wall Street, none of it seemed to have anything to do with our family's life. Even, after the crash, when I began to hear my parents discuss the tragic news of some acquain-tance who had lost all his money and had killed himself or heard Eddie Cantor or some other comedian on the radio make jokes about all the people who were jumping out of windows on Wall Street, no one in our family gave Warren and me any reason to think that what was going on was of any more importance to us than events that might be taking place among some unfortunate people in a foreign country.

Soon afterward, however, things changed quickly. Layoffs and closings started a downward economic spiral. Evictions of people from their apart-ments and brownstone homes and pitiful jumbles of bedding and furni-ture on the city's sidewalks; the appearance of jobless apple sellers, breadlines, Salvation Army soup kitchens, and raggedly dressed unemployed and homeless men in sandwich boards advertising their need for work; the proliferation of tar paper–shack settlements called Hoovervilles in the parks all around us—all were signs of the steadily worsening hard times and the onset of the Depression. Still, though classroom and other discussions at Horace Mann and my reading of an increasing number of magazines and newspapers in the school library made me more aware of and interested in what was happening and in the causes of the Depression and panaceas like technocracy that were being proposed to end the crisis, it all seemed strangely abstract and intellectual to me, for there was yet no evidence that the Depression had, or would, hit our family. Everything at home seemed to be running its normal course, as it had always done. My father still went to his business, there was no talk of giving up, cutting back, or retrenching, and, since I had outgrown Camp Androscoggin, we had even begun renting summer homes again in Pleasantville.

At Horace Mann, meanwhile, after a brief try at football that ended with my being briefly but painfully injured, I made the cross-country team in the fall and ran the mile and half mile with the track team in the spring. On winter afternoons, to keep in training, some of us took the subway down to Columbia University and worked out on the college's outdoor board track at 116th Street off Broadway, joining the Columbia runners as well as prominent amateur and professional track and field stars like Ray Conger and Glenn Cunningham who had come to New York from various parts of the country to compete in the Millrose and other winter games at Madison Square Garden.

One afternoon in December 1930, I came back to the Columbia locker room to find several of the star runners in somber conversation, all of them grouped around one disconsolate man whom they were trying to buck up. The latter had just learned that the big and supposedly safe Bank of United States in New York City had failed, and he had lost all the money he had in the world. The news, it turned out, was real, and it affected thousands of families, including mine. In those pre–New Deal days, there was no Federal Deposit Insurance Corporation, and when a bank ran out of money and closed its doors, that was it. I had no idea at first that our family was involved, and at home I never even thought to mention the bank's closing or the sad episode in the locker room. But a few nights later, my father and mother got Warren and me together and told us that all the money that had been put aside for our college education had been lost in the failure of that bank and that there was no chance that we'd ever recover any of it.

I had a sick feeling, as if a stone were sinking in my stomach, but before

I could say anything, my mother told us that, despite the loss of the money, everything was going to be all right, because they had had a conversation with S.K., her father, and he had told them that he was determined that Warren and I go to college and that he would pay all the costs, so we shouldn't worry. By the big smile of satisfaction that she gave us, I knew that we were saved and that everything was going to be all right, but I felt a sudden sense of shame, as well as of relief, go through me. Warren, who was two years behind me in school, didn't look so confident as my parents continued to talk, telling us that, despite my grandfather's generosity, things were getting harder and we would have to watch our expenses and maybe make some cutbacks. As it turned out, the immediate cutbacks were very few and hardly noticeable, except for one of them. And that one was terrible. It soon became apparent that there was not going to be enough money to send Warren, as well as me, to Horace Mann, and he ended up shortly having to go to George Washington, a public high school in New York City. It hurt him badly and filled me for a long time with guilt over my advantage.

With my college education secured, I went back to life as usual, although I now felt a vicarious bond with those who were experiencing the effects of the Depression. Still, the general bad times continued to touch us in only the slightest ways. Because of dwindling business, my mother, who with one of her cousins had been running a successful neighborhood retail bookstore and lending library that delivered and picked up books at customers' homes, closed down the shop. At the same time, during the Christmas holidays, I went to work at my father's business, earning some money to save for college by manhandling heavy barrels and crates of dressed poultry from refrigerated railroad cars on West 14th Street to waiting trucks of the steamship lines and wholesale customers. As far as I could tell, those were our only accommodations to what was going on in the country, and I actually felt good earning my way with the longshoremen and other rough types who worked regularly on the Hudson River docks and around the markets.

Meanwhile, largely at the instigation of Mr. Baruth, who thought I had some talent for writing and barked at me, "You ought to want to be a writer, and if you want to be a writer, write!" I joined the staff of the school's weekly newspaper, the *Horace Mann Record*, and found—in journalistic reporting and writing, in the drama of a composing room and the processes of laying out and putting together a paper, and in the smell of ink and newsprint and the noise of the presses where we printed the paper—the lure of journalism as an exciting, adventurous career.

Most of the articles we wrote were routine reports on school issues and

activities and detailed accounts of sporting meets with other schools, but
in 1931, a school friend named Billy Watters and I began writing a series
of jointly signed interviews for the *Record* with important authors of the
day. The series grew out of my idea of an interview with H. L. Mencken,
and both Mencken and my grandfather had something to do with it—my
grandfather because I wanted him to see that maybe I could become a
writer rather than a publisher, and Mencken because the impact of the
Depression was making me more skeptical of much that I had always
accepted without question, and both from meetings with him, which were
becoming more common at my grandfather's office, and from reading his
devastating ridicule of hypocrisy and sham in American life, I had become
his fan and felt that an interview with him would be an interesting feature
in the school paper.

Mencken did not let us down. Watters and I sat for more than an hour
with him at the long table in my grandfather's office while he puffed on
the stub of a cigar and enjoyed himself immensely, entertaining us with his
acerbic opinions, some of them uproarious, some outrageous, on everything from the state of American education to the reason for the popularity of tabloid newspapers. "If you tried to open a *New York Times* in the
subway," he observed humorously, "you would probably get injured. And
then when you ride in the subway, notice the class of people who are reading tabloids. All they can do is figure out two-syllable words, and look at
the pictures." On education, he dismissed the teaching of Latin and foreign languages as useless in later life, "like most of the rest of the stuff
taught in school today." (Being in my third year of both Latin and French
at Horace Mann, I gulped quietly at this.) "Pedagogy is a hundred years
behind," he continued. "It is one of the slowest things on earth. . . . The
only thing that has advanced is physics. . . . Take geometry. What does
that teach you? It's the same stuff they taught a hundred years ago. And
English. In Shakespeare's time the grammar teacher wasn't as dumb as he
is today. . . . He still believes what he was taught in 1880, and he is too
thick to expand this knowledge. . . . Most of the pedagogues are merely
stupid, romantic people who love to teach, anyway."

When we ran the interview, with all of Mencken's jeers and derisions
intact, it caused an expected furor among some of the faculty members at
the school, but the student body and other faculty members read it with
delight, and it became the start of a series of heady, though less controversial, interviews with other prominent literary figures of the day. Among
our quarry were André Maurois, the best-selling French biographer of
Shelley, Byron, and Disraeli, who received us, along with a covey of adult
reporters, in his stateroom on the French liner *Paris* an hour before it

sailed for Europe; Albert Payson Terhune, who related to us in his River-side Drive apartment that he had first started writing books and stories about dogs because an editor at a magazine had urged him to try to do so after Mrs. Terhune's pet collie, Lad, had taken a liking to the editor ("A great story about a common thing is better than a common story about a great thing," the author, whose book *Lad: A Dog* had made him famous, reminded us as the interview ended); and G. K. Chesterton, the huge gray-haired English poet and author of the Father Brown detective stories, wearing a long black cloak and a soft black hat, whom I interviewed while sitting on a couch in the lobby of the St. Moritz Hotel on Central Park South, crushed between Chesterton and his courtly, more famous friend, the British author of *The Forsyte Saga*, John Galsworthy, who was also staying at the hotel. Although Galsworthy, tall, slender, and extremely polite, felt he was intruding on Chesterton's appointment with me and begged off being interviewed himself, he promised to autograph one of his books for me and then accompanied us into Rumpelmayer's, a tea shop off the lobby, for a dish of ice cream.

After that, Watters and I interviewed Rupert Hughes, who was writing the third volume of a controversial, debunking biography of George Washington; Donald Ogden Stewart, the humorist, playwright, and screenwriter, who announced to us sagely that "the talkies" were "definitely an established thing in Hollywood"; and Guglielmo Ferrero, an intense Italian historian, recently released from detention by Mussolini to lecture in the United States, who told us that the world would not have another great war until it got over the economic troubles caused by the last one—"and that will need a long period of world peace." Communism, he assured us, had little power anywhere in Europe except in Germany, and there "they have another group to put them down, the Nazis."

In addition, we met, but were unable to interview, the huge, uneasy Theodore Dreiser, a household name of the day, white-haired, with thick lips, glaring eyes, one of which seemed to float in its socket, and famous for *Sister Carrie* and *An American Tragedy*. He welcomed us to his Manhattan apartment opposite Carnegie Hall, but he was too ill—or hungover—to field questions from us (most literary critics at the time thought that he had deserved to be the first American to win the Nobel Prize for literature, an honor that had just gone, instead, to Sinclair Lewis). We were also disappointed by Robert Frost, who was too busy preparing to give a poetry reading in Greenwich Village to do more than speak to us for a few moments and sign copies of his books that we had brought with us.

We ended the series, however, with three rewarding interviews. The first was with the literary critic and Yale English professor William Lyon

Phelps, in his dressing room before one of his lectures at Town Hall, near Times Square. He told us to take H. L. Mencken seriously—"He knows what he's saying"—then differed with Mencken by telling us that it was important to study foreign languages in school so we could "read the literature of the world." We met with Edwin Arlington Robinson, a lonely, soft-spoken, and tragedy-ridden poet, called by many critics at the time the best of his generation, in his third-floor walk-up apartment in a dingy house on East 42d Street, in Tudor City. Wearing his smoking jacket, puffing on Sweet Caporal cigarettes (he was soon to die of cancer), he told us that although he doubted that a true appreciation of poetry could be taught, he thought that all young people should be encouraged to read Shakespeare: "It is the best thing any young fellow can do," he said quietly. And finally, we interviewed Edwin Markham, the poet of the once-popular "The Man with the Hoe" and "Lincoln, the Man of the People," which Chief Justice of the Supreme Court William Howard Taft had had read as part of the dedication ceremonies of the Lincoln Memorial in Washington, D.C., in 1922. We met with Markham, who looked like an Old Testament prophet with long-flowing white locks that merged with a heavy white beard, at his Staten Island home, which was cluttered with manuscripts, papers, and thirteen thousand books. Edwin Arlington Robinson was on a par of greatness with Rudyard Kipling, Markham announced to us, and then, as if lost in thought, he added, "Boys, what we want is a world in which all workers shall think and all thinkers shall work. Put down that quotation. It's one I abide by."

I sent copies of each of the interviews to my grandfather and to Mencken. My grandfather acknowledged them in a grandfatherly way, calling them "admirable," but Mencken made my spirits soar by encouraging me to think of going into journalism, but only, as he advised, for a few years to learn "to write fast" and to "get experience by going places and meeting people." He had said much the same thing in an answer to one of our questions during our interview with him: "The reporter gets used to a set of rubber-stamp phrases which he employs over and over," he had told Watters and me, "but a few years of reporting won't hurt if you're intelligent and leave." Now he was offering this advice to me personally, and I liked hearing it. Talking with famous authors had influenced me greatly, and I began to think seriously of becoming a newspaperman. At the end of the school year, I took a first step down that road by being named the next year's managing editor of the *Record*.

That school year, 1931–1932, was my senior year at Horace Mann, and also the exciting year of the buildup for the 1932 presidential campaign. Once again, I wrote a series for the *Record*, this time a group of biographical sketches of the leading presidential candidates, employing quotations from their speeches and papers and explaining their positions on major issues, such as the continuing Depression, the repeal of the Eighteenth (Prohibition) Amendment, and the payment of a bonus to needy World War I veterans. Those I wrote about included President Hoover, as well as Al Smith and Franklin D. Roosevelt, who were the former and current governors of New York State, respectively; the then Speaker of the House of Representatives, John Nance Garner of Texas; Albert C. Ritchie, the Democratic governor of Maryland; and Newton D. Baker of Ohio, who had been President Woodrow Wilson's secretary of war during World War I. I interviewed none of them, but I drew amply on the literature that the campaign headquarters of each man sent me and on what additional research I could do in the school library's newspaper and magazine files or in those of the New York Public Library. Although a conversation with Mencken had persuaded me that his Maryland friend, Governor Ritchie, was the best man in the field, because he would end Prohibition (which to Mencken was the campaign's principal issue) and was also fiscally conservative and not a "charlatan" or "imbecilic"—Mencken's views of most of the other candidates—I tried to be entirely objective in the series and played no favorites.

My father, who often told me that he had to be a Democrat, contributing to Tammany Hall and to Democratic candidates and functions in order to conduct the business he was in in New York City and to avoid the strong-arm extortion of mobsters and corrupt American Federation of Labor union leaders, was for Al Smith. During that winter, he frequently got into arguments with my grandfather, who, despite his opposition to Prohibition, was a strict Republican constitutionalist who supported Herbert Hoover and Hoover's contention that the federal government had no constitutional power to pass social legislation to assist individuals who were being hurt by the Depression. That, he said, was the duty of the states. I didn't get into their friendly combat, and although I had fallen so under Mencken's influence that I felt sure that Ritchie would be seen as the best man and would win at the Democratic convention and then defeat President Hoover, a number of faculty members at Horace Mann praised my series for its nonpartisanship, while various student friends condemned me for not supporting this or that favorite candidate of their own. In short, the series was a success and drew another heartening letter of encouragement from Mencken.

During all this time of moving into my later teens, I had been traveling around parts of New York on weekends with classmates and other friends, becoming familiar with many of the different sections of Manhattan

Island, like Greenwich Village, the Bowery, City Hall Park, Harlem, Hell's Kitchen, Chinatown, Madison Square, the Battery, the Lower East Side ghetto, and Times Square, and falling in love with the excitement and action of the bustling city. Almost every night, during winter holiday weeks, there were formal teenage dances to attend in the full dignity of white tie, tails, and collapsible opera hats at the Waldorf-Astoria or another midtown hotel where the bands of Smith Ballew, Vincent Lopez, and Paul Whiteman held sway. Of much greater interest and entertainment, however, were Friday- and Saturday-night rendezvous at other times of the year in Times Square with ten or more of us Horace Mann seniors, who played everything by sudden impulse and, after taking in Minsky's burlesque, Hubert's circus of trained fleas on West 42d Street, and other amusements, could end up hours later "slumming" at the Cotton Club in Harlem, crossing moonlit New York Harbor on the Staten Island Ferry, or drinking sloe gin fizzes and listening to a jazz pianist in a West 52d Street brownstone speakeasy, named Tony's or Leon and Eddie's or the Kit Kat Klub or whatever else.

At times, we "plunged," paying minimum and cover charges to drink cheap whiskey in false-bottomed shot glasses and gawk at gorgeous, half-naked showgirls in extravaganzas at Nils T. Granlund's huge, crowded nightclub on Broadway, and on one notable night the driver of a Chinatown tour bus turned about ten of us into helpless suckers. "Want to see naked women?" he asked us. "One buck a head." When we paid him our dollar bills, he drove us to an unmarked door on West 48th Street off Times Square and, turning us over to a doorman, sped away in his bus. After demanding and collecting another dollar a head from each of us, the doorman conducted us inside, up a staircase, and, after rapping three times on a door for someone to open it, into a narrow, dimly lit room filled with spectators sitting at small tables against the walls. Someone pulled a couple of tables together for us, but before we could sit down, a team of two tough-looking bouncers came over and, eyeing us suspiciously, asked what we wanted to drink, volunteering the information that the drinks would cost us ten dollars apiece.

Someone in our party said we didn't want any drinks, and after that, I don't remember much. The two bouncers, joined by a third one, said, "Out! We don't serve kids here! Out!" and like a herd of cattle we were suddenly driven out the door, down the stairs, and back into the street. The doorman was nowhere in sight; luckily, we were each out only two dollars, and that was the end of that evening.

What was more our speed were the ten-cents-a-dance dance halls like the Orpheum and the Tango Palace, whose garishly lit entrances on

Broadway were lined with studio portraits of some of the choice dancing partners waiting for us upstairs. After climbing the stairs, one bought a wad of ten-cent tickets, picked a partner from among the girls waiting for customers in the semidarkness, paid her a ticket, and, after the music began, either danced her out on the floor or maneuvered her into a darkened booth or to the bar to try to make time with her. After a couple of minutes, the music stopped, and the customer could stay with the girl and keep on paying her his tickets for the two-minute bursts of music or he could say good-bye and look for another partner. The girls worked on commission for the establishment and did whatever they thought was necessary to hang on to a customer and keep collecting his tickets, as well as get him to buy watered-down drinks which were served at the bar or brought by a waitress to the booths, where a good deal of fondling was generally going on.

Once in a while, the hostesses' ardor to keep us as loyal customers inflated our egos and seduced us into ephemeral romances. On one occasion, at the Tango Palace, which was among our favorite dance halls, several of us fell for a rather shy young girl who didn't look like she belonged there and who told us that she had only recently come to New York from her parents' corn-and-hog farm in Indiana to join her older sister, who was a veteran ten-cents-a-dance hostess. After a few weeks of getting acquainted with her, and learning that she dreamed of going someday to one of the neighboring legitimate theaters and seeing a live performance by a movie star, I made a date with her for a Saturday matinee. I picked her up in a taxi at the West Side apartment where she lived with her sister and took her to see the French star Maurice Chevalier, who was appearing at one of the theaters in an afternoon concert of his famous songs, like "Louise" and "Sweeping the Clouds Away," and was accompanied on the bill by the European pianists Jacques Fray and Mario Braggiotti. My companion liked Chevalier's sparkling personality, but I could see that she was a little bewildered by it all and had never seen or heard of this particular star and had no idea who he was. But after the performance, we had a soda, and she seemed extremely pleased by the afternoon. We took a taxi back to her building, and I went upstairs with her to her apartment. When she opened the door, she started to introduce me to her older sister, a frumpy-looking bleached blonde who was standing in a slip in a bedroom doorway. The sister never gave my companion a chance, but let loose a screaming barrage of vile language, reminding her that it was against the rules to make dates with customers of the Tango Palace. In return, my shy date, to my surprise, started to scream also, aiming even more vulgar language at her sister and, as if transformed suddenly into one of *Macbeth*'s witches, making obscene gestures at her. I beat a fast retreat down the stairs and out of the building, and when I next returned to the Tango Palace, I was told that the frumpy blonde and her sixteen-year-old sister had been scratched up in a taxi accident and no longer worked there. No one knew where they had gone, and I never saw or heard of either of them again.

As my senior year at Horace Mann approached its end, my mind was increasingly on getting into a college. My grandfather wanted me to try for Harvard; my father, who might have been expected to steer me to Cornell, thought, instead, that Cornell had gotten too big and wanted me to go to a

I don't know when this was taken, but it may be a Horace Mann class portrait.

small college; and I wanted to go to Dartmouth, where many of my best friends at Horace Mann had applied. Apparently, too many from Horace Mann had applied, for Dartmouth sent me an early rejection, and my list was down to two. During the spring vacation of 1932, I drove with my father to upstate New York to inspect Hamilton College and be interviewed by the admissions people. It was a successful trip, first because I liked Hamilton and came away with the impression that it liked me and that I could probably be admitted, and second because my father let me take the wheel of our Marmon automobile for long stretches along the Hudson and Mohawk river valleys, so that at the trip's conclusion I was competent and confident enough to get my driver's license.

My enthusiasm for Hamilton, however, did not daunt my grandfather, who overlooked no opportunity to try to persuade both my father and me that throughout my life I would benefit from the unmatched opportunities and advantages of a Harvard education. At Horace Mann, I conveyed what was going on to one of my Latin instructors, who had also been my football coach in my freshman year, an extraordinarily compassionate and well-liked older teacher named William J. Nagle, who took a personal interest in the destiny of his students and knew how unhappy I had been when Dartmouth had turned me down. "Harvard or Hamilton?" he asked. "Why Harvard, of course! It has no peer in this country. You take College Boards for it, and you'll get in and you'll do wonderfully well there." He waggled a finger at me. "If you don't try for it, your entire life will be one of regret, because you'll never know if you could have made it."

That settled it, and it made my grandfather happy. I would take the College Board exams that Harvard required, and if I failed, I would fall back on Hamilton as my second choice. My father seemed satisfied enough with the decision, and I sent my preliminary applications to both institutions and began to study for the College Boards. At the same time, I had become the leading miler on our school's track team, and about a week before graduation, my mother and grandfather drove up to Riverdale to watch me run in our last important meet. I won the mile in what was record time for me, coming in well ahead of the nearest runner, and after the race, my grandfather came up to me, beaming with pride, and congratulated me. As he took off his pince-nez and pumped my hand, I noticed that his cheeks were very pink, in a way that I had never seen them before, and I thought that it was probably from his excitement at seeing me run and win. The following week, he was back at the school, accompanying my mother and father to my graduation ceremonies. When they were over, he rubbed his hands together heartily. "Now for Harvard," he said, and I noticed that the strange pink color was still in his cheeks.

That was the end of May. On June 11, at 7:15 in the morning, as he was about to get out of bed, he suffered a fatal heart attack, having had no previous warning that anything was wrong, and died at once. It was a terrible shock. My mother cried and cried as I had never seen her cry before, and my grandmother lay on a couch for days, with tears rolling from her eyes into a handkerchief that she kept pressing against her face. It was my first experience with the death of someone I loved, and for a while I sobbed privately and thought that the end of my world had come. After the funeral, I realized that I simply had to pass the College Boards for my grandfather and get into Harvard. The exams—Latin, English, history, and physics—were almost upon me, and it was hard doing the studying. At night, my mind drifted off to memories of my grandfather, who had loved me so and was proud of me, maybe because he thought I was going to be like him and carry on all his goals and values, and whom I would never see again, and tears blurred my eyes and fell on my books, and I didn't know how I was going to take the tests and pass them, because my eyes kept on being so blurry. But they cleared, and I got through all the exams, and early in the summer, Harvard accepted me. I wrote Mr. Nagle, and he wrote back, "Good boy! So much for Dartmouth!" and I saw my father and I knew that he was proud too. If I had thought hard, I might have wondered whether he was worrying if we now would have the money for Harvard. But in my elation, I put such questions into the future. Besides, there was suddenly something else to think about. Harvard had required letters of recommendation, and, at my request, several people had written in my behalf. None of them, however, was an important person whose name would have been familiar to or have carried any particular weight with the Harvard authorities. I now learned vaguely from one of my grandfather's lawyers—as if I were not to know about it—that one of the last things my grandfather had done was to ask Henry Mencken to send Harvard a letter of support for me, and that Mencken had done so. From the grave, my grandfather, it appeared, had gotten his way and seen me into Harvard.

II � BREAKING OUT

4 ❖ INNOCENT AT HARVARD

The first genuine westerner I think I ever met was a strangely dressed fellow freshman at Harvard with a purple porkpie hat on top of his head who was so awkward and bumpkin-appearing as to seem painfully lost and out of place. I came upon him in the middle of his struggle with the chaos of registration day, at a moment when he needed some friendly help.

That morning, I had arrived at Harvard Yard in Cambridge after an overnight train ride with other Harvard-bound freshmen from New York and had found my quarters—a cheerfully white-walled suite of bedrooms, a study, and a bath that I would share with two other freshmen—in one of a pair of long, narrow colonial-looking dormitories known jointly as Wigglesworth Hall, with rows of chimneys and third-story dormer windows, snuggled along the Massachusetts Avenue wall of the Yard behind the massive bulk of the Widener Library.

Everything on that early fall day in 1932 was exhilarating, intimidating, and, as I conveyed in an enthusiastic letter to my father and mother, "swell." I made a cautious tour of the Yard, exploring other dormitories and classroom buildings covered with ivy and hallowed by history and age, running into old friends among the arriving freshmen and making new ones, attending to the business of registering for classes, paying in advance for meals at the Harvard Union and for athletic association and other dues and obligations, and braving a gauntlet of independent hucksters who, turning a part of the cavernous Memorial Hall into the semblance of a wild, yelling Oriental bazaar, signed us up for laundry, daily milk deliveries, and shoe shines during the semester (40 shines and 120 suit pressings for twelve dollars), for subscriptions to the college newspaper, the *Harvard Crimson*, and other publications, and for a host of different undergraduate services, organizations, and activities.

Gradually, as I mastered the confusion and coped successfully with the required routines, whatever apprehension I had started out with fell away, and I headed back to Wigglesworth Hall, feeling confident that I was on my way to becoming "a Harvard man," not really knowing what that meant, but vaguely conscious that I was learning some of its leading hallmarks. Most prominent were a sacred respect for the many college traditions established by generations of Harvard men—most of them apparently founders and presidents of the nation and other prominent Americans now long dead and buried—and an up-nosed, self-confident feeling of superiority known and nurtured as "Harvard indifference" by freshmen from Groton and certain other New England prep schools whose fathers had gone to Harvard and had familiarized their sons with Harvard beliefs and values, including the well-worn boast, "You can always tell a Harvard man, but you can't tell him much," which I must have heard ten times or more that day.

As I reached Wigglesworth Hall, I noticed that the walk in front of its entries was empty save for one wild figure who was grappling with the blowing contents of an exploded cardboard suitcase and with sheets of paper forms, receipts, and other notices and documents he had acquired during the day and which now had cascaded from his arms and were flying all around him. I took a moment to size him up—the flat-topped porkpie hat high atop his round, desperate-looking baby face, a black-and-white-checked jacket and tiny red bow tie that seemed to be choking him, and pants legs that ended far up on shiny cowboy boots. Then I rushed across to help him. When we crammed everything back into his suitcase and strapped it up again, he was all over me with thanks and told me he was "real grateful." He said he had just arrived and was from "out west," and he wanted to know who I was and where I had come from. Then he thanked me again profusely, said it had been a pleasure making my acquaintance, and shuffled past me with his load, seeming to walk a little bowlegged and embarrassed, and disappeared into an entry.

I rarely saw him again, but later on, I learned that "out west" to him meant the western edge of Minnesota, where his family had a farm rather than a ranch, and I thought of my father doing business for years with poultry shippers from Minnesota and of my never having equated them with my romantic ideas of westerners, and I felt confused and disappointed. But I felt sorry for him, too. He hadn't lied to me. Minnesota was out west from Massachusetts, and maybe western Minnesota, not far from the storied plains of the Dakotas, was part of the West. At any rate, people talked about him as being overly friendly, and maybe he wasn't sophisticated enough for them and they, in turn, weren't friendly enough for him.

Often in later years, I heard the complaint that "eastern kids aren't as friendly as western kids" from one of my own grandsons and from other students who were raised in the West and sent east to school. In this respect, my classmate from Minnesota was, in truth, my first westerner. Sometime during the year, however, something—poor grades, the hard times, or perhaps homesickness—caused him to drop out of Harvard, and he was seen no more.

Meanwhile, amid my mounting sense of freedom and of being more on my own than ever before, my life filled fast with new experiences and interests. Some of them had taken root during the sad summer after my grandfather's death, before I had left for Harvard, and others even earlier. Two years before, in 1930, when I was fifteen, my mother's younger brother, Edwin Knopf, who in the early 1920s had "gone into" the legitimate theater in New York City as an actor, director, and producer and by 1930 had become a movie director and writer at Paramount studios in Hollywood, thrilled me by trying to persuade my parents to let me stay with his family in California during the summer and visit his studio.

Edwin, or Eddie, as he later preferred my calling him, was only sixteen years older than I and apparently almost from my birth had felt a companionable attachment to me as his firstborn nephew. On my part, he was the most romantic and exciting member of the family. He was handsome and superdramatic, and he had a cultured, worldly wise manner and impressively expensive tastes in clothes, wines, and food. He knew famous movie stars like Greta Garbo and John Gilbert, musicians like George Gershwin and Jerome Kern, and playwrights and authors like Noël Coward and F. Scott Fitzgerald. He had been married for a couple of years to Mary Ellis, the glamorous star of the stage hit *Rose-Marie*, and in the late 1920s, running a repertory company in Baltimore, he had hired the then-unknown Katharine Hepburn and started her on her acting career. He lived in the magical world of stage and movie sets and New York and Hollywood parties and traveled extensively to exotic spas and watering places in Europe. And he had been a hero. In a German store in 1922, he had seized a live explosive device from World War I, which a little boy had picked up innocently. He had tried to rush it out of the store, but he had been too late. It exploded at the door and blew off his left hand, making him something of a curiosity to gawking children for the rest of his life as someone who could cut his meat, tie his tie, play bridge, and do everything else expertly with one hand.

There was only one thing wrong with his invitation of 1930. My grandfather quietly did not approve of the theater as a career for his son—and certainly not Hollywood, which he regarded as a cesspool of depravity

("Actors are pimps, and most actresses are whores," Edwin claimed that
S.K. once growled at him)—and he convinced my mother that I was too
young to be exposed to the immorality of the movie capital. So, hiding my
anguish and disappointment, I did not go to the West that year.

But Edwin did not give up. He had a great respect for writers, wrote
and sold screenplays himself, and, I think, felt that I was showing signs of
becoming a kindred soul, since I was writing three-act plays in Mr.
Baruth's class at Horace Mann; perhaps I might like to write for the
movies one day under his tutelage. Two years later, in 1932, when I would
be seventeen and about to enter college, the Summer Olympic Games
were going to be held in Los Angeles, and knowing of my interest in track
and field events, he gradually wrung from my grandfather agreement and
a promise that I would then be old enough to visit Hollywood and could
go to the Olympics. My grandfather's death in June 1932 abruptly ended
those plans. For what was to be the last time, my parents had again rented
a house for the summer in Pleasantville, and instead of being in California, I listened to the games played in the Los Angeles Coliseum on a tall
standing radio in our living room in the country, staring now and then
gloomily through a western window at the familiar dark wooded ridge
that rose toward the clouds and that still seemed to bar me from knowing
what lay on its other side.

One unexpected development—an intense two-year romance by mail
with a girl I had never met—came out of the aborted trip to Southern California. Edwin's wife, our Aunt Mildred, a huge-hearted woman with
many talents who busied herself in writing plays and cookbooks, making
quilts for Irene Dunne and other friends in the movie industry, and generally thinking up good works to do for others, had arranged for me to meet
and have as a companion during my visit a very lovely high school senior
who was the daughter of a friend of someone my parents had met during a
trip to California in 1929. When my trip was called off, Mildred sent me
some pictures of her. She was indeed lovely, and I was crushed. I wrote
her, she wrote back, I replied, she responded, and I was smitten. Her letters were buoyant, charming, and, to come quickly to the point, we shared
so many interests and points of view that the correspondence continued
warmly for two years, sustaining me during difficult times at Harvard,
enticing me with the prospect that eventually we would meet, and then
finally ending in ashes when she wrote me of her engagement to somebody else.

There were other things, also—ominous, threatening matters—to
think about that summer of 1932. Throughout the country, the Depression was worsening, and tensions were increasing. In a shocking episode

reflecting how bad things were becoming, a large number of unemployed and homeless veterans of World War I who marched on Washington, demanding the immediate payment of a bonus that Congress had promised them, were routed from their shabby encampment on President Hoover's orders and driven mercilessly from the capital by the tanks, gas, and bayonets of a new generation of young soldiers, commanded by General Douglas MacArthur. Meanwhile, thousands of other jobless men, who had abandoned their families in shame because they could not provide for them, were stealing rides on freight trains, crisscrossing the country as hoboes in search of work and restored self-confidence, while at the same time, in parts of the Middle West, desperate farmers, unable to make a profit from what they produced, were organizing into the militant Farmers' Holiday Association, preventing sheriffs' sales of bankrupt farms, dumping milk and burning other commodities to try to push prices higher, and threatening revolution against the federal government.

Early in the summer, soon after I learned that Harvard had accepted me, my father took me aside and, with the same painful embarrassment he had once displayed when trying to tell me about the birds and the bees and sex, looked awkwardly at his hands and his shoes and the walls and out the window and everywhere else and explained hesitantly that times were not improving, that with my grandfather's death, the future income of our family had become really uncertain, and that I would have to be careful of my spending and maybe even consider ways of earning some money or applying for scholarships or loans to help out with expenses at college. The seriousness of the session jolted me into taking action, and I immediately enrolled in shorthand and typing courses in a secretarial school in White Plains, the county seat near Pleasantville, thinking that someday at college I might find those skills handy in bringing in some income. Each weekday for a month or more, I took a bus from the Pleasantville railroad station to the school in downtown White Plains, but although I tried hard, I failed to master either course in the limited time I could give to them before leaving for college, and I finally gave up, still typing faster with two fingers and knowing little more Gregg shorthand than the curves and squiggles of brief phrases like "Dear Sir" and "to the" and "from the."

Meanwhile, the journalistic articles I had written on the presidential candidates for the *Horace Mann Record*, plus the impact of the Depression and the deteriorating situation in the country, had made me increasingly interested in politics. Under the influence of my grandfather, I had been more Republican than Democratic. But while I had been writing the *Record* articles, I had become aware that somehow in the previous years, the stature of Theodore Roosevelt, whom I had been taught to admire when I was younger as the second greatest Republican president after Lincoln and a role model for all Americans, had been downgraded. His birthday was no longer a holiday, and the new Roosevelt who was running for president seemed to have eclipsed his fame. Few people still looked on the great T.R. as an heroic figure or even seemed to remember much about what he was like or what he had done. I inquired among Republican party publicists and staff officials at their New York headquarters about what had happened to Theodore Roosevelt's mighty reputation and heard with surprise that it was Republicans themselves who had done him in, that few of them had any love for his memory, and that all "real" Republicans had never forgiven him for his "radicalism" and for splitting the party in 1912 with his Bull Moose party, or Progressive party, thus allowing Woodrow Wilson to win the presidency. Although in 1920, after Roosevelt's death, the Old Guard conservative, or "real," Republicans had regained power, "troublemaking" Roosevelt Progressives within the party had continued to fight them, and part of the way the party leaders had fought back was to disparage and downplay the stature and memory of Theodore Roosevelt, which they had done vigorously and with success during the administrations of Presidents Harding, Coolidge, and Hoover.

It was a cynical and disillusioning tale, but over at Franklin D. Roosevelt's campaign headquarters at 331 Madison Avenue, in Manhattan, I met a number of aging Bull Moose party veterans who still revered Theodore Roosevelt's memory and were working for his Democratic cousin, Franklin D. Roosevelt. They readily corroborated what I had been told their enemies, the Old Guard Republicans, had done to smother the memory of T.R. True or false, it was plausible, and it soured me on the stiff-necked, petulant President Hoover and the Old Guard mossbacks who controlled the Republican party.

After my grandfather died and our family's financial future began to darken, I became more personally bitter about the president, who clung stubbornly to his conviction that the Constitution prevented him from doing anything about the Depression except to provide money to banks and large corporations and hope that it would "trickle down" to everybody else. Meanwhile, counting on the usual workings of the business cycle to end the slump, he urged people to hold on, proclaiming that "prosperity is just around the corner," which convinced no one but provided a theme for one popular song's lyrics, "Just around the corner, there's a rainbow in the sky," to join the haunting "Brother, can you spare a dime?" Andrew Mellon, Hoover's disagreeable-looking multimillionaire secretary of the treasury, was more blunt and cruel than the president and did not seem to care what the American people felt or thought. "Let the slump liquidate itself," he told the country with unbelievable disdain. "Liquidate labor, liquidate stocks, liquidate the farmers. . . . People will work harder, live a more moral life. Values will be adjusted, and enterprising people will pick up the wrecks from less competent people."

In Pleasantville, as the hot, humid summer began, I listened with disgust to the Republican convention in Chicago, which renominated President Hoover but offered no hope for an end to the Depression, ignoring the suffering that was destroying the country, and spending almost all of its time arguing over the repeal of Prohibition. The Democrats, who my father thought would come up with some fresh ideas, were hardly better. My father was for Al Smith, and in New York, he said, the Democrats led by Smith had always been good for business. Nominate and elect Al Smith, he assured us, and the Democrats would bring prosperity back to the whole nation. But Al Smith wasn't nominated. We listened to Will Rogers joke with the delegates, to a fight over seating Huey Long, to the roaring adoption of a plank in the platform for repeal of Prohibition, and at last to Al Smith speaking on what he called "the raddio" in his grating New York accent and to the cheers that followed his speech while the mighty pipe organ in the Chicago convention hall sent chills up and down our spines with the blasts of Smith's theme song, "The Sidewalks of New York." But that was about it. The Democratic delegates promised to take some vague measures to end the Depression and then watched an angry Al Smith and his supporters "take a walk" and leave the convention in a huff after a dramatic secret deal behind Smith's back threw Speaker John Nance Garner's votes from Texas and California to Franklin D. Roosevelt and gave him the nomination. In return, Garner was chosen to run as vice president.

My father and a lot of people—including H. L. Mencken, whose candidate, Governor Ritchie of Maryland, also went down the drain—were furious, and so was I. Mencken, Walter Lippmann, and many other columnists, editorial writers, and radio commentators who had hoped to get rid of Hoover and end Prohibition felt personally thwarted by Roosevelt's deal and spread their belief that the Democrats had nominated their worst candidate, a spoiled, uninspiring rich man's son who had a lackluster, do-nothing record as governor of New York and, to boot, was a cripple who could not be expected to wage a winning campaign against the Republicans.

To me, the worst thing about the conventions was that there now seemed to be no hope of anyone being able to end the Depression. When I finally left for college, all I could wish for was that my family's financial situation would get no worse and that, between the periodic checks that my father would be able to send me and my ability to stick to a tight budget and in an emergency get a loan, a scholarship, or a job, I would be able to stay at Harvard. At the same time, the prospect of having to drop out hung over me like a sword, and, as if I feared that the sword might fall at any time, I tried to experience Harvard's opportunities and the many facets of its life to the fullest.

Intending to concentrate in the field of government, history, and economics, I started off with basic required courses in English, science, Latin, French, and Western European history (from the latter days of the Roman Empire to the Treaty of Versailles), and I never studied harder in my life. Still, I had plenty of time for athletics and a variety of extracurricular activities. I had my mother ship me my old football gear from my first year at Horace Mann and went out for freshman football, but I only weighed 125 pounds, and the trainer told me I'd be killed and that I should go out for manager of the team instead. That meant competing as a water boy against about twenty-five other candidates at the varsity games on Saturdays by taking turns rushing out on the field during time-outs in the game to carry water, cups, and towels to the haggard players. It all seemed simple enough, and I never did discover the criteria by which we were judged for the job of manager, but each week a bunch of us got the ax without any explanation, and after two or three games, it fell on me. Since the trainer hinted to me that the whole thing was stacked and the winner had been selected from the beginning, I didn't much mind it. I had enjoyed sitting on the bench with the players, getting a free field's-eye view of the games and of the excitement of the cheerleaders with their megaphones, the Harvard band playing "Wintergreen for President," and the crowds in the stands that loomed up behind me in Soldier's Field.

I still had time to do something else in the fall, so I joined the freshman cross-country squad under coach Jaako Mikkola, pleased him by coming in ninth on the squad in my first four-mile race on the course along the Charles River, and qualified for the team for the rest of the season. I failed to go out for track the following spring, however, being lured instead to lacrosse, which left me with a jumble of memories of doing more running up and down a field than I would ever have done as a miler on the track team and getting banged every which way on all parts of my head and body day after day by other people's sticks. I also remember that another member of the freshman lacrosse team was Theodore Roosevelt III, who had gone to Groton and was also a good soccer player and was more used than I to running endlessly up and down a field and getting kicked in the shins and tripped up in the legs. I was aching to talk to him about his grandfather, but I was too preoccupied with holding my own in the violence on the field to do so, and I never really got to know him. The following year, as a sophomore, I chose sports more wisely, running varsity cross-country in the fall and the mile and half mile on the track squad in the winter and spring.

By the end of my freshman year, my close encounter with a member of the Roosevelt family had become typical of what one might expect at Harvard. If one were looking for celebrities or sons of celebrities, they were there. On Halloween night in the fall of 1932, Franklin D. Roosevelt, on his way to campaign in Boston, stopped in Harvard Square near Wigglesworth Hall and, as I wrote my parents the next morning, got "the grandest razzing" from the mobs of students who poured out to see him. A few days earlier, Hoover had won a straw vote at Harvard, but I was sure that the poll was out of step with the majority feeling in the rest of the country. People might have been unhappy with FDR, but they hated Hoover.

A couple of nights later, I went to a Democratic campaign rally, met the mayor of Cambridge, and succumbed to his plea that I help the local Democrats. That got me involved in a rally for Newton D. Baker, one of the unsuccessful candidates for the Democratic nomination for president. He had come to Boston to campaign for Roosevelt, and after Baker made what I thought was a great speech, I met him and decided to get into the fight to get rid of Hoover. Some of the more activist Democrats induced me to join the Harvard Liberal Club, and there I met John D. Rockefeller's grandson David. A very reserved but friendly classmate, he had graduated from Lincoln School, a progressive institution in New York City that, like Horace Mann, had been founded by Teachers College. Over the course of the next two years, I discovered David to be extremely compassionate about others, and I became very fond of him. He said that after graduation, he intended to go into social work among the poor, but he veered instead into a distinguished career that mixed civic service with banking and finance and that many years later would bring us together again through our mutual interest in American Indians.

Meanwhile, on election day in November, I worked at a Cambridge voting poll as a checker for the Democrats, verifying the names and addresses of the voters for the local district boss, a florist by the name of Galgay, who was so sure of his own victory that he threw a party that night and then discovered that he was about the only Democrat who had lost. After leaving Galgay's grim party, I joined Cambridge's Democratic Mayor Russell and some politicians and toured the polling places, exulting in the Democrats' national victory over Hoover. The next morning, truly converted to the excitement of political life, I wrote my parents that I intended to join the Harvard Democratic Club.

As if this were not enough on my platter, I sang with the University

Instrumental Clubs, tried out for the Harvard *Crimson*, and, landing on somebody's list as an extra Harvard man, maintained a busy social life on weekends, accepting invitations to "coming out" dances of Massachusetts debutantes at the Brookline Country Club and other clubs and hotels. As for the Instrumental Clubs, everyone in my family thought I was tone-deaf and unable to carry a tune, but I was judged just adequate enough in my audition to make the vocal group within the Instrumental Clubs and, submerged among stronger voices than mine, participated in concerts at various schools and organizations in New England and, all dressed up in tuxedo or white tie and tails, sang Gilbert and Sullivan and old barbershop ballads with words like "Broadway's a tame street compared to our Main Street." Once, returning from a concert to Harvard in a blinding snow-storm after midnight, the snappy roadster in whose rumble seat a friend and I were huddled in freezing cold and misery skidded and smashed into a tree. I was hurled like a somersaulting acrobat out of the rumble seat and into the snow, seeing stars and crushing my derby hat as I landed, but suffering no serious injury. The windshield broke into shards that fell in on the owner of the car and two companions who were in the front seat and the car was demolished, but no one was too badly hurt, and overlooking how close we had come to getting killed, we thumbed rides back to Cambridge and made it to first class the next morning.

The competition, or "comp," for the honor of being invited onto the staff of the *Crimson*, Harvard's daily paper, was brutal. Originally, I, along with some fifty journalistically inclined classmates, tried out for three editorial positions that were allocated to freshmen. We carried out reporting and writing assignments, brought in ideas and stories of our own, and were judged for quantity of work as well as journalistic ability. The competition ran for eight weeks, and from time to time, candidates were rejected and the field was narrowed. While it lasted, it was almost a full-time job, leaving little time for studies, and there was a saying that every freshman who made the *Crimson* paid for it by going on probation. I was already cutting classes, my marks were falling, I faced getting failures in more than one of my courses, and I was feeling guilty about wasting the money of my hard-pressed parents. When there were only five of us left in the comp, I decided to drop out and try again in my sophomore year. I stayed for one final assignment that seemed too interesting to pass up—an interview with the great Polish pianist and first prime minister of Poland, seventy-two-year-old Ignace Paderewski, who had come to Boston for a concert and was living with his staff in a private railroad car in the yard of the Back Bay station. Paderewski was frail and seedy-looking, like an old man with a crown of long, straggly white hair who dropped crumbs all over himself. He greeted me kindly but, claiming that he was too busy and had to write a lot of letters, refused to give me an interview and turned me over to one of his managers, who handed me a few sheets of publicity about their tour of the United States. I thanked them and left, and the next day retired from the *Crimson* competition.

Meanwhile, I had been writing occasionally to Mencken, keeping him informed of some of my activities and views at Harvard and of my continued interest in journalism. He usually responded very promptly and encouragingly, and sometimes with great humor, enclosing in one of his letters a form of bequest to himself, which he asked me mischievously to convey to Professor Irving Babbitt, who taught French literature and was one of his friends. He was also interested in my freshman English course and hoped I would go on to take Bernard De Voto's advanced writing class. I was not at Harvard long enough to take De Voto's course, and after having taken Mr. Baruth's exciting class at Horace Mann, I told Mencken that I thought that the freshman English course at Harvard was a stuffy bore taught by uninspired teachers. One classmate who shared my view was Deric Nusbaum, a big, sturdy fellow who had been a hero to me in my Boy Scout days because as a boy author he had written one of my favorite books, *With Deric in Mesa Verde*, about his adventures with his father, a prominent National Park Service archaeologist, in the Indian ruins of the Southwest. Despite the fact that he was a published author, Deric had constant trouble with our English teacher, getting poor marks on his papers and coming close to failing the course. At the same time, another classmate, William Burroughs, who was destined for future fame, sat quietly and presumably contentedly through the course, absorbing something that I must have missed. Burroughs, who told me that after Harvard he thought he might go into the advertising business, was quiet and unassuming, with a large head, pale, washed-out skin, and slicked-down hair above a high forehead. He wore bow ties, was pleasant and friendly, and gave no hint that one day he would be a beatnik guru and, with *Naked Lunch*, one of the most influential American writers of the twentieth century. After graduating, he did some work in anthropology, then went to New York and, from Harvard's point of view, simply vanished. While he roamed in Mexico, South America, North Africa, and elsewhere, experimenting with drugs and with writing, our periodic class reports listed him off and on as "Lost—Address Unknown," leaving us to wonder at times who was lost, he or we?

After our Christmas holidays, the sense of emergency about the Depression became greater, and the long winter weeks at Harvard, a dreary montage of snow, gray skies, and unrelieved study for midyear examinations, seemed to become increasingly bleak. In the nation, unemployment hit a new high of 15 million, breadlines got longer, banks started to fail, Congress did nothing, and people were talking communism and revolution. Promising action as soon as he was inaugurated, President-elect Roosevelt spoke stirringly about "the forgotten man" and the evils of greedy interests that had brought on the Depression, and though he was not specific about what he intended to do, his optimism and jaunty, reassuring personality induced increasing numbers of people, including myself, to believe that he might really do something to save the country if we could only hold on long enough for him to take over. At times, it seemed questionable. In Miami, a deranged unemployed bricklayer named Giuseppe Zangara took shots at him, missed, fatally wounded the mayor of Chicago, and shocked the nation. Roosevelt remained incredibly calm, and shock gave way almost immediately to relief and then to a great wave of admiration for the president-elect. A strong new skipper, of a kind we had long needed and could count on, seemed about to take the helm.

Roosevelt did not let us down. Shortly before his inauguration on March 4, banks began to fail and close their doors all over the country. My father had just told me that the time had arrived for me to start trying to get a scholarship or a college loan that would help see me through the rest of the year. With the banking system about to crash, no one could talk about a loan, and anyway, it was the wrong time of the year to apply for scholarships, which were few in number and were generally available only to applicants who could meet a donor's narrowly drawn restrictions, such as, for example, requiring that an applicant be a descendant of the donor, one Ephraim Cox of Malden, Massachusetts, who would use the scholarship at Harvard only for the study of early Puritan New England.

On Inauguration Day, feeling an omen of doom, I crowded into the Harvard Union, which was packed with classmates, to listen to the swearing-in ceremonies for the new president on loudspeakers attached to a radio and, like almost everybody in the building and probably in the nation, was electrified by the vigor and eloquence of Roosevelt's assurance that "This great Nation will endure as it has endured, will revive and will prosper," and that "the only thing we have to fear is fear itself." People were nodding enthusiastically to one another and shaking their fists in approval. For a moment, my own eyes filled with tears. From that time on, Roosevelt had me.

Right after that, Roosevelt closed all the banks in the country for four days to shore them up so they could reopen, and there was something of a holiday spirit around Harvard Square. Everybody ran out of cash, and there was a feeling of a jointly shared experience, where everybody was in the same boat, and somehow, with IOUs and scrip that stores quickly issued, we got by until the banks opened again. Soon after that, I got the first of several short-term loans, guaranteeing that I would stay at Harvard for the rest of the year. Meanwhile, FDR and Congress went into action and, passing one bill after another in a whirlwind of unity and determination, restored confidence, started relief agencies that provided jobs, repealed Prohibition, and, as I and many others saw it at the time, saved the capitalist system in the United States from complete collapse.

In the middle of the excitement of the start of the New Deal, I was named to the Freshman Jubilee Committee, which had charge of putting on our class's big dance of the year. My major contribution was getting as entertainer for the event the sophisticated lyricist Johnny Green, who had cowritten "Body and Soul" and other hits for singers like Libbie Holman and was then at the peak of his popularity. Johnny, who had gone to both Horace Mann and Harvard about eight years ahead of me and now lived and worked in Hollywood, jumped at my invitation, but he asked if I could get him a date for the evening. I did so, but he really didn't need one. He turned out to be a charming celebrity, and both at the piano and at tables, he was constantly surrounded by my classmates and their dates.

I finished all my courses in good shape that semester, and near the end of the school year, my father came up to see me before I returned home. I knew from his face that there was something wrong. He told me that things had really gotten bad in his business and that I might not be able to return to Harvard that fall. But he tried to reassure me and added that he didn't know yet for sure how things would be during the summer. What he really wanted to tell me was that a bridge-playing friend of his who was the part owner of a resident-buyers' firm in New York City had offered me a job in his company for the summer and that I ought to take it and save some money and maybe by fall he'd be better off and I could return to college after all. "Jobs are scarce, you know," he added wistfully.

I told him that of course I'd take it and save all that I could. And, with a kind of reassurance for him on my part, I told him it wouldn't be the end of the world if I didn't get back to college. Lots of kids were dropping out for money reasons, and if things improved, maybe I could return the following year. But even as I talked, there was an awful lump in my stomach, and my head seemed to spin.

My father nodded, seemingly relieved that he was through delivering his unhappy message, and he said, "We'll see how it works out."

5 ▪ INNOCENT IN POLITICS VERSUS HUEY P. LONG

While I was growing up in New York City, it seemed to be general knowledge that if your family was going to move, they did it on October 1. Each year, that day was moving day, the day when leases ran out and the streets were filled with moving vans that were backed obliquely in toward the buildings, and furniture was piled all over the sidewalks. On October 1, 1932, just after I had started my freshman year at Harvard and was far removed from the turmoil of the packing and unpacking, my parents, with Warren to help them, had moved across Manhattan Island from West 92d Street, where I had spent my formative years, to another apartment building on East 71st Street and Lexington Avenue. One block from fashionable Park Avenue and three from Fifth Avenue, it was a quieter and more sedate neighborhood than the one we had left, with solemn-faced doormen and elevator operators in winged collars and white gloves, but it was also duller and gloomier, without the spaciousness and airy feeling of grandeur and freedom that the sweeping views of the Hudson River conveyed to the neighborhoods of Riverside Drive.

Although I never knew for sure why we moved, I assumed that it was a matter of economy and that we were paying less rent for the new apartment, which was slightly smaller than the old one. At any rate, on my return from Harvard in June 1933, I missed something and at first thought it had to do with my fantasy world of the American West and Oregon that had been symbolized for me for so long by the memory of the little red lighthouse and the ever-present majestic views of the Palisades, which, along with the West Side and the friends and ties of my youth, we had left behind. But it was more than that. The independence and new interests that had marked my growth at Harvard during the year's absence from living at home made me feel strangely indifferent to my parents' new residence. As if I were expanding out and away from my family and had become something of a boarder who had lost his roots and a place to which to belong, the new, unfamiliar apartment felt less like a permanent home and more like a temporary bedroom, which I left every morning for the East Side subway, the 42d Street shuttle, and the summer job in an office building just south of Times Square that I hoped would help get me back to college in the fall.

My job, which had been created generously for me as a favor to my father by his bridge-playing friend, turned out to be that of an office boy and general helper in the mailroom of one of New York's leading resident-buyers' firms, which provided office space and assistance to department- and specialty-store buyers from all over the country when they came to New York on their periodic purchasing visits to manufacturers or to attend their sales shows, and which at other times of the year, when the buyers had gone back home to their stores, serviced them with information and representation. The mailroom, a hot interior room without any windows, was presided over by a gangly, good-natured Yankees baseball fan in his middle thirties named Eddie, who had a big, toothy grin, imagined himself a comic who might end up in vaudeville one day, and kept his staff of five or six younger men in their late teens or early twenties, all of whom seemed to live up in the Bronx, laughing uproariously at his wisecracks and jokes as they emptied the mailbags each day and sorted the letters for the different staff people and visiting buyers into pigeonholes in racks along the walls.

A good part of my job consisted of running errands through the hot, humid streets of the city, taking the Pitney-Bowes stamp machine for servicing at the main Manhattan post office, picking up theater, sporting-event, and railroad tickets for the buyers, bringing back paper-bag lunches of pastrami and chopped chicken liver sandwiches, pickles, and Dr. Brown's Celery Tonic from a Times Square delicatessen and packets of Squibb's bicarbonate of soda from a drugstore for Eddie and his staff, and delivering or picking up packages all over town. Much of the firm's business was with companies in the Garment District of midtown Manhattan, and in my errand-running, I got to know the hard, tough world of Seventh Avenue and the bustling streets south of Times Square that were jammed with trucks and with yelling people who pulled open racks of garments on wheels through the honking traffic and in and out of freight elevators and rabbit warrens of workrooms in the tall office buildings and lofts where hats, coats, dresses, and other articles of clothing were manufactured for all of the United States.

Sometimes my errands took me to the the city's other boroughs. Once, I had to deliver a parcel to someone near Cortelyou Road in Brooklyn. I got off at the wrong subway station in that borough and panicked when I couldn't find anyone who had ever heard of Cortelyou Road. The more I wandered around, the more lost I became. A lot of good my Harvard education was doing me, I thought desperately. Finally, I found my way back to the subway, returned to Manhattan, and, starting over again, got off eventually at the right station and located the address I had been looking for. There they told me that the subway station I had first gotten off at was only three blocks away from Cortelyou Road in a different direction, and they didn't know why nobody had been able to direct me to it. "Maybe you weren't speaking in Brooklynese," one of them said. When I told Eddie in the mailroom how nobody in Brooklyn had recognized the name of a street that was only a few blocks from where I was talking to them, he and the others went into gales of laughter. "That's Brooklyn for you, kid," Eddie exclaimed, tapping the side of his forehead with his fingertips. "You gotta be careful. You come up from the subway into a strange place over there and you could get lost forever and never be heard from again. They're all coconuts in Brooklyn. They never know where they are."

Everyone in the mailroom regarded me as a greenhorn who needed their advice and protection, and they referred to me as "the kid from Harvard." They all knew that I was going there, that my job was an unnecessary one and had been specially created for me by one of the firm's partners who was a friend of my family, and they assumed that I would be going back to college in the fall. Although none of them had gone beyond high school, no one was resentful or envious of me, and, like my father's friend, they all went out of their way to help me and make my stay a pleasant one. In turn, I was grateful for their tolerance and concern and kindness, but kept my fingers crossed that I'd be out of there by September.

Luck was with me. I had been hired at a salary of nine dollars a week, and because I lived at home, where I had breakfast and dinner, I had been able to save about half of what I earned. But one Monday morning late in July, I came in and found everybody in the firm milling around in excitement. The code of conduct of Roosevelt's newly passed National Recovery Act, or the NRA, as it was known, had been approved for our company, posters with the blue eagle emblem and the patriotic legend WE DO OUR PART were tacked up all over the place, and, in line with the NRA's goal of putting more spending money, or "purchasing power," in the pockets of working people so they could buy more things and get the wheels of production rolling again, all of our salaries had been raised over the weekend without advance notice, mine included. From then on, I would be making the exciting sum of thirteen dollars a week! My father's eyes lit up when I told him what had happened, and he smiled and said, "I think things are getting better," and I got a feeling that maybe he was also signaling to me a new optimism about his own business.

Meanwhile, despite the time that I had to give to my job, my interest in President Roosevelt's efforts to end the Depression had not faded, and I wanted to play some kind of an active role in the historic events and changes that were taking place. I could tell all around me in New York that people like myself loved and trusted FDR, and I gathered from the newspapers, newsreels, and radio that it was also true among people throughout the country. A small number of wealthy and powerful men in the nation were bitterly attacking the NRA and the other New Deal emergency legislation as communistic and loaded with governmental regulations, but it seemed obvious to me that the new laws were not being imposed on the overwhelming majority of the American people against their will. Instead, their great support for Roosevelt indicated clearly that they needed relief and wanted Congress to enact the new laws and regulations to pull them out of the suffering of the Depression and protect them from the greed and abuses of the forces that still clung to Herbert Hoover's disastrous faith in a laissez-faire, survival-of-the-fittest society.

At the same time, many of Roosevelt's powerful and influential enemies in banking and business were almost daily discrediting themselves and their cause by public admissions of fraud, theft, embezzlement, and other crimes in sensational hearings before the Senate Banking and Currency Committee in Washington. The president of the New York Stock Exchange, the heads of the Chase National Bank and the National City Bank, and Samuel Insull, the most famous builder of holding companies, were among many who were involved in shocking scandals that sent some of them to prison in handcuffs and others, like Insull, fleeing from the country. The revelations during the tumultuous months of 1933 of the wholesale misdeeds of the once-respected business and financial leaders of the nation played into Roosevelt's hands and helped him end the Horatio Alger myth that being wealthy and powerful was synonymous with being virtuous and right.

In the contest between good and evil or right and wrong, as I saw it, there was no national campaign in which I could participate that year. But in New York City, front-page exposés and scandals had also been rocking Tammany Hall, whose Democratic bosses had been an unwanted millstone around FDR's neck, and Fiorello La Guardia—a short, charismatic Roosevelt supporter and former congressman who had been a World War I flyer and was still known formally by his wartime rank of Major—was running for mayor on the reform ticket of the Fusion party, vowing dramatically in an impassioned, high-pitched voice to "eradicate the pestilence" of Tammany Hall from New York life. I wrote La Guardia, offering to help his campaign against corruption in any way that I could, and after receiving an appreciative reply from someone on his staff, I ended up for a few weeks in August doing research in my spare time for a Columbia University professor who was writing campaign speeches and articles that in November helped La Guardia win the election and oust Tammany from power.

In the meantime, my father informed me one evening in August that his business had improved, and sitting down with me, he went over a budget that, along with the help of my summer savings and a loan and a job at Harvard, would make my return to college possible. We both let out a long sigh and, with the strain of uncertainty off of us and my education settled for another year, we shook hands happily. The next week, there was still more good news. Among my oldest and closest friends was a wealthy young New Yorker named Lester Hofheimer, whose grandfather had apparently made a fortune from his inventions. I had first met Lester at Camp Androscoggin when we were both about twelve years old. Our parents were friends, and Lester and I had ended up living in the same bunkhouse at the camp. He was sturdy and strongly built, with shiny black eyes that always seemed to be fastened intently on your face, as if he were studying you. The truth was that years earlier, a serious mastoid operation had left him totally deaf in one ear and partly so in the other one, and he had learned to read lips. During our growing-up years, we became fast friends, sharing numerous interests and adventures. He was bighearted and compassionate and was uncomfortably aware of the advantages he possessed from his family's wealth, and he was always giving money to charities and trying to help other people. The previous June, he had graduated from Phillips Exeter Academy, where he had been on the wrestling team, and he was slated to enter Harvard in the fall.

During the summer, I saw him often in the evenings and on weekends, and he worried about my money problems, which made it uncertain whether I would be going back to college. Generously, he wanted me first to allow him to have his family pay my tuition, and then he offered to lend me enough money, interest-free, to pay it myself, but I would have nothing to do with either proposal and was glad when I could tell him that my father and I had solved the question ourselves. Then he threw another proposal at me. He had a car and wanted me to drive with him at his expense on a few days' trip to the Chicago World's Fair before college began. By taking turns driving, he said, we could make the thousand or so miles each way without stopping.

When I discussed the idea with my parents, they surprised me by agreeing that it was a great opportunity and that I had earned it by working hard all summer and to go ahead. My father even said that I should offer to pay for my own expenses with a little money that he would give me. In view of our financial situation, his enthusiastic support puzzled me, but I remembered all the travel he had looked forward to doing earlier in his life and had not been able to do, and the wonderful stories he had told Warren and me about the St. Louis and other world's fairs when he was a kid, fantasizing about them as if he had seen them himself, and I thought sadly that although he would miss this fair, too, he perhaps wanted to experience it vicariously through me.

At any rate, on September 1, my job ended, and a few days later Lester and I took off for Chicago, crossing the Hudson River on a ferry and leaving the Palisades far behind us. I knew that none of this trip would be through the Far West of my imagination, but it led toward it, and the country we would see would all be new and exciting to me. Before we started, Lester told me that another friend of his had decided to join us and that we would pick him up at his home in Lewistown, Pennsylvania. It was long before the day of high-speed four-lane interstates, and after we made good time across New Jersey, fierce downpours with thunder and lightning slowed us to a crawl on narrow two-lane roads in Pennsylvania that climbed, descended, and twisted in hairpin turns on the sides of dark wooded mountains.

In Lewistown, Lester's friend joined us, and we continued on through a stormy night, taking turns driving and sleeping. At dawn, we passed through towns in western Ohio on roads paved with red bricks that gave a rumbling sound to our tires. The storm was gone, and from there almost to Chicago, the flat prairie land was carpeted with fields of densely planted corn, some of whose stalks had already been picked and whose yellowing leaves looked dry and torn. Here and there were barns with Mail Pouch tobacco advertising signs painted on their sides, and near them were the homes and buildings of farm families, many of them dilapidated and seedy and looking unpainted and badly in need of repairs, with missing shingles, broken steps, partly collapsed porches, and mounds of earth piled for insulation against rotting foundations. We all observed the dreary, poverty-stricken scenes of this fertile farm country, and Lester's friend reminded us that these people had been suffering a depression since the end of World War I. Overproduction and low prices had brought them to the verge of revolution the previous spring, and they were just now beginning to be helped by the New Deal's emergency farm acts.

Chicago was a lusty, adventurous city. I don't remember much about the fair, whose theme was "A Century of Progress." I bought a program to take back to my father, and we spent a whole day at the fair, visiting one exhibition building after another, drinking newly legalized Pabst Blue Ribbon beer with a 3.2 percent alcoholic content, and seeing Sally Rand doing her famous nude dance behind big feathery fans that she flipped around teasingly in front of her body. But Chicago itself, endowed with a dramatic reputation of being the dangerous city of Al Capone's mob, was more exciting and entertaining. We stayed at the home of a relative of Lester's friend. He had two extra bedrooms and a number of girlfriends, and with them we roamed State Street and other crowded streets in the Loop and along Michigan Avenue, seeing the sights, looking unsuccessfully for the haunts of gangsters, eating Polish sausages and Greek and Italian meals, and lingering with other tourists at the open doors of taverns, listening to the music of famous jazz bands, pianists, and blues singers who were performing inside. The grand climax of our stay was a feast of big juicy steaks in a jam-packed, festively decorated restaurant at Chicago's huge, smelly Union Stock Yards.

Leaving Chicago finally, we took a route home through some of the industrial sections of the Midwest and western Pennsylvania, passing the steel mills of Gary and Youngstown, stopping for meals in cafés near automobile, rubber, and wire and cable plants, and driving along secondary roads through scores of depressing-looking, run-down company-owned towns of factory workers and coal miners, whose company stores, pool halls, and ranks of drab weather-beaten row houses covered the sides of scruffy, eroded hills. During World War II and in the years that followed it, large numbers of the kind of working people we were seeing in these towns would rise economically, principally through federal government spending and union-labor activity, to become members of a strong, burgeoning American middle class. But in 1933, millions of them, including large numbers of foreign-speaking immigrants from Eastern and Southern European countries, constituted part of an enormous blue-collar class in the nation. Living almost as serfs of the corporations that employed them, few of those in the towns we were driving through harbored any expectation that one day they might own their own house, possess such a thing as an insurance policy, or have a family member go on from high school to college.

In the Lehigh Valley of eastern Pennsylvania, after we had returned Lester's friend to his home, we came on a scene of labor excitement in a small, muddy coal-mining town named Mauch Chunk. Angry-looking members of John L. Lewis's United Mine Workers who were on strike had taken over one of the streets and were throwing rocks and bricks toward a line of helmeted company policemen on horseback. Back at Harvard the previous March, Bob Playfair, the captain of the freshman cross-country team, who had become a friend of mine, had introduced me to his father, who was the managing editor of the *Boston Evening Transcript*, one of the leading papers in that city. I had told Mr. Playfair of my interest in journalism and my trying out for the *Crimson*, and I suddenly remembered that he had offered to pay me space rates for anything I submitted that the paper bought. The *Transcript* already had a regular student campus correspondent, and it turned out that I had been too busy at Harvard to hunt for something unusual to write up and submit, but now I thought that here was a chance to do an exciting eyewitness story of a battle between striking coal miners and the police that the *Transcript* might buy. I told Lester to pull over, and I jumped out and started down the block toward the crowd that was yelling and throwing rocks. As I neared them, the mounted policemen started to move toward the crowd, some of the miners backed up in my direction, and all of a sudden a rock from somewhere hit me on the side of the head, and I went down.

Lester and a couple of miners got me into a store and then to the home of a doctor, who stopped the blood that was flowing from a gash above my temple. He shaved the hair from that part of my head, stuck a bandage over the wound, gave me some pills, and, telling me that I would probably have a scar there for the rest of my life as a memento of my visit to Mauch Chunk, said that Lester and I could go on but that I shouldn't do any of the driving. By the time we got back to the middle of town in the car, the confrontation was over and the last of the miners were drifting away. Lester and I went on toward New York, I never did write a story about the disaster, and years later, I learned that there was no more Mauch Chunk; the town had changed its name to Jim Thorpe, honoring the famous American Indian athlete. But I still had the scar as a remembrance of the aborted attempt to cover the strike.

In the middle of September, Lester and I drove up to college. I had been assigned to a double suite in the recently built Lowell House, one of the new grandly magnificent Georgian-style undergraduate houses along the Charles River, sharing it with Arthur Fields, who had been one of my two roommates in Wigglesworth Hall the previous year, and whom I liked immensely. When I was at Horace Mann, I had run the mile against Art, who had lived in New York and had gone to Hackley School, one of our rivals. He was a big strapping fellow, a good student, and an all-around athlete, but several times during the two years that I roomed with him at Harvard, he got scary, out-of-control skin infections that ended up in blood poisoning. In 1935, after his third year at Harvard, he got an appointment to Annapolis and transferred to the Naval Academy. There, just before his graduation, he got blood poisoning again, and this time the doctors were unable to treat him successfully, and he died. It was a great tragedy, for a few years later, penicillin became available, and it would have saved his life.

At Harvard, I was now living very close to the bone, not only pinching pennies but hustling to increase my income. During the year, by making and staying on the dean's list, I was lucky to be awarded two fifty-dollar grants and some additional fifty-dollar loans by the college's Committee on Scholarships and Other Aids. These grants and loans helped me meet Harvard's bills, but I also had to scrounge for jobs that would contribute to my budget

Hard at study in Lowell House, Harvard, 1934. The picture was taken by Alonzo B. Kight, a classmate and friend, who found it among some of his papers more than sixty years later, just in time to be included in this book.

for meals, laundry, clothing, books, athletic tickets, movies, travel home, and various out-of-pocket incidentals. At one time or another during my sophomore year, I earned a 7 percent commission from soliciting contracts from undergraduates for a laundry firm; waited on tables and washed dishes in return for my own lunches at an eating club for law students in Cambridge; saved twenty-four dollars on my college bill by carrying out the chores of a monitor in one of my classes; and got my dinners free by rushing into Boston in my tuxedo to a fish restaurant late every afternoon to work as a headwaiter for three hours. Sometimes I was employed in two or three of these and other jobs, like personal tutoring, simultaneously, but they frequently clashed in timing with one another or with one of my classes or other college activities, and I often had to drop a job and look for another one.

Meanwhile, in the outside world, the Depression continued despite the efforts of the Roosevelt administration to restore prosperity, and my father's business took a sudden turn again for the worse, thus reviving our worries. Still continuing to regard Harvard as a wonderful experience that might end for me at any moment, I apportioned my time anxiously among classes, athletics, and other college activities. I took courses in government, economics, and philosophy, and an advanced class in English composition that aimed at helping us to produce marketable books, plays, articles, stories, or whatever we wished to write. Hoping to sell something, I launched into research for a three-act play on the life of Robert Burns, and I also tried my hand at some short stories and essays. In December, my English professor routed one of my stories to a Boston agent, who paid me three dollars for it and got it printed in a local magazine. It was my first sale, and I was so cheered by it that to celebrate the event—and also, incidentally, to observe the final repeal of Prohibition, which went into effect the same week, although not in Cambridge, which remained dry—I spent almost ten dollars throwing a party with cigars and bootlegged beer and Canadian ale in my rooms and getting woozily drunk with a lot of friends on the smoky mixture of alcohol and the strong cigars.

At the same time, during the year, I turned down invitations to join several clubs and fraternities, principally because their dues were beyond my means, but I ran varsity cross-country and track, sang again with the Instrumental Clubs, played touch football on a Lowell House team against one from the Civilian Conservation Corps, which we defeated, and tried out once more for the *Crimson*. This time, I dropped out of the competition for the *Crimson* to join some rebelling editors of that paper in founding a more lively college daily, a tabloid called the *Harvard Journal*. Although it was great fun competing with the *Crimson*, which we considered stuffy and too conservative, the *Journal* had no financial staying power and was short-lived.

My principal interest, however, gradually became centered beyond Cambridge, in the colorful political leaders of the New Deal and the affairs of the NRA, FERA, AAA, CCC, and the other new "alphabet" agencies in Washington that were trying to pull the nation out of the Depression. During the summer, both my government professor, Arthur N. Holcombe, and my economics professor, Harold H. Burbank, had served in Washington as advisers to the Roosevelt administration, and I looked upon them with awe and envy, wanting ever so much to find a way to get into the dramatic world of the New Deal myself, to support and be a part of Roosevelt's inspiring crusade against what I saw as the stupidities and evils of my parents' generation that had brought on the Depression, and to help create a new and better world.

Much of my political passion was kindled and kept aflame by two of Professor Holcombe's stimulating courses in government that I took during the year. In both of them, he applied our studies of the problems and actions of previous administrations, of landmark Supreme Court deci-

sions, and the writings of sharp-eyed observers of American political institutions—including a recently published best-selling autobiography by
Lincoln Steffens, a sensationally, "muckraking" journalist who had found
corruption almost everywhere in American political life—to discussions
and analyses of the current scene in Washington, as well as in the European democracies and the ideological "ism" dictatorships of Communist
Russia, Nazi Germany, and fascist Italy. I was still a member of the Harvard Liberal Club, which presented interesting speakers and discussions at
its meetings but avoided becoming involved in overtly political activity.
Professor Holcombe knew of my membership in the club and also of my
interest in politics. He was a slim, youngish-looking man of about fifty
with dark-rimmed eyeglasses and a severe, intimidating expression, but he
was a thoughtful liberal activist, often urged me to think about public service as a career, and at length proposed that I consider giving leadership to
members of the Liberal Club who wanted to engage in political activities.

It was an exciting notion, and I leaped at it eagerly, expanding his suggestion within a few hours into a huge, dramatic plan, which I wrote down
on paper, to organize students in colleges all over the country into a
national student political movement with ties to no party but able to discuss and take united, independent action on individual issues. The first
step, however, was to form a base within the Harvard Liberal Club from
which to launch such an ambitious enterprise. Before I could do anything
about it, Professor Holcombe surprised me by telling me of a National
Conference on Students in Politics that was going to be held in Washington during the Christmas-week holidays. Under the sponsorship of a
number of different government and private agencies, it had scheduled as
speakers many New Dealers, as well as members of Congress, political
and religious leaders, educators, newspaper publishers, and officers of
prominent national organizations. Invitations had gone out to student
groups throughout the country, and Professor Holcombe thought that
this might prove to be an attractive opportunity for interested Liberal
Club members to become active in political affairs.

He gave me some literature on the conference, and at the next meeting
of the Liberal Club I presented the subject and found more than a dozen
members, including the club's president, Raymond Dennett, eager to
attend the Washington gathering. Because of my enthusiasm, the members appointed me chairman of the group and authorized us to represent
the Harvard Liberal Club at the affair. So on December 28, during our
Christmas-week vacation at home, one of our members who had a car
drove three of us from New York to Washington. There, we joined the
rest of our party at the YMCA, where those putting on the conference had

arranged for many of the delegations to sleep on cots and be fed. The next day, the conference opened in the packed auditorium of the U.S. Chamber of Commerce Building on H Street, and we listened to a barrage of speeches, some more inspiring than others, from Henry Wallace, the secretary of agriculture, and other administration officials; Norman Thomas, who had gotten almost a million votes as the Socialist presidential candidate against Roosevelt and Hoover; several senators and congressmen; Eugene Meyer, the publisher of the *Washington Post;* Reinhold Niebuhr of Union Theological Seminary; Ed Murrow, the future radio and television celebrity, who was then an officer of the International Student Service; and many others on why American students should play an active role in the political affairs of the country. The pleas of all of them struck deep, responsive chords in me. It was just what I had been hoping to hear, and it reinforced my emotional belief that the time was right for a plan like the one I had devised.

The conference became most interesting that night and the next two days when we discussed and debated among ourselves what students ought to do. Although we in the Harvard delegation thought of ourselves as political middle-of-the-roaders, neither conservative nor radical, it turned out that the conference became divided between what we called "the radicals" and all others. We were part of the "all others," and we quickly made friends and alliances with like-minded liberal delegations from Vassar, Princeton, Wellesley, the University of North Carolina, and several other colleges. The radicals, who were arrayed against us in many of the debates and votes on resolutions, comprised a majority of the delegates, and they were led principally by a combative, tough-talking officer of the Communist-run National Student League and by Joe Lash, a more civil and less dogmatic member of the Socialist party's Student League for Industrial Democracy, who later became a close friend of Mrs. Roosevelt and, later still, an award-winning author of books on the Roosevelts.

Most of the time, our opponents, the Communists and the Socialists, who had no love for each other's brand of Marxism, fought between themselves, and the conference ended without creating unity or forming an ongoing organization. But in a number of ways, the meeting had been worthwhile for our delegation. We had had a chance to present, debate, and win enthusiastic support from the Vassar, Princeton, and several other college groups for my plan for a nonpartisan national student movement made up of autonomous groups on college campuses throughout the country. We had also aroused interest in the plan among the press and various administration officials who attended the conference, including an aide to Secretary of Commerce Daniel Roper, who had been working for the administration on an idea for a National Laboratory on Public Affairs for students, to be conducted by a consortium of government agencies in Washington. Finally, the wide visibility we managed to gain for the plan had won the attention and support of the powerful nonpartisan National Student Federation of America, the country's leading student organization, composed of student governments and campus organizations at almost four hundred member colleges in the nation and headed a few years before by Ed Murrow. Although the NSFA, as it was known, had not participated in our conference, its president, John A. Lang, a graduate of the University of North Carolina, and other officers, who were working with the administration in planning the National Laboratory on Public Affairs for students, attended as observers.

At the same time, Huey P. Long, the demagogic, arm-flailing senator from Louisiana who was beginning to seem ominously like an American Mussolini, had learned of some attacks made against him at our meeting in the U.S. Chamber of Commerce Building and chose to return the compliment on the Senate floor, likening our student conference to an assembly of pestiferous fleas that could be scattered by a wave of the hand. The result was predictable; hostility to Long was about the only thing that united all the student delegations. But before I left Washington, I met Mrs. Hilda Phelps Hammond, who was the head of a women's committee in Louisiana that had been fighting Long and who had read in the newspapers both of our verbal exchange with the senator and of my plan for a nonpartisan national student movement. She wanted us to help her group fight Long, and, thinking that this might eventually make an important issue for our projected national movement to consider, I promised to contact her when we were organized.

After I returned to Harvard, I received many letters, interviews, and articles about my plan for a national student movement, first by Eunice Fuller Barnard, who had covered the Washington conference for the *New York Times*, and by wire-service reporters who had been there, and then follow-up stories in Boston and elsewhere and articles in *Literary Digest* and other magazines began to appear across the country. The membership of the Harvard Liberal Club swelled, and eventually I was named chairman of a political action committee that was authorized to undertake any popular cause that might interest students and bring new members into the club. The mail and publicity we were getting had me on a heady roll, but more was to come. A phone call to Mrs. Hammond in Washington requesting information about her committee's campaign against Senator Long brought us several manila envelopes bulging with newspaper clippings, affidavits, and sworn testimony that convinced us that the

Louisiana "Kingfish," whom many Americans tended to dismiss as simply a noisy clown, was indeed a ruthless political dictator who terrorized, imprisoned, and destroyed the reputations and livelihoods of opponents within his state, and a power-hungry bully whose demagoguery on the national level and the mushrooming number of his "Share-the-Wealth" clubs constituted a growing threat to the whole country.

Claiming that Long had stolen the Louisiana election that had sent him to the Senate, Mrs. Hammond's group, made up of many of the state's most prominent families, had been trying unsuccessfully to persuade the Senate Committee on Privileges and Elections to hold hearings in which they could submit evidence that would force the Senate to unseat Long, and they were now asking the students of America, through us, to support their fight. After reviewing Mrs. Hammond's material, our committee suggested that I first try to get the opinion of one of our Massachusetts senators, David I. Walsh, who had once spoken to the Liberal Club and was friendly to us. Walsh was intrigued by my call and implied that he would like to help us, but he said that the Senate was afraid that Long would turn a hearing into a "circus," and besides, Long had certain "goods" on two members of the committee that would hear him, and most of the rest had no stomach for a confrontation with the man.

That settled it for us. After giving Mrs. Hammond the gist of our conversation with Senator Walsh, we sent fat packets of copies of all of Mrs. Hammond's documented material against Long to more than one hundred student councils and undergraduate clubs in colleges throughout the country, asking them to join in a national student movement to unseat Senator Long by demanding that the Senate Committee on Privileges and Elections hear the charges against him. We told the press what we had done, and in the following days, when student organizations at more than fifty colleges from New England to Southern California wrote, phoned, or telegraphed us and announced in their own local papers that they were joining us, the story of college students taking on Huey Long became front-page national news.

Mrs. Hammond was ecstatic, and one day she called me excitedly to report that the Senate committee had agreed to hold hearings and that she wanted me to come down to Washington and testify for our group, and she would pay all my expenses. I felt pretty scared about what I might have to face, but I took an overnight train to Washington and met Mrs. Hammond at the office of her lawyer, a burly, red-faced Texan in a white suit and a black string tie, who told me right off that he hated Long's guts. He briefed me about the Senate committee and what its members might ask me about our student "crusade" and how I should reply, and the next morning we went to a hearing room in the Capitol. My heart was pounding with nervousness, and I was trying to think of what I would be saying to the committee. But I never had a chance. When we got to the hearing room, it was empty, and we were told that no hearing was scheduled. Mrs. Hammond's lawyer was good and mad and hurried us to the office of a friend, Senator William E. Borah of Idaho, who was a member of the Senate committee, and there we learned that my trip was fruitless. The chairman of the committee had changed his mind, Senator Borah told us, and there would be no hearing. "You're fortunate," he said to Mrs. Hammond. "It would be nasty, and Long would win."

Eventually, our Harvard group dropped the anti-Long campaign and went on to others, including one in support of voting rights in state elections for all college students over the age of nineteen. Nevertheless, mail and publicity kept alive our fight against the Louisiana senator, and we continued to receive support throughout the rest of the college year from churches, chambers of commerce, editorial writers, and NSFA, whose tall, lean president, John Lang, became my friend, visiting me on several occasions at Harvard and arranging for me to write an article on our campaign for his organization's publication, the *National Student Mirror*, which brought a number of other colleges into our movement. But we had satisfied ourselves that we had done all that we could do. Our national protests had educated a lot of people about Long, and sooner or later, we hoped, the Senate committee would do its duty and investigate the charges against him. Of course, it never did, and a year later an aggrieved Louisiana citizen shot and killed Long in the state capitol at Baton Rouge.

In the meantime, the Liberal Club had turned much of its attention to the rise of Adolf Hitler and the Nazis in Germany. One night, a refugee professor, newly arrived from Germany, spoke to the club. The hall was crowded, and the poor old man got thunderous applause as he delivered his remarks. He tried to hide his emotions, but he broke down and cried as he asked rhetorically, "Why did they shoot my friend so-and-so? Why did my friend so-and-so hang himself? Why did they burn my books?" The dead silence in the hall was stirring.

During the year, hatred of Hitler and disgust at what was happening in Germany built up among a large part of the faculty and the student body at Harvard and resulted in embarrassment and riots in the spring when Ernst "Putzi" Hanfstängl, a German alumnus of Harvard and an intimate friend of Hitler, appeared in Cambridge to promote the Nazi regime, followed by the arrival in Boston Harbor of a German cruiser bent on a similar mission. Many at Harvard snubbed Hanfstängl, a sophisticated, gentlemanly-appearing figure whose supposed role in the Nazi world was to play the piano to soothe Hitler's nerves, and he soon left, resentful of his treatment by his American alma mater. Later, it was said that Hitler turned against him, and he and his family were forced to flee for their lives across the Alps to Switzerland. The presence of the cruiser led to large anti-Nazi and antiwar demonstrations in Harvard Square and near the ship's berth in the Navy Yard at Charlestown, which turned to riots and arrests when police tried to break them up, which resulted, in turn, in charges of police brutality and denials by the police in inconclusive hearings that dragged on into the summer, long after the German cruiser had departed.

A couple of months before the end of the school year, it became apparent to my parents as well as to me that it was going to be almost impossible financially for me to return to college the following fall. My father's business was doing so poorly that even with jobs and loans, and despite my having acquired good enough marks to stay on the dean's list and therefore be in a good position to apply for a scholarship and renewed aid, it would all amount to very little, and I would not be able to make ends meet. I had been writing steadily but had sold nothing. During one of my trips to New York, I visited an editor at Street and Smith, the publisher of many pulp magazines, and he encouraged me to submit some stories to him. His great need seemed to be stories for western and risqué romance magazines, and I tried concocting a story for each category, dreaming of the money they would bring me. Both came back with sharp notes. The romance lacked enough "molten fire and zip," and as for the western, didn't I know that maple trees did not grow in a waterless desert? In other words, write about something you know—advice that I had received earlier from Mencken and Alfred Baruth!

I tried again, this time writing a comical story called "The Frame-Up" about Man Mountain Dean and some other professional wrestlers whom I had gotten to know during occasional attendance at their matches in Boston. Just as I finished it, I received a visit from Kenneth Holland, who had been the director of the Christmas-week students' conference in Washington and was now an educational director of the Civilian Conservation Corps. Through our mutual friend John Lang, I had gotten to know him well, and at dinner Ken informed me that John had told him of my uncertainty of being able to return to Harvard. If that was so, Ken said, he wanted to offer me a full-time job working for him.

It seemed too good to be true. Hiding my excitement at this stroke of good luck, I told him that it sounded great and that I'd let him know as soon as possible. I wrote at once to my parents about this break, but a day or so later, I received an unexpected letter from Uncle Edwin in California. I guess that my mother had written or spoken to him about my financial difficulties, for he asked me to send him immediately copies of any stories, plays, or books that I had written, and told me that MGM was starting a new unit of staff "junior writers" and was hiring recent college graduates and perhaps they might like my work and consider offering me a contract. I couldn't believe it, but I sent off to him at once "The Frame-Up" and two or three other stories—*not* the rejected romance and western—and waited.

On June 14, after I had taken my last examinations, said good-bye to Art Fields and others who were departing from Cambridge, and was preparing to pack and send my belongings to New York and leave for home, my mother phoned excitedly and read a telegram she had just received from Edwin: "Have definite job for Al writing here at MGM stop six weeks at thirty dollars weekly followed by three months at fifty comma six months at seventy five comma one year at one hundred stop executives well impressed by his stories stop ship him on as soon as possible stop congratulations."

I stood transfixed at the phone, again seeing momentarily in my mind a flashing memory of the little red lighthouse and the Palisades. All I could say was, "Wow!"

6 ✠ INNOCENT IN HOLLYWOOD

A few hours after my mother's call, I left college in a whirl, scarcely knowing what I was doing in my relief and happiness at the unexpected turn of events. But it was a tough decision. One road that had been opened to me so suddenly led to a tempting position in the New Deal and to a possible career in politics and public service. The other led to glamorous Hollywood, to writing, and to the American West, the romantic country I had wanted to see for so long. That evening, I took the night boat down from Boston to New York, and as we sailed along the Massachusetts coast and went through the narrow Cape Cod Canal into Buzzards Bay off Rhode Island, I paced around on the ship's darkened deck, turning the two options over in my head.

Although I was still little more than an eager college sophomore, I felt that politically I had matured immensely. My sheltered conservatism, like the comfortable security and stability of my youthful middle-class environment in New York, had vanished during my two years at college. The continued anxieties of the Depression and the influences of my government and economics classes had played important roles in my change, but they had been only partly responsible for it. The memory of President Hoover driving World War I veterans out of Washington; the sight of helmeted company police riding down miserably poor striking anthracite coal miners in Pennsylvania's Lehigh Valley; the cynicism of the Huey Long episode; the brutality against the anti-Nazi students in Boston who were demonstrating fear and defiance of Hitlerism; and an almost-daily, sickening diet of congressional and newspaper exposés of criminality, collusion, and greed among rich and powerful bankers, industrialists, and other leaders whom I had regarded as great Americans in my growing-up years (the latest headlines were coming now from a sensational Senate investigation led by North Dakota's Gerald P. Nye, a Progressive Republican, of the profit-driven role of the munitions industry in getting the United States into World War I) had each contributed to a profound overall impression. It was that my father's generation had bequeathed to mine a fundamentally unjust and unsound society, with whose disastrous results President Roosevelt was trying to cope, and that my generation would have to help him reform it if the America of our Founding Fathers was to survive and we were to avoid having a Hitler of our own.

The number of Communists and Socialists in the country who were also trying to change things appeared to be growing, but I was not one of them. To me, Marxism was something foreign and threatening that I knew little about and that seemed to have no relevance to America's constitutional traditions. Also, the few students I understood to be Marxists were too conspiratorial and dogmatic, and I resented them and did not want to have anything to do with a dictatorial system that ordered others what to do, to say, or to think. Instead, while college and Mauch Chunk and Mrs. Hilda Phelps Hammond had taught me a lot about the difference between idealism and the real world, I was still an idealist, but a reformist liberal of the optimistic FDR variety, rather than a radical or an extremist, and I wanted to be involved in politics and the New Deal as a mainstream American and a Democrat.

President Roosevelt had just published a book entitled *On Our Way*, which reviewed his aims and accomplishments during his first year in office. In the book, he wrote: "The almost complete collapse of the American economic system that marked the beginning of my administration called for the tearing down of many unsound structures, the adoption of new methods and a rebuilding from the bottom up.

"Three steps, all interrelated, were necessary," he continued, referring to the challenges as he had seen them, "first, by drastic measures to eliminate special privilege in the control of the old economic and social structure by a numerically very small but very powerful group of individuals so set in authority that they dominated business and banking and government itself; second, to war on crime and graft and to build up moral values; and third, to seek a return of the swing of the pendulum, which for three generations had been sweeping toward a constantly increasing concentration of wealth in fewer and fewer hands—a swing back in the direction of a wider distribution of the wealth and property of the nation."*

I thought that that was saying it pretty much on the nose, and as I recalled it amid the throbbing rhythm of the engine on the boat going

---

* Franklin D. Roosevelt, *On Our Way* (New York: John Day Co., 1934), pp. xi–xii.

from Boston to New York, I felt lucky and somehow proud that Ken Holland had offered me a chance to join FDR's revolution and play a role in the Civilian Conservation Corps, one of the president's new, innovative agencies.

But there was more to think about. Above everything, I wanted to make enough money to return as soon as possible to Harvard and complete my college education. No matter what kind of a government job Ken Holland was going to offer me, I knew instinctively that it could not be too important or well-paying, or even lead to anything bigger, because I was really half-baked and had no degree, and until I completed college, I would always be that way. On the other side of the coin, the Hollywood offer was enormously seductive. In my optimistic mood, the prospect of making one hundred dollars a week after just a few months of lesser salaries could not be dismissed. With that kind of money rolling in, I could delay going back to college in the fall, continue to work at MGM for a year and pile up my savings, and then have more than enough in the bank to see me through my final two years at Harvard. In addition, earning all this money in Hollywood, working at a studio among stars and well-known writers, living with my uncle and his family, and seeing at last a part of the real American Far West would be no punishment.

When I arrived home at our apartment in New York, I found that my parents had already made up their minds that I should go to California. I could tell that my mother was more than a little wary of the brashness of my political activities at college, of the publicity that I, her nineteen-year-old, still-wet-behind-the-ears son, had been getting taking on a United States senator like Huey Long, and concerned that I might be falling under the influence of the wrong people at college and becoming some kind of a radical. Though she didn't say it straight out, she made it clear that if I were to leave home to take a job somewhere else in the country, she much preferred knowing that I would be under the guiding wing of my uncle. My father didn't say anything about my politics—that, he felt, was my business—but his thinking about my economic future kind of paralleled mine. "Financially, you might do well enough in the movies to afford to go back to college," he said. "But at your age and without experience, I'm afraid that might not be true in a government job where you'd probably be on the bottom rung." In the end, I finally agreed with my parents that the MGM offer was in black-and-white in a telegram, that it was definite and solid, and that it needed immediate decision and action, while Ken Holland's offer, still undefined as to where, what, when, how much, and for how long, was very kind and generous, but still, as my father put it, "a pig in a poke."

With the decision made, I sent my thanks and regrets to Ken, and on June 22, after saying good-bye to my parents and to Warren, I climbed aboard a Greyhound bus at the West Side terminal in midtown Manhattan and set off for California. It was 1934, the year of the popular movie *It Happened One Night*, which featured a memorable Greyhound bus ride with Clark Gable and Claudette Colbert, but my first day was much worse than theirs. We traveled in convoy with another bus, and both of them, bound for Pittsburgh, were old and rickety and full of carbon-monoxide fumes from the exhaust. We went through the Holland Tunnel under the Hudson River, and by the time we reached the New Jersey side, with three thousand miles still to go, I was carsick. I stuck it out gamely until we made what the driver called a "comfort stop" at a roadside restaurant, but worse lay ahead. During the day, each of the buses got two flat tires and engine trouble and had to stop for repairs, and after dark, as we wound through the Pennsylvania mountains, we had a tremendous electrical storm like the one Lester and I had experienced the previous summer.

The thunder crashed and the rain washed down in torrents over the bus's windows, and several times one or the other of the straining vehicles went off the narrow, twisting road and got stuck in mud and debris, and some of us had to get out and get drenched, helping to shove a board under the wheels and push. The grand climax came about midnight, not far from Pittsburgh, when we careened down a hill in the flood and, with an explosive crash and a ripping, screeching noise above us, went under a low railroad overpass in the pitch-blackness and sliced off the baggage belonging to half of our passengers. While this luggage had been lashed to a carrier on the roof of the bus, my bag, fortunately, had been stowed inside the bus. All of us tumbled out in horror, scrambling around in the rain, and by the light of the buses' headlights and sudden flashes of lightning, and amid the din of the thunder and of people screaming, crying, and cursing the bus driver and the Greyhound company for packing things so high up on the roof, we retrieved shattered and opened suitcases and packages, articles of clothing, shoes, hats, books, toothbrushes, photographs, and other soaked possessions that were scattered all over the place.

After that, things had to get better, and they did. At Pittsburgh, I changed to an almost-empty bus for St. Louis, and at a stop in Indianapolis, we took on a number of college students from the University of Indiana who were on their way back to their homes for the summer. Some of them had guitars and harmonicas, and it was no time before everyone knew everybody else, and even the bus driver had a great time through half the night, singing with us such old chestnuts as "My Gal Sal," "A

Bicycle Built for Two," and "You Are My Sunshine" as he piloted us on to St. Louis. I had drawn as a seatmate a beautiful coed with long black hair and a southern accent who was on her way home to Lubbock, Texas, where her father had a cotton plantation. When the singing finally ended and the bus lapsed into silence, we snuggled down in the darkness and talked through the rest of the night, interrupted only by the bus's comfort stops, which were made about every two hours at all-night cafés with rest rooms.

At St. Louis, we both changed to another bus and continued riding together to Kansas City, where her older sister was waiting at the terminal with a car to drive her to Texas. By that time, we had become close friends, had exchanged addresses, and had promised to write to each other, but she had told me that she had plenty of boys after her in Lubbock, and as she and her sister left the terminal building, I knew that I'd never see her again. From Kansas City on, all the way to Los Angeles, I had a new seat-mate, a large, amusing woman in her fifties, handsome and well educated, who was head of the California Republican Women's Club and claimed she had once been an opera singer. She was chatty and entertaining, got into spirited conversations with everybody on the bus, and was soon leading us in singing to the accompaniment of a guitarist and a girl with a squeaky violin.

Before we left Kansas City, our new bus driver, a big bald-headed man of about three hundred pounds who had taken off his cap and jacket and rolled up his sleeves to reveal tattoos on his forearms, announced that despite the repeal of Prohibition, Kansas was still a dry state, and that if anyone wanted to make a purchase, he knew a store on the Missouri side of the border that sold beer and liquor, where he would be glad to make a brief stop before we crossed into Kansas. Everyone shouted, "You bet!" and we left that liquor store with several cases of beer tucked beneath some of our seats, and wondering how much of a kickback the store owner had given our driver.

Since leaving New York, I had hardly slept, and after a bottle of beer, not even my seat companion's operatic singing could keep me awake. I missed stops at Topeka, Salina, and Dodge City, and when I awoke, we were in the real West and in the middle of a frightening dust storm that was roaring all around us. I had read and heard a lot about these terrible windstorms that were at their peak in that summer of 1934. Caused by years of drought and destructive farming practices, they were blowing away the topsoil of farms and ranches, but I had no idea how scary they were. To those of us in the bus, it was like being in a brown closet cut off from the outside world, amid a fearful roar beating against our heads and with grit blowing in through cracks and up through the floor, threatening to smother us. The bus driver was hollering reassuringly not to get scared, that we'd soon be coming out the other side of it, and that he'd been through a hundred of them. He said if anyone suffered from claustrophobia, they should just close their eyes and think of something nice. We soon did get through it, emerging somewhere around Garden City, Kansas, in some pretty empty-looking plains country with a few low weather-beaten houses that seemed to be falling down, occasional knots of scrawny cows around old windmills, and hardly any trees. This was the cowboys' West, I thought, and there was nothing romantic-looking about it. But my seat companion shook her head as if she had seen my disappointment. "They're terrible, just terrible," she said. "These dust storms. They're driving everybody out of here, turning this part of the country into a desert." We didn't know it then, but within a few years, the dust storms would virtually cease. Strip and contour farming, the planting of trees in shelter belts against the wind, and other New Deal soil-conservation programs would begin effectively to combat the erosion of the soil, saving many farm and ranch families from further suffering and ruin and helping to restore stability and prosperity to that part of the United States.

In eastern Colorado, we went through two more dust storms, then climbed up to the clear, fresh air of nine thousand feet at the Raton Pass before descending into New Mexico. The driver told us that we were now following the exact route of the old Santa Fe Trail, and I suddenly took a new interest in looking out the window, and, sure enough, as we went past a place called Wagon Mound and headed toward the ruins of Fort Union, everything began to look old and historic and also Spanish. Some of the buildings in the small villages we passed through were made mostly of sunbaked brown adobe. There was little or no green grass or landscaping like in the East, but there were lots of brightly colored patches of flowers, strings of red chilies, smoky-looking shrubs with yellow pods, and even gnarled and twisted clumps of prickly pears, and around many of the yards were tightly made walls of tall, woody boughs and branches of what my seat companion guessed were cedar trees stuck side by side into the ground to form a barrier protecting the property. Many of the inhabitants looked like pictures I had seen of Mexicans, the women in dark dresses or blouses and big skirts and with black shawls over their heads, and some of the men in wide-brimmed straw sombreros, white pants and shirts that looked like pajamas, and sandals known as huaraches, and carrying bright-colored folded ponchos, or serapes, over their shoulders. Some with sticks drove burros heaped high with firewood, baskets of charcoal, or other loads.

With the explanatory help of my knowledgeable seat companion, the Republican clubwoman and operatic singer, who apparently had made this trip many times and on occasion had stayed in New Mexico, I took it all in with a feeling of exhilaration, as if I were seeing history come alive and had become a participant in it. It was fascinating and wonderful, because everything from the bus looked almost as I imagined it had looked in the last century. Approaching Santa Fe, we went through a small brushy canyon and past a rocky area known as Glorieta, where the driver told us a big battle of the Civil War, called "the Gettysburg of the West," had taken place about seventy years before, in which Union volunteers from Colorado and New Mexico had turned back an army of Texans who had been bent on conquering all of the Southwest and its gold and silver mines for the Confederacy. The site was private property, not a national battlefield or a park drawing tourists, and it looked exactly as it had looked at the time of the war. Some old ranch buildings that had been on the site when the battle was fought were still standing there, lonely, undisturbed, and forgotten, and I figured that some of the men who had fought around those buildings were still alive, and I wondered where they might be. This was what I had envisioned for years the West would be like—something so close to adventurous history that it was not history, but still real life, the real thing—and it was exciting.

At the bus terminals in Santa Fe and Albuquerque, we were surrounded by Indians with deeply lined, leathery faces who tried to sell us beautifully made pottery, katsina dolls, and pieces of silver and turquoise jewelry. They were about the first "real" Indians I had ever seen, and I felt very sorry for them. They were Pueblo Indians, short and rather portly, from villages along the Rio Grande, and they looked poor and distressed and nothing like the bold, proud Plains warriors of my father's stories and the books I had read. Not knowing anything about modern-day Indians at the time, I concluded that in a short while, they, like most other Indians, were going to vanish, simply die out or be absorbed in the American melting pot, as just about every person who was an "expert" on Indians said was destined to happen. It would be many years before I would know better.

After we left Albuquerque, we got onto Route 66 and headed straight west. I was so groggy from lack of sleep that I kept dozing off in the bus, but every so often, something would wake me up, so that the rest of the trip became a kind of series of impressions and dreamy events. First off, I became aware that there were many old cars on this new road, full of poverty-stricken-looking people of all ages crammed among their furniture, bedding, and other possessions, some of the cars out of gas or stuck for repairs by the side of the highway, others tooling along with us toward

California. At times, it was like a parade, and at one of our comfort stops, we learned that these families, who were becoming known as Okies and Arkies, had abandoned their farms and homes to dust storms in Texas, Oklahoma, Arkansas, and other places and had been following Route 66 on their way to find work and new homes in California.

Then we began to have a seemingly endless series of troubles with our bus, which became almost as helpless and forlorn as the flivvers and jalopies of the desperate columns of refugee families who were lurching along with us. Twice we came to a halt while we helped the bus driver change a tire. The first time, we were in sagebrush country, in a flat plain of huge, awesome distances, and I woke up enough to stand off alone at the edge of the road, smelling the sagebrush in the brittle air and looking around at the vast expanse, realizing that, other than our road, there was no sign of anything but the wonderful, wild, empty land as far as I could see in every direction. Our second stop was at the edge of the Petrified Forest, which skirted the black ribbon of Route 66 in eastern Arizona. Several of us who were not needed to help the driver picked our way into the desert, where among large chunks of petrified wood we caught some lizards and beat a fast retreat from a rattlesnake. Both stops brought me face-to-face again with a West I had long imagined, and that still existed, and I was determined that I would come back and see more of it.

During the rest of the way to California, we continued to make so many stops for repairs, rest rooms, and meals at the roadside filling stations, camps, and cafés, whose menus offered little besides chili and chicken-fried steaks, that we had plenty of time to meet and talk with some of the Okies and Arkies, as well as with waitresses and other footloose folks who were drifting across the largely empty Depression-ridden Southwest from one job to another. Like the dust storms that we had gone through, the nomadic and migrating people were history in the making, but I was so numb from weariness and so intent on the western landscape and its past history, and particularly, now that we were approaching California, on my writing and my desire to be a successful screenwriter, that I ignored the social chaos around me. By the fourth morning of the trip, I was so sleepy that I left my raincoat at one of the stops. Forty miles farther on, I discovered my loss, and at the next halt, the driver phoned back and told me that they had found my coat and would mail it to me. He gave them my address, but I never got the coat back.

When we crossed the Colorado River and started across the deserts of Southern California, the weather got much hotter. Once, in eastern Arizona, we had had to stop at a guard station while a state agricultural officer came aboard briefly to be sure we didn't have any fruit, vegetables, or seeds on the bus. He was friendly and courteous, and after a minute he wished us all a good trip and let us go on. Near Barstow in California's Mojave Desert, when we had to pull over for an inspection in that state, the guard who came aboard was not so polite. In fact, he wore a pistol and seemed threatening, appearing to be more interested in our personal lives than in what agricultural products we might be carrying. He asked some of the people on the bus where they were going and what they intended to do in California, and then he made a speech to all of us, warning us that California did not look kindly on vagrants or "Reds" or other "trouble-makers" and that we should remember that they had a criminal syndical-ism law that was enforced throughout the state against radicals. It all seemed raw and unpleasant, but when we pulled away, my seat companion tried to explain to me that among the tens of thousands of newcomers who were arriving in California were many "anarchists" and union organizers who were making trouble for the farmers and businesspeople of the state, and the criminal syndicalism law had been passed to control them. I nod-ded, but her explanation was ominous, and I did not forget the episode.

Nearing the end of the trip, everybody on the bus came wide awake. There was no smog in the Los Angeles Valley in those days, only clear, brilliant air that made everything look sharp and bright. After San Bernardino, we passed mile after mile of picture postcard–like scenes of orange groves backed by the dry, rugged mountains of the San Gabriel range. Some of our passengers started singing "California, Here I Come" and getting real chummy and exchanging addresses. By the time we rolled into the terminal in downtown Los Angeles, we all felt a close attachment to one another, as if we had been in a battle together, sharing common challenges and experiences in a strange frontier land.

Uncle Ed had driven down earlier from his home in Santa Monica and was waiting for me. The first thing he did after giving me a hug with the arm that had lost its hand was to tell me not to call him Uncle Ed, that I was no longer a little boy, and to call him Eddie like everybody else did. That was fine with me. The drive out to Santa Monica on the coast was a long one, but it was full of wonders. As we talked, I had impressions of clean wide boulevards with no sidewalks or pedestrians but bordered for blocks by citrus groves or bean fields worked by Japanese-American farm-ers; of sparkling sunlit buildings, none over a few stories high for fear of earthquakes; of palm trees and bungalows and Spanish-looking stuccoed houses fronted with vines of blazing red bougainvillea or orange trumpet flowers and by lawns of pink and white geraniums; and of dry, warm air and bizarre-looking, attention-grabbing sights like a restaurant built in the shape of a brown derby hat and tall radio towers advertising evangelist

Aimee Semple McPherson's gigantic Angelus Temple. Overall, everything looked fresh and new, contrasting starkly with my recollections of the dismal grayishness of the older, often run-down, and dowdy East and seeming to say, This is the place to start life all over again.

Eddie, my Aunt Mildred, an expansive, creative woman full of love and the desire to help and to please everyone, and their two little children, my cousins Christopher, aged about six, and his sister, Wendy, a year and a half younger, lived in a large stuccoed house with Spanish-style balconies and a red-tiled roof on a hill overlooking Santa Monica Canyon and the Pacific Ocean. Eddie, who was MGM's story editor, was on leave from that studio, working on an original screenplay of his own, which he sold shortly afterward to the producer Samuel Goldwyn as a movie for Anna Sten, a blonde Russian actress who was a neighbor of the Knopfs and whom Goldwyn had under contract.

During the first few days, Eddie and Mildred (I also quickly abandoned calling her "Aunt") drove me around much of the countryside, to Beverly Hills, where they showed me Pickfair, the home Mary Pickford and Douglas Fairbanks had built themselves, and the estates and mansions of other movie greats; to Lake Arrowhead, five thousand feet high in the San Bernardino Mountains east of Los Angeles, where the studio people went for relaxation; and up the magnificent Coast Highway, past long, rolling ocean waves to the Malibu beach home of the family of B. P. Schulberg, previously the powerful head of Paramount and the father of Budd Schulberg, the soon-to-be-celebrated author of *What Makes Sammy Run?* Budd, who had gone to Dartmouth, was at a Writers' Congress in the Soviet Union at the time, but we had lunch and played tennis with an impressive group of other guests, including Claudette Colbert, the heroine of the movie bus ride in *It Happened One Night*, who seemed in real life just as she appeared on the screen, bubbling and fun-loving, and John Gilbert, whom I remembered as the star of *The Big Parade*, the epic film about the World War that I had seen when I was about ten. In later years, after talkies replaced silent pictures, Gilbert began to lose his popularity, and his career was apparently reaching its end. Although he had recently played opposite Greta Garbo in *Queen Christina*, he made a number of self-deprecating remarks that day that seemed to me to be brave, but sad, attempts to make light of his awareness that he was becoming a box-office has-been.

All this introduction was topped by the excitement of my first visit with Eddie to MGM, where I was thoroughly dazzled by being brought into intimate contact in the commissary and on soundstages with some of MGM's most famous stars who were friends of Eddie's. The noisy,

An aspiring, nineteen-year-old MGM junior writer pictured at the Knopfs' home in Santa Monica, in 1934.

bustling commissary—famous in the movie industry for its huge thirty-five-cent bowl of chicken soup, thick with matzoh balls, chunks of white meat, and chicken fat (no one at that time knew anything about cholesterol) and made supposedly from a recipe of the mother of the studio head, Louis B. Mayer—was filled with actors, actresses, and extras in layers of makeup and all sorts of costumes who had streamed in from the different sets to have lunch. Eddie introduced me to the British actor Charles Laughton, to Fredric March and Lionel Barrymore, to Myrna Loy and Joan Crawford, and to a pretty young star named Jean Parker, and after lunch we visited some of the soundstages and met Wallace Beery and Jackie Cooper, who were filming a scene for *Treasure Island*, and Maurice Chevalier and Jeanette MacDonald, who were making *The Merry Widow*. After a while, the heady novelty of meeting movie stars began to pale, and when Eddie whispered to me that Chevalier was very conceited, and I started to watch the French star and noticed him pacing around nervously and picking at his chin in a mirror, I lost some of my sense of awe and reminded myself that actors were humans like the rest of us, with worries and problems of their own, and that as likely as not they were bullied and pushed around by their employer, Mr. Mayer, who was known as a tyrant and was feared and hated by many people at the studio.

I started in my new job right after July 4. My boss was an autocratic little man whom I will call Jeremy Rivers. He wore expensively tailored suits, slicked his hair down flat on his head, and smelled from too much aftershave. He struck me as being something of a no-talent bureaucrat who, for lack of anything better to do with him, had been put in charge of the junior writers, who then numbered about seven or eight. He also seemed kind of lewd and gave me a lot of crazy directions on how to write for the movies, such as "Write your smut subtly so the censors can't do anything about it." Instead of assigning me one of my own stories to work on, he surprised me by directing me to turn William McFee's novel *The Harbourmaster* into a treatment for a movie and then had a secretary install me in a small office in a steaming-hot green-and-white wooden building that looked like a barracks and housed a number of writers far off near the exterior sets of false-front buildings, jungles, and city streets in the back lot at the studio.

I soon found out from one of my writer neighbors in the building, Irvin S. Cobb, a heavy-jowled Kentucky humorist who was a veteran in Hollywood and had written many of Will Rogers's movies, that about a dozen writers, more experienced than I, including the playwright Laurence Stallings, the coauthor of *What Price Glory?* had already tried and failed to "lick" McFee's book, which simply lacked elements necessary for a movie. Nevertheless, I tried, but I also failed. It didn't bother Mr. Rivers, who seemed to have expected my failure and had assigned it to me either as a test of some sort or because he didn't know what else to do with me.

Mr. Rivers was also in charge of MGM's Junior Actors' Division, which groomed young contract actors and actresses and put on plays at little theaters in Los Angeles, where they could get experience and develop their talents. Following my wasted time on *The Harbourmaster*, he assigned me to write an original three-act play for this group, based on the life of a flamboyant Beverly Hills restaurant owner who called himself Prince Mike Romanoff. I hung out for a while at one of the little theaters, where I met and received advice from a popular MGM comic actor, Edward Everett Horton, who was directing some of the young stock players for Mr. Rivers; then I went to work on the Romanoff play. When I finished the first act of what I considered another puzzling assignment, Mr. Rivers liked it so much that he switched my orders and, expecting apparently that we might ride to success together, directed me to forget the play and write it as a treatment for a movie for Robert Montgomery, an MGM star for whom the studio was trying to find a vehicle. I did so, and Mr. Rivers liked the result and submitted it to his superior, Harry Rapf, a senior producer. After a couple of weeks, during which I had nothing to do but wait for a reaction, Mr. Rapf sent back word that the studio had found another property for Montgomery, and my project ended up on a shelf.

By then, the initial six weeks' term of my contract was about over. I had accomplished nothing, and there was no reason why MGM would have any interest in taking up my option and keeping me at an increase in salary for another three months. Suddenly, I was in a fix. On my small salary, I had been able to save very little money, and returning to Harvard that fall was impossible. Without a studio job, moreover, I would have to return home and try to find work in the East. Just at that moment, however, Mr. Rivers discovered my short story "The Frame-Up," which had been lying somewhere around the studio. At that time, movie programs in theaters usually included a number of one- and two-reel short films, including comedies, brief musicals, travelogues, newsreels, cartoons, and so forth, and Mr. Rivers liked "The Frame-Up" so much that he persuaded Mr. Rapf, who, among other things, headed MGM's busy shorts department, to let me write it as a two-reel short. I received no increase in pay, my contract was allowed to expire, and I continued at the studio on a week-to-week basis as a thirty-dollar-a-week junior staff writer. But I persuaded myself that as long as I could stay on the payroll, I would have a chance to write something big and important that would bring me a large increase in salary and the funds with which to return to Harvard the following year.

Still, all was not happy. I wrote the screenplay for "The Frame-Up" as a two-reel comedy, which was to star the professional wrestler Man Mountain Dean, playing himself, but when Dean demanded $25,000 for his performance, MGM said it was too much and canceled the project. Later, I was told that the studio had sold my screenplay to Hal Roach, an outside producer of comedies, but I never learned if it reached the screen. Mr. Rivers continued me on salary, however, and after that project, he put me together with three other junior writers, more irreverent and cynical than I, and assigned us as a team to turn a story by Corey Ford in *College Humor* magazine about a campus winter carnival into a play entitled *Joe College* for his junior actors.

My three collaborators, a wonderfully funny and harmonious group, all seemed to have a protracted toehold on the bottom rungs of the movie industry. The oldest was a woman named Nikki Justin, who knew various veteran performers on the lot and introduced us to some of the greatest and most endearing of them, including Jimmy Durante and Buster Keaton. Keaton, a sad-faced little man, had been one of the great comic stars of the 1920s. He had had his own unit and independence at MGM and his silent pictures had been famous for their long sequences of wonderful sight gags, which he had often made up while the movie was being filmed. In recent years, Irving Thalberg, the head of production at MGM, had ended Keaton's unit and freedom, making him a coach of other comedians and putting him into uninspired two-reel comedies with Durante

We never got anywhere, but we had a lot of fun. Our irreverent team of junior writers (from left: Bobby Lees, Fred Rinaldo, Nikki Justin, and me) on the MGM lot in Culver City.

that wasted the talents of both of them. From time to time, Keaton would drop into our office to vent his frustrations and anger at the studio and reminisce about some of the wonderful chase scenes and other original and uproarious gag sequences in the films he had made in the past.

Nikki was herself something of a carbon copy of another of her friends, Patsy Kelly, a tough-talking, wisecracking, heart-of-gold comedienne. Nikki couldn't write, but her barrelhouse humor, delivered out of the side of her mouth, contributed greatly to our scripts and to our own entertainment. The other two on our team were Fred Rinaldo, a Dartmouth graduate, who seemed to know a lot about how to get on at MGM, and Bobby Lees, who had been a dancer in the movies and who introduced us to some of Mr. Rivers's junior players.

Borrowing from President Roosevelt, our foursome called itself facetiously "the Brain Trust," and the other three members, commiserating on our lowly status at MGM under Mr. Rivers, gradually straightened me out on what I had gotten myself into in becoming a part of the motion picture industry. As I had already figured out, there was a rigid caste system in Hollywood based on how much money a person was making, which, in turn, was based on one's most recent success and perceived importance. The junior writer, a title that became known as a front for nepotism, was at the very bottom of the heap, unknown, unwanted, and just barely paid. Because he or she was unknown, without screen credits or status, no producer would give him or her anything to write. If the writer wrote something on his or her own, no one would read it. No one, that is, but Mr. Rivers, who, according to Nikki, used his job for affairs with chorus girls and starlets in the Junior Actors' Division and needed us junior writers working busily on anything at all to justify his own job.

So there it was—an answer to my puzzling assignments and the dead ends of my work. I wondered how we junior writers could ever get ahead, to write something important, to get producers to read it, and to stop being unknowns. "Let's set fire to the place and burn everything down," Rinaldo joked. "That'll get some attention." Lees was more serious. "Listen," he reminded us, "there are hundreds of hungry writers out there who would love to have our jobs. There's a Depression on. All we can do is keep plugging and do what Rivers wants us to do, and the breaks will come."

And that was what we tried to do. We developed *Joe College* into a three-act play for Mr. Rivers and then, without hearing anything about its fate, went right on to other projects. One of them was a one-page scene that we wrote for a movie named *Wicked Woman*, which had been previewed and found to have a sequence that was too long and serious and needed a humorous break. We supplied the break by writing a scene in which a talkative, comical radio repairman, played by a squeaky-voiced comedian named Sterling Holloway, arrived unexpectedly on a service call and, interrupting the seriousness for a minute or two, jabbered away idiotically while trying to fix a radio in the room. Our scene was shot immediately, and it was the first thing that we ever got on the screen, but it didn't save the movie.

After that, we wrote and submitted a lot of ideas for short comedies and musicals and finally caught Mr. Rapf's attention with one of them about dummies in a department store window that came alive during the night. When Mr. Rapf decided to make it, we determined with a mixture of resignation and disgust that we had discovered the secret of success: write for twelve-year-old minds. Rinaldo and I wrote the lyrics for several songs for the picture, including one for the villain to sing for our imagined twelve-year-old mentality of average movie audiences; it began: "Fee, fi, fo, fum, I smell the blood of an Englishman." We then discovered the reason for Mr. Rapf's enthusiasm for the script. Among a number of European refugees from Hitlerism whom MGM had hired recently and brought to Hollywood was Bronislau Kaper, a brilliant composer who had written some international hits, including a very beautiful waltz, "Two Hearts in Three-Quarters Time." MGM needed something immediate for him to do, and our story, which did have some charm to it, filled the bill. Assigned to our little two-reel musical, he became an honorary member of our Brain Trust and provided marvelous lilting music for our lyrics. Our luck ran true to form, however, and everything ended in disaster. The script called for a lot of trick photography, including one scene in which a display of ladies' bras and panties danced by themselves. In reality, they were being worn by dancers who were painted with something that supposedly would make them invisible to the camera so that the audience would only see the bras and panties. The technical people in the camera department at the studio had assured Mr. Rapf that the trick would work. It didn't. The scene came out looking like an orgy of dark-painted people in their underwear, and after gobbling up a lot more money in unsuccessful retakes, the picture was shelved.

For a while, we struggled to present more ideas for shorts—for a "crime does not pay" short for Robert Taylor, whom the studio was grooming for stardom, for a series of shorts built around Pete Smith, Chic Sales, and other MGM featured players, and for more two-reel musicals, with singers, bands, and brief appearances by top supporting actors at the studio like Ted Healy, a brassy comedian, and Leo Carillo, a descendant of the original settlers in California, who owned a Spanish land grant in Santa Monica Canyon and had become an ethnic actor with a comic Spanish accent. Then, mysteriously, we were put back on *Joe College*, the winter-carnival story, and were ordered by Mr. Rivers to change it from a play into a treatment for a movie. It seemed like another exercise in futility, reminding me of the Prince Mike Romanoff play that Mr. Rivers had had me rewrite as a movie for Robert Montgomery. Nevertheless, we plugged along dutifully until one day we learned that Mr. Rivers had been fired. The rumor was that he had tried to romance a young actress in whom Louis B. Mayer was interested. Other startling changes followed. The Junior Writers Division was officially ended, the junior writers themselves who were not on assignment were let go as soon as their options came up, another producer, Jack Chertok, succeeded Mr. Rapf as head of the shorts department, and our Brain Trust disintegrated as each of us concentrated on finding an assignment or selling one of our stories so that we could keep working.

Fortunately, Jack Chertok kept me on, assigning me the task of writing shorts and original feature-length stories and giving me a chance to get an assignment from a senior producer. At the same time, however, I was finally becoming convinced that I had made the wrong choice the year before. First of all, I was on an economic treadmill that was solving nothing. For a number of months in the beginning, I had lived happily with Eddie and his family, paying no rent, having few expenses, taking the

Southern Pacific's Red Car, which looked like a big speeding trolley car, from Santa Monica to the studio at Culver City each day, and managing to save some of my thirty-dollar paycheck each week. During that period, the Knopfs moved twice, and I went with them, first to Malibu and then to La Mesa Drive, a quiet, eucalyptus-lined residential street in Santa Monica, on the lip of a canyon across from Will Rogers's home and above the Riviera Club's field, where Rogers played polo. It was a short street, but one of some status: Greta Garbo lived at one end of it, the actor Pat O'Brien near the other end, and Joel McCrea and his actress wife, Frances Dee, right across the street from us.

After a while, my increasing activities and Los Angeles's huge distances made it impractical for me not to have my own car, and I invested $130 of my savings in a used 1929 Chevrolet roadster with a rumble seat. Soon afterward, as I approached my twentieth birthday, I decided during a spell of optimism about my future at the studio that I had mooched on my uncle and aunt long enough and ought to be paying for a place of my own. Mildred, who had grown up in France and was sometimes not overly astute in trying to be of help, wrote my mother, reassuring her that she and Eddie had met and approved of many of my friends and that I was old enough to have privacy if I wished to entertain young ladies. Eddie barked at her in shock, "How could you?" but he laughed and defused my mother's concern, and I took a furnished apartment in the small village of Westwood, near the fairly recently established campus of UCLA. For thirty-five dollars a month, I had a bedroom with two beds, a large living room with a pull-down Murphy bed, a kitchen and dining alcove, big closets, a bathroom, all utilities, daily maid service, and a weekly change of linens. So everything turned out fine, except for my savings account, which, with added weekly costs for food, the car, and the apartment, and without an increase in salary at the studio, quickly dwindled away to monthly balances of zero, leaving me nothing to show for the months I had been working to acquire funds for Harvard. In short, I was no better off than the day I had arrived in California, and until and unless I got a raise at the studio, I would no longer be able to save anything and, in fact, would be hard put just trying to meet my monthly expenses.

But that was not all that was troubling me. In retrospect, 1934 and 1935 have been viewed by history as among the golden years of Hollywood and particularly of MGM. And indeed they were. Time and again, as I waited for an assignment or a reaction to a script from Mr. Rivers or someone else, I visited an outdoor set or one of the huge MGM soundstages with writers or other friends after lunch and watched with deep awe and respect the filming of scenes with W. C. Fields, Clark Gable, Myrna Loy,

Nelson Eddy, the Marx Brothers, Ronald Colman, and other great stars for pictures like *David Copperfield, Mutiny on the Bounty, The Thin Man, Naughty Marietta, A Night at the Opera, A Tale of Two Cities,* and other MGM classics of those days. While I was struggling with the Brain Trust on idiotic scripts about dancing bras and panties and dreaming up other silly ideas for MGM's short films, others were writing these glorious features, and I was naturally envious.

But there was even more to it than that. Dramatic political events and real-life human conflicts were occurring in California and across the nation, but in general, they were being ignored as story material by the movies. Almost from the beginning, I had urged Mr. Rivers to let me try to deal with such subjects and write a screenplay about real-life people and their problems. But he kept saying that Mr. Mayer would not allow that kind of a movie to be made at MGM, that MGM made movies to entertain people and help them escape from their troubles, not depress them with stories of more problems. And so, if I stayed in Hollywood, I had to face continuing to deal with, and write, trivia.

But a strange thing happened. I began to think about things that were still important to me, like President Roosevelt's New Deal and public service and writing about serious subjects and seeing Oregon, the place of my boyhood imagination. And as I thought about whether I would ever see Oregon and more of the American West, I remembered the dust storms and the impoverished Okie families and migrant job-seekers along Route 66 and the California border guard who had come aboard our bus near Barstow and warned us about vagrants and Reds and the state's criminal syndicalism law, and the truth suddenly struck me. I had rubbed shoulders with history, and I was far more interested in it than in the make-believe world of MGM and Mr. Mayer.

7 INTO THE REAL WORLD

During my problems as a junior screenwriter, I had not given up my interest in politics. In the beginning of my work at MGM, I had sometimes found time to meet over lunch or in the evenings or on weekends with college undergraduates and others in the Southern California area who had written to me at Harvard about my proposal for a national student political movement or had joined in the campaign to unseat Huey Long. Some of them, like the leader of the student government and the graduate head of the alumni association at the University of Southern California, had already been active in the National Student Federation of America, and at their invitation I addressed a weekend regional conference of NSFA at a private club on the coastal highway in Santa Monica. I also spoke at undergraduate gatherings at UCLA and Pomona College, and to a dinner meeting of the California League of Municipalities, where I was the guest of Ernst Leibacher, a twenty-four-year-old city councilman of Inglewood, California, who had written to me at Harvard with enthusiastic support for student involvement in politics.

California at the time was reeling from the effects of the Depression, and many parts of the state were experiencing political and social turmoil. One provision of the NRA had encouraged labor to organize for collective bargaining, but in California's cities, as well as on the great corporate farms in the state's interior agricultural valleys, where employers were trying to cut their labor costs, the attempts of workers and migrant pickers to form unions, raise wages, and end unfair practices and substandard working and living conditions were being met by beatings, murders, and the arrest and imprisonment of labor organizers as vagrants or criminal syndicalists.

Until 1969, when the Supreme Court finally ruled it unconstitutional, the criminal syndicalism law, California's catchall legal net, made it a crime to advocate or belong to an organization that "advocated or aided terrorism [read union activities] as a means of accomplishing a change in industrial ownership or control or effecting any political change." Anyone—employers, company and state police, county sheriffs, city "Red squads," local vigilante groups, and judges—could read the criminal syndicalism law any way they wished. Usually, they did so, keeping wages low and the workers under control by using the act to punish "troublemakers" who complained about working conditions or unfair treatment and to prohibit strikes, boycotts, picketing, soapbox speeches, demonstrations, the distribution of handbills and other publications, and even on occasion the public reading by union organizers of sections of the Declaration of Independence or the U.S. Constitution.

The most serious situation at the moment was on San Francisco's waterfront, where the militant longshoremen, joined by the seamen and Teamsters, and led by Harry Bridges, a tough Australian-born dockworker, had defied the police and gone on strike in May to end a score of abuses by their employers. The strike spread to other ports, and on Thursday, July 5, the same day I started work at MGM after having arrived in California, the employers in San Francisco used strikebreakers to try to end the longshoremen's walkout. A bloody battle ensued in downtown San Francisco, resulting in more than 260 casualties, including two deaths, and inducing the employers and their supporters among California's industrialists, politicians, radio stations, and newspapers to spread panic by announcing that the state was on the verge of an insurrection and a "Red revolution." The governor, an elderly, frightened Republican named Frank Merriam, known irreverently by the Democrats as "Moonface," responded by ordering out the National Guard, which resulted, in turn, in the calling of an unprecedented general strike in support of the longshoremen by almost every union in San Francisco.

It was a dramatic turn of events. I remembered the mounted police attacking union members at Mauch Chunk and the threatening California border guard warning us about "Reds," but being new in the state, I didn't know what to make of the San Francisco fighting or who was right or who was wrong. Earlier, I had written my parents unhappily that the trunk with most of my clothing and possessions, which they had sent to me by a Grace Line boat through the Panama Canal, had reached the Los Angeles port at San Pedro but could not be unloaded because of "a terrible dock strike." A few days later, I could write more, reflecting the fears surrounding me and my own confusion: "A general strike has hit San Francisco and is threatening all coastal cities. Things farther north, we hear, are terrible.

Aunt Mildred laid in $60 worth of groceries in case the general strike comes here (which I'm sure it won't), because once the strike comes, there is a mad scramble for food. All day yesterday soldiers were marching through here on their way up north. A lot of people are afraid of a red uprising, as the Communists are very strong here. However, I think the danger is very overexaggerated."

The general strike lasted only four days, and eventually the longshoremen, with Bridges leading them, won their strike. Peace returned to the coastal ports, and I got my trunk and my clothes. But elsewhere in the state, the impact of the Depression mounted. At the League of Municipalities dinner with Leibacher, the principal talk was of towns going bankrupt, unable to provide essential services, defaulting on their debts, and seeking desperately to find new things to tax that would not outrage the voters. But to most of those who were at the dinner, it seemed clear that the voters were worse off than the towns and were threatening a revolt against the taxes they were already paying. A large part of the population in Southern California was lower-middle-class retirees from Iowa and other midwestern states who were being hurt badly by the Depression. Many of them were losing their homes and life's savings, and in their fears and insecurity about the future, they were talking of desperate measures or were turning to all kinds of movements that promised an end to their troubles.

Some of the "cure-all" panaceas were advanced by quacks and promoters, and others by well-meaning reformers, the most popular of whom was Upton Sinclair, a mild-mannered fifty-six-year-old Socialist and muckraking author of the early part of the century, whose book *The Jungle*, published in 1906, had been largely responsible for the passage of the Pure Food and Drug Act. In 1933, Sinclair had registered as a Democrat in California and, announcing that he would seek the Democratic nomination for governor, had written a smash-hit book entitled *I, Governor of California, and How I Ended Poverty*.

The book had pointed out that while millions of unemployed in the cities were going hungry and losing their homes, the goods and produce that they needed but were unable to buy were lying idle in stores and rotting in fields and orchards. Containing a program that Sinclair claimed would end poverty, the publication had made an immediate impact on masses of angry, demoralized California families. Almost a thousand EPIC (End Poverty in California) clubs had sprung up to help Sinclair launch a crusade to gain the governorship and carry out his program, which basically promised to give California two different economic systems. One of them, the existing private-enterprise system, would continue to produce for profit, while a second one, a new state-run system of cooperative farms and factories, acquired by eminent domain or with tax monies, would put the unemployed to work producing for use rather than for profit. The details were fuzzy and seemed more idealistic than practical, but Sinclair's writings and speeches were simple and persuasive, and hundreds of thousands of starry-eyed volunteers were working zealously throughout the state for his election.

In August, to the surprise and consternation of the political and business leaders of California, Sinclair won the Democratic primary by a landslide over eight opponents. As it began to look like he would go on to win the governorship in November, the Republicans and the monied interests of the state, fearful that Sinclair's schemes would ruin them, set out to destroy him by a massive, all-out public-relations campaign conducted in large measure by the media empire of William Randolph Hearst and by the head of MGM, Louis B. Mayer, who could commandeer and direct the creative talent necessary for a smear campaign.

Hearst and Mayer had once been friends and collaborators. Hearst's movie-producing company, Cosmopolitan Pictures, distributed its films through MGM, and when I first went to work there, Marion Davies, the very talented comedienne with whom Hearst had been conducting a long-time affair, was esconced as MGM's highest-paid star (ten thousand dollars a week) in a large fourteen-room private bungalow that sat among the soundstages in the middle of the MGM lot. But soon afterward, there was a blowup, accompanied by the sudden departure of Marion Davies and her bungalow from MGM. Somebody at the studio, claiming to know what had happened, told us that Hearst had come on the lot to see Davies and had found the door of her bungalow locked. When the autocratic media tycoon knocked impatiently, a male visitor inside, unaware of who was knocking, had called out in jest, "Don't come in! We're all naked!" This had so infuriated Hearst that he had wanted nothing more to do with MGM and had moved Davies off the lot. The true story turned out to be less theatric: Despite Hearst's demands, Mayer, it appeared, had given prized leading roles in two major moving pictures to producer Irving Thalberg's wife, Norma Shearer, rather than to Davies, and in high dudgeon, Hearst had moved her, the bungalow, and Cosmopolitan Pictures out of MGM and over to Warner Bros. Now, however, Mayer and Hearst joined hands in common cause against Sinclair.

While Hearst turned his papers full blast against Sinclair, printing only adverse material about him, Mayer helped mobilize publicity and advertising experts, directors, writers, actors, and extras to produce false and scurrilous newspaper and billboard ads, radio spots, fake newsreels, and anti-Sinclair posters and flyers, depicting Sinclair as a dangerous imbecile, an unwashed, bearded, bomb-throwing anarchist, an atheistic Communist, an enemy of religion, a crazed vegetarian, and a supporter of free love. One night, I accompanied Eddie and Mildred to a dinner at the home of their friend Herman Mankiewicz, a hard-drinking former New York newspaperman and one of Hollywood's best-known screenwriters, who years later would incur Hearst's wrath by writing the script for *Citizen Kane*, the unflattering movie based on Hearst's life. Mankiewicz, a cynic and wit who had nothing but scorn for Sinclair as a "crackpot idealist," told us that Mr. Mayer had his younger brother, Joe Mankiewicz, a talented writer at MGM, busy writing spots for radio that would frighten people "out of their minds" and turn them against Sinclair.

At the same time, Felix Feist, a director of screen tests at MGM and a friend of some of us junior writers, was turning out phony newsreels on the MGM back lot, which theaters all over the state included in their programs. Many of them showed hordes of horrible-looking alleged bums played by hired film extras who supposedly were pictured on their way to California from other parts of the country, announcing happily to the camera that Sinclair had promised to take care of them if they helped him get elected. The venomous campaign soon began to have its effect, and I reported examples to my parents. "Everyone with any money," I wrote them, "is becoming scared sick of Sinclair. One of Uncle Ed's friends who owns a huge plumbing supply manufacturing firm told him the other night that he fired 400 of his men because they announced they were voting for Upton Sinclair. And the newsboy in front of this studio has been barred from the grounds because he sells Sinclair's paper, the *Epic News*."

To help finance the smear campaign, Mr. Mayer pressured every MGM actor and employee making over one hundred dollars a week to contribute one day's salary, putting out word that if Sinclair won, the studios would move out of California. As a junior writer making only thirty dollars a week, I was spared at first, but one week I found in my pay envelope a pledge form volunteering a donation to the Merriam campaign. All I had to do was sign it and hand it in. I held the form for a day or two, then tore it up and threw the pieces away angrily when I saw my first shocking example of the anti-Sinclair forces' obscene handiwork on a towering billboard that loomed above an intersection on Wilshire Boulevard. Depicting Sinclair as a hairy apelike monster with blood dripping from his fangs, it showed him advancing with a bomb and a gory knife in his hands toward a heroic Governor Merriam, who was posed defiantly like a modern-day Horatio at the bridge, protecting a frightened, cowering mother and her children from this oncoming ogre.

The vicious campaign of deliberate lies and distortions, orchestrated by Mr. Mayer and the Republicans in every medium of communication, was an ugly forerunner of the wholesale use of hired public-relations and advertising experts to help candidates smear opponents, a practice that would become familiar in "negative" American political campaigning in the future. This first exposure to it so upset my sense of decency and justice that I wrote to Sinclair, offering to help his campaign in any way that I could. He replied on October 10, inviting me to "come and join our EPIC movement." Despite my feeling that he was too idealistic and impractical to make a good governor, I thought he would be better and more honest than Merriam, and I joined up and for a couple of weeks found time to write some campaign news articles for Rube Borough, the editor of Sinclair's newspaper, the *Epic News*, on South Grand Avenue in downtown Los Angeles. The brief stint was a learning experience for me, too, for I saw up close the power of the reactionary anti-Roosevelt Republicanism that hammered Sinclair and his campaign into the mud, and I also met many of California's growing number of dedicated and courageous progressives and reformers whom the Republicans demonized. Among them was one whom I came to admire greatly, Carey McWilliams. A quiet, thoughtful writer with an intense curiosity for the truth, he was covering the campaign for *The New Republic*. A few years later, his landmark book *Factories in the Field*, about California's migrant farm labor, played an important role in helping to bring California's liberals to power and improvements to the lives of agricultural workers.

Sinclair lost, the hysteria of his opponents evaporated, and in the heat of defeat and anger, I spent a bitter weekend after election day writing a slim satirical book entitled *How to Bait Reds*, a tongue-in-cheek volume of immoral and unscrupulous advice based on the tactics that had been used by Louis B. Mayer and the kind of people who had beaten Sinclair. It was my first try at a full-fledged book, and I sent it off to several publishers in New York—not including Alfred Knopf or Mencken, neither of whom, I was certain, would look kindly on it. Ben Huebsch at Viking Press, a noted civil libertarian and one of America's most respected publishers at the time, wrote me a personal letter praising the manuscript, but nobody published it, which was probably a good thing, because I had written it with more of the fury and self-righteousness of a nineteen-year-old than with wisdom and restraint.

Having gotten it off my chest, my ardor cooled quickly, and I returned to concentration on my writing career at the studio, gradually devoting less and less time to my political contacts and interests and more to social activities among a widening circle of movie-industry friends. They ranged from the studio barber at MGM, with whom I played golf occasionally on Sundays, to young writers, directors, actors, and actresses, including Olivia and Joan de Havilland, whose ladylike bearing and exquisite diction, drilled into the girls by their mother, Mrs. Lilian Fontaine, made all three of them seem to me like wondrous characters out of a Jane Austen novel. The two sisters, distantly related to the British builder of the de Havilland aircraft, were in their late teens when I first met them at a party in Hollywood and were stunning, bright, and full of devilment toward each other. Olivia was already launched on a movie career, and Joan, who to go it on her own dropped the "de Havilland" and became first Joan Burfield and then Joan Fontaine, was not far behind her. I became very fond of Mrs. Fontaine and her daughters and, for several months, until I left California, was frequently in their company.

With them and with many others, I lived in a happy, youthful, inexpensive world of parties in people's homes with games of charades, bridge, and sardines; of wienie bakes, toasting frankfurters over fires on the ocean beach at night, and midnight grunion hunts in the foaming surf with flashlights and tin pails; of sneak previews at theaters around the county and private showings of movies in projection rooms at the studios; of dancing to the smooth big-band orchestras of Ted Fio Rito or Jan Garber at the Coconut Grove in the Ambassador Hotel and more of the same on weekend trips by boat to the big round dance pavilion on Catalina Island, where admission for the whole evening was only twenty-five cents; of music under the stars at the Hollywood Bowl and the New Year's Day Rose Bowl football game in ninety-six-degree heat at Pasadena.

Late in the winter, I ran into my friend from Horace Mann, Bill Watters, who had conducted the literary interviews with me for our school newspaper. Bill had developed theatrical ambitions and had transferred from the University of Arizona to a school for actors in Pasadena. He had also fallen in love with the West and had spent a lot of time just driving around, visiting different places. His talk of ghost towns and historic sites that he had seen set my imagination afire and rekindled my own urge to see more of the West and, if possible, get to Oregon, the fabled goal of my boyhood dreams. Bill thought we could make it to that state and back easily on a weekend, and one Friday afternoon, equipped with a desert water bag for the car's radiator and maps from the Automobile Club of Southern California, we set off in his '34 Chevy coupe.

Bill wanted to go through Death Valley, which had just been established as a national monument in 1933, and then head straight north through Nevada to Oregon, so we drove first to San Bernardino and Barstow on the strip of Route 66 that my Greyhound bus had followed coming to Los

Angeles. It was after dark when we got to Barstow. We stopped for the night at a little auto camp off by itself, and when we awoke at dawn, we saw that we were out in the middle of the Mojave Desert. For a few brief minutes of awesome splendor that held me spellbound and overcame me with a spiritual feeling for the astonishing powers of nature, the little whitewashed shacks of the auto camp and the whole empty land around us were bathed in the fiery redness of the rising sun. It was a moving and unforgettable experience, and so was our drive that morning through a wild, unearthly landscape of dry lake beds, steep, rugged mountains of naked rock, and weird eroded formations streaked with bands of different-colored earth, mostly reds, yellows, and brown and black. Occasionally, we drove past a lone prospector with his pickax, coffeepot, and other possessions loaded on a burro, or the rotting black timbers of hillside entrances to abandoned gold, silver, and borax mines, but for long stretches as we headed north beyond the desert hamlet of Baker on a dirt road that eventually became little more than two wheeltracks, we saw no other car or any sign of civilization, except a cardboard warning stuck on a stick saying not to drive any farther without plenty of oil, gas, and water.

We ignored the sign and went on, and everything we had seen during the morning turned out to be a prelude to a sudden hard, twisting climb between encompassing walls of rock, followed high up by our breaking into the open, with steep drops on both sides of the rough, narrow road and huge mountains towering ahead and behind us. Rounding a turn, we came abruptly to the road's end at Dante's View, a breathtaking, windswept overlook of all of Death Valley's floor of sand, clay, and salt beds a mile below us. It was the most stupendous view I had ever seen. Straight down from our mountain perch was Badwater, the lowest point in North America, 282 feet below sea level, while westward in the haze beyond Death Valley and its dark western wall of the Panamint Mountains, which had trapped a party of California-bound emigrants during the gold rush of 1849, we could make out the Sierra Nevada range and the snow-covered 14,500-foot-high summit of Mount Whitney, the highest peak in the forty-eight states, which, with the noncontiguous territories of Alaska and Hawaii, comprised the United States at the time.

In the fierce wind, we clung to the door handles of our car and tried to take some pictures, and then we turned the car around and found a road lower down that led us to the floor of the valley. On the way, we passed a series of abandoned borax mines and numerous old, broken-down wagons in which twenty-mule teams had once pulled the borax out of the valley. There was so much to see, driving around the valley and stopping at places like the Furnace Creek Inn and the national monument headquarters to pick up some food and maps and historical pamphlets, that it was late in the afternoon when we finally drove out of an eastern entrance of the monument on a dirt road that would take us to Nevada and a highway running north to Oregon. We had to drive very slowly because the road was dangerous, sloping off at its edges to frightening plunges on both sides, and soon it began to get dark. When we tried to put on our lights, however, we found, to our horror, that they didn't work. Our map showed a town named Bullfrog a few miles away, and in something of a panic we increased our speed and hurried toward it. We could tell from the many abandoned gold and silver mines that we passed in the fading light that we were driving through historic country that had once teemed with miners, but we didn't dare stop. Bullfrog turned out to be a ghost town of crumbling buildings and no people, and our fears increased. We hurried on to the next town on the map, Rhyolite, and it, too, was a ghost town, though a bigger and more substantial-looking one, which included a large and elegant stucco railroad station and a number of roofless shells of three-story buildings that stood silently in the gathering gloom among the once-rich mineral-bearing hills.

Just as it was becoming so dark that we could barely see the road ahead, we glimpsed lights in the distance, and slowly and carefully we felt our way to Beatty, a little mining center of about seventy-five people, left over from the gold and silver rush that had brought tens of thousands of fortune-seekers to this part of Nevada only thirty years before. We put up at a small hotel, which was really an old saloon and gambling house, with its main floor lined by a long bar facing a row of green-covered poker tables and a staircase leading to a second floor of several almost-bare, timeworn bedrooms, the keys to which hung on a rack downstairs behind the bar. Almost all the walls of the building seemed cracked and loose from the dry air and neglect. Many of the outside walls creaked and slapped and banged in the wind all night, and the thin weathered boards of our bedroom walls were so warped and split and pulled away from each other that one could easily see through them.

We could find no one in town who could help us fix our lights, and every place on our route for the next day's drive through the Nevada desert to Oregon also looked on the map like a ghost town or close to it. After dinner, we sat around a fireplace, talking to some elderly Swiss miners who had come to this country in the late 1890s, had helped establish both Rhyolite and Beatty, and had been there ever since. After they confirmed our fears, telling us that we would probably have to go far out of our way to Reno, or back south to Las Vegas, to find someone who could take care of our problem, I agreed unhappily with Bill, who wanted to get home the next night before dark, that we'd better forget Oregon on this trip and explore north just a little ways through Nevada and then circle back into California and hurry back to Los Angeles in the afternoon.

The next morning, I awoke early, still feeling unhappy that I was not to get to Oregon. It was fantastically clear and brittle outside, with the temperature at eleven below zero and the air seemingly dry enough to shatter glass. With a little time on our hands before we could get breakfast, we drove back a few miles to Rhyolite, exploring the empty buildings, figuring where a bank, a saloon, a jail, and a dance hall and whorehouse might have been and about how many thousand people might have lived in the town, and picking up from the ground as souvenirs a few scattered bottles that had lain in the sun for years and turned purple or greenish blue. Don Quixote and Sancho Panza had nothing on us as our imaginations peopled the abandoned town with miners and others who had once lived in Rhyolite and helped us visualize the booming frontier history that had taken place there.

From Beatty, we drove north, still in freezing weather, to Goldfield, which was also almost a ghost town, then turned west, hoping to get across a mountain pass, back into California. The road climbed steadily, and at five thousand feet, we ran into twenty-foot-high snowdrifts and had to turn back. On the way, we towed a lady whose car had frozen up on her. Although she operated a gas pump in Goldfield, she couldn't fix our lights, but she gave us two gallons of gas and a big lunch. We sat around in her house, getting warm, and when Bill let slip to her that I worked at MGM, she told us that she was a cousin of Jeanette MacDonald, who, she said, had been born in Goldfield in 1907, when the place was a big, flourishing mining center with large brick buildings and was known as the capital of southern Nevada, more important than Las Vegas. Miss MacDonald's father, she said, had been an important financier in Nevada, and Miss MacDonald had gone off to be an opera singer. While we finished eating, she wrote a quick note and gave it to us to mail to her famous alleged cousin, explaining that in winter, mail pickups at Goldfield were sometimes few and far between.

Not knowing whether to believe her tale, or whether she was just a lonely, hallucinating movie fan (the latter proved true), we left her and continued farther north, looking for a road to California, and finally reached Tonopah, locked in snow and with nobody in sight. We went through the town, with the wind buffeting our car, and turned off on a road leading west to Montgomery Pass and California. It took us to lower and warmer country and to a sandy stretch that threaded through a vast region of salt flats. For a while, the temperature soared, then dropped again as the road climbed into a range of mountains on the Nevada-California border and twisted precariously on the edge of cliffs past stands of three-thousand-year-old bristlecone pines gnarled by centuries of windstorms. It started to snow, and the snow became a blizzard, and all of a sudden the road was filled with mountain goats that ignored our car's horn and barely moved aside to let us creep forward among them. For a while, it was like a desperate nightmare, with the mountain peaks surrounding us, the terrifying drop-offs on both sides of the narrow road, the driving snow almost blinding us, and the mountain goats, ghostly in the storm, trying to deny us passage.

At last, we got through the barrier and out of the snow, descending eventually into California's Owens Valley, where we passed a number of settlements of Paiute Indians, set too far back from the road for us to see what they were like. Again, we were in an area where much history had occurred. In the nineteenth century, settlers assisted by American troops had seized the Owens Valley from the Indians who for centuries had lived off the seeds and wild foods of its fertile, well-watered fields. Many Indians had been killed resisting the invaders, but in the end, the survivors had been thrown off their lands and reduced to poverty. But the settlers' victory was short-lived. Early in the twentieth century, engineers and lawyers, seeking more water for Los Angeles, managed to win the rights to the water of Owens Valley and, constructing a great aqueduct that diverted the valley's water more than two hundred miles to Los Angeles, visited a revenge of sorts on the settlers, whose farmlands dried up.

The story of the drying up of Owens Valley was well known in California, and I wanted to stop and try to visit with some of the Indians and other people in the valley. But Bill was in a hurry to get home before it got dark, and we raced south along the eastern side of the massive Sierra Nevada, through Bishop, Independence, and other settlements, and finally reached the town of Mojave, where a man who ran a gas pump and a garage finally managed to sort out some wires under the dashboard and get our lights working again. Much relieved, we took it easier the rest of the way, and Bill dropped me off at home in time for dinner, after we had driven more than a thousand miles, seven hundred of them on this last day.

The adventurous trip, with its enduring memories of spectacular country and places and people right out of the frontier past, whetted my appetite not only to take more automobile trips through the West but also to read western American history, particularly diaries, journals, and other old accounts of places I thought I would like to see. During the spring and summer, I spent several weekends with friends on auto tours to places I read about, driving north to the Santa Barbara Mission and then into the rugged coastal mountains behind Santa Barbara; visiting the San Diego World's Fair and crossing into Mexico's Baja California to spend a night in a cabin on a deserted moonlit beach at Ensenada, a scruffy little fishing and canning town that years later, after World War II, would become a crowded tourist resort; and even heading far north again in California, this time on a planned long holiday weekend drive through the state's interior valleys and the 1849 gold rush country on the western slope of the Sierras with an out-of-work MGM senior screenwriter who vowed to me that we would make it into Oregon before we had to go back.

Again, I was frustrated. It was a beautiful drive through the largely undeveloped San Fernando Valley and across parklike hills dotted with luxurious live oaks where ferocious grizzly bears had once roamed in huge numbers, then past vast irrigated farms, the present-day scene, I knew, of bitter migrant labor strife, and on up to Sequoia and then Yosemite National Parks. At Yosemite, we entered the rustic Ahwanee Hotel to check in for the night, only to be handed a telegram for my companion from his agent back in Hollywood with the news that Irving Thalberg at MGM wanted him to work with him writing the new Marx Brothers picture, *A Day at the Races,* and to come back right away. My companion was so excited that he could scarcely eat his dinner. We stayed the night at the Ahwanee and, abandoning the plans for Oregon, turned around the next morning. The return trip was uneventful except for a case of vapor lock that stalled our car for an hour on our way out of the mountains and had my companion biting his fingernails with worry until we got going again. Once more, I was disappointed and figured that I was fated never to see Oregon.

When summer arrived, Harvard classmates and other eastern friends who were touring the West on vacation began dropping by. It was good visiting with them, showing them around the studio, and hearing what I had missed during the past year. When my classmates said good-bye and left me to finish their trips and return to Harvard in the fall, now as seniors, I felt kind of sad, knowing that again I would not be going back to college with them, and would probably never be able to return—even if I wanted to, which was beginning to be a question in my mind, since my classmates were moving so far ahead of me. At best, if I managed to go back at any time in the future, I realized that I would be at least two years behind them.

As I brooded about it, things began to come to a head. I was getting nowhere at the studio, and it appeared increasingly evident that sooner or later I would have nothing to do and would be dropped. When my old friend Lester Hofheimer arrived for a few weeks' visit, we talked it over. Lester wanted me to drive back with him to the East, and again he urged me to let him lend me the money to go back to Harvard in the fall. My pride refused to allow me to accept his offer, but I began to think seriously of giving up at MGM and driving back with him and trying to do better among my family in the East. One night, I got very sick. I was driving Joan Fontaine to dinner at Edwin and Mildred's and suddenly felt violently nauseous. Pulling over, I bounded out of the car and threw up uncontrollably at the curb. Joan jumped out and held my forehead, and though she was extremely concerned and caring, I was terribly embarrassed. The next day, the doctor said I had had an attack of appendicitis. An operation would be premature, he said, but sooner or later I would probably need one.

That did it. I wrote my parents that I'd had an appendicitis attack and would eventually need an operation, and that I wanted to have it in the East and would be coming back with Lester and the friend who had accompanied us to Chicago two summers ago and who this year had driven west with him to California. I also told Edwin and Mildred of my decision, and although they were disappointed by the way things had gone for me, they accepted the realities of my situation.

After checking out of MGM, engaging in hugs, kisses, and tears at a round of farewell parties among all the many good friends I would leave in California, and saying good-bye to Eddie, Mildred, and my cousins Christopher and Wendy, all of whom had been so kind and generous in sharing their lives with me, I departed with Lester and his friend on August 31.

We had planned a route that would include a lot of interesting sight-seeing, and we were not disappointed. We wanted to see the new, almost-completed Boulder Dam (later renamed Hoover Dam), and our first destination was the nearby desert center, Las Vegas, which had not yet become a gambling metropolis but, although run by Mormons, had a prominent red-light district of long green buildings containing the "cribs" of prostitutes who catered to the dam-builders. It was oppressively hot in Las Vegas, and we stayed at a small hotel that proudly advertised that it was air-cooled. Its homemade system consisted of the frame of an old ice-box without front or rear panels and a large fan that blew at some exposed cakes of ice in the icebox, sending cold air down the hallway outside our rooms. With the added help of smaller fans in our rooms, we got some sleep, then were told in the morning that the temperature was expected to get up to 134 degrees in the sun. It made us decide quickly that we better get moving and get out of there.

Lake Mead, the reservoir behind Boulder Dam, was still filling up, and to cross it to the road that would lead us to the dam and then on to Route 66 at Kingman, Arizona, we had to take a scow that acted like a temporary ferry. Late in the morning, we got to the beach where the scow would put in and found that the only other people waiting for it was a family of Japanese tourists. In the baking heat, they had started a fire with some kindling and wood they had carried, and were cooking their lunch over the flames. We watched them in amazement, though we quickly followed their example of soaking our handkerchiefs in the lake and draping them on our heads to try to keep cool.

After we crossed the lake, we stopped to view the new dam and caught our breath in wonder and not a little visceral fear at the awesome sight of the concrete wall rising with strength and beauty from the dark, terrifying depths of the Colorado River's Black Canyon. Then we continued on to the Grand Canyon and to Albuquerque and Amarillo, Texas, where I had another attack of nausea and vomiting. The United Daughters of the Confederacy were holding a convention in Amarillo, and we couldn't find a place to stay overnight. I didn't feel too well, and the others were too tired to keep driving, so we slept in the car that night. In the morning, I felt fine again, and we went on to Oklahoma City and Kansas City, passing increasing numbers of hoboes and "bindle stiffs" (migrating workers with their bedrolls and bundles of clothing and possessions) clustered in woods or along streams in smoky wayside camps, or "jungles," as they called them, or trying to thumb rides from cars headed west. They were shabby-looking men and women, defeated and homeless, bound, like this year's continuing army of dusted-out Okies, for the winter warmth of California or Arizona. Leaving them behind and arriving eventually in Pennsylvania, we dropped off Lester's friend and finally reached New York, where I had a happy reunion with Warren and my parents.

During my absence, they had moved to a new apartment building on East 72d Street near Second Avenue, and after a while, I went out for a walk under the noisy Second Avenue elevated with Warren and my father to get acquainted with the neighborhood. After the brightness and colors of California, everything looked gray and dingy, exactly as I had remembered the East. But there were more sober things to think about. In May, the Supreme Court had ended the NRA and many other New Deal programs as unconstitutional, the Depression in New York was as bad as ever, with millions still unemployed, and I had no job.

III ✖ EXPANDING HORIZONS

8 ✠ DEPRESSION DAYS

The first thing I did was head into a hospital and have my appendix taken out. It was no emergency, but our family doctor said that it might soon become one if I didn't get rid of it. While I lay in the hospital recuperating, I thought a lot about what I should do next. I was stone-broke, my parents were just getting by, and a return to college was out of the question. There was no money for me to think of anything except to make money and support myself. At the same time, I had a cocky sense of confidence that I would soon get a good job and everything would be all right. Far from feeling dejected or defeated by my experience at MGM, I was full of optimism, trying to sort out my varied interests—journalism, politics, public service, playwriting—and decide which one I should now try to make my career.

By the time I left the hospital, I had it pretty well figured out. I was homesick for my friends, the fresh air, the spacious landscapes, and the vibrancy of the way of life in California and the West, all of which I missed very much, and I wished desperately that I could return to the exuberant, mostly outdoor existence that I had come to love in that part of the country. But I would not go back as a junior screenwriter, working without respect on what I considered trash and trivia. I had brought back with me a lot of first drafts of plays and ideas for plays about the economic and political concerns and struggles of real-life people that I had tried to write while I was at MGM, but whose subjects Mr. Rivers had persuaded me would not win Mr. Mayer's approval as the kind of problem-free family-entertainment pictures that MGM made, and which might even cause him to fire us both. In New York, I now decided that, with my little-theater experience writing material for Mr. Rivers's Junior Actors' Division at MGM, which I had enjoyed doing and from which I felt I had received some satisfying recognition, I would try to become a professional play-wright. I would get one of those plays or a new one produced on Broad-way and would work to establish a reputation that would take me back to Hollywood as an important, well-paid senior writer, one whom studio producers would have to take seriously.

It was the pipe dream of an ambitious twenty-year-old, but during the fall weeks of 1935, while my parents and Warren put up with me patiently, I pursued the art and skill of playwriting with a single-minded intensity, working all night at my typewriter in the kitchen of our quiet, darkened apartment and then sleeping until noon every day. Through Hollywood writer friends who had come back to New York, I met several agents and was soon represented by one of the best. He liked much of what I had written, and eventually, he came excitingly close to interesting the Group Theatre, the producer of Clifford Odets's work, in one of my plays, a con-temporary political story called *As Maine Goes.**

But nothing sold. I hung around Times Square and became part of the theatrical scene, reading casting notices and producers' announcements of new plays in *Variety* and meeting out-of-work young actors, actresses, directors, and writers who clustered in the bars of the Piccadilly and other side-street hotels and in a bustling Broadway drugstore on a corner in the Forties where some of them held temporary jobs while they waited for tryouts and good news from casting directors or from their agents. Despite the glamorous environment in which we wanna-bes imagined ourselves to be important theatrical figures with stardom and celebrity status guaranteed to be just around the corner, time ran out for some of us, including myself, and I soon decided that while I waited for something to sell, I would have to find a paying job that would put some money in my pocket and end my reliance on the small financial support my father was able to give me.

When my parents learned of my new decision, they seemed pleased that I was going to give up the "playwriting business" and seek a steady nine-to-five job like most other people, and Warren, who had such a job with a textile firm downtown near the Woolworth Building, cheered me on, not altogether in jest, saying, "Good! So you're going to quit loafing." Remembering my grandfather's plans for me, my mother said I should see her brother, Alfred, who knew of their father's wish that I join Alfred's publishing company and who should now have a place for me in the firm. At first, I balked. I had had enough of nepotism, and besides, I had no

---

* The title was part of a well-known political-campaign saying that ended, "So goes the nation." The next year, 1936, Roosevelt shattered the old adage by winning every state in the Union *except* Maine and Vermont.

interest in becoming a publisher, but my mother told me that she owned stock from her father in Alfred's company and urged me to go and talk to him. My father's face took on a stern look as he reminded me that "jobs are pretty damn scarce these days." So I went to see Alfred in his office in the Heckscher Building at Fifth Avenue and 57th Street. I was relieved when he told me brusquely that he and his wife, Blanche, had to keep a place in the firm for their son, Pat, but that the company was doing so badly in the Depression that they had had to let some loyal employees go and they couldn't afford to take on any new person, not even me.

I was also relieved not to run into Mencken at the office. The previous year, he and Alfred had sold the *American Mercury*, which had been losing money, but Mencken had continued as a stockholder in the publishing firm and was still Alfred's close friend and consultant and made the Knopf office one of his New York bases. At the same time, he had become an increasingly angry Roosevelt-hater and a thorough enemy of the New Deal, and I had had no correspondence with him since leaving Harvard. The truth was, I was still grateful to him and would have been embarrassed to see him again, preferring not to risk his scorn of my liberalism and support of Roosevelt, but to remember him as the man I had known and admired, my grandfather's warm, kindly friend who had generously encouraged and helped me during my school years.

After I told her what had happened, my mother was upset with her brother for a while, but I didn't care and felt confident that I would find a job much more to my liking. However, the episode was the opening act of the darkest days of frustration and gloom in my life. While I was in California, I had kept up correspondence with many of those whom I had met through my interest in political affairs and the national student movement during my last year at Harvard, and I now sent off letters to Ken Holland, John Lang, and others, asking about public-service job possibilities, inside or outside the government. Back came a stream of disheartening replies— all tentative or negative: "No openings right now"; "Our budget's been cut, but I'll keep my eyes open for you"; "There's a long waiting list"; "Try after the first of the year." Meanwhile, many relatives and family friends gave me letters of introduction to people in all walks of life, and I called on one after another of them, receiving polite and sympathetic interviews and, from some, encouragement, advice, and letters of introduction to others—but no steady job.

As the weather got colder, I trudged the streets of New York from one appointment to another, trying not to get despondent. I talked without success to executives at Young & Rubicam, Batten, Barton, Durstine and Osborn, Blackett-Sample-Hummert, and other advertising agencies about writing radio soap operas or advertising copy for products like Ipana toothpaste or Carter's Little Liver Pills; to McGraw-Hill in their big green building on West 42d Street about a magazine job on a construction-industry trade journal; to our old Pleasantville friend Pendleton Dudley about public-relations work for one of his clients, the Corn Products Refining Corporation; to a *New York Times* friend of a friend of one of my uncles on my father's side about a newspaper job; and to NBC officials in the RCA Building in Rockefeller Center about any kind of work. Some talked to me for half an hour, then said flat out that although they would like to hire me, there were absolutely no openings, but they would keep me in mind. Others, like McGraw-Hill, said they could only consider older men with experience and specialized expertise, and then they would prefer to hire married men with children to support.

By November, I was pretty low. I found myself scouring the meager "Help Wanted" employment columns in the daily newspapers, finding a few ads for lathe operators or others with specialized skills that I didn't have, then in discouragement walking up and down Sixth Avenue under the elevated tracks, examining the rows of job-opening cards tacked up on bulletin boards outside the doors of seedy little employment agencies that lined the avenue in old firetrap buildings north of 42d Street. Almost all those cards were for temporary menial or manual-labor jobs like restaurant dishwashers and construction-project ditchdiggers. They paid almost nothing, and in some cases only a meal or two and no money, but all but the worst had been snatched up early in the mornings by crowds of unemployed that had congregated outside the agencies and filed up a flight of stairs to the second-floor employment offices in the buildings to sign up for a day's work. For several days, I searched the bulletin boards in vain for a job for someone who could use a typewriter or something else I could do.

As my leads played out, my confidence flagged, my self-esteem vanished, and I began to feel frightened and ashamed of myself. I had little money in my pocket, and my daily food routine had become a ten-cent breakfast at the counter of a Nedick's hot-dog stand, consisting of a glass of watery orangeade, a cup of coffee, and two doughnuts; a ten- or fifteen-cent lunch of a bowl of chili with plenty of free saltine crackers at a Horn and Hardart Automat or at some hole-in-the-wall around Times Square; and a good, nourishing dinner with the family in the apartment in the evening. At home, at the same time, I started saving and squirreling things away—empty boxes, string, thumbtacks, rubber bands, broken pencils—everything that cost money and that looked like it might have some future use.

One cold, sunny morning, I sat on a Fifth Avenue bench with Central Park at my back, feeling so desperate that I was close to tears. A city street-cleaner in a white uniform and visored cap went slowly past me along the gutter, pausing to unlimber his broom, sweep up some litter, and dump it in the trash can on wheels that he was pushing along. I suddenly found myself envious of him. How terribly, terribly lucky he was, I thought—he and other employed people whom I watched from my bench: a conductor on the rear steps of a passing double-decker Fifth Avenue bus, a uniformed doorman in front of an apartment building across Fifth Avenue from me, the policeman in the middle of the intersection. All of them had steady jobs, steady take-home pay, and the self-respect of being needed or wanted by somebody.

For a while, I felt guilty and disgraced, thoroughly conscience-stricken, as if there were something wrong with me that kept me from getting a job. It must be my fault, and everybody knows it, I thought. In addition, I felt suddenly lonely—everybody I knew—everybody in my family, including my mother, was working. I walked back down Sixth Avenue from 59th Street and under the rumbling elevated, outside one of the employment agencies, tried to break my dreadful loneliness by striking up a conversation with two unemployed men in caps and old ragged secondhand overcoats from the Salvation Army that almost dragged along the sidewalk. Their good humor and my hunger for the companionship of people who were in the same boat with me cheered me up, and I soon found myself ambling along with them to Union Square just above 14th Street, where they knew a place to get a free meal.

A huge demonstration of unemployed men and women and people on relief was under way in the Square, and in the crush and confusion of the crowd and the yelling of different speakers, I lost my companions. I stood in the mob, alone, listening for a while, but made out a lot of fiery talk against capitalism and President Roosevelt, and about how Russia had solved its problems, and demands that the United States government create more jobs, and I got uneasy and finally pushed back out of the crowd and through a line of bored-looking New York policemen holding on to their billy clubs but not threatening anybody. On Fifth Avenue, beyond the edge of the throng, a few people were fighting furiously over some placards that read BLACK AND WHITE, UNITE AND FIGHT and FIGHT WAR AND FASCISM. Some policemen started to walk over, and not wanting to get involved, I decided to leave the area quickly and got on a Fifth Avenue bus that was going uptown.

I climbed the curving rear steps to the open-air top deck and went forward to an empty seat in the front row. For some reason, I didn't get off at

72d Street to walk east to our apartment, but with fears, frustrations, and worries all mixed together with happy memories of bus rides over this route with my mother and Warren when I was a kid, I watched everything absentmindedly until suddenly we were on Riverside Drive, headed toward the recently built George Washington Bridge. Then I got off and walked uptown to the bridge and as far under it toward the river as I could. The house on the hill above the Hudson where my mother had lived when she was a little girl was gone, but the little red lighthouse was still there, dwarfed by the huge bridge above it and standing all alone like a tiny sentinel at the river's edge. Memories of fantasies and books and adventures and stories my father had told Warren and me long ago flooded through me.

I dawdled in the area for a long time, gazing across at the Palisades and thinking of driving without any lights through Nevada ghost towns with Bill Watters, of the Spanish villages around Santa Fe, and of many of the other western places I had been and the different experiences I had had in the huge country beyond that rocky wall. I still had not reached Oregon, but I was suddenly sure that sooner or later I would get there. When I finally left, I felt better, but then I had to pay another dime on a bus to get home and I lost my self-confidence again. That night, I had a hard time hiding from Warren and my parents my depression and feelings of shame and guilt at still not having found a job after all the advantages—Horace Mann, Harvard, working in Hollywood—that had been given to me.

A few days later, things suddenly started to brighten a little, and I wondered superstitiously at the coincidence of my visit to the little red lighthouse and whether this relic from my childhood was going to be something of a lucky symbol for me. I remembered Ben Huebsch at Viking Press, who had liked the manuscript of my satirical book, *How to Bait Reds*, which I had written after the Sinclair campaign in California. Mr. Huebsch, a very warm and friendly man, granted me an interview and turned me over to Marshall Best, one of the editors, who greeted me kindly and offered me a fifteen-dollar reader's fee to read and report on a manuscript that an author had submitted to Viking. I accepted the offer with enthusiasm and went home with raised spirits.

Several days later, while I was writing my reader's report for Mr. Best, I received a postcard telling me to call the employment office of Macy's department store, one of the places where I had left an application for a temporary Christmas job. When I phoned them, they said they could use me and told me to report for training the next day. I was suddenly on a roll! The job was in Macy's Junior Stamp Department. A section within the regular stamp department on the cavernous main floor of the store, it was set aside for little kids who were just starting to save stamps. After a brief training that dealt mostly with how to make out sales slips and how and when I could leave the counter to go to the employees' men's room, I started work.

I was extremely grateful to Macy's, principally because the job restored my self-confidence and made me feel that somebody wanted me after all, but my first bloom of happiness did not last long. First of all, I was getting a minuscule salary, with the understanding that most of my pay would come from commissions from my sales. That might have been fine in the regular stamp department, but most of my customers seemed to be very demanding ten-year-olds in knickerbockers and caps who took half an hour studying individual stamps with a magnifying glass at the counter and then bought a single stamp for just a few cents. My average sale, in fact, totaled about a dime. Second, I was not used to standing on my feet all day long, and after a day or two of the resulting torture, I had to resort to all kinds of maneuvers to try to ease the excruciating pain, such as standing on the sides of my feet behind the counter or on one foot at a time. Eventually, it got better, and as Christmas and the end of my employment approached, an unexpected opportunity came my way from out of the blue for a new, permanent job.

This one was on Wall Street. It would start right after New Year's Day, and the offer came from another bridge-playing friend of my father named J. Horace Block, who was one of three partners in Maloney, Anderson and Block, a stockbrokerage firm way downtown at 50 Broadway, near Bowling Green and the southern tip of Manhattan Island. Mr. Block, who had been following my difficulties in landing a job, told my father that his firm was about to begin putting out a weekly financial newsletter for their clients, and writing it for them might be right up my alley. The statisticians in the company would give me all the material I needed, and I could get other ideas and suggestions for articles from the partners and the "customers' men," as the firm's brokers were known.

I was thrilled to have a steady job, even though the starting salary was microscopic. But I was promised a raise after I got going, and I liked Mr. Block—or Horace, as everyone called him—a big, amiable man who loved and followed (and probably bet on) most major sports events and whose recently deceased father, Benjamin Block, had once been a minor celebrity as one of the owners of a thoroughbred horse named Morvich that had won the Kentucky Derby in 1922. The firm's other two partners seemed always preoccupied with their own affairs, and I never really got to know them. P. J. Maloney, a bustling, red-faced man, was well known on "the Street" for a wild but unsuccessful attempt to corner, or gain monopoly control of, all the stock of the Radio Corporation of America in the 1920s. He spent most of his time on the floor of the New York Stock Exchange, and on the occasions when he was in our office, he was usually huddled in private with friends, planning, according to some of the firm's veteran employees, grandiose schemes to outwit the market. Mr. Anderson, the third partner, was a formidable man in his sixties, tall, bulldog-jawed, and unsmiling. He was a whiz at arbitrage, came in very early each morning to trade between the London and New York stock exchanges, rarely emerged from his private office, and never said anything more to me than a solemn "Good day."

Every morning, I took the Second Avenue el or the faster Lexington Avenue subway down to the Wall Street area and my new job, and for several months I had a private glass-enclosed office overlooking rows of desks of the firm's customers' men. Here I wrote a weekly financial letter filled with tidbits of inside news, analytical articles about market trends, and information and advice concerning the prospects of individual companies and their stocks and bonds. The facts, substance, and opinions of everything I wrote were supplied me by the head statistician or one of his assistants, and each week Horace Block read my articles before the newsletter was printed and mailed. It was regarded as a service to the firm's customers, but its purpose, of course, was to encourage them to give the company more business by buying or selling on the newsletter's recommendations and advice.

At times, the sudden change in my fortunes seemed ironic and weird. Without any financial background, experience, or interest, I had gone within a few months from a Hollywood junior writer, an aspiring playwright, a member of the unemployed, and a clerk in Macy's Junior Stamp Department to something of a Wall Street financial adviser. But, as a newcomer, almost everything I observed about Wall Street, which I had previously regarded as a mysterious bailiwick of the world's most knowledgeable and powerful financial leaders, seemed a little bit strange.

In buying and selling stocks, for instance, everyone appeared at times motivated by some kind of irrational mob psychology, rushing without knowledge or sense to do what they thought that everyone else, or some Wall Street leading figure, was doing, although they usually didn't know why. Moreover, aside from the partners, the statisticians, and the veteran telephone clerks who formed the principal links between our customers and the traders on the floors of the different exchanges, few of our members and clients appeared well informed on anything going on in the world. Dour-looking customers with apparently nothing better to do sat all day long like mummies in clusters of chairs among the desks of the customers' men, staring up at magnified images of a slow-moving ticker tape and a scratchy Dow Jones news ticker, and turning in panic to their customers' man for an explanation of any Dow Jones item that referred to a stock that they held or in which they were interested.

As purveyors of timely and relevant wisdom on which a client's entire financial destiny might depend, most of the customers' men, in turn, were unabashed frauds. During my weeks of seasoning, I began to eat lunch regularly with some of the statisticians at a neighborhood quick-meal cafeteria called the Exchange Buffet, known more familiarly in the financial district as the "E and B," or the "Eat It and Beat It," and they warned me not to take items for the newsletter from the customers' men. "In this industry, it's who you know, not what you know," one of them said. "The customers' men really don't know anything. Most of them are spoiled Ivy League rich men's sons who couldn't get a job anywhere else. The company tells them what stocks to get their customers to buy or sell, and they come running in to us to find out what they should tell the client. You just watch them."

The comment hit a raw nerve in me, for it could have been aimed squarely in my direction as well. I knew that the hardworking statisticians, whom I liked and respected for their intelligence and integrity and who generally had no customers of their own to provide commissions for them, were poorly paid and were sometimes resentful of those, including me, who lived on their research and knowledge. But there was nothing I could do about it, and for a brief time that afternoon, I took their suggestion and stood outside my office observing one of the customers' men, a youthful-looking, nattily dressed broker with a carnation in his buttonhole who appeared frequently in Walter Winchell, Louis Sobel, and other newspaper gossip columns and was known to the telephone clerks as a Park Avenue café society playboy.

One of his clients, an elderly woman, had come in to see him after lunch about investing some money, and, on the advice of one of the statisticians, he had recommended that she buy one hundred shares of Melville Shoe. She asked him what Melville did, and he said, "They make shoes." But that seemed to be all that he knew about the company. She kept asking him questions about where the company was and how much profit it made, and after most questions, he had to get up and hurry into the statisticians' office and return with an answer. Finally, he came back with a blue-printed information sheet about Melville's finances and told her to read it. I had to go back to my work before she made up her mind what to do, but I thought a lot about the episode and wondered uneasily what kind of a career I was now embarked on. When people go to a doctor, I thought to myself, they put their lives in the hands of an expert. When they go to a lawyer, they put their legal problems in the hands of an expert. But when they go to a broker, they put their money, perhaps all their life's savings, trustingly into the hands of someone who could be a nincompoop. Although it didn't seem to bother our clients, I found it nothing to laugh about, and it made me question seriously, once again, where I was heading.

An answer came abruptly a couple of months later when Horace Block came into my office one afternoon after the market had closed and paced around, smoking a cigarette nervously. He told me that business had not picked up during the first quarter of the year the way the partners had hoped it would, and they had decided that the newsletter had been a good idea but that it had not produced enough results. They had to adopt some cost-cutting measures, he said, and they had agreed reluctantly to end the newsletter. But, he added quickly, they all wanted me to stay on and learn to become a customers' man because they felt that with my background and experience I must have a lot of young friends from families with money who would be potential investors and whom I could bring into the firm as customers. If I agreed, he concluded, I would be given a small raise while I got experience and training, and after that, the sky would be the limit. "You could make a lot of money," he assured me.

While he talked, I could feel the blood draining out of me, and I went weak in the knees with fear. The last thing in the world I wanted to be was a customers' man, not only because I wanted to do something much more with my life than sell stocks and bonds but also because I shrank at the prospect of losing my self-respect and becoming a salesman or, worse still, someone like a racetrack tout living off friends like Lester Hofheimer. I wanted to be productive, I wanted to be in public service and help end the Depression and do some good in this world, and I wanted to be a writer. But I also didn't want to be unemployed again. I was afraid. I knew that I needed the job, that I needed it badly until I could find something else. I liked Horace immensely; he was a good friend, a good, decent person to work with and for, and I could read in his face that he wanted me to stay. Almost without thinking of my words, but knowing what I had to say, I finally thanked him and assured him that I would certainly like to stay on and get trained to become a customers' man, but my voice sounded hollow to me, as if it were in some kind of a box far away.

So I put on armbands, a green eyeshade, and a gray alpaca jacket like those all the salaried employees wore and began my training, first as one of the board boys, running up and down on a platform in front of a huge blackboard that covered the front wall in the room where the customers' men and their clients sat. The blackboard listed the New York Stock Exchange symbols of major corporations and the price of the last sale of their stock, and it was our somewhat-breathless job to watch the ticker tape high up above one end of the board and with eraser and chalk keep the sales figures on the board up-to-date. It was a tense, nerve-racking job, requiring quick recognition of the stock symbols on the tape and rapid changes of prices on the board, and several times I wanted to quit. But in a corner near an entrance to the room stood a little knot of down-and-out former employees of the firm who had been let go in the years after the crash of 1929 and who had been unemployed ever since. They were all family men with children, and they seemed to come in almost every day, seeking comfort and security among familiar people and surroundings and hoping that a vacancy would occur in the firm and they would be rehired. Their presence gave me second thoughts about quitting. There, but for my job, I convinced myself, go I.

In time, I was moved up through the different routine jobs in the office, processing and recording buy and sell orders that were handed in by the customers' men or phoned in from our uptown branch office in the Biltmore Hotel, near Grand Central Station. Late in the spring, I was assigned to the Commodity and Curb Exchanges and finally, as a telephone clerk, to the floor of the New York Stock Exchange to work with Horace. Each assignment was interesting, but the one on the floor of the Stock Exchange was the most exciting. As a telephone clerk, I manned a wall phone with a direct line to a clerk in our office at 50 Broadway, who relayed to me buy or sell orders. I noted them with a pencil on little pads headed BUY in black ink or SELL in red ink and handed them to Horace, our floor trader, whom I had summoned from wherever he was on the exchange floor by pressing a button that illuminated his number on a big board high up on one of the walls above the mob of brokers, traders, and clerks. After the trade was made and Horace returned the slip to me, I confirmed the purchase or sale, as well as the price, to the clerk at 50 Broadway, who communicated the information to the customers' man or the client. Eventually, computerized trading would make a mockery of this ponderous system, but at the time, the pace of fulfilling orders on the floor seemed speedy and often, during heavy trading periods, tense and frenetic.

By late summer, the novelty and excitement of working on the floor of the New York Stock Exchange began to wane, and I started to worry again. I realized that I was getting bored, but now my training was over and there was nothing else for me to go on to except to become a customers' man—a ludicrous thought, because I didn't want to be one, and I had no customers and didn't want any. Horace probably realized that I wasn't ready to be a customers' man, and he let me go on being a telephone clerk, but I knew that that, too, wasn't what I wanted to do forever, either, and that somehow I would have to get out of my predicament.

Meanwhile, after work, in the late afternoons, in the evenings and late into the nights, and on the weekends, I was still writing plays and occasional short stories, hoping to sell them, and keeping up my interest in political affairs. The Depression continued to hang heavily over the country, and although my Wall Street job, like the one I had had in Hollywood, insulated me from involvement in what I thought of as the world of conflict, my period of unemployment had affected me considerably. I could not forget the demonstration in Union Square and the two unemployed men in long, ragged overcoats from whom I had sought companionship, and I read in magazines and in the New York papers of the continued vicious oppression of agricultural workers in California and other news stories of people's sufferings. I found myself, as well as a number of friends and others my age whom I knew or met in New York, moving left politically to a surprising extent, identifying with the Depression's victims, both morally and emotionally, and wanting in some way to join and help them in their struggles.

At the same time, although Hitler, Mussolini, and the Japanese militarists were becoming more expansionist and warlike, they did not seem to threaten the United States, and my friends and I also tried to adopt an isolationist and pacifist stance, reflecting both our determination that the United States not get embroiled in another foreign war like that of 1914–1918 and our opposition to what we identified as dangerous fascist mimics at home like Father Charles Coughlin and Gerald L. K. Smith, a demagogic successor of the recently assassinated Huey Long. Meanwhile, my faith in President Roosevelt and in the constitutional heritage of freedoms bequeathed to us by the Founding Fathers, particularly Thomas Jefferson, who, in my avid reading of history, was becoming my most inspiring American hero, continued to keep me from being entangled in the policies and intrigues of the growing number of Communists and their proliferating organizations among the political activists.

In the middle of July, as a result of recommendations by John Lang and other friends in the Roosevelt administration to whom I had written the previous fall about a job, I received a letter, and then a visit, from a Washington official of the Works Progress Administration, who wanted me to join in organizing a national movement of college students to help President Roosevelt win a second term in the November elections. It was a temporary job and would mean a lot of travel, which, in turn, would require quitting my Wall Street job, something I was not ready to do. Our interview ended, instead, with my being put in touch with officers of the Roosevelt First Voters League at the headquarters of the Democratic National Committee in the Biltmore Hotel in New York who enlisted me to organize a chapter of the league on the Upper East Side, the part of Manhattan where I lived.

Like almost every firm doing business in Wall Street, Maloney, Anderson and Block was overtly dedicated 100 percent to the defeat of Roosevelt. Everyone, from the partners to the board boys, wore prominent, extralarge yellow Alf Landon sunflower buttons on their lapels, proclaiming their support for the Republican candidate, Kansas's governor, who had been nominated largely because he had managed to balance that state's budget, and all the employees got the word that if Roosevelt won, we would all find pink slips in our next pay envelope and the firm would go out of business. No one knew of my organizing work for Roosevelt, and somehow it was after the election before anyone learned what I had been up to, despite the fact that on a number of occasions I had spoken along with others at street corners and from the back of trucks at different places on the East Side. Generally, however, our meetings were in private apartments and school buildings. With original lists of potential members supplied by the Democratic National Committee, the few of us who had begun the chapter enrolled increasing numbers of young people who would vote for the first time and, equally important, would work enthusiastically for the Democratic ticket as volunteers on election day, getting other Roosevelt voters to the polls.

As election day approached, everything seemed solemn and hushed on Wall Street, as if the fate of everyone and every firm hung in the balance. On the eve of the election, Roosevelt planned to drive up Broadway from the Battery to midtown in a dramatic last-minute campaign appearance. Toward noon of that day, crowds of Wall Street workers, all wearing their bright Landon buttons, lined the curbs of lower Broadway or filled the windows of the buildings overlooking the president's route, everybody ostensibly ready to boo and jeer FDR as he rode by in his open car. Standing with friends in the crowd, I felt terrible. Surrounded by a sea of Landon buttons, I, too, wore mine, though I had pinned a Roosevelt button underneath the lapel of my jacket. On schedule, the motorcade began south of us, and as it headed north, we began to hear a roar that got louder and more frenzied as the president's car approached us. Everyone assumed it was the sound of massive booing and jeering, until suddenly, straining to see what was happening, we saw the air south of us filled with ticker tape coming down from every office building. We realized with a start that the roar, now engulfing us like a storm in the Broadway canyon, was from people along the sidewalks and in the office buildings cheering at the top of their lungs as the president rode by, waving happily at them from his car.

In a moment, he was gone, on his way up Broadway, accompanied by the huge roar that rolled along with him like an ocean wave. But behind him, where we were standing, and up and down Broadway as far as I could see, Wall Streeters were pulling off their Landon buttons and throwing them with defiance and glee into the middle of Broadway, where they littered the pavement until street cleaners swept them up. That afternoon, I and a startling number of other people, including leading brokers and traders, returned to work wearing red-white-and-blue Roosevelt buttons, and nothing happened. In the election, Roosevelt won every state but Maine and Vermont, and no firm on Wall Street went out of business. On the East Side, I and our young workers of the Roosevelt First Voters League cast our first ballots in an election and then spent the day in the precincts as poll watchers, checking off the registered Democrats as they voted and telephoning and helping others who needed a reminder to vote or assistance in getting to the polls.

When I went back to my job at the exchange after Roosevelt's landslide victory, the excitement of my involvement in the political world and the campaign had convinced me that I had to get out of the brokerage business and into something that would be more stimulating and dynamic. Throughout the year, I had hoped that one of the plays or stories I wrote would sell, but I had no success. I had a play agent who liked much of what I wrote and labored hard, although in vain, to interest a producer in my work. Early in the summer, I signed on with a second agent, Mrs. Sewell Haggard of the William Morris Agency, to handle my short stories and articles and get me freelance radio-writing assignments. Edith Haggard worked hard for me, too, and things began to happen. Bob Hope needed an additional gag writer for his weekly radio program, and she sent me for an interview with him and some of his writers in an office overlooking Times Square. It was a pleasant meeting, filled with wisecracks and laughs, but it didn't take long for all of us to agree that I had not been born to be a gag writer.

Next, I was sent to Louis de Rochemont, the producer of "The March of Time," Time, Inc.'s documentary film series for theaters, and my luck at last began to change. De Rochemont assigned me to write a segment on Farouk I, the young king of Egypt, who was just succeeding his father on the throne. It was a combination of news and film writing, and working at night after returning home from Wall Street, I completed a script on schedule and hoped for more "March of Time" assignments. But Mrs. Haggard had other work for me, writing five- and ten-minute guest-appearance spots for Fifi D'Orsay and other entertainers on such popular nighttime radio variety shows as "The Rudy Vallee Hour." The pay was good, but the occasional assignments could not be counted on for steady income. Nevertheless, I began to think that this sort of freelance writing for the radio would eventually help me get out of Wall Street.

I was not wrong. During the year, I had also done some writing for Jerry Danzig, an old friend from Horace Mann, who had become a director of news and special features at WOR, a popular fifty-thousand-watt independent radio station owned by L. Bamberger, a Newark, New Jersey, department store that was a subsidiary of Macy's. Among other duties, Jerry was responsible for supplying the program department with special onetime, sustaining, or noncommercial, programs, and at Jerry's invitation, I had written a few of them. He knew of my restlessness on Wall Street, and one day near the end of 1936, he told me that WOR and the prestigious *New York Herald Tribune* had made a tie-up, and beginning after the first of the year, WOR was going to carry a new weekly series for the paper, and the paper needed a writer for the series who could join the *Tribune*'s staff full-time and work over there, and was I interested?

I certainly was, and after I beetled over to the *Tribune* on West 40th Street and was interviewed by people in the Promotion, Circulation, and Editorial departments, I was hired at thirty-five dollars a week to begin work right after New Year's Day. I was ecstatic. I was going to be working full-time—and for one of New York's two greatest newspapers.

9 🔳 OF MEXICO AND LEON TROTSKY

My departure from Wall Street was painless. Horace Block, the statisticians, and all the friends I left at Maloney, Anderson and Block had finally
come to accept me good-naturedly as a fish out of water, knowing I was
more bent on becoming a professional writer than a customers' man, and
our office Christmas party, ringing with good-luck toasts to my future,
doubled as a cheerful end to my career in New York's hustling financial
district.

At the same time, in view of all the frustrations and rejections I had
experienced during my job-hunting the previous year, I could scarcely
believe that I had actually been hired by a metropolitan daily newspaper,
and by one with the eminence of the *Herald Tribune*. In 1924, the *Tribune*
had purchased the *Herald*, and the paper resulting from the merger, with a
history of ownership by some of America's greatest journalists of the past,
including Horace Greeley, James Gordon Bennett, and Whitelaw Reid,
was known as the country's leading Republican mouthpiece and by many
people as perhaps the best-written, best-edited, and typographically the
most attractive paper in the nation. Its daily circulation of 350,000 was
almost 70 percent of that of its chief rival, the *New York Times*.

In 1937, the *Trib*'s high standards were still imposing. Although reflecting the conservative Republican partisanship of its owners and management, the paper was fair-minded, civil, and objective, and its reporters,
writers, editors, and correspondents, some of the most literate and colorful figures in American journalism of that day, included liberals and radicals as well as conservatives. Among them were Walter Lippmann, the
formidable left-of-center political pundit; Dorothy Thompson, a celebrated foreign correspondent turned columnist, who was married at the
time to the Nobel Prize–winning novelist Sinclair Lewis; Joseph Alsop, a
stylish, socially connected member of the Washington bureau, who later

coauthored an influential column of political commentary; and Stanley Walker, a slightly built man from the small town of Lampasas, Texas, who, directing the *Herald Tribune*'s daily coverage of the sins and delights of New York, had become the country's best-known city editor and was now an assistant managing editor.

Immediately after New Year's Day, I reported to my new boss, a personable young Louisianan named Jim Barnett, who had graduated from Princeton and who, as educational director in the Circulation Department, was responsible for boosting the paper's subscriptions in colleges and high schools. One of his projects, designed to promote sales in New York City's public high schools, was a citywide Biggest News of the Week contest, conducted by the *Herald Tribune* among students in English, current events, and other classes who competed for cash prizes from the paper for essays on what they considered the week's most important news story. In addition to awarding the weekly prizes, the *Tribune* publicized the winning authors and their schools and classes, publishing the best essays and the runners-up every Saturday morning on the first page of the paper's second section.

The teachers did all the work in screening the essays and sending the best ones on to the *Trib*. But someone on the paper had to choose the final winners and take responsibility for preparing the essays, as well as stories about the winners and their schools, that the makeup people needed for the Saturday edition. On the paper, it had become a largely unorganized weekly chore, shared by the Circulation Department, which had no trained writers, and the rewrite men and others around the city desk. The first thing Jim did was relegate it all to me, giving me the title of education editor and putting me in charge of the project, with responsibility for writing and getting to the city desk everything it needed on the contest for the Saturday paper.

Some of Jim's staff broke me in, taking me around the city's boroughs to Stuyvesant High and other schools, where we met teachers and principals and gave out awards in assemblies to the pre-Christmas student winners and runners-up. During my first week, as another batch of essays came in to the paper, I breezed through the assignment until Friday afternoon, when for the first time I took all the copy, including the stories I had written about the winners, downstairs to the city room for the next day's section page and gave them to Stanley Walker, who was slouched down in a chair at the city desk, sitting in that day for the city editor. He looked up at me quizzically, as if wondering who I was, and I told him. Then, a little scared in the great man's presence, I started hurriedly back for my desk in the Circulation Department.

Walker could not have read more than a couple of sentences of my lead story when he rasped, "Josephy!" in a voice that must have been heard by half the city room. I went back to his desk, trembling inside and sure that I was about to lose my job. But by the time I reached him, he had calmed down and seemed almost kindly. His eyes were narrowed, and I noticed that his badly stained and eroded teeth looked like he had been chewing on betel nuts. They were about the most repulsive set of teeth I had ever seen, a fact that helped me regain some confidence.

"Are you the product of a journalism school?" he asked me. "No," I told him. "Well, that's good," he said. "I wouldn't hire anybody who went to a journalism school." He held up one of the pages I had written and waved it at me as if challenging me, and again my knees weakened. "You used the term *most outstanding* here," he announced. "You can't compare the word *outstanding*. There is no such thing as *more* or *most outstanding*. A person is either outstanding or he's not. Don't do it again." He turned away from me, and I slunk from the city room, aware of amused smiles from some of those around the city desk. I felt humiliated, but saved in my job, and it was a good lesson. From then on, with the specter of Walker looking over my shoulder, I paid careful attention to my writing and, indeed, to every word that I wrote.

The second thing Jim Barnett did—and the principal reason he had hired me—was to put me in charge, also, of the new Saturday-morning promotional *Herald Tribune* radio series that would start on WOR in a couple of weeks. Titled "The Thrills Behind the Story," the programs, which I wrote and produced, were interviews with *Herald Tribune* writers and editors by members of a WOR–*Herald Tribune* High School Radio League. The project, which had the interviewees talk about the nature of their jobs on the *Tribune*, as well as discuss their opinions and relate anecdotes of their careers, gave me access to almost everybody on the paper, for I could select anyone to go on the shows and received introductions to them from the Promotion Department.

Once started, the weekly fifteen-minute programs at WOR's studios went smoothly. The first program, a dramatic account by Lewis Sebring, the *Tribune*'s night city editor, of the chaotic night an earthquake struck New York an hour before the final edition deadline, was followed by an engaging session with Emma Bugbee, a veteran reporter of twenty-six years with the *Tribune*, who recounted her current adventures in covering Mrs. Roosevelt's activities and in trying to keep up with the nation's fast-traveling First Lady. Succeeding programs featured, among others, foreign correspondent Joseph B. Phillips, who had just returned from Moscow and gave us the first eyewitness account of Stalin's brutal "treason" trials, which were horrifying the world; Dorothy Thompson, who, although an ardent New Dealer, lambasted FDR on our program for the president's current attempt to control the Supreme Court by "packing" it with additional members; and John O'Neill, the *Tribune's* Pulitzer Prize–winning science editor, who, without a crystal ball that could tell him about Hiroshima only eight years in the future, predicted to his high school interviewers that within the next decade scientists would produce "the biggest story in the world," smashing the atom and releasing enough energy to make power cheaper than water, revolutionize civilization, and "bring untold benefits to mankind."

Gradually, as the radio series caught on, I met and became friends with editorial people throughout the *Tribune*, working with them over scripts, coming in late in the morning, as most of them did, and staying with them until the bulldog edition came out at 11:00 p.m. When I had nothing else to do, I hung out among them amid the clacking of typewriters and the calls for a copyboy on the busy editorial floor, which to me was the most exciting place in the building. At mealtimes I ate, drank, and joined with some of them in playing the match game (a guessing game of the number of matches hidden in our fists, the loser being responsible for paying the bill) in Jack Bleeck's next-door Artist and Writers Restaurant, whose long front-room bar with its "free lunch" of pickles, cheese, and other snacks was sometimes three-deep with a convivial crowd of *Tribune* people, including the paper's usually inebriated owner, Ogden Reid, along with playwrights, Broadway press agents, and thirsty stragglers who wandered over from *The New Yorker* and other midtown publications.

In a way, I was something of a freewheeling maverick on the paper. Although I did a lot of writing and editing in connection with the Biggest News of the Week contest and gave my copy to the city desk, I was not responsible to the city editor, and although I reported to Jim Barnett and maintained my desk close to his in the Circulation Department, I was not considered, strictly speaking, a circulation man, but an editorial person. Nevertheless, I became quite friendly with the night city editor, Lew Sebring, and even with Stanley Walker, who went on one of our radio programs and then agreed one day to write for me a short foreword to an illustrated promotion portfolio entitled "Aids in Newspaper Writing," which I was preparing for Barnett's staff to distribute in college and high school journalism classes.

While I stood over him, Walker pecked at his typewriter and in about three minutes produced as a foreword this tongue-in-cheek characterization of a stereotypical journalist of the 1930s as popularized by *The Front Page* genre of movies, plays, and books:

What makes a good newspaperman? The answer is easy. He knows everything. He is aware not only of what goes on in the world today, but his brain is a repository of the accumulated wisdom of the ages. Moreover, he is somewhat psychic, and is able to sense what the news will be tomorrow, and next month, and even next year. He writes prose that is crisp but graceful. He can perform any job in journalism. He is not only handsome, but he has physical stamina which enables him to perform great feats of energy. He can go for nights on end without sleep. He dresses well and talks with charm. Men admire him; women adore him; tycoons and statesmen are happy to share their secrets with him. He takes a drink, but never gets drunk. He is good to his family, if any. He hates lies and meanness and shams, but keeps his temper. He is loyal to his paper and to what he looks upon as his profession; whether it is a profession, or merely a craft, he resents attempts to debase it. When he dies, a lot of people are sorry, and some remember him for several days. He leaves little money, but he had a pretty good time.

Although we used Walker's little essay in our promotion piece, it was never reprinted elsewhere, perhaps with good reason.

As summer approached, I began to wonder what Barnett would have me doing when the schools closed for vacation. I did not want to do circulation work, and I began to hope that somehow I could get on the editorial side of the paper, covering and writing the news. Important developments, like the Spanish Civil War, the growing threat of the Nazis, the formation of an international Popular Front against fascism, and in our country the sit-down strikes of automobile workers in Michigan and Ohio and the swift emergence of the CIO and its huge militant unions of miners and auto, rubber, clothing, and other workers, were reshaping the world, and I envied writers who were at the scenes of action, witnessing and reporting the history-making events. From time to time, thoughts of the labor developments reminded me of the continuing class strife in California. In turn, memories of that state and of my drives with Billy Watters and others made me nostalgic again for the air and mountains and skies of the West, and, although I knew it was far-fetched, I wished there would be a way for me to return to that part of the country as a *Tribune* correspondent.

One night, a friend named Jimmy Loeb, whose economist father had been one of the early figures in the pre-FDR technocracy movement, which some people had thought would cure the Depression, took me to a party where I met Fred Leighton, a well-known New York importer of Mexican arts and crafts. Leighton, who went to Mexico frequently on buying trips for his Greenwich Village shop, fascinated me with an account of what had been going on in that neighboring but little-thought-about country to our south. In general, I was aware that Mexico had been a land of turmoil since 1911, when a revolution by Francisco Madero, a liberal reformer, supported by armies of poor workers and farmers, had overthrown a dictator named Porfirio Díaz, who, allied with the hierarchy of the Church, wealthy landowners, bankers, and foreign concessionaires, had ruled Mexico with an iron hand for more than thirty years. A few years after Madero's triumph, he, in turn, had been murdered by American-supported reactionary generals. It started a twenty-year period of revolution and counterrevolution marked by assassinations of leaders on both sides and by almost unceasing warfare between the reformers and their opponents.

Now, in 1937, the reformers were on top, and the struggle, according to Fred Leighton, had reached a climactic stage. After years of little but violence and rhetoric, many properties of the big landowners were finally being expropriated and redistributed to poor Mexican farmers; the nationalization of railroads, oil, and other basic industries was being planned or had already taken place; and priests and nuns had been driven from the country or into hiding and their churches and other properties seized and converted into schools, orphanages, and even garages as part of a vigorous anticlerical campaign that the revolutionists had waged intermittently to break the political and economic power of the Church. In addition, as a sidelight to all of this, the firebrand Russian Marxist leader Leon Trotsky, who as a partner of Lenin had built and commanded the Red Army during the Russian Revolution and Civil War and whom Stalin had viewed as a dangerous rival and expelled from the Soviet Union, had recently been granted asylum by Mexico's current president, Lázaro Cárdenas, a full-blooded Tarascan Indian. Trotsky was living in exile in a section of Mexico City called Coyoacán, in a house borrowed from the Mexican artists Diego Rivera, and his wife, Frida Kahlo, whose family owned the building.*

Leighton told me that although the *New York Times* and many European papers had correspondents in Mexico, who were getting their arti-

---

* At the time, the building was known to most people only as the home of Diego Rivera, who hid Frida Kahlo, his wife, in the immense shadow of his own personality and accomplishments. In later years, after she had gained international recognition as a talented artist and an important and interesting individual in her own right, the house became known as the Frida Kahlo Museum, dedicated primarily to her memory and life.

cles about the country printed almost every day, the *Herald Tribune* had sent no one there, and its coverage of all the dramatic events going on in Mexico was almost nonexistent. "Why don't you get the *Tribune* to send you down there?" he asked me suddenly. "I could give you a lot of introductions."

The notion seemed ridiculous, but also very appealing, and in the ensuing days I thought about little else. Then Jimmy Loeb told me that he was going to drive to Mexico City for the summer and asked if I would like to go along with him. After that, things moved quickly. I consulted with Jim Barnett, who told me that he could spare me for the summer, but he advised me that the *Tribune* traditionally didn't spend much money on foreign correspondents, even in Europe, and that if I went to Mexico, I'd probably have to pay all my expenses myself. At his suggestion, I saw George Cornish, the Sunday editor, a soft-spoken, kindly Alabaman, who told me that the paper was suffering from a downturn in business activity caused by President Roosevelt's attempt to balance the national budget and could not afford a staff correspondent in Mexico. When I announced to him, however, that I intended to go down there anyway and get exclusive interviews with Leon Trotsky and President Cárdenas, he beamed at my enthusiasm and agreed to give me credentials as a *Tribune* correspondent and pay me space rates for anything the paper bought from me. But for the time being at least, I would have to pay all my expenses myself.

Jimmy had to go first to Santa Fe, and we made plans to meet in San Antonio. Meanwhile, I got shots for typhoid, paratyphoid, cholera, and half a dozen other diseases and spent hours in the *Tribune*'s morgue and the New York Public Library boning up on Mexico as well as on Leon Trotsky. I read about the dictatorial days of Porfirio Díaz, only some twenty-five years earlier, when about 2 percent of the Mexican people owned more than 80 percent of the land, when less than 15 percent of the population could read, and the landless and uneducated farmers and their children were bound by debt in a system of perpetual peonage to the landowners. What the Mexican Revolution was largely about, it seemed clear, was freedom, as well as land, education, and human dignity, for the peons, and my sympathies were aroused for them and for legendary figures like Emiliano Zapata and Pancho Villa who had led them in their agrarian uprisings earlier in the century. In those years, the peasant armies had won victories and had been given promises of land redistribution by such men as Venustiano Carranza and Alvaro Obregón, whom they had placed in power as leaders of the Revolutionary party and as presidents of the country but who then enriched themselves, temporized, and went back on their word to the poor people. Finally, in the Indian revolutionary general Cárdenas, they seemed to have found a humanitarian president of ramrod integrity and determined will who was making the promises of what had become known as the Revolution come true. He was their trusted and beloved hero, not a Communist or socialist or grafter, but "Mexico's Abraham Lincoln," as Fred Leighton called him, the sympathetic champion of the little people and the Indians who comprised three-fourths of Mexico's population.

As for Leon Trotsky, he appeared to be a bomb in a pail of water, an angry world revolutionist who had given his word to Cárdenas to refrain from agitation and political activity while he was a guest of Mexico. But this had not defused him. The previous January, the same month that Trotsky arrived in Mexico, old Bolshevik colleagues and friends of his—arrested by Stalin, tortured, and facing execution as Trotskyite traitors—"confessed" in one of Stalin's sensational purge trials in Moscow that Trotsky had led them in a conspiracy with the Germans and Japanese to destabilize the Soviet Union with acts of sabotage and terror and then overthrow Stalin's government. Almost immediately, Trotsky, joined by a number of followers and neutral intellectuals, including John Dewey, the American philosopher and educator, staged a weeklong "inquiry" in the Kahlo house in Coyoacán of the charges that had been made against him in Moscow. Crowds of international correspondents flocked to Mexico City to cover the proceedings, which Trotsky, still a gigantic historic figure, stage-managed like a countertrial of Stalin, talking, talking, talking and arguing, arguing, arguing, as one correspondent complained, painting Stalin as a monstrous betrayer of the Russian Revolution and trying to convince world opinion of the fraudulence of Stalin's charges against him.

The proceedings soon became repetitive, and the attempts of the bored and cynical correspondents to convince Trotsky that they had already written everything he had to say and that he was no longer supplying them with news got them into unpleasant wrangles and fights with him, and gradually the correspondents, accused of being pro-Stalin "enemies" by Trotsky, who would no longer talk to them, went back to their home countries or to their offices in Mexico City and ignored the Russian exile.

The "inquiry" was now over, a report favorable to Trotsky was expected to be issued early in the fall by John Dewey's group, and the word was that Trotsky, suffering from headaches and high blood pressure from the "trial," viewed all correspondents in Mexico City as hostile or Stalinists and refused to trust or see any of them. As soon as I had decided to go to Mexico, I had written directly to him at his Coyoacán address, telling him of my trip to Mexico for the *Herald Tribune* and asking for an interview with him, and I worried that the days for press people seeing him were now over, even though there had been no *Herald Tribune* man to anger him at the proceedings at the Kahlo house. It turned out that I had nothing to fear. I would be a totally new correspondent in Mexico, he still needed sources to carry his words to the outside world, and why not try me? Shortly after July 4, a letter came from Bernard Wolfe, one of his American secretaries in Coyoacán. Mr. Trotsky was going away for a vacation in the mountains, he wrote, but would be back toward the end of August. Please call when I got to Mexico, and "I shall be happy to arrange a meeting for you."

It was good news, and as I got ready to leave New York, I felt relieved. With the help of C. B. Allen, the *Tribune*'s aviation editor, I wangled free airplane tickets on TWA, then known as Transcontinental and Western Airlines, from New York to Kansas City, and on Braniff from there to San Antonio. It was my first airplane trip, and the flight seemed exciting and romantic until the diving and bucking of our small propeller planes in the rough air of the low altitudes at which they had to fly made passengers start throwing up. The awful sound of their retching surged through the plane, making others feel suddenly sick, and soon everybody aboard was heaving into the little white bags provided for the purpose. The cabin attendants of that early day of commercial aviation were like nurses as well as travel guides. They squeezed in sympathetically beside us, gave us little vials of something strongly medicinal to smell and bring relief, and then tried to divert us, now pale-faced, emptied, and covered with perspiration, with a lecture about some river or other landmark over which we were flying.

At San Antonio, Jimmy was waiting for me in a shiny new Ford sedan, sporting a large metal PRESS sign, which he had affixed for my benefit above the front license plate. We visited the Alamo and then drove to Laredo, on the Mexican border, where we spent the night. Jimmy was a small, footloose, and happy-go-lucky individual who was an expert, self-confident driver. His parents were divorced, and his mother, whom he had just visited, was a member of Mabel Dodge Luhan's avant-garde circle of artists and writers in Taos, near Santa Fe, where Jimmy's mother lived in bohemian style with a talented black writer named Jean Toomer. Neither she nor her ex-husband paid much attention to Jimmy, who lived on a trust fund established by his grandfather and spent most of his time driving around the country visiting friends. Later, in World War II, he became a navy pilot, flying planes off carriers in the Pacific, and when the war was over, he founded an aviation taxi company in New Jersey and was killed when his plane fell into New York Harbor.

But he liked speed, and after we crossed the Rio Grande and headed down the first leg of the recently opened Pan-American Highway, which ran in a long straightaway through the desert of northern Mexico toward Monterrey, Jimmy accelerated to ninety miles an hour and kept it there. Past Monterrey, we continued on through a sweet-smelling region of citrus groves, sunny fields of cactus and maize, and dense stands of sugarcane, staining our radiator guard and windshield with smashed bugs and the wings of small yellow butterflies and feeling occasional thuds as we struck long-eared jackrabbits that popped out of nowhere and raced blindly under our wheels.

We had been filled with grim stories about bandits waylaying tourists in the Mexican countryside, but throughout our almost-thousand-mile drive to Mexico City we saw neither bandits nor tourists and, outside of the bigger towns, almost no traffic at all, only horse-drawn carts, local people on horses or on plodding burros, and an occasional old truck or beaten-up bus. At a government checkpoint in the desert south of the Rio Grande where we had to stop for inspection, a contemptuous official complained that because of President Cárdenas's expropriations and the threat of renewed violence in the country, very few American tourists had "the *cojones*," meaning "balls," or "courage," to visit Mexico these days, and the absence of their—or any other—automobiles made long stretches of the highway very lonely.

That night, we stayed in an auto court in Ciudad Victoria, where we were the only customers, and we ate breakfast the next morning at a Coca-Cola stand in the main plaza. After we left town, the road descended gradually into lower and warmer country of thicker vegetation and even jungle. Brightly colored birds and swarms of butterflies filled the air, and from frequent rises in the road, we had spectacular views of unbroken tropical growth extending like a green carpet toward distant storm clouds and mountains. Occasionally, we passed hamlets of primitive-looking thatched huts clustered among banana and palm trees along the roadside or above the banks of muddy streams and seeming to shelter pigs, chickens, and cows, as well as very poor-looking people who were barefoot or who wore sandals made of pieces of old rubber tires.

At one point, the pavement of the highway appeared littered with dozens of large hard-shelled desert tortoises. Jimmy did his best to slow down and steer through them, but he was unable to avoid scrunching a few of them. Farther on, we rounded a bend and caught an abrupt, heart-stopping glimpse of a large jaguar, which immediately turned from the edge of the road ahead of us and disappeared into the jungle. It suddenly made me feel the strangeness of this drive. We were now less than five hundred miles from Texas, yet ever since we had crossed the Rio Grande, we had been in a truly foreign country, totally unlike our own and so undeveloped that it could have been on another continent thousands of miles distant from the United States. How unreal, I thought: a next-door neighbor to our powerful and corrosive culture, but so unaffected by it and so different. There must be something enormously strong and resistant in these people of Hispanic and Indian background, I felt, but it would be years before I would know what it could be.

Shortly after seeing the jaguar, we entered a hilly region of sugarcane fields and suddenly faced disaster. Our car, for some reason, began to shake and shimmy and make dreadful grinding noises. Jimmy slowed it down and, making a terrifying racket, we limped fourteen miles farther on, into a small town. There was no gas station or garage, but we found a man who was a mechanic at a nearby sugar mill that happened to be on strike, and he said he could probably help us. He had us drive the car to an open shed next to his house where he had some tools and some kind of a homemade winch made out of chains and secured to the roof of the shed. Word of what was going on spread through the village, and dozens of small boys arrived, clustering around the car in wonder and watching intently while, to our horror, the mechanic separated the body of the car from the chassis and winched it into the air. The mechanic assured us that he knew what he was doing and proceeded to take the car apart, ignoring our protests and laying bits and pieces of the transmission in a mess all over the place, so that it seemed impossible that he would ever get it back together again. As Jimmy and I began to wonder where we were and how we would ever get out of the town, the mechanic extricated the long main driveshaft of the car and showed us one of its ends, which in some way had become roughened and nicked.

It was no problem, he told us, but the next morning he would have to take it over to the sugar mill, where they had a file with which he could smooth the damaged surface of the shaft. The car, he promised, would be ready for us by noon. Meanwhile, he urged us to go with one of the little boys to a small hotel in town and have a good night's sleep. There was nothing else we could do, and though we were up half the night, worrying that we might have to find another car, the man was as good as his promise. At noon, we returned to the shed, and he had all the car's parts reassembled and the engine running smoothly. "See, no problem," he said, laughing. We paid him gratefully and started off again, and for some miles, Jimmy drove cautiously and slowly, certain that the man had not reassembled everything correctly and that some part of the transmission would suddenly fall onto the road. But nothing happened, and finally Jimmy again picked up speed.

A day later, after a spectacular crossing of eight-thousand-foot-high mountains on a twisting, unfinished section of the highway that was still unpaved and had no guardrails, we descended onto the central Mexican plateau and, driving past picturesque fields of huge maguey plants and the ruins of derelict churches, burned and partly destroyed during the violent years of the Revolution, reached Mexico City and the Villa International, a pension near the capital's principal avenue, the Paseo de la Reforma, where Fred Leighton had reserved a room for us.

Mexico City was exhilarating and exciting, with nothing like the huge population, the dense traffic, the noise, or the stifling pollution it would know in the second half of the twentieth century. The air was clear, the skies blue, the climate crisp and sunny, and the sights strange and won-derful—a radiant architectural, cultural, and historical mosaic of the grandeur and majesty of Mexico's Indian and Spanish colonial pasts and of the fiery anger and conflicts of its present. This was a time again of the Indians, long stamped upon and ignored, but now favored by Cárdenas, one of their own, who listened to their pleas and tried to help them. The signs of their newly recognized importance were everywhere—in Diego Rivera's great murals on the walls of the National Palace, which fronted on the Zócalo, the capital's enormous central plaza, and in the respect given to the Indians by the gray-shirted militia of Communist-led union-ized workers, many of them proud at last of their Indian heritage. They marched in parades, ready to fight domestic or foreign fascists, and stood guard in the Zócalo over a huge flag laid out on the pavement every day, onto which passersby threw coins or peso bills to be sent to the Spanish Loyalists. The signs of the Indians' ascendance were even in the hushed chapels of the brooding National Cathedral, built by the Spaniards on the ruins of the Aztecs' principal temple, overlooking the Zócalo and opened now by Cárdenas to anyone who wished to pray within it, although it was now shorn of its former authority because under the country's laws the Catholic Church was supposedly no longer permitted to control, educate, or administer to the Indians or to anyone else in Mexico.

Fred Leighton was away in the countryside somewhere, but George Cornish had given me the name of Jack Starr-Hunt, who ran a small advertising agency in Mexico City and had once sold stories to the *Tri-bune*. He had not been very good, and the *Tribune* had stopped using him, but he was knowledgeable and obliging and knew a lot of people in the capital, and Cornish had told me to look him up if I needed any help. I did so, and after we had met, he took me around on introductory visits to a few of the government officials he thought I ought to know.

Through one of them, Ramon Beteta, the undersecretary of foreign relations and a principal adviser to President Cárdenas, I hit the jackpot. Beteta, an eager young intellectual who spoke perfect English, was delighted to know that the *New York Herald Tribune* had sent somebody to his country, and he was anxious to assist me. He had no use, he said, for Frank Kluckhohn of the *New York Times*, the only other important American newspaper with its own correspondent in Mexico, because all he did was pick fights and criticize Mexico and the Cárdenas administration. Kluckhohn, he told me, was running true to form. He had come to Mexico from Spain, where first the Loyalists and then Franco had allegedly ordered him to leave. Now he was making trouble in Mexico, writing articles that inflated the importance of a disgruntled former member of Cárdenas's cabinet named General Saturnino Cedillo, who had resigned and returned to his home state, where, according to Beteta, he was conspiring with right-wing fascistic elements, including American oilmen, to lead a revolution against Cárdenas.

Beteta urged me to travel around the country and judge the Mexican situation for myself. I would have to go see Cedillo on my own, but he offered to arrange for me to interview Cárdenas, and he would also get me on a weeklong train trip through much of Mexico with the minister of finance, who would be leaving in a few days to visit some of the lands that the government had expropriated and redistributed to landless farmers. Both proposals were exciting, and I welcomed his help.

In the meantime, I did not forget Trotsky. I phoned his home and got Bernard Wolfe, the secretary who had written to me in New York. Trotsky was still on vacation, but Wolfe directed me to write down my questions and drop them off at the house in Coyoacán as soon as possible. I began to feel uneasy. Would I not be able to see Mr. Trotsky? I asked. Wolfe assured me that that was still going to be possible, but Mr. Trotsky would want to read my questions first and supply written answers. Then we could arrange a personal meeting. There was no sense arguing. Trotsky, I assumed, was making sure that I was not "a Stalinist" or another "hostile" journalist, and maybe the news of him still being away was a cock-and-bull story and just a way of keeping me at arm's length umtil he could judge me by the questions I submitted.

At any rate, obliged to play along with this legendary master of intrigue, I typed up a list of fourteen questions, about which I had given considerable thought during the previous weeks, and Jimmy and I drove to Coyoacán and found the house, a low blue-painted building on Avenida de Londres, a quiet residential street with no one about except a drowsy policeman, who was sitting with a dog at his feet outside the front door of

Trotsky's home, half-asleep in the shade of a tall tree. We exchanged nods, and he watched me indifferently as I rang the bell. It was answered in a moment by Bernard Wolfe, who introduced himself and accepted the envelope containing my questions. "Please call us in about ten days," he said, and that was it. He closed the door, and Jimmy and I took off.

A couple of days later, after a call from Ramon Beteta, I said good-bye to Jimmy and went down to the railroad station to join the train trip around Mexico with Eduardo Suárez, the minister of finance, a tall, trim, mustachioed man in a snap-brimmed white hat and a white jacket buttoned tightly at his throat. Suárez had organized the junket to sell Cárdenas's agrarian program to representatives of important Mexican and European banks and financial interests by showing them the successful results of individual projects where lands had been expropriated and redistributed to poor farmers, and to persuade them to help the government fund their continuation and expansion as a development beneficial to all of Mexico. In addition to the financial people, Suárez had gathered a pack of correspondents, mostly fat and tired European and Latin American over-the-hill hacks who seemed to live on bottles of carbonated water and were constantly belching. Besides myself, there were two others from the United States, Betty Kirk, a young freelance stringer for several American publications, and Frank Kluckhohn, the correspondent from the *New York Times*, a tall, thin man in a gray fedora and white shoes. The latter's criticisms of Mexico, which had angered Beteta, turned out to stem more from a desire to create news by provoking controversy than from any ideological or political convictions of his own.

We had a special three-car train pulled by a locomotive, the first car of which was occupied by Suárez and members of his staff. The middle car was a club and dining car, where we lounged with cold drinks and got to know one another during the long rides between stops, and the rear car was an aged Pullman sleeper with a small observation platform and upper and lower berths that were crammed at night with all the correspondents and financial people on the trip.

We zigzagged around the country, pulling onto sidings at small towns and being greeted by government officials, crowds of enthusiastic peasant families, brass bands, and troops of mounted men in big sombreros. Armed with guns and wearing bandoliers full of cartridges across their chests, the soldiers carried huge red flags emblazoned with gold hammers and sickles and the words TIERRA Y LIBERTAD. The riders sat on their horses in the summer dust and heat near giant cement versions of the sculpture of a defiant clenched fist on a pedestal, copied by local artists from the original by Diego Rivera. To some of our party, the scene appeared communistic, although it was unlikely that any of the horsemen knew the slightest thing about communism.

From the stations, we were taken on tours to the agricultural projects, which were operated partly on the basis of a pre-Columbian Indian form of collective farming. The cotton, wheat, and other farms we saw had been expropriated from English, German, American, and other foreign corporations and divided among the peons, who were organized into ancient-style community groups, *ejidos*, that worked the land collectively. Special labor chiefs oversaw cultivation and organizational matters, the National Bank of Ejidal Credit financed the projects with loans for seeds, machinery, maintenance, and livestock, and the government marketed the crops and divided the profits among the members of the *ejido*, according to the work that each had done.

In the evenings, we gathered under the moon in a gaily lit town plaza or schoolyard as guests of the local political chiefs and *ejido* families at a lively fiesta given in our honor, during which Suárez, in a ceremony of elaborate speeches, distributed the *ejido's* profits. Under the influence of abundant food and alcohol and the piercing guitar and trumpet music of "La Cucaracha," "Adelita," "Jesusita en Chihuahua," and other songs of the revolutionary armies, the singing and dancing went on half the night, highlighted on one occasion in a small northern town near Torreon by the presence of an honored group of aging veterans of Pancho Villa's army, who kept shooting off their pistols in fun and scaring everybody on the dance floor. On the way back to Mexico City, I wrote some stories and remembered it all. Not long before, these people had been peons, bound to those who owned the land, paid them wages, and kept them in perpetual debt. Now, as owners of the land that they worked, they were free, with pride, dignity, and self-esteem, and the *ejidos'* powerful sense of community and cooperation, stemming from their Indian background, might create the basis for a modern Mexican rural middle class. I did not know whether it was going to work, but this was the Revolution that Cárdenas was trying to achieve.

Back in Mexico City, I called Trotsky's home again and was told that he had returned and would now see me. I drove out to Coyoacán, rang the bell, and was admitted by another American secretary, Rae Spiegel. She introduced me abruptly to Trotsky himself, who was standing near the door, peering at me through a pair of small round-rimmed spectacles. For a moment, it was a shock to realize that I was face-to-face with a towering figure of the twentieth century, a man who until then had been for me only the subject of history books and of photographs in which he was pictured haranguing immense crowds of soldiers, sailors, and workers during

the Russian Revolution, or taking the salute from massed ranks of Red Army troops during Russia's civil war, or standing at the walls of the Kremlin side by side with Lenin. Up close in the entranceway, he looked like a family doctor, I thought, though I tried to see him more realistically as still humanity's most feared revolutionist. He was tall, a commanding-looking man, with upswept gray hair, a high forehead, blue eyes that squinted slightly from behind his glasses, thick lips, and a mustache and small goatee.

The peaceful setting outside Leon Trotsky's home during my visit to him in Coyoacán—a couple of dogs, a dozing policeman at the front door, and Jimmy Loeb, who had come with his car to get me after my interview. Trotsky stayed at this house as the guest of the Mexican artists Diego Rivera and his wife, Frida Kahlo, whose family owned the building. Later, the Russian revolutionary moved to another, nearby home, where he was assassinated in 1940.

Speaking in heavily accented English, he welcomed me courteously and, leading me into his study, waved me into a chair at a long rectangular table where the two of us would talk. Sitting down opposite me, he watched while I received and read quickly a six-page single-spaced manuscript of my questions and his answers, both written in English.

I had not wanted to repeat with him subjects that had been thoroughly aired in the John Dewey countertrial a few months earlier, so I had submitted questions that I hoped would plow fresh ground. I had asked him, for instance, the conditions under which he would be willing to join with Stalin and the Western democracies, in Spain or elsewhere, in a united front against Hitler; his opinions about the democratic struggle against the Franco fascists in Spain; what changes he would bring to Russia if he returned there; and whether he would agree that many people, despite the purge trials, supported Stalin against Trotsky because they wanted to see the defeat of Hitler and felt it was no time to antagonize Stalin and disrupt efforts to build a united front with the USSR against fascism. Finally, while Trotsky denied vigorously that he had conspired to overthrow the Soviet leader, almost everything he wrote or said attacked and threatened Stalin, frequently urging his overthrow and assassination. Should it not be expected, I had asked, that Stalin would fight back and try to save himself by "liquidating" Trotsky and his followers?

In a few moments, I finished reading the document, and our conversation began. As we talked and he disposed of my questions, he became increasingly impatient and short-tempered, indulging in sweeping Marxist generalizations about the "toiling masses," "social contradictions," and "the revolutionary vanguard." In the course of two hours of discussion, he covered all the major points I had raised, sometimes courteously and with restraint and at other times snapping at me with the fierceness of a fanatic. No, he would not join a united front with Stalin and the liberal democracies of the West against fascism, in Spain or elsewhere, because without an honest social revolutionary program that "rallied the proletariat and the oppressed masses of petty bourgeoisie," such a united front "deceives the masses" and could not win. But, yes, if the USSR were in a war with a fascist government, then "all my partisans and all real revolutionaries would support with all their strength the USSR and the Red Army *in spite of* the Stalinist dictatorship."

Occasionally, he kept coming back to his enemy in the Kremlin, demonizing him but denying vehemently the charges of the purge trials that he, Trotsky, had followers in the Soviet Union with whom he conspired to overthrow Stalin. At one point, however, he told me the details of some of Stalin's brutalities in an area of the Ukraine, and I asked him how he had gotten his information. "I have partisans there," he replied. "They are able to keep me informed." When I asked whether Trotsky's threats might not have forced Stalin into a fight to the death between the two men, Trotsky brushed the question aside and turned to something else. Finally, he talked at length about the Spanish Civil War, which was still undecided, declaring a fascist victory "completely unavoidable," because the Loyalist leaders "compromised too much with the capitalist governments of western Europe," but he gave me the lead to my story by adding that when and if the Loyalists felt that the time was ripe for a genuine social revolution like the one that had brought victory to the Bolsheviks in Russia, he would be glad to go to Spain and throw himself into the Spanish struggle.

The interview was the highlight of my stay in Mexico. It provided a hard-news story for the *Herald Tribune* and a long article for *Ken*, a handsome but short-lived periodical published by the owner of the more successful magazine *Esquire*. For all his vanity and arrogance as a world revolutionist with practically no constituency among the working class or poor farmers of any country, Trotsky had been something of a prophet. During our meeting in 1937, he rightly predicted for me the tragic end of the Spanish Civil War, the failure of the antifascist united front, and the inevitability of World War II. After my interview, Trotsky had a personal falling-out with Diego Rivera and moved to another house in Coyoacán. There, in August 1940, three years after I saw him, he was assassinated. It was ironic that fifty years later, when communism collapsed in the Soviet Union, he was all but forgotten.

In the following weeks, with the help of Ramon Beteta, I met more members of the Mexican government, including President Cárdenas, with whom I had a brief interview in a small town near Mexico City where he was listening to the requests and complaints of a long line of poor, humble-looking people. One by one, they came up to a table at which he and a number of government officials were seated, and as scribes recorded their problems, Cárdenas ordered this or that member of the government to look into the matter and assist the person and his family. A big, broadshouldered man with the dark skin of an Indian, he spent much of his time in this manner, traveling through the countryside to the little people and listening to their problems. I could talk to him only briefly. He was reserved and straightforward, indifferent to the complaints of foreign interests opposed to the expropriations of the Revolution. "In 1500, all Mexican land belonged to the Indians," he said to me through an interpreter. "From 1500 to 1910, that land was stolen from them by foreigners without compensation." As far as he was concerned, he added, all land in Mexico still belonged to the Indians.

Toward industry, he was equally blunt. "We mean to raise the standard of living," he said, "and unions can do it better than government decrees. If foreign interests won't recognize our workers and their right to high wages, then let them hand over their investments and we'll take care of them ourselves." The threat of a conservative counterrevolution or an intervention by the United States Marine Corps did not worry him. He had already armed the Mexican workers and peasants, he said, and the Spanish experience would not be repeated in Mexico. Moreover, he declared, he trusted President Roosevelt to live up to the Good Neighbor Policy and not intervene. On the subject of religion, he noted frankly that the Revolution had successfully broken the power of the hierarchy of the

Mexican Catholic Church. Opposition to organized religion had now eased off, he claimed, and the large cathedrals were open.

I tried soon afterward to see General Saturnino Cedillo, the man who was rumored to be preparing an uprising against Cárdenas. I traveled north to his headquarters at San Luis Potosi, a dusty old silver-mining city in bleak desert country, but after waiting a day at the government office among local politicians and pistol-packing hangers-on, I was told firmly that the general was at his ranch in the mountains, about a four-hour drive away, and refused to see any foreign newspapermen.* There were a number of foreigners sitting around the town, as if waiting for something to happen, and before I left to return to Mexico City, I met a few Americans who had learned that I was with the *Herald Tribune* and who wanted to know why newspapers in the States weren't demanding that President Roosevelt send marines down to Mexico to get rid of this "communistic" government on its border. They were representatives of oil companies and, worried that Cárdenas was going to expropriate their oil wells, were clustering around Cedillo and offering him their backing. The next year, Cedillo did revolt, but was killed in a few days. He had waited too long. A short time earlier, on March 18, 1938, President Cárdenas had aroused the patriotic fervor of most Mexicans against "the gringos" by nationalizing the foreign-controlled oil fields, and had doomed Mexican support for a counterrevolution.

In the meantime, I continued to visit different parts of Mexico, vacationing briefly at Taxco and on the primitive and still-undeveloped beaches at Acapulco, and spending a lot of time studying the Indian background and religions of Mexico, which, particularly after my meeting with Cárdenas, fascinated me. The Spaniards, I learned, had used the excuse of the mass human sacrifices of the Aztecs' religion to justify their conquest and its own mass barbarisms, but, I wondered for the first time, what justified all the centuries of brutal warfare and dispossession visited by European and American capitalism and imperialism on Indians throughout the western hemisphere?

Although I was writing and selling articles on Mexico to magazines, including the *Literary Digest* and *The Statesman and Nation* in England, as well as to the *Tribune*, the paper was still not paying any of my expenses,

* About six months later, the British author Graham Greene, who wrote that he got to "hate the Mexicans," managed to conduct a rather testy interview with Cedillo at his ranch outside San Luis Potosi, ascribing his success to the fact that he was a Catholic. ("I could never have got leave to visit him otherwise, for he didn't receive foreign newspapermen," he wrote.) At the same time, to get to see Cedillo, Greene gave "interminable assurances that I . . . would let no one in Mexico know that I had seen the General." See Graham Greene, *Another Mexico* (New York: Viking Press, 1982), pp. 46–48, 58.

and I knew I would soon have to be returning to my job with Jim Barnett. The end of my stay in Mexico came faster than I had planned. I suddenly got sick. It was diagnosed as amoebic dysentery, and with Jimmy, who had continued to keep me company in Mexico City, I started back to New York, as miserable as a person can be. As we headed north, I felt sorry to be leaving, but I carried with me a love for Mexico and its people and an interest in the history and continuing struggles of the country's Indian population, subjects that would grip me again many times in the future.

In 1936, President Roosevelt rather grandly told the delegates to the Democratic convention who nominated him for a second term that their generation had "a rendezvous with destiny." Three years later, in his annual message to Congress in January 1939, he repeated the prediction, and in the ominous atmosphere of the increasing Nazi threat to civilization added that the prophecy was coming true. For me personally, the fateful "rendezvous" did not happen all at once, but sort of built up in a diffused, spread-out fashion in a number of different places during the tumultuous years 1938–41, when I was in my mid-twenties and passed definitely from youth to seasoned adulthood.

I remember very little of the last months of 1937, following my return to New York from Mexico. It took weeks and the help of a medical specialist in tropical illnesses to get me over my dysentery. Meanwhile, the business recession of 1937 had continued to force cutbacks at the *Tribune*, among them a decision made while I was in Mexico not to renew the radio series in the fall. But as soon as my strength returned, the paper took me back, and at first I worked again with Jim Barnett, writing special articles for various sections of the *Tribune* that helped him promote subscriptions among the Ivy League colleges of the Northeast, after which I got a crack at doing some general reporting in Manhattan for the city desk. At the same time, I met frequently with friends at WOR, especially with Jerry Danzig, who kept me busy as a freelance writer in my spare hours, writing spots for variety and other WOR radio programs.

In December, Jerry was promoted to a new job at WOR, and his assistant, a heavyset, cigar-smoking radio journalist named Dave Driscoll from Fergus Falls, Minnesota, moved into his vacated position as director of news and special features. That left Dave's old spot open, and Jerry invited me to fill it. I liked the *Herald Tribune* immensely. I had been very happy there among professionals for whom I had great admiration and respect, and a decision to leave it was not easy to make. But, in addition to an increase in salary, the radio job sounded much more exciting than anything I could hope for at the *Tribune*, at least in the foreseeable future. As a staff writer on the paper, I could expect to be assigned to relatively unimportant stories for some time, covering at best only one subject, one part of the city, or one beat, like a particular one of the city's departments, at a time and possibly enduring weeks or months of boredom in doing so.

A radio news and special-features man had a far livelier agenda. His beat was literally the whole world. At WOR, which was the key New York station of the Mutual Broadcasting System and which considered itself in heated competition with the New York stations of the three other coast-to-coast radio chains, the Columbia Broadcasting System and the Red and the Blue networks of the National Broadcasting Company, the fields of responsibility of the news and special-features men broke into several categories. First, they were in overall command of the coverage of news, not only supervising the station's daily newscasters and commentators but also gathering and editing news bulletins and, in on-the-scene broadcasts, describing news as it happened from where it happened. Second, they scheduled and managed the radio coverage of speeches, banquets, sports events, parades, and other prearranged news occurrences, as well as public-service broadcasts by religious, civic, patriotic, and other nonprofit organizations. Finally, they planned and executed stunt, human-interest, and novelty programs to enliven the station's schedule and attract more listeners, which, in turn, attracted more advertisers and revenue. Far from the job being one of tedium and routine, each broadcast was different, posing its own opportunities and problems, and no two days were ever the same.

I finally made up my mind to accept Jerry's offer, and over the Christmas holidays I again changed jobs, settling in with Dave Driscoll at WOR's studios on the top floors of an office building at Broadway and 40th Street, only a couple of blocks from the *Herald Tribune* and from Jack Bleeck's restaurant, where I continued to eat most of my meals and visit with friends from the paper. The new job started out mildly enough. I spent much of my time with publicity directors and press agents of almost every sort of public and private, national and local organization, accepting or turning down their requests for free radio time on WOR to publicize their causes and seeing that the programs that we did accept were as interesting and well done as possible. Often, Driscoll or I helped them plan and write their scripts and even participated in the broadcasts as a

moderator, commentator, or interviewer— particularly when the programs originated from "remote," or outside-the-studio, locations like a laboratory, a hospital, or the scene of some ceremony.

A radio news and special-features director. In my office at WOR in New York City in the late 1930s.

One of my first of such preplanned broadcasts was of a poignant visit by schoolchildren to abandoned puppies in the New York City animal shelter of the American Society for the Prevention of Cruelty to Animals. Scheduled in connection with the ASPCA's annual Be Kind to Animals Week, the program was filled with the sounds of the puppies' yelps and the delighted squeals of the children and was done to help focus sympathetic attention on the organization's work and on its need for financial support from the public.

Frequently, Driscoll and I dreamed up human-interest programs of our own, scheduling them in connection with a holiday or a news peg. During my first months at WOR, I described a Valentine's Day party among indigent elders at a city institution for the homeless on New York's Welfare Island in the East River; climbed aboard a new Holland America transatlantic liner from a tugboat in New York's outer harbor to describe the city's gala reception for the luxury ship's arrival on her maiden voyage; dressed myself in a cutaway coat and a top hat containing a shortwave radio transmitter to describe Fifth Avenue's Easter Parade from atop a celebrity-packed tally-ho coach drawn through the throngs on the avenue by a team of four horses; and on a sweltering hot day entertained a crowd in Times Square while I described to the radio audience how fast the steaming sidewalk would fry an egg.

Sometimes things went awry. To mark the closing of Manhattan's old Sixth Avenue elevated prior to its being demolished and replaced by a new subway line, I rode downtown on the last elevated train filled with city officials, intending to get off with them at a certain station where Driscoll would be waiting on the open-air platform with a microphone to interview them for a few stories and a bit of history and nostalgia. For some reason, the engineer failed to stop the train at the designated station, and I and the political dignitaries rode blithely past Driscoll, who in consternation had to end the program without the interviews. On another occasion, President Roosevelt's lateness in arriving to give an important speech at the dedication of the Federal Building on the site of the New York World's Fair, which was to open the following year, forced me to ad-lib to our radio audience about anything and everything I could think of for forty-five torturous minutes. All four networks were covering the event, but WOR was determined to hold on to its listeners and not lose them, as the other networks were doing, by "returning" the audience to the studio for forty-five minutes of listening to stand-by music until Roosevelt appeared. So I had to talk and talk without a script until I could finally say, "Ladies and gentlemen, the president is arriving. His car has just pulled up at the rear of the platform," and so on.

By and large, this kind of onetime special-feature broadcast, including fairly routine coverage of late-night speeches by prominent persons from black-tie banquets in the grand ballroom of the Waldorf-Astoria or another New York hotel—always guaranteed to irritate large segments of the younger members of our audience by knocking out Mutual Broadcasting System pickups of the popular dance music of Benny Goodman, Guy Lombardo, or another of the nation's big bands—continued throughout my years at WOR. But soon we found ourselves beginning to give greater spontaneous, on-the-scene coverage to unplanned news events, and the excitement of the job increased. Early in the spring, there was a disastrous explosion, resulting in casualties, at the Horton brewery in the heart of Manhattan. Rushing to the scene and getting through the police lines with our press passes, Driscoll and I commandeered a public telephone in a nearby drugstore and phoned the studio's master control, which put us on the air. During much of the day, we used up a lot of coins supplying WOR and Mutual stations throughout the nation with eyewitness descriptions of the catastrophe from our perch in the phone booth.

On another, more horrifying day, the wire service that provided our Teletype machines with news sent through word about noon that a man named John Ward—who we later learned had become distraught over domestic troubles—was standing on a narrow ledge on the seventeenth floor of the fashionable Gotham Hotel at Fifth Avenue and 55th Street, threatening to jump to his death. Hurrying uptown, where large crowds had already collected to watch police and firemen try to talk Ward into coming back from the ledge through a window into his hotel room, Driscoll and I, accompanied by studio engineers, set up our equipment in an office building opposite the Gotham and for the next nine hours broadcast eyewitness reports of the rescue efforts.

About ten that night, we learned that Ward was about to give himself up to the police and would be taken down a back stairway in the hotel and driven to a hospital. With one of our engineers and a shortwave transmitter and hand microphone, I started hurriedly across the street to the hotel and its back stairway. We had just reached the Gotham's front entrance, which was covered by a large iron and glass marquee that extended over the sidewalk, when there was a loud cry from the crowd in the streets and above us a terrible crash and the sound of broken glass showering down from the marquee. Ward had changed his mind and jumped from the ledge, his body smashing onto the marquee and then dropping lifelessly into the gutter at the edge of the sidewalk, only a few feet away from us. In the horror of the moment, I failed to notice that the poor man had come so close to me that my clothes were wet from his bladder, which had filled during his long stand on the ledge and had burst when he hit the marquee. It was a dreadful scene of death and one that rose to haunt my memory for weeks to come.

Gratefully, not all our news coverage was of tragedies. Early in the summer of 1938, we joined the other networks in covering an attempt by Howard Hughes to set a new record by flying around the world in four days. The flight, a major news event of international interest, which WOR and Mutual expected that Dave and I would cover from beginning to end, proved a personal cliff-hanger for me. On July 15, the day after Hughes planned to arrive back at his starting point in New York, I was to be married at St. Thomas Church on Fifth Avenue. I had met my bride-to-be, Rosamond Eddy, a tall, lovely high-fashion model, the year before through her cousin, one of my friends who worked for Jim Barnett at the *Tribune*. After months of dating, we had decided to get married and had made all our plans for the wedding and for a honeymoon trip to eastern Canada. Both of us decided stubbornly that Hughes would not let us down. He had to get back on July 14 before our wedding date to achieve his goal of a four-day flight and, crossing our fingers, we assured ourselves that he would make it and that our coverage of his flight would be ended in time for the wedding to be held on schedule.

There was a second problem. Two years of intensive planning and cooperation between Hughes and NBC's parent company, RCA, which had supplied Hughes with his radio engineer and with RCA transmitting equipment for the plane, gave NBC an understanding that, in return, it would have exclusive rights to carry all progress reports that Hughes would broadcast as he circled the world. But the charismatic Hughes and the drama of the flight had a great appeal to the popular imagination, and in the competitive atmosphere of the day, neither Mutual nor CBS intended to let so important a news story be NBC's exclusive property. But how to horn in? In a master stroke of skullduggery, CBS provided the answer, persuading Hughes to allow the New York World's Fair, which was still a year away, to be the official "sponsor" of the flight. It followed that as sponsor, the fair could not favor one network over the others, and in short order NBC was forced to abandon its right to exclusivity. But it was up to Driscoll and me to figure out how to get the most newsworthy broadcasts from the plane and, if possible, get them exclusively for WOR and Mutual.

We had luck beyond anything we could have imagined. After much haggling, it was decided that once the flight got going, the networks would take turns in carrying Hughes's reports from the plane. NBC and CBS drew the first two broadcasts from over the Atlantic, but they were full of static and conveyed nothing newsworthy. When it was our turn in the predawn hours of the morning, Hughes came through loud and clear and startled listeners by voicing a fear that he was running out of fuel and might not make it across the ocean. The late editions of the morning newspapers ran the alarming news in eight-column headlines, crediting WOR and Mutual with the scoop. Our luck continued as Hughes landed safely at Paris and went on to Moscow, Siberia, and Alaska, with fine broadcasts picked up for us from Hughes's plane by the powerful short-wave facilities of Press Wireless on Long Island. At one point, over the Soviet Union, a technical mistake by NBC personnel allowed us to carry a broadcast that should have gone exclusively to NBC, and after that, inter-network relations broke down completely.

In the scramble that followed, contact with the plane was lost as it headed south from Alaska, bound, according to various versions of Hughes's plans, for Winnipeg, St. Paul, Detroit, or Cleveland. As tension built rapidly throughout the country over the whereabouts and safety of the fliers, we and NBC sent crews to cover the airports at each of the cities, but when Hughes's plane arrived suddenly at St. Paul, the NBC team there had gone someplace to have breakfast, and we at WOR had another eight-column scoop.

Three days, nineteen hours, and eight minutes after he had started his trip, Hughes finally got back to New York, and the next day, Roz and I were married on schedule. One day after our marriage, Hughes's flight was all but eclipsed by the feat of another aviator, Douglas Corrigan, who had been denied a permit to fly the Atlantic to Ireland in his nine-hundred-dollar plane, but who flew it anyway from New York to Dublin, maintaining merrily that he thought he was flying to California. By that time, Roz and I were in Canada on our honeymoon, but we got back in plenty of time for me to cover the hero's welcome that New York extended to the grinning, pixieish "Wrong-Way" Corrigan when he returned to the United States on an ocean liner.

Throughout the fall, the tempo and variety of our on-the-scene news coverage increased. In the middle of August, I began daily coverage of the sensational four-week trial of James J. Hines, a powerful New York political boss of Tammany Hall, who was charged with having protected the rackets of the late notorious gangster Dutch Schultz. The trial in New York State Supreme Court—presided over by Judge Ferdinand Pecora, one of the country's most prominent jurists, and prosecuted by Thomas E. Dewey, then New York's up-and-coming young district attorney—was full of drama and colorful, headline-making personalities from politics and the underworld and drew the attendance of some of the best and most widely read reporters and columnists in the United States. No microphones were allowed in the courtroom, but twice a day, after each morning and afternoon session, I hurried breathlessly with a handful of notes from the courthouse to the nearby dowdy studios of the city-owned radio station, WNYC, which patched me through over a telephone line to WOR, to whose audience I broadcast fifteen-minute recapitulations of the trial's latest developments. The proceedings ended abruptly in a farcical mistrial, resulting from an error that Dewey, an overconfident lawyer with a soft voice and an unpleasant, condescending smile, made during his cross-examination of one of the mobsters, but in a retrial Dewey won and Hines was convicted. In the intervening time, however, most people had lost interest in the case, and we did not cover the second go-round.

By that time, indeed, there were far more compelling events to cover, including a war crisis in Europe and a catastrophic hurricane and tidal wave that whipped north from the Caribbean in September 1938 and clobbered the unsuspecting, heavily populated coast of southern New England. Largely because it was unexpected, the severity of the hurricane—the worst to strike New England in more than a century—created turmoil from New York to Boston, isolating and flooding cities and towns, killing more than six hundred people, and bringing normal activity to a halt. To report what was happening while the end of the storm was still raging, I helped equip a truck with a shortwave transmitter, as well as with saws and axes to get us through the devastation. Accompanied by a couple of studio engineers, I made my way east in heavy gusts of wind along the Boston Post Road from New York, broadcasting from town after town that was still cut off by fallen trees, tangled telephone and power lines, flooded roads, and the wreckage of buildings that had been smashed flat. In New London, Connecticut, I described fires still raging out of control in the center of town; near Stonington, we saw but could not reach passengers on a New Haven Railroad train that was still stranded on a partially submerged causeway in an inlet of Long Island Sound; and in downtown Providence, which had been hit by a tidal wave, we came on bodies still floating in muddy water up to twenty feet deep. After two days on the road, we returned to New York, shaken by the terrible scenes of destruction and death that we had described to the country.

Among all our broadcasts that year, however, those that covered the growing threat of war in Europe drew the greatest number of listeners. In March, Hitler startled the world by toppling the democratic government of Austria and annexing that country to Germany. With translators sitting in headphones in our New York studios to interpret shortwave radio pickups from Europe for our audience, Driscoll and I directed the coverage of developments almost hour by hour, broadcasting official German transmissions of Hitler's tirades, which Press Wireless relayed to us from Berlin, as well as speeches by frightened government leaders in Vienna, Paris, and other European capitals and eyewitness descriptions by foreign correspondents of the grim takeover of Austria by the German troops. People stayed up all night to hear our reports of the dramatic events, but it proved to be only a prelude to our coverage in September of a new and more ominous crisis that Hitler precipitated when he demanded that Czechoslovakia—which Great Britain and France had promised to defend—cede to Germany the section of her country known as the Sudetenland.

By then, the networks' engineers had perfected an ability to pick up broadcasts from almost any place on land, sea, or in the sky, as well as to transmit three- and four-way conversations among people who were located in different parts of the world. For several weeks, as the size of our audience swelled amid a renewed fear that another world war was about to start, we again stayed on the air around the clock, broadcasting news bulletins, the desperate speeches of government leaders at the League of Nations in Geneva or in their own capitals, and four-way conversations among Mutual commentators in New York, London, Berlin, Paris, Rome, and Prague. The crisis finally ended at Munich, where England's prime

minister, Neville Chamberlain, and the French premier, Edouard Dala-
dier, gave in cravenly to Hitler and Mussolini. Warning the helpless
Czechs that if they opposed the agreement to give Hitler the Sudetenland,
they would have to fight the Germans alone, Chamberlain boasted in a
hollow statement to the English people, which we carried live to American listeners, that he had achieved "peace in our time." Although I, like
most Americans, felt relieved that war had been averted, Hitler's new triumph dismayed me, and everyone I knew agreed with my fear that giving
in to him was only going to lead to more trouble.

We were right. The frightened attempt at appeasement did not work,
and the following March, Hitler humiliated England and France again by
ignoring the Munich agreement and seizing all the rest of Czechoslovakia.
Meanwhile, many of the talks and other onetime special-feature programs
that Driscoll and I were scheduling were reflecting a deepening concern
among the American people over the international situation and a growing confusion and division over how to deal with the German dictator. For
some years, the reaction to the horrors and senselessness of World War I
had made many Americans, including myself, embrace isolationism, hoping that the United States would stay out of any future foreign war. Even
the shockingly evil Hitler seemed at first to be Europe's problem and not
ours. Then came the Spanish Civil War and the intervention of Hitler and
Mussolini on Franco's side, and there began to grow among some people,
again including myself, harrowing beliefs that Hitler was bent on world
domination and that the only nation that would stand up to the Nazis was
another dictatorship, the Soviet Union, which, with its followers in other
countries, had formed the so-called International Popular Front to combat fascism.

In Mexico, where I had seen people throw coins for the Spanish Loyalists onto a Spanish Republican flag that lay on the pavement in the Zócalo,
I was impressed by Ramon Beteta and other Mexicans in different walks of
life who told me with great passion that they supported the Popular Front
for unity against fascism anywhere in the world, and for the first time it
had made me question my isolationism. Later, in New York, I met friends
and other people who, like me, were Roosevelt liberals but were becoming
unhappy with FDR's inability to get Congress to repeal the Neutrality
Act, which prevented the supplying of arms to the Spanish Loyalists. With
some of them, I began to go to parties and meetings to help raise money
for the anti-Franco forces or to say good-bye to an idealistic volunteer
who was leaving for Spain to join the Abraham Lincoln Brigade and fight
the fascists. In retrospect, for some like myself who were shedding isolationism, it gradually became a romantic and stirring era of causes and new

friends and companions, of watching colorful united-front parades on Seventh Avenue that lasted all day, with labor-union bands playing "Solidarity Forever" and the Spanish Loyalists' song, "No Pasaran," and marchers waving to cheering crowds on the sidewalks. It seemed to me to be a time when everything in the world was black or white, when there were victories to be won, and when most people whom we got to know believed in a future that belonged to us and was worth fighting for. So I changed. I did not abandon my opposition to communism, but I scuttled my isolationist views and agreed that there were good wars that were necessary, and one of them would be a war against Hitler.

Not everyone saw eye-to-eye with me by a long shot. Isolationists were still politically strong in the country, and the influence of Hitler, seemingly a winner, was growing among many of them. But at radio stations and networks like ours, requests for airtime were coming increasingly from civic, religious, patriotic, and other groups that were worried about the international situation and either wanted the United States to stand up to Hitler or wanted the nation to stay out of Europe's affairs. As the polarization of the country became more pronounced, Driscoll and I did our best to be evenhanded, giving equal time to both sides, and drawing the line only at an extremist with his own agenda, such as the nakedly Nazi propagandist Fritz Kuhn, the jackbooted leader of the German American Bund.

Nineteen thirty-nine, the year that war finally came, was not entirely a somber one. With pleasure and excitement, Driscoll and I spent much of our time that year covering events at the New York World's Fair, which opened to huge crowds on April 30 and, looking forward optimistically through the gathering storm clouds, celebrated the "World of Tomorrow." Three of the fair's many highlights remain most vividly in my memory. In June, England's King George VI and Queen Elizabeth, after first visiting Canada and Washington, D.C., arrived at the fair. The trip of the British monarchs was precedent-making, and all four networks labored long on elaborate plans for a full coverage of their every move. Save for a bit of tongue-twisting by an excited announcer who told our audience that the royal couple had received "a twenty-one-son galoot" from cannons on their arrival at the fair, everything went well until a formal reception and lunch in a large hall within one of the fair's central theme buildings, the Perisphere.

Although the networks had received permission to cover the reception and lunch, describing the king and queen shaking hands and eating democratically with the hundreds of assembled American dignitaries, we were forced to do so from behind a long folding screen along one wall, which was supposed to hide us and our messy wires and equipment from the guests but which also hid them from us. As might have been expected, the worst happened. During one of the quietest moments of the formal luncheon, an announcer from one of the other networks tried to peer around the end of the screen and lost his balance. With an enormous clatter, he and the entire screen went over, revealing to the startled king and queen and the fair's officials and guests our hitherto-concealed cluster of equipment, wires, awkward-looking announcers, and shirtsleeved engineers in headphones. As waiters rushed to help us set the screen upright again, the room rocked with laughter.

In the following month, the fair witnessed high radio drama of another sort. At the request of a Mrs. Rushmore Patterson, the daughter of the man for whom Mount Rushmore had been named and a member of the Daughters of the American Revolution, I had scheduled in connection with the observance of Flag Day a fifteen-minute late-night patriotic program from the DAR's building at the fair, a small replica of George Washington's Mount Vernon, erected at the edge of the fair's amusement area. The program featured an interview between Mrs. Patterson and a young writer named Howard Fast whom she had met and whose recently published book, a patriotic novel about the American Revolution, had captivated her. On the night of the broadcast, I went to the fair with Mrs. Patterson and Howard and his wife, Betty, and broadcast the program following the eleven o'clock news. During the broadcast, I received an alarming news flash from our master control at the studio that two people at the Parachute Tower in the fair's amusement area, only several hundred feet from where we were broadcasting, had become stuck 125 feet in the air on a seat whose parachute had jammed and would not come down.

After Mrs. Patterson's program was finished, it took me only minutes to confirm the accuracy of the flash about the couple stranded on their perilous little perch high above the fairgrounds and to decide to start covering that story as quickly as possible. Accompanied by the Fasts, my engineer and I strung a microphone wire from the DAR's building directly across the amusement area's Nude Ranch, where fairgoers were ogling scantily clad models, to the base of the steel-girdered Parachute Tower. Within ten minutes, I was on the air, informing WOR's late-night audience of the emergency at the fair. Throughout the night, until 4:45 in the morning, when mechanics finally got the couple down, I continued to broadcast from the site, describing the attempts to rescue the trapped pair and attracting to the scene a huge crowd of people who had heard my broadcast at home or in cars and had hurried to the fairgrounds to see the drama for themselves. As for the Fasts, the tense emergency we had shared

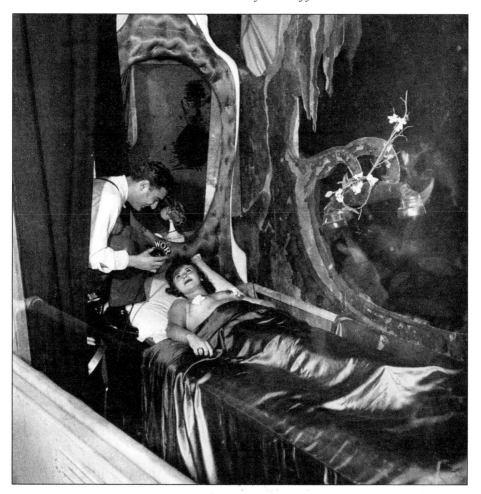

acted as a bond, and we became good friends. Howard was a gentle, kind, and outgoing person. When the war came, I lost contact with him, and after the war, as a prolific, successful author honored for his writings by the Soviet Union, he became internationally known, and I read regularly about him. But he had gone out of my life, and we did not see each other again for more than fifty years.

To observe the closing night of the New York World's Fair in 1940, we "interviewed" participants in some of the fair's most popular attractions. Here I am, with a WOR handmike, conversing for our radio audience with a "sleeping beauty" in Salvador Dalí's surrealist exhibit in the fair's amusement area.

Finally, by all odds, the most popular industrial exhibit at the fair was General Motors's immense Futurama, designed by Norman Bel Geddes, which inspired me and many others with its vision of the fair's "World of Tomorrow" theme. To spectators in moving chairs that circled a huge working model of an enormous urbanized landscape, the Futurama exhibit portrayed how Americans of the future, with advanced science and technology, would be able to conquer and control all "obstacles" of nature and the wilderness and build their cities, homes, and highways on every type of terrain, covering with their improvements each square inch of deserts, mountains, forests, and other heretofore "inhospitable" parts of their land.

It was a dramatic portrayal of the final "conquest" of the continent—a vision of nature as an enemy, a vision whose roots lay in nineteenth-century Manifest Destiny, as I then knew and celebrated it, and a vision that was consistent, as I saw it at the time, with the best thinking of Roosevelt's New Deal and its stirring building and development projects like the Tennessee Valley Authority and the great dams and irrigation projects of the West. The Futurama, I thought, surely prophesied for me and for millions of others how we could pull ourselves finally out of the years of stagnant Depression and portrayed the direction in which we as a nation had to go, which was to continue the old traditions of the generations of my grandfather and father in building an ever-bigger, better, and greater America. The sermon of development and more development and of the subjugation of the natural world made a profound impact on me and was to be a major influence on my thinking about our country until well into the postwar years.

Late in the summer, Roz and I, who were living in a top-floor apartment on Waverly Place near Washington Square in New York's Greenwich Village, took off on a brief vacation in the Southwest, where we visited Eddie and Mildred Knopf, saw several of my movie friends at Malibu Beach, and then, ironically oblivious of a conflict with the vision of the Futurama exhibit, found joy and exhilaration in getting away from civilization and exploring some of the then-still-unspoiled beaches, deserts, and haunts of wildlife in the northern area of Baja California. When we returned to New York with our batteries recharged, as it were, Hitler was rattling his sword again, demanding the cession of part of Poland to Germany and threatening war against Poland if his demand was not met. England and France had learned their lesson, and this time, when they promised to defend Poland against the Nazis, they gave every sign of meaning it. But now they were too late. In an unexpected development, Stalin demonstrated that he no longer trusted the Western democracies to stand together with him against Hitler and signed a mutual nonaggression pact with the German leader that in an instant threw the world into confusion, ended the united front against fascism, as Trotsky had predicted, and gave Hitler a free hand to go at Poland. On September 1, German tanks rumbled across the Polish border, and the long-feared war finally began.

As during the Munich crisis, we at WOR remained on the air around the clock for many days, picking up dramatic shortwave broadcasts from the European capitals and covering the English and French declarations of war and each additional development with trenchant analyses by Raymond Gram Swing and other Mutual commentators. Swing, with a scholar's sense of history, a distinguished journalistic background in Europe, and a calm but authoritative radio personality, was extremely popular among our listeners and helped to build up the largest audience WOR had ever had. From time to time during the winter, as we continued covering the world's fears and confusions during the inaction of Hitler's so-called phony war with Britain and France, I slept on a cot in the studio. The German-Soviet pact, followed by the two former enemies' joint carving up of Poland and Stalin's aggressions against the Baltic states and Finland, temporarily bewildered me, but by the following spring, when Hitler invaded Denmark and Norway and then the Low Countries and France, my drift back to isolationism halted. Along with many other Americans who watched the tragedy at Dunkirk and the German air assault on England, I came to believe that, with or without the Soviet Union, Hitler had to be stopped and ultimately we would have to help do it.

The United States, however, was still divided. Week after week, we were barraged by appeals for airtime from the America First Committee and other groups that wanted us to stay out of the war and from William Allen White's Committee to Defend America by Aiding the Allies, the Fight for Freedom Committee, and other groups that wanted us to help Britain. Meanwhile, Hitler's successes were spurring us on to prepare our own defenses, and Driscoll and I began to do an increasing number of broadcasts from ordnance factories, army bases, military planes, government defense agencies, and submarines and warships at practice out at sea. During one busy period, I covered the commissioning of a new battleship, the USS *North Carolina*, at the New York Naval Shipyard and some realistic National Guard defense maneuvers on a Long Island beach at night; rode in a B-17 Flying Fortress bomber over New York during a trial blackout; and described the production of bomb fuzes by women workers at the Picatinny Arsenal in New Jersey and the retraining of other workers for defense jobs in an airplane factory.

Although it was exciting work, it was also often tense and grueling, requiring my living by the hand of a stopwatch that timed every split second of our programs. The stress was stimulating rather than bothersome, but in the summer of 1940, Roz and I took another break and drove to

Mexico City down the Pan-American Highway, which Jimmy Loeb and I had traveled three years earlier. Mexico was in the middle of a presidential campaign, and as we made our way through rural areas, most of which were still desperately poor, I worried about what I was told would happen to Cárdenas's agrarian program. Cárdenas's term was ending, and the two men vying to succeed him were more conservative than he. Exploiting the international situation, moreover, the United States government, I learned, was persuading the candidates and other Mexican politicians to disarm American hostility to Mexico by halting the expropriations and other leftist actions that Americans opposed and ally their country with the United States if war came. The leading presidential candidate, General Avila Camacho, who ultimately won the election, had already announced that he would end Cárdenas's land-redistribution program, and eventually that is what he did. Before Mexico would have had time to solve the economic plight of the Indians and other poor farmers, who constituted the bulk of the country's population, Camacho's newly installed administration aborted the forward motion of the Mexican Revolution and in large measure left the problems of the rural population to fester through the years, unsolved, like a cancer on the nation.

Back in the United States that fall, President Roosevelt, who was reelected over Wendell Willkie to an unprecedented third term, continued meanwhile to respond to Hitler's victories in Greece, Yugoslavia, and elsewhere with bold, positive actions and fireside chats, which slowly diminished the influence of the isolationists and increased support for the embattled British and their allies. In succession, Driscoll and I concocted programs that covered, among other fast-moving developments, the speedup of arms production, which turned the United States into what FDR described as the "arsenal of democracy"; the inauguration of America's first peacetime draft; the debate over the Lend-Lease Act to help Great Britain; the declaration of an unlimited national emergency; and the mobilization of the National Guard. My brother, Warren, who had joined and become a sergeant in the New York National Guard's 258th Field Artillery, was called up for active duty early in February 1941, and my mother and father, Roz, and I went up to an armory in the Bronx to see his outfit off for training at Fort Ethan Allen in Vermont. It was a highly emotional evening, climaxed by the band playing "The Caissons Go Rolling Along," the familiar song of the field artillery, as the troops marched out of the armory to the subway that would take them to a train at Grand Central Station. The next day, my father, aged fifty-four, had a heart attack, and in accordance with medical practice of the day, he was ordered to bed for six weeks of absolute rest.

At the time, I had begun writing short plays and skits for some of the national programs that we carried for war-relief organizations, and on a program for British War Relief, Peggy Wood, a well-known actress, read one of them—"Have You Ever Seen the Boys Leave?"—which I had written about Warren's departure. It was an uninhibited tearjerker, but it fit the popular mood of a nation on the edge of war and drew many requests for copies from our listeners. Even more popular was an affirmation of patriotism called "Young Man in Search of a Faith," which I wrote for another program. A cantata, set to an original score by Robert Russell Bennett, later the arranger for *Oklahoma!* and other Rodgers and Hammerstein musicals, it received several airings and ended up being published in two anthologies.

One Saturday night in June, the war took another dramatic turn when Hitler unexpectedly invaded the Soviet Union. On Sunday, Roz and I had had a date to accompany our friend Jerome Weidman, well known at the time for his book *I Can Get It for You Wholesale*, to New Jersey's Fort Dix with a cheese cake from Lindy's Restaurant in Times Square for our mutual friend Jimmy Cannon, a New York newspaper sports writer, who had been drafted into the army and who, as a lowly and hungry private, was pining away in his barracks for one of Lindy's famous cakes. I had been up all night directing our coverage of the war's latest turn, and I was exhausted, but it was too exciting a day to go home and sleep. The Soviet Union was now on our side, not Hitler's, and everything had been turned upside down again, and I suddenly felt at last that the Nazis were going to get beaten.

I went with the others to Fort Dix, where I found that Jimmy Cannon was more skeptical than I and had the future figured out differently. "It's what Churchill has wanted all along," he said to us. "He won't help the Commies. He's been against them all his life. He'll just sit back and watch Hitler knock out Stalin, and that will be that." He was wrong. On the way home, we kept the car radio tuned to WOR, and we heard Churchill talk to the people of the British Empire about the new situation. "Any man or state who fights on against Nazidom will have our aid," he declared firmly. "Any man or state who marches with Hitler is our foe. . . . It follows, therefore, that we shall give whatever help we can to Russia and the Russian people." Inside the car, we cheered. The united front against fascism, now one of nations and not of individuals, seemed reborn.

When August came, Roz and I took a United Fruit boat to the Central American countries of Honduras and Guatemala. The trip was part pleasure and part business. The United States, I had learned, had finally awakened to the presence in those countries of small but longtime, strongly entrenched German populations that numbered among them many influential owners of coffee *fincas* and banana plantations and directors of banks, businesses, and exporting firms. These individuals had been pushing Nazi propaganda and building a secret fifth column of pro-Hitler military and intelligence-gathering organizations that threatened the Panama Canal and our ties with Central and South America. In preparation for war, American officers of the State Department and of intelligence and inter-American affairs defense agencies were now busy exposing and destroying the Germans' influence, and on assignment from Transradio, our news-gathering organization, I headed south on vacation with Roz to see if I could do a story on what was going on.

The high point of our outward voyage from New York was a sudden, unexpected surfacing of a German submarine from the sparkling, sunlit waters off the Atlantic coast. It rose in ominous silence close to our ship, like a steel gray monster slithering up through the waves and shaking off the foam from its body preparatory to looking us over. German seamen emerged from the conning tower, regarded us for a few minutes through binoculars, then waved at us cheerfully and filed back into the conning tower. They coasted along on the surface with us for a while, then submerged and were gone. It was an eerie feeling, knowing that at last we had seen close-up a face of the war and of our potential enemy from far-away Europe.

After a stop at Havana, we sailed on to Honduras and stayed a few days, taking on bananas at Puerto Cortés, where I spent the time meeting government officials and acquiring information for my story. Next door, at Puerto Barrios, Guatemala, we boarded a train for an all-day ride to Guatemala City, the capital in the highlands and the seat of power of Jorge Ubico, the country's tinhorn dictator, who, under the influence and pressure of the U.S. government, was in the throes of changing from a pro-Nazi to a pro-American. At the old colonial city of Antigua, nestled under slumbering volcanoes and still largely in ruins left by eighteenth-century earthquakes—where we discovered, to our amusement, that no one had yet heard of the fairly recently invented product known in the States as tomato juice and a bewildered waiter served me instead a glass of iced catsup—I learned about a German communications headquarters in town that had linked Nazi agents and activities from Mexico City to Lima, Peru. Under the prodding of the U.S. State Department, the headquarters had recently been exposed and put out of business and those running it had been forced to leave the country.

When I had acquired all the information I needed to relate how the Germans in Honduras and Guatemala were being isolated and rendered powerless, politically and economically, by being dropped from boards and barred from the ability to export their large coffee crops, to engage in businesses based on imports, or to continue their German business, social, or educational organizations, I wrote and sent my story to Transradio. Then, becoming simply a vacationer, I drove with Roz through the majestic volcano and lake scenery of Chichicastenango, Lake Atitlán, and other highland centers of the Mayan Indians.

It was a spectacular tour of an ancient and colorful countryside, but the highlight for me was the powerful experience of glimpsing the deep spirituality of the Indians at Chichicastenango, who had been conquered by the Spaniards more than four hundred years earlier but who, with the addition of a slight overlay of European influences, still—to my wonder—maintained the religious beliefs, forms, and values of their pre-Columbian ancestors. Garbed in brightly colored head scarves, blouses, jackets, short pants, and other articles of clothing fashioned from their own stunning weavings, they crowded the stone steps leading up to the door of Chichi's whitewashed Church of Santo Tomás, creating clouds of pungent smoke from their swinging incense pots and communing with the spirits who presided over the church's entrance. A short distance away, in the hills, we were led to a stone idol dating from pre-Columbian days. Several Mayan Indians were on their knees in front of it, deep in prayer. At the time, I knew nothing of what I was witnessing and wondered if this were all theater, designed for tourists like Roz and myself. I kept my thoughts to myself, and later I was glad that I had done so. In a word, it was real, and I was profane and blasphemous—one among the very many non-Indians who too quickly found one reason or another to dismiss or demean Indian spirituality as not being a religion because it was not like any of our own.

In time, Guatemala's Indians were destined to suffer greatly. In 1954, after the Cold War set in, the CIA engineered the overthrow of a democratically elected liberal president of Guatemala and helped install and maintain in his place a series of ruthless dictators who with the support of "human rights" assistant secretaries and other functionaries in the U.S. State Department set out to dispossess the Mayas from their lands by waging a genocidal war against them "in the name of God, progress, and the struggle against communism." They failed. There were, and still are, too many Mayas—so many that I am sure that one day they will again run their own country.

When Roz and I got back to New York, the United States seemed closer than ever to war. American naval vessels were convoying military supplies to England and Russia, and German submarines were threatening to torpedo the convoys. On September 16, Roosevelt ordered the U.S.

Navy to fire upon Axis vessels "on sight." We were creeping awfully close to hostilities, and I thought of the German submarine and realized with a plunging feeling in my stomach that one day soon bombs might be dropping on New York as they had on London. But the incremental steps, short of all-out war, continued. On September 23, the Nazis sank the first U.S. merchant ship, and Congress debated a bill to arm the American merchant marine. During October and November, more merchant ships, as well as the first American destroyers, were torpedoed, some with heavy loss of life. In the face of what was going on, the ranks of the steadfast isolationists thinned, and many of those who still opposed getting into the war became increasingly desperate. On October 30, the America First Committee scheduled a large antiwar rally at New York's Madison Square Garden, and we agreed to carry an address at the rally by an isolationist senator, Burton Wheeler of Montana. Soon afterward, the public-relations office of the America First Committee called up to cancel our broadcast of Senator Wheeler's speech, and the next thing we knew, Colonel Robert McCormick, a leading midwestern isolationist, who published the *Chicago Tribune* and owned WGN, our Mutual affiliate in Chicago, thundered into our New York office, demanding to know why we had refused to schedule Charles Lindbergh from the America First Rally.

Despite uproars over the anti-Semitic coloration of some of Lindbergh's speeches, we had carried him once or twice and had suffered angry criticism from our offended listeners. But the choleric Colonel McCormick had his facts wrong: We had not been offered Lindbergh from the October 30 rally, and we had not rejected him. We finally pacified McCormick, whom Dave and I already personally resented because, as a part owner of Mutual, he had made us carry as network commentators some of the *Tribune*'s foreign correspondents, several of whom, such as Donald Day, in Berlin and occasionally in Helsinki, sounded as if Goebbels had written their copy.

At any rate, Colonel McCormick got his facts straight and retreated, and soon afterward the America First Committee called us back and rescheduled Senator Wheeler. I went to the rally, whose speakers represented a hodgepodge of Socialists, FDR-hating Old Guard Republicans, German-American Nazis, isolationist senators, right-wing Christian Front crackpots, followers of Father Coughlin, and gentle, idealistic liberals and pacifists. The meeting had hardly begun when the entire auditorium was filled with fanatical cries of "Hang Roosevelt!" I could hardly wait to get Wheeler on and off so I could get out of the madhouse. The senator finally went on, and rabble-roused as well as the best of them there. "We are safe now, and we're safe for years to come!" he bellowed to the cheering audience, evoking the image of an America protected from the rest of the world by the Atlantic and Pacific oceans.

That was October 30. Less than six weeks later, early on the afternoon of Sunday, December 7, I was at home, shaving and listening to a concert of classical music on WNYC, the city-owned station. At intermission, they returned us to the studio for a rundown of the latest news. One of the items hinted at deepening trouble with Japan. Then suddenly, the announcer said in a flat, casual voice, "Here, I've just been handed a flash. Japanese planes are bombing Pearl Harbor. We return you now to the concert."

That was all. I thought it was a gag, and a pretty bad one, but to make sure, I called WOR's master control. One of our announcers answered and said he hadn't seen such a bulletin on our machines. Everything was very quiet. I told him to look at the machines and call me back. A few minutes later, he phoned, all excited. Transradio had it, and he was putting it on the air. I still had lather on my face and had only a towel around me, but for the next hour I stayed on the phone, amid mounting confusion. I couldn't reach Mutual's traffic people, so I called our contact at WOL, the Mutual station in Washington, D.C., for an immediate broadcast for the network on what was known in the capital, then ordered pickups from our Mutual stations in Los Angeles and San Francisco and had the studio try to reach Hawaii and Manila for broadcasts from those locations. I finally dressed and rushed to the studio. During the afternoon, people began coming in, and by 8:00 p.m., the whole staff was at work. We carried reaction-type commentaries by Vincent Sheean, a foreign correspondent who had just returned from the Far East, and by Clare Boothe Luce, a prominent playwright and journalist, as well as a vivid report from our correspondent in Manila. But Hawaii was cut off—no communications for radio.

The war at last was really upon us.

11 ◈ "GOD BLESS THE BOYS OF NINTH AVENUE"

Late that night, still starved for details about the attack on Pearl Harbor, we took a microphone into Times Square and broadcast the reactions of people in the streets. Although the famous lights of Broadway were still bright, a strange hush, compounded of grim disbelief and anger, lay over the area and made it seem that everyone was whispering and that some-body ought to turn off the glare from the billboard ads and the movie theaters—and do it quickly.

Americans' feelings about the Japanese had always been heavily laced with bigotry. Now the racism was unrestrained. Every hostile image and contemptuous stereotype of the Japanese was evoked as people grasped our microphone and recorded their patriotic shock and fury that the "grinning little yellow men" whose prewar industry had "produced cheap, third-rate, defective imitations of American and European manufactures" and "who fought like nearsighted monkeys in trees and with their slant eyes couldn't be expected to shoot straight" had had the nerve, the audac-ity, to take on the United States. The treacherous nature of their attack, launched while our attention was focused on Hitler, made their action seem all the more "despicable."

At the same time, the night's bravado and tough talk overlay a feeling of insecurity and fear of what was going to happen next. As a nation, we were united at last, but we knew that we would now be at war as well with the other Axis countries—Germany and Italy and their allies—who had prob-ably known of what Japan was up to and would soon follow with their own attacks against us—maybe even that night. As some of us finally hailed taxis at 3:00 a.m. to go home for a few hours of sleep, we caught one another looking anxiously up at the dark sky, and for a moment I imagined that we in New York might now know what the people of Madrid, Warsaw, Rotterdam, London, and dozens of other aerial-bombed cities around the world had already lived through.

The next day, apprehension and fright, sometimes bordering on hysteria, got the upper hand over the previous night's bluster. President Roosevelt's solemn war address to Congress, which we rebroadcast four times that day and evening, breathed defiance and courage, but "hostilities exist," FDR reminded us, then added in sober warning, "There is no blinking at the fact that our people, our territory and our interests are in grave danger." The president told us nothing about our losses at Pearl Harbor or our military situation in the Pacific, and in our ignorance of precisely what had happened and what we were doing about it, the nation suffered a brief spell of the worst fear of all—that of the unknown. Free to run wild, imaginations bred confusion and terror.

The night of Roosevelt's address and Congress's declaration of war was a sleepless one, as the news services carried word that the West Coast was being threatened by enemy planes from a Japanese aircraft carrier off San Francisco. I returned to the studio, and after switching our audience several times to Mutual's San Francisco station for breathless descriptions of an American city that was about to be attacked by planes coming from no one knew where, we gave it up as a false alarm. The next day, it was New York City's turn. Driscoll and I were in a program meeting at WOR, protesting that panicky episodes like that in San Francisco the night before were spreading confusion and fear all over the country, when our own master control called us with a press association bulletin that unidentified planes were heading for Manhattan Island.

Sure enough, the news Teletype machines were ringing with flashes from Mitchell Field on Long Island and from the New York City Police Department, reporting that East Coast army interceptor planes had gone up and that an air alert was being sounded. What this meant for us to do at WOR, no one knew, as we had never had any experience like it, nor had we received instructions from the army or from city authorities, telling us who would be in charge of keeping the broadcasting industry officially informed during a crisis.

I suddenly became scared. My stomach turned over, and I began to shake with nerves. Within ten minutes, the whole thing became a frightening shambles of confusion in the studio, with us getting contradictory information from the military at Mitchell Field, the press associations, the New York Police Department, the other networks, and Morris Novik, Mayor La Guardia's liaison man with the networks at the city-owned station, WNYC. There was an alert, there wasn't an alert. At the same moment that the police announced that the alert was over, Novik called us with an excited request from the mayor to get the noise of a siren from our sound-effects department and play it through a microphone over the air. New Yorkers were not clearing the streets, going into doorways and designated shelters, Novik yelled at us through the telephone, but were ignoring the city's air-raid sirens, thinking that they were the familiar sounds of police cars, ambulances, or fire engines trying to get through traffic on routine everyday business.

Since Novik assured us that the alert was not over and that German planes had already been sighted at Montauk, headed our way from eastern Long Island, we got our sound-effects man to broadcast his recording of the piercing wail of a siren. Then Driscoll and I, wearing brown World War I steel helmets loaned to us by a studio engineer who had brought them in from a memorabilia collection at his home for just such an emergency, bounded up one flight of stairs and out onto the flat roof of our office building. An engineer and his equipment followed us, and for twenty minutes, as my fear subsided, Dave and I, peering through binoculars, described to WOR's audience our fruitless search for German planes in the clear wintry skies above Manhattan's towers. The sound-effects man finally joined us, relieving us with word that the alert was officially ended and that an army spokesman thought the "German planes" must have been seagulls. I felt silly and embarrassed in our World War I helmets, and Dave was furious, especially when a friend called and said, "I understand that brokers are phoning their wives that they had an air-raid drill on Wall Street." But it determined us to get our relations with the military and civilian information offices tightly organized.

Before we could do anything, we had another night of nerve-racking alarms from the West Coast, which again experienced the terror of warnings of imminent enemy attacks. Blackouts were ordered, California radio stations went off the air, and rumors leapt around like wildfire. Armed Japanese bands, landed from submarines, were reported to be marching north from Baja California to seize San Diego, and at Tijuana, an electrical switch was thrown by alleged Japanese fifth columnists, plunging that Mexican border town into darkness. In San Francisco, a fire broke out on Angel Island during a blackout, and in the Northwest, mysterious flaming arrows were found pointing toward Seattle like direction beacons for invaders. I was again in the studio in New York most of the night, and the steady stream of bulletins, plus the hysterical descriptions coming to us from the West Coast, keyed us up again to a feeling of near panic.

Then, during the couple of days that followed, the atmosphere of tension receded and vanished. Realization that there had been no air raids or enemy invaders, only a wilderness of false rumors, sank in throughout the nation, restoring a realistic calm and a determination to win the war and save civilization from Hitler and the Japanese empire. Crowds of volunteers, including many of my unmarried friends and relatives, flocked to the recruiting centers. Department stores, preparing for air raids and fires, advertised stirrup pumps and sandbags, as well as blackout material to hang over windows, and newspapers ran notices of men who claimed they could build air-raid shelters or make homes blackoutproof and bombproof. My father became an air-raid warden in his apartment building, and my mother, who had developed chest pains from angina, perhaps from worrying about Warren, who had been commissioned and faced going overseas, busied herself making blackout curtains for Roz and me as well as for herself. At the same time, the superintendent in the seven-story building where Roz and I lived in Greenwich Village tried unsuccessfully to persuade us to move from our top-floor apartment to an empty one lower down, where he claimed we'd be safer from German dive-bombing airplanes.

At WOR, meanwhile, where we straightened out procedures to follow in future air-raid alerts, agreeing to make no announcement unless it came from police headquarters or from Mayor La Guardia's office, we received a stream of government and military directives from the army, navy, and federal agencies. Most of them dealt with matters that now had to be censored—no broadcasts about troop movements or the strength of military units, no casualty lists or reports of damage from enemy action, no more remote quiz or ad-lib interview shows where an unknown person could get near an open microphone to deliver secret messages or codes, and no more uncensored international cablegrams or radiograms. The Coordinator of Inter-American Affairs, who was trying to get Latin American countries to join us in declaring war on the Axis powers, urged us to be positive and friendly in any commentary or news item that we carried about those nations, and the War Department's Military Intelligence Office ordered us sharply to stop referring on the air to "the yellow race," which was insulting to China and to allies we had in Thailand, Indonesia, the Philippines, and other Asian countries.

Some of the censorship directives were troublesome, and others were unenforceable at times. Knowledge of weather conditions, for instance, was deemed potentially valuable to the enemy, and all weather and temperature reports, including traffic and road conditions, forecasts, and the like were banned and dropped from our schedules. But slipups were frequent, particularly on the part of our radio sports announcers at stadiums, who in that pretelevision era would exclaim thoughtlessly into their microphone something along the lines of "It's a beautiful day here in Boston," or "The rain's beginning, and the field is getting muddy."

More difficult for us to accept was an occasional questionable application of a blanket prohibition on the location or movements of merchant or naval ships. Many tankers and freighters along the Atlantic coast were being torpedoed by German submarines, frequently within sight of horrified onlookers watching from the beaches of New Jersey or of other coastal states. Nothing could stop them from telling other people of the loss they had witnessed, although we could not mention it. But on February 9, when the huge French luxury liner the *Normandie*, taken from Vichy France and renamed the *Lafayette*, caught fire and turned over in its dockside berth in the Hudson River, where it was being converted into a troopship, there was no way for Driscoll or me, who covered the disaster, to hide the fact that this was the *Normandie* burning. Everyone in New York City knew it was the *Normandie*, though the navy at first tried to keep us from revealing the ship's identity.

Such bureaucratic officiousness, though irritating, caused the least of my grumblings. In the Pacific and the Far East, the war unexplainedly went from one disaster to another. Supposedly, we and England had been preparing for a long time in that part of the world to put the belligerent Japanese in their place. We deprecated them and talked ourselves into thinking that when and if the time came, we could defeat them easily. Now that the war was on, the Japanese in great force seemed suddenly to be everywhere, moving quickly and winning stunning land and naval victories in Malaya, Thailand, the Philippines, the Dutch East Indies, and the Pacific Islands. In addition to whatever they had done to us at Pearl Harbor (and we still didn't know), three days after the attack on Hawaii their torpedo planes and bombers sank two of Britain's mightiest warships, the *Prince of Wales* and the *Repulse*, in the Gulf of Siam in Southeast Asia, opening the way for the inconceivable—a Japanese attack on Singapore, the British Empire's legendary Far Eastern stronghold.

As the Japanese advances continued, President Roosevelt and Prime Minister Winston Churchill, who visited the United States over the year-end holidays, talked confidently but seemed unable to stem the enemy tide. In the new war zones, Japan's Zero airplanes ruled the skies, her ships ruled the seas, and her army was surprisingly well prepared and equipped. There were many impatient questioners, and I was one of them. How had the Japanese been able to achieve so easily and quickly an overwhelming air superiority? How could they so easily invade the Philippines with such a large fleet of ships—perhaps, according to our Manila correspondent, two hundred or more, and with so many hundreds of thousands of troops? What kind of resistance were we able to offer? We knew that American and Philippine forces were fighting bravely, but their backs were already to the wall around Manila, and that city was on the verge of falling to the

Japanese. Why were there no reinforcements for the Philippines? Where was the American army? Where was the fleet? Where were American planes? We asked these questions of one another, read the headlines, and got no answers. Nothing was told to us, and as a result, we at home could only sit by and wonder—becoming at length almost indifferent to the whole business, as if those who were in combat with the Japanese in the Philippines and elsewhere were participants in a far-off encounter that had nothing to do with us at home. We were not whipped up, and we did not fret overly about Manila's fate, simply because the government kept it all mysteriously distant and unattached from us. Eventually, there would be reports of large groups of skilled shipyard workers departing for Hawaii and then the release of official revelations of our crippling losses at Pearl Harbor, and the causes of our helplessness during the first weeks and months of the war became at last clear. But during the time that censorship kept us in the dark lest the Japanese learn anything that they did not already know, our frustrations and questions went on.

At the same time, fear of the Japanese-Americans in our own country reached a sordid climax in the federal government's unprecedented relocation program, which had them rounded up and forced into concentration camps in the western American deserts. Many people, including myself, were for a long time indifferent to the brief newspaper reports of this wartime action. Paranoia at the time, however, ran widely and deeply in the United States, and a majority of the American people, filled with suspicion and hatred of anyone Japanese, wholeheartedly supported the relocation program, especially when a Japanese midget submarine appeared suddenly off the coast of California. Firing shells at an oil refinery near Santa Barbara in the first enemy attack on U.S. continental soil since the War of 1812, it scared the country anew and raised hysterical demands from isolationists to bring all American troops back home to defend the United States mainland. Years later, after the war, I was deeply ashamed of the relocation program and the terrible, unreasoning injustice to the Japanese-Americans that I and my generation had let stain our country's history, but at the time, memories of the help given to Hitler by pro-Nazi fifth columns within the nations he had attacked determined us to protect ourselves against the possibility of the same thing occurring among spies and saboteurs of Japanese ancestry in our own country and blinded us to what we were doing.

Because of my position and work at WOR, my draft board at the time had placed me in a deferred status as engaged in communications activities "essential to the war effort." But as time went on, I itched to get into one of the armed services and see action. Married and almost twenty-seven years old, I thought I could do better than enlist for twenty-one dollars a month, and one day, after talking to an officer friend in the navy, I applied to that branch of the service for a commission. Occasionally, I still suffered from mild asthma attacks, and the navy, in the person of a pompous young ensign interviewer at the downtown headquarters of the Third Naval District, decided quickly that it could not use an asthmatic. Besides, he noted that I wore eyeglasses for a slight case of nearsightedness. "What would you do if you fell on a deck at sea and broke your eyeglasses?" he asked me. It sounded too silly for me to try to reply, but as I rose disappointedly to leave, he seemed to have a change of mind. "Do you speak Moro?" he asked, suggesting that the navy could use officers who spoke the language of some of the people of the Philippines and therefore might be useful in the desperate defense that was being waged for those islands. I had to tell him unhappily that I didn't speak Moro, and that ended my attempt to gain a commission in the navy.

Several days later, a telegram arrived from out of the blue, lifting my spirits unexpectedly with an invitation to come to Washington to discuss filling a position in the Radio Bureau of the Office of Facts and Figures, or OFF, a wretchedly named but very high-powered, proactive government war propaganda agency, which was led by Archibald MacLeish, the distinguished American poet and the head of the Library of Congress, and staffed by many well-known writers, editors, and leading figures in radio and other creative fields. Feeling greatly excited, but not knowing what it was all about, I took a crowded train to Washington, standing in an aisle throughout the five-hour-long trip, crushed among suitcases, people in uniform, and other standees, and in the capital hurried to the OFF, which was located temporarily in the Congressional Library's newly built Annex Building.

Spun off from the Office of Civilian Defense in October 1941, before Pearl Harbor, to coordinate the publicizing of America's defense efforts, the OFF was now charged by President Roosevelt with planning and coordinating the dissemination of all government war information to the American people. Since our entry in the war, almost every executive department and agency in Washington had independently been bombarding newspapers, the radio networks, and other branches of the media with pleas to give top priority to their own news and informational materials and to their requests for publicity, and the harried media, in turn, were now demanding that the administration take a hand in establishing priorities among the various competing agencies. MacLeish and an array of assistants, deputies, divisions, and bureaus were now in the early throes of doing so, trying to impose on the other government departments and agencies, ranging from the jealous and powerful State, War, Navy, and Treasury departments to upstart war agencies like Selective Service, the Office of Emergency Management, the War Production Board, and the War Manpower Commission, a system of priorities in which the OFF would determine whose messages would be accepted and scheduled for dissemination. In addition, it might recommend how best to present the information and might even initiate campaigns and prepare material of its own on subjects like holding down inflation or the nature of the enemy, topics about which it felt the American people needed to be better informed.

In meetings with Archibald MacLeish and William B. Lewis, who had left a senior executive position at the Columbia Broadcasting System in New York to head the OFF's Radio Bureau, I learned that in this complex war information machine, I was being offered the position of one of its central technical cogs. With the title of time clearance officer, and with my background and experience at WOR and Mutual, I would be the Radio Bureau's liaison with the networks' program and news and special-events departments, from whom I would seek mutually satisfactory air-time for every government program, including talks, ceremonies, and special events, all of which would first be submitted to the OFF by the different departments and agencies and approved for broadcast. At the same time, I would be expected to work with the government depart-ments, bringing them together for joint special-event programs and mak-ing recommendations to them that would assure the high quality of their broadcasts.

After consulting with Roz, I accepted the OFF's invitation, partly per-haps in rebound from my turndown by the navy, but largely because it seemed that in this new government position I would be able to make the best use of my special experience and abilities to serve the country and contribute to the war effort. Resigning from WOR and then joining the migration of people flocking to Washington to fill new jobs in the expand-ing war agencies, I rode another crowded train back to the capital, this time identifying myself proudly with all the many signs I saw of Americans involved in winning the war—a troop train headed south and loaded at every window with soldiers in long winter underwear, who flashed us the V-for-victory sign as they went past us; one big new trackside war plant after another, their chimneys darkening the skies with black smoke and their huge parking lots edged with flags and jammed with the automobiles of thousands of workers; the hulls of new merchant ships sitting tall and almost finished in the Sun shipbuilding ways near Wilmington, Delaware; and in the aisle beside me, settled on their suitcases and struggling to talk to one another over the noise of the train, a knot of adventuresome young Red Cross women on their way from their homes in New England to assignments in Washington.

Roz, meanwhile, had stayed behind temporarily in New York to sublet our apartment and put our furniture and other possessions in storage while I found a furnished place for us to live in Washington, a task that at first seemed almost impossible. Renting a small hotel room, I chased around during the days in buses or in borrowed cars, answering newspaper ads for apartments that were already taken by the time I got there, or that turned out to be uninhabitable, filthy hovels, or were outrageously overpriced and unaffordable. During one of my searches, I was stopped by a policeman for turning right on a red light, which was against the law in the District of Columbia. When he heard that I was trying to find a place to live, he became friendly and attempted to interest me in a studio room that his wife was trying to rent. I told him I'd look into it. We parted the best of friends, but unfortunately for him, I needed an apartment, not a room. At another time, I learned of one of MacLeish's deputies at the OFF who wanted to get out of his lease and was looking for someone to take it over. When I called on him at his home, however, it developed that he had a small run-down house in a part of Georgetown that was unrestored and still a slum and that he was wearing a bandage on his face where a rat had bitten him one night while he was asleep.

In desperation, I finally got out of the hotel, moving into a dark, seedy apartment near Washington Cathedral. Its single bedroom was already shared by four young men, three of whom worked at the Washington airport at night, leaving their cots empty for use by others during the nighttime hours. They were glad to welcome my sharing the apartment's rent with them in return for use of one of the cots. It was not a satisfactory arrangement, but it was only temporary. In the Radio Bureau at the OFF, I met Frank Wilson, one of the country's most successful big-time radio writers, whom Bill Lewis had also just hired and brought to Washington and who, like myself, was searching fruitlessly for a decent place to live. Frank, who had written for the Jack Benny, Fred Allen, and other top weekly shows, and who possessed a charming, soft-spoken sense of humor, had an idea of how we could settle our problem jointly. We would pick out the part of the city, the exact building, and the precise apartment in which we wanted to live, then go there and offer the present occupant two thousand dollars in cash to move out and another two thousand dollars for his or her furniture.

There were several things wrong with the proposal. To me, Frank was talking big money; in addition, while Frank's wife, Wanda, had an executive position in New York with the Major Bowes Amateur Hour, one of radio's most popular weekly programs, and had no intention of coming to Washington, Roz was coming, and I would need our own place. In our desperation to get temporarily settled, however, we agreed to try Frank's scheme, but it didn't work. From a sidewalk in the stately Kalorama Road area off Connecticut Avenue in the northwest section of Washington, we picked out a corner apartment on the top floor of a handsome building and went up to visit its tenant. When he heard our offer, he exploded with laughter. "Where am *I* supposed to go?" he exclaimed. "Get out of here!" And that ended the experiment.

A day or two later, Frank somehow discovered a sublet that we could share until I found something for myself. It was a furnished double with two bedrooms, a living room, and a kitchen in a fortresslike old stone apartment building on 16th Street. Known as the Chastleton, it had once been notorious throughout the capital as the abode of President Harding's mistress, but its long, dark hallways were now grubby and dingy, reeking from the smells of tenants cooking sauerkraut and other pungent dishes in their apartments. Nevertheless, we moved in and occupied the place for two months, until Roz was ready to come down. During that time, our living room became practically a hotel for friends who were visiting Washington and were unable to find anyplace else to sleep. One of our lodgers, who occupied our sofa for almost a week, was Alan Jay Lerner, a small and delightfully cheery guest, whom both Frank and I had known as a radio writer and who in postwar years would become the internationally known writer and lyricist of such great theatrical hits as *Camelot* and *My Fair Lady*.

Despite the traffic through our apartment, Frank and I had both missed our wives, and by the time Roz was to come down, Frank had had enough of his loneliness and had decided to quit the OFF job and go back to his commercial radio writing in New York. He waited to help greet Roz, then moved to a hotel for a night or two and finally said good-bye to all of us and returned to New York, where he was soon writing a new network hit show, "Stage Door Canteen."

In the meantime, during his stay in Washington, Frank and I, working usually every night until 9 or 10 p.m., then stopping for a drink and dinner at a late-night restaurant in one of the city's hotels before going back to bed at the Chastleton, had participated in many of the busy formative stages of the OFF's Radio Bureau. Under Bill Lewis, the bureau's aim had become one to get as many daily and weekly radio programs as possible to accept a system of priorities and allocations in which they would take turns working into the routines of their programs whatever war-related government messages the OFF policy makers had decided should be disseminated to the American people. Thus, during one week, the radio spectrum from coast to coast might be saturated, for example, with a message about a growing need for help in hospitals and with exhortations to young women to become nurse's aides. The message would be repeated on radio stations in the form of simple announcements or as a part of longer talk programs or panel discussions, as items on the evening news, or in special-event broadcasts; it would also be integrated one way or another in the story lines of many daily soap operas, as well as in the scripts of the prime-time weekly comedy, variety, musical, and dramatic programs, such as "The Jack Benny Show."

From week to week, our informational campaigns and their messages varied greatly. Many of the early ones, reflecting our need to convert quickly to a wartime economy, explained decisions to halt the production of new automobiles, typewriters, refrigerators, and other consumer goods for the civilian market and to impose rationing on such items as rubber tires, sugar, shoes, gasoline, and meat. Others were designed to induce women to take jobs in war industries, to persuade men to switch from nonessential work to jobs in war plants, and to break down the prejudice of white male workers against women and blacks in war jobs. There were campaigns to clarify new draft regulations, to explain the freezing of wages and prices to control inflation, to combat absenteeism, to halt gossip that could help the enemy, to increase the sale of war bonds, to conduct scrap-metal drives ("Turn it in, turn it in, turn it in"), to save bacon fat, to enlist a large reserve body of civilian pilots, and to grow victory gardens. And there were campaigns for meaningful national observances of special occasions like Army Day, I Am an American Day, Flag Day, and Labor Day and campaigns to combat antiblack racism and help the American people better understand such topics as "What We Are Fighting For," "The Nature of the Enemy," and "The United Nations," which was a new, idealistic concept for wartime and postwar unity that stemmed from a New Year's pact that twenty-six nations that were at war with Hitler had signed at the beginning of 1942.

Frank's role seemed to have been that of a liaison with the big weekly network comedy and variety shows, where he could have helped the writers and principals insert a message into the comic situations or into the dialogue between the stars and their guests and thereby contribute to the show's entertainment as well as to the OFF's informational needs. I, during the same time, was in a somewhat independent position, working strictly with the government agencies, clearing time on the networks for the agencies' OFF-approved onetime programs, such as speeches and informational special-event broadcasts, which might or might not have been relevant to a current OFF campaign and some of which included the participation of President Roosevelt.

At WOR, I had put the president on the air at banquets and ceremonies many times, but now, responsible for the scheduling and production of his broadcasts, I had opportunities to see him up close. One rainy night, when he was scheduled to address John L. Lewis's union of coal miners, urging them not to go on strike and cripple the war effort, I went to the White House to see that his radio appeal went off all right. The broadcast was from the privacy of the downstairs Oval Room, a small egg-shaped room with a red carpet, a fireplace, a couple of windows hung with red drapes, and pictures of former presidents and their wives on the walls. A bank of newsreel cameras and compartments for the radio announcers, which looked like telephone booths with red felt curtains and little windows, were set up facing an old desk and a chair in front of one of the windows. Except for the network men, the cameramen, and a few members of the Secret Service, the room was empty until a little before broadcast time, when people came downstairs—Harry Hopkins and his wife, Supreme Court Justice James Byrnes and his wife, the playwright and presidential speechwriter Robert Sherwood, some young army and navy officers, and a few servants and secretaries—and sat down in a tight cluster of chairs against one of the walls.

Less than two minutes before airtime, Steve Early, the president's assistant, entered the room, followed by the president, who was wheeled in on a dinky little chair on wheels. He was sitting way forward, with his long cigarette holder tilted jauntily upward from the corner of his mouth. In a second, he was shifted to the chair behind the desk, and a moment later, the NBC announcer startled him by saying that he had only ten seconds to go. As the president quickly fumbled with his notebook for the first page and took his cigarette holder out of his mouth, the announcers went into their booths and suddenly began by saying, "Ladies and gentlemen, the president of the United States."

The president was on the air, breathlessly at first, then more and more at ease, raising his voice slightly and looking angry during his reading of forceful passages to the miners. When the twenty-minute broadcast was over, he posed for half an hour, repeating some of his talk for the newsreel cameramen. In the bright lights of their cameras, he looked extremely strong and well. I noted that his head seemed massive, out of proportion to the rest of his body. His face was tanned a pinkish brown from a recent trip, his hair was gray, and his eyes were light blue. They were all pastel colors and made him look handsome, especially in the glaring lights. When he seemed finished rereading from his talk, he surprised the newsreel men by continuing to talk, reading a thank-you note to the newsreel editors for their war effort. It was unplanned, and the newsreel men, who hadn't expected it, kept their cameras going, not knowing what was coming next. As FDR finished and roared at his joke, everyone laughed except the cameramen, who complained that the government gave them only so much rationed film and the president had now "wasted" some of it. It didn't ruffle the president, who next tried to open a drawer in his desk and found that the old White House antique had a false front and there were no drawers. One of the newsreel men asked the president where he had gotten it, and FDR, clenching his cigarette holder back between his teeth, replied mischievously, "It was an Easter gift. The Easter bunny laid it."

As the president said good-bye to everyone and was wheeled from the room, I thought how hard it was going to be for anyone to follow FDR as president. It would have to be a dynamic personality who could command respect and obedience from as many different kinds of people as FDR did—from a sensitive Robert Sherwood, to a tough Tony Muto, the Fox newsreel director who adored and joked with the president, to a shrewd and powerful politician like Justice Byrnes, who, it seemed generally known, had his eye on the presidency. All of them called FDR "the Chief"—and with reason. It was comforting to me, and inspiring, knowing that we had such a leader.

In mid-June of 1942, the OFF was combined with several other government information offices to form a new, greatly enlarged agency called the Office of War Information, or the OWI. Elmer Davis, a veteran newsman and one of the country's most respected radio commentators, left CBS to replace Archibald MacLeish as our new head, and we of the old OFF continued without interruption doing what we had been doing, although our staffs jumped in size—the Radio Bureau, for example, going from eight to sixty people. Earlier, the OFF had moved from the Library of Congress Annex to share a building with the Lend-Lease Administration. Now, to accommodate our swollen ranks, we moved again, this time to a huge new air-conditioned office building that had been intended to house the Railroad Retirement Administration. At almost the same time, Roz and I found a wonderful new air-conditioned apartment on Woodley Road, next door to the old Wardman Park Hotel. After bringing down our furniture from storage in New York, we finally moved out of the Chastleton and into what was to be our home for the duration of the war.

The coming of Elmer Davis, a tough-willed, pragmatic Indianan with white hair and heavy black eyebrows who before Pearl Harbor had gone through a transition from isolationist to interventionist, reflected to some extent the fact that all had not been sweetness and light in the policy-making level of the OFF and that Archibald MacLeish had had his troubles. First of all, the heads of many other government agencies, particularly the secretaries of the State, War, and Navy departments, resented having to clear the dissemination of their information through the OFF and often clashed with MacLeish, especially during the period when we were suffering military defeats, over what should and should not be told to the American public, MacLeish usually arguing to trust the American people with bad news as well as good. Second, both within and outside of the OFF, there were two types of people, one of which felt strongly that the OFF should never try to make policy or editorialize, so to speak, on such basic subjects as what we were fighting for or what kind of a postwar world we wanted, but should limit its activities strictly to helping other agencies provide in a coordinated fashion whatever practical information they felt the American people needed in order to win the war as quickly as possible. In this camp—along with some conservative, anti-Roosevelt members of Congress who from its start had viewed the OFF as a dangerous pro-Communist propaganda agency, and with Secretary of War Henry L. Stimson and Secretary of the Navy Frank Knox, both of whom were prominent, long-standing Republicans and had joined FDR's cabinet in a show of unity during the war emergency—were a number of MacLeish's own assistants and deputies who, like Bill Lewis, had come to Washington from top positions in different professions and fields of business and were used to the hard-nosed sales-promotion ideas and practices of the advertising world. The second camp, in which I and many of the more liberal and idealistic staff members of the OFF's different working bureaus numbered ourselves, recalled how Tom Paine's writings during the American Revolution and Lincoln's Emancipation Proclamation during the Civil War had each told people what they were fighting for and had helped inspire them to win victory for a cause. We were dead sure that MacLeish was right in including in our charter the purveying of information that would lead the American people to support a war that was being fought for the end of the evils of fascism everywhere and for the achievement of a better postwar world in which the Four Freedoms (of speech, of worship, from want and from fear), enunciated several times by FDR and Winston Churchill, would flourish.

MacLeish, the idealistic, visionary poet, lost out and for a while, before he finally resigned, was relegated to a subordinate position in the OWI. But in many ways, the dissension went on, frustrating and hampering the agency's work. In the Publications and Graphics divisions, the conflict became so stormy that several of their leading members, including Henry Pringle, a Pulitzer Prize–winning author, and the young historian Arthur Schlesinger, Jr., resigned with a blast, some of them complaining, in a dig at the advertising-industry mentality to which they felt they were being subjected, that they refused to "sell" the United Nations like Jell-O "in five delicious flavors."

Although my job, whose title had been uplifted to the Radio Bureau's chief of special events, specifically embraced my securing radio time for agency programs that dealt directly with inspirational war and postwar themes and for talks by FDR and others, in and out of government, who spoke on such subjects, I did not stay free of occasional enmeshment in the ideological and bureaucratic warfare. On one occasion, I cleared time on CBS for a broadcast for the Industrial Morale Division of the War Department to announce the giving of new incentive awards, called the Army-Navy Joint E Awards, to war plants that were doing outstanding jobs in producing for the war. Against the OWI's decision, the War Department wanted the program to run on all four networks. Without telling us they bypassed us, going instead to the other three networks, but amid considerable confusion, they were rebuffed. Then they refused to let us or CBS see the script in advance or tell us the details of the contents of the program, and suddenly we learned from Donald Nelson, the head of the War Production Board, that there was more to the program than we had been told. Soon after the giving of the Army-Navy awards, some twelve hundred war plants in the country were going to be ordered to slow down production or to shut down temporarily because of acute shortages of raw materials caused by War Department procurement foul-ups. The broadcast's real purpose, we learned, was to prepare the American people for the bad news and to shift the perception of the blame to labor by implying falsely on the program that if workers in the plants to be shut down had worked harder and also won the Army-Navy awards, the plants would not have had to be shut down.

With one of the OWI deputies, I took the matter to Elmer Davis, proposing that we take over the program ourselves, rewriting the War Department's script at the OWI and telling the radio audience the whole truth of the production crisis. The white-haired and black-eyebrowed Davis, strikingly picturesque in a white suit and black bow tie, sat there humphing and then fully agreed with us. He wrote us a note, saying that he wanted the OWI to put on this broadcast and tell the whole truth, then called Donald Nelson at the War Production Board and Undersecretaries Robert Patterson of the War Department and James Forrestal of the Navy and asked them to go on the show with him. They agreed to do so, and he followed by having the program rebuilt from top to bottom to include the participation of General Eisenhower from England, Admiral Nimitz from Pearl Harbor, Admiral William D. Leahy, the president's chief of staff, from Washington, and the heads of the American Federation of Labor and the CIO, and getting the script rewritten by *New Yorker* magazine writer Philip Hamburger, who was a member of the OWI's Publications Division. The revised program—saluting the winners of the Army-Navy Joint E Awards, explaining frankly the shortage of raw materials and the forthcoming war-plant shutdowns, and promising immediate better planning and increased effort by everyone—was a big success. The whole episode left me feeling that Davis was a great guy for getting things done. He used few words, thought fast, came straight to a point, and took a firm and thoroughgoing position—no compromise or quibbling. In the Washington arena of infighting, he seemed to me a much stronger and abler administrator than MacLeish had been.

Meanwhile, the drama of the war itself was claiming more and more of my attention. In the great naval battles of the Coral Sea and Midway and the Marine Corps landings on Guadalcanal, we had turned the tide of war against the Japanese, and in North Africa and at Stalingrad, Hitler had met his first major defeats. Warren, who had married and was now a first lieutenant, was in England with his field artillery unit. Many of my friends were also overseas, and some of them had already been killed or wounded in the Pacific or in North Africa. When I went to New York to visit the networks and see my parents, I noticed with a renewed feeling of guilt the service flags hanging in so many windows, displaying a blue star for each family member in service and a gold star for each son, brother, or husband who had given his life for the country. On Ninth Avenue in the Fifties, a banner, strung high in the air across the busy thoroughfare, read imploringly, GOD BLESS THE BOYS OF NINTH AVENUE. It made a big impact on me. When I got back to Washington, I told Roz that I just couldn't stay out of the service much longer, that I had an obligation to the future of the whole country and the world, to her and to our families and to my beliefs, and to the good people of the world who were the victims of fascism, and that I was feeling ashamed of myself for not being in uniform. Roz was several months pregnant with our first child, but we knew a number of couples like us, where a wife had been pregnant when her husband had gone into service, and Roz said she understood and was sure we would make it all right. For several months, however, I did nothing about it. Then one Sunday evening, Roz and I attended a small party at the Shoreham Hotel following the weekly broadcast of Mutual's program "The American Forum of the Air," on which I had placed a government participant. Among the guests was Dick Neuberger, a well-known journalist from the Northwest and a future senator from Oregon, whom I engaged in an enthusiastic conversation about our mutual regard for his state. I still had not been there, but I told him of my youthful fantasies about going there and of my early fascination with everything about Oregon, including its name and its colorful history. For a minute as we talked, my head filled with fleeting images of my father soaking in a bathtub and telling stories to Warren and me and of the little red lighthouse and the Jersey Palisades. Then Neuberger asked me for my address, and he suddenly moved on and I was talking to another guest, Captain Arthur Engel, a Marine Corps public-relations officer for whom I had previously placed a couple of Marine Corps broadcasts.

For some reason, I told Engel that I was thinking of giving up my civilian job and enlisting, and he said, "In the Marine Corps, I hope." I suddenly remembered my infatuation with the Marine Corps at Camp Androscoggin, where "Chief" Healy had filled us with stories of his brother's exploits in the Corps at Château-Thierry and in other battles in World War I, but I also recalled the navy recruiting officer who had rejected me for a commission because I wore eyeglasses. "What about my eyeglasses?" I asked Engel. "What about them?" he said. "Carry an extra pair or two." Then, as I apparently began to look serious to him, he told me about a combat correspondent unit in the Marine Corps that I ought to look into.

The next day I did so, traveling to Marine Corps headquarters in Arlington, on the Virginia side of the Potomac, and meeting Engel, who introduced me to a small, rotund, and rather jolly brigadier general named Robert L. Denig. General Denig, a veteran of World War I, had come out of retirement after Pearl Harbor to head up the Corps's Public Relations Division, whose principal component was now a group of a couple of hundred combat correspondents. Mostly former newspaper and radio newsmen, they had enlisted in the Marine Corps, gone through boot camp at Parris Island, South Carolina, or in San Diego, and then been assigned to the combat correspondent unit, ordered to Marine Corps headquarters for orientation, and given the rank of sergeant. They were then sent to join a Marine Corps combat unit in the Pacific to fight with the outfit but also to send back stories of the men and the fighting that General Denig's office could place in the media.

I had an interview with General Denig, who said that Captain Engel had talked glowingly about me, which was good enough for him, and before I realized how fast things were moving, I was told by the general's deputy, Major Van der Hoef, to have my draft board reclassify me for enlistment and to be sure the enlistment office accepted me for the Marine Corps. I would then go to Parris Island for training, and I was told to keep General Denig informed of my platoon number and when I would be through with my training. The general would then request that I be ordered back to headquarters at Arlington for assignment as a combat correspondent.

It took almost two months to get reclassified, to take my physical, and to be sworn in as a marine at a recruiting center on Pennsylvania Avenue in Washington. Then I had to wait until I was told to report for transportation to Parris Island. During that time, I got my affairs in order and accepted an offer from my father to send a monthly check to supplement my allotment and help support Roz, who was about to take a maternity leave from a nice-paying job she had gotten in Washington with the publisher of the weekly Kiplinger financial letter. I also received a letter from Elmer Davis thanking me for my service with the OWI and releasing me from the agency. Shortly before I said all my good-byes and left, I received a package from Dick Neuberger, who, I believe, had gone back to Alaska, where he had been living. It was a book of excerpts from diaries of pioneers who had crossed the country in covered wagons on the Oregon Trail in the 1840s, and it looked fascinating. But I had no time to read it. I put it in a closet, wrote a note of thanks to Neuberger for his kindness, and left for the war.

IV ❖ NEW BEGINNINGS

Everything worked out as planned. In June, July, and part of August, I went through nine weeks of intensive marine recruit, or boot, training at Parris Island on the Atlantic coast of South Carolina. About all I remember were perspiration and thirst in the excruciating summertime heat and humidity of the base and a stream of intimidating punishments and threats dished out by tough, brutal-faced drill instructors, or "DIs," whose efforts to turn us quickly from soft, flabby civilians into hardened, disciplined marines involved around-the-clock mental and physical torture. The first weeks of incessant marching on painfully blistered feet were the worst ones for me, because for years my life had been largely a sedentary one with little or no physical activity, and I was overweight and in poor physical shape. I recall previously arrived boots hollering, "You'll be sorry" at me and at other newcomers on our first day at Parris Island, but in truth I never did get to feeling sorry, and after it was over and I had dropped a lot of pounds, I felt proud that although I was approximately ten years older than most of the other boots around me, old enough to be called "Grandpa" by many of them, I had endured the ordeal and gotten through it all right.

Nevertheless, in the wartime rush to move us through, there was a lot of petty cruelty of various kinds, above and beyond what, in retrospect, seemed necessary. For example, when our platoon of recruits was engaged in close-order drill one day, a runner brought a telegram to our DI. He tore open the envelope, read the telegram to himself, and stuffed it in his pocket. An hour or so later, he announced casually to the whole platoon that the telegram had been for me and that it said that my wife had given birth to a son. Later, when he finally handed me the telegram, I read that Roz had given birth not to a son but to a daughter, a beautiful little girl baby whom we would name Diane. What was in the DI's mind, I wouldn't know. But I was too joyous and too anxious to telephone Roz to worry about the stupid little sport that the DI had had with me.

About the eighth week, as our graduation from boot camp approached, I was promoted to PFC and was offered a chance to go on to Officer Candidate School at the Marine Corps base at Quantico, Virginia. But I wanted to go back to Washington and become one of General Denig's combat correspondents, and I couldn't do both. So I turned down the OCS offer and a week or so later, trim, tanned, dressed in freshly starched khakis and a "piss cutter"—our name for the jaunty fore-and-aft overseas khaki cap that we perched along the side of our heads—I took a train back to Washington, carrying orders to report to the Marine Corps barracks at the Navy Yard in the capital for assignment to the Public Relations Division at Marine Corps headquarters, where a member of General Denig's staff, true to Major Van der Hoef's promise, had remembered to requisition me at the end of my boot training.

For several months, I remained in Washington, receiving combat correspondent orientation and a promotion to sergeant. While I waited for assignment to a combat unit overseas, I was able to live at home with Roz and our new daughter and at night visit with our many friends in the capital, but during the days I worked in uniform at the combat correspondent office in the Marine Corps headquarters building in Arlington, overlooking a part of the National Cemetery, where almost every day we observed a military funeral for somebody important who had died or been killed in the war. Our office was filled with combat correspondents—some, like myself, waiting for their first field assignment, but many who had already been overseas and had served as fighting reporters at Guadalcanal, Tarawa, and other battles. Once a week, we all went to the Navy Yard to report to the unit at the Marine Corps Barracks to which we were officially attached and to take part in drill on the parade ground, but the rest of the time we were responsible to General Denig at headquarters and were kept busy copyediting and preparing for publication the eyewitness descriptions of marines in battle and other news and feature stories that came in from the CCs, as we were known, who were serving with Marine Corps units throughout the Pacific.

By the time I had become a combat correspondent, General Denig and his staff had created a unique, highly professional news organization of former civilian reporters and editors that not only brought the Marine Corps much day-to-day publicity and provided it with material for the historical record but that also raised morale on the home front and among the troops abroad by providing stories to the national media, as well as to hometown newspapers and radio news programs, about the heroism and activities of thousands of individual marines and their units. Almost every type of marine combat organization, from air wings and island defense battalions to the six large divisions of the Fleet Marine Force, which leapfrogged north, island to island, from the Solomons to Iwo Jima and Okinawa, had combat correspondents among its ranks, living, fighting, and sometimes dying with their fellow enlisted men, but carrying in their transport pack, in addition to everything else, a lightweight portable Hermes typewriter and paper and carbons, and pausing, sometimes under fire but whenever and wherever possible, to knock out a story about what was happening around them.

The American media were hungry for these kind of eyewitness stories and, after they had been quickly censored, snapped them up, usually giving bylines to the marine combat correspondents who had written them. Because the Marine Corps CCs were among the men who were doing the fighting, they were usually in the middle of action in the front lines, far out ahead of the civilian correspondents, many of whom during the invasion of an island remained aboard the command ship until it was relatively safe to come ashore. In the meantime, the civilian reporters were given access to what the CCs were writing and could quote from them in their own stories or use their stories in their entirety with appropriate credit to the CC. If a story was not taken immediately, it moved on to a progression of Marine Corps centers, including Pearl Harbor, San Francisco, and Washington, where General Denig had placed public-relations officers and CCs who distributed it to appropriate wire services, press associations, daily and weekly newspapers, magazines, and other national, regional, state, and local elements of the media. The whole complex distribution operation had been fashioned by the professionally experienced CCs and some of General Denig's public-relations officers and enlisted men and was a tribute to a warm relationship that existed between General Denig and the CCs.

All the CCs loved and worshipped the sixty-year-old general, who was like a father to many of them. One could always see him, talk to him, and get a sympathetic reaction from him. He was a short, paunchy, fun-loving man, decorated with rows of ribbons and stars for pre–World War II Marine Corps campaigns and battles, and in conversations at his desk, he would sometimes spin around merrily in full circles in his swivel chair, continuing to talk as he did so and giving one the feeling that he was having fun in his public-relations job and wanted everyone else to have fun too. To him, we were professionals in our field, and he let us know that he needed and appreciated us. More than that, some of us knew that he had many enemies, or at least critics, among the brass at headquarters, and that he didn't give a damn for any of them. He always backed and defended the CCs when they got into trouble, and many times he got called on the carpet about one or more of them whose independent conduct had scandalized some line officer. It didn't upset him. He was our protector, and we all knew we could count on him. It had a lot to do with the morale and performance of the CCs, and therefore of the success of the operation.

He had overlooked very little. Along with combat correspondents, others whom he helped organize and support were marine combat photographers and combat artists, officers and enlisted men who in civilian life had been professional photographers or established illustrators and artists. In September, Captain Ray Henri, one of the general's public-relations officers, requisitioned me to help him handle the many paintings and drawings that were coming into headquarters from combat artists in the field. We arranged some shows in Washington and in other cities, including one at the Museum of Modern Art in New York, and got some of the best works published in a book distributed by Charles Scribner's Sons and titled *Marines at War*. For weeks, I lugged paintings, frames, paraphernalia, and publicity materials for the exhibits and the book all over the place, but I liked working for Captain Henri. He was rather stiff-necked on the surface, but underneath he was a wonderfully sensitive man, a commercial display designer in civilian life and also a talented poet who had published in *The New Yorker* and other well-known magazines. He was decent and gentlemanly and got on well with enlisted men like myself, whom he treated with friendship and respect.

Late in November, I finally got my orders to go overseas. I was to relieve one of the combat correspondents with the Third Marine Division, which was then engaged in wresting Bougainville, one of the densely jungled Solomon Islands in the South Pacific, from the Japanese. At the same time, Captain Henri was also ordered to the Third to relieve its current public-relations officer. Before I left, General Denig, who was aware of my radio background, called me into his office and told me that in addition to my typewriter, he wanted me to take some recording gear with me. He explained that some "music man" from the Library of Congress had been around, stating that he wanted an authentic record of World War II songs for his archives and was offering to give recording equipment to each branch of the armed services if they would assign personnel to make records for the Library of Congress of the songs the men were singing overseas. General Denig said that both the army and the navy had told this man to go to hell, that they were too busy fighting a war for such nonsense, but that he had agreed that the marines would take the equipment. Then he told me, "Get some records of the men singing if you want, but don't worry about that. What I want are combat recordings that we can get the networks to play. I want the sounds of marines in battle."

For about a week, I went over to the Library of Congress, reporting to the "music man," who turned out to be Dr. Harold Spivacke, the head of the Music Division. Before the war, he had directed a pioneer operation, sending folk-song experts like Alan Lomax around the United States with portable equipment to make records of folk songs for the Library of Congress. Now Dr. Spivacke wanted the same thing done in the war, and he instructed me happily in the use of the machine that I was going to take with me. Developed by the Armour Research Corporation in Chicago and secured within a small carrying case, the recorder used an endless spool of special 35-mm film that revolved beneath a needle in a fixed head that scratched parallel sound grooves into the film's surface as it traveled past the needle. Although the machine weighed fifty pounds and had to be powered by a heavy twelve-volt storage battery and a converter, for the combat conditions in the Pacific it was a vast improvement over other portable units, including wire recorders, whose brittle wire often broke, and large flat turntables whose ungainly bulk, fragile disks, and moving needle that jumped tracks when disturbed made them impractical for battlefield use.

As I learned to use the machine, all kinds of other activities went on around me in Dr. Spivacke's department. Alan Lomax was still there, fiddling with his folk-song collection, a Dr. Smith was making instruction records for American GIs in how to speak Russian and other foreign languages, and an enthusiastic group of sound engineers was studying a secret new technique that had been used on a recording of President Roosevelt's message to the French-speaking people of North Africa on the eve of the Allied invasion of that area, retaining Roosevelt's unmistakable voice and delivery but changing electronically the words that came out of his mouth from English to perfectly spoken French.

When I finished my orientation at the Library of Congress, I returned to Marine Corps headquarters and got ready to leave for the Marine Corps barracks on Treasure Island at San Francisco, where I would be assigned transportation across the Pacific to the Third Division. Captain Henri, who would depart for the same division soon after I left, helped me ship the heavy recording gear, which would await me at Treasure Island, and around the first week in January 1944, I finally said good-bye to my family. In the meantime, I had received the grievous news that Lester Hofheimer, one of my closest friends since childhood and the person with whom I had gone to the Chicago World's Fair in 1933 and who had been commissioned in the Air Corps after Pearl Harbor, had been killed while flying "the hump" over the Himalaya Mountains from India to China. I learned, in addition, that Lester, who had tried so often, generously but without success, to persuade me to accept his financial help to continue my education at Harvard, had left money for me in his will. Knowing that I could not thank him added to the gloom and sadness of my departure, but as I started my long train ride from Washington's Union Station to California, I thought about it and had an eerie feeling that I had reached the end of one life, with all its friends and jobs and experiences, and was starting a brand-new one, which would have a minimal connection to the first.

The four-day train trip across the country, most of it aboard the Santa Fe Railroad's luxurious Super Chief, roused my spirits. The famous train was jammed with young men and women in uniform who, traveling alone as "casuals" on special assignments or to join various units, crowded the aisles in the Pullman cars and made friends easily. Standing together for half the morning on long lines that stretched back through most of the train for breakfast in the single dining car, then returning to the end of the line to stand again all afternoon for dinner, the only other meal served on the train, was made bearable by impromptu group singing of "Mairzy Doats," "My Gal Sal," and other popular songs, and by the good-natured baiting of army MPs and members of a Naval Shore Patrol who were aboard the train and came forcing their way through the cars from time to time with their billy clubs to break up any horseplay.

After a brief stopover at Los Angeles, where I said good-bye to Mildred and Eddie Knopf and to friends from my days in the movie industry, I continued on by train to San Francisco, arriving late in the evening and finding no place to stay that night but on a cot among some groaning drunks in the Turkish bath in the dank basement of the St. Francis Hotel. The next morning, I continued on to the Marine barracks on Treasure Island, located beneath the Bay Bridge, which led to Oakland and Berkeley. I had to wait there for a ship that would take me across the Pacific. There were a lot of other marine casuals on the island, also waiting for transportation to the war zones, and while we waited, there was nothing for us to do. Every day, we were let off the island with liberty from 4:00 p.m. until roll call at 8:00 a.m. the next day. By a stroke of good luck on my first day of liberty, I ran into two girls who had been with the OWI in Washington and had been transferred to its San Francisco office, and they invited me to use an extra bedroom in their flat. After that, I had their companionship for an occasional dinner and to see the sights of San Francisco at night and then a place to stay until I had to be back at Treasure Island in the morning.

San Francisco excited me greatly, because it seemed like the only American city that was really at war. The streets, the hotels, and the bars were full of men and women in uniform who had just come in from "out there," meaning the western Pacific Ocean, where the war against Japan was raging, or who, like myself, were just going "out there." The great San Francisco Stage Door Canteen, rocking to the singing of "Bell-bottomed Trousers," and "Bless 'Em All," was a thrilling place of war talk, war humor, war uniforms, and war music, where everybody, men and women alike, were buddies for the moment, able to share stories and emotions that would be hidden from families at home.

But there was more to it than that. One night, I escorted the two OWI girls up to the genteel Top of the Mark bar in the Mark Hopkins Hotel on Nob Hill, where we had a round of drinks. There were no other enlisted men in the place, only officers and civilian couples. Then we toured Market Street, and in one of its seedy bars, stuffed with enlisted servicemen, I started a fight with a bartender, who charged us three times the Top of the Mark's price for one-third the amount of liquor, which was sold to us in false-bottomed glasses. The enlisted men, in other words, could have done far better on all counts to have patronized the elegant Top of the Mark. The bartender sputtered and bellowed at me, but others took my side, accusing the bar of exploiting and gouging servicemen and of other alleged crimes, and when tempers subsided and we left, I felt thoroughly happy and secure. I had made my point, and enlisted men, among them some marines, had rallied to support me. I was drunk in wonderful wartime San Francisco, but I also luxuriated airily in an exuberant feeling that I was back in the West and relishing again its adventurous atmosphere of freedom and self-assurance.

One afternoon, without warning, I was directed to get ready to go and not to leave Treasure Island again or make or receive any more telephone calls. Before dawn the next morning, a large canvas-covered Marine Corps truck transferred me and all my gear, including my seabag, blanket roll, transport pack, weapons, typewriter, recording machine, storage battery, converter, and bag of hand microphones, films, and wires to the Oakland docks, where a cargo-carrying Liberty ship was waiting to sail for Nouméa, the capital of Free French New Caledonia, an Allied base in the South Pacific.

The deck of the gray-painted, heavily armed freighter was crowded with lashed-down new P-38 fighter planes, but because the ship's holds were loaded with high-explosive shells and other ammunition, we had to travel across the Pacific alone and not in a convoy, which our cargo might endanger if a Japanese submarine or airplane attacked us. The ship had a civilian merchant marine crew, a Coast Guard gun crew assigned to man the gun tubs that lined the decks, and a detail of eight enlisted marines traveling, like myself, as casuals. Some of the marines were already combat veterans who had been wounded and sent back to hospitals in the States and were heading across the Pacific again for their second tour of duty overseas, but because as a sergeant I outranked them all, I was placed in charge of them. Assigned to occupy bunks in an airy wooden superstructure that had been built on the deck among the P-38s near the ship's fantail, we were ordered to reinforce the Coast Guard crew and stand watch during the voyage in some of the gun tubs, keeping a lookout for enemy submarines, planes, or surface craft.

We had heard that as we sailed out of San Francisco Bay, the last sights we would have of the United States would be of a painter, working high above us on the Golden Gate Bridge, who would wave his brush in a farewell salute to us. Sure enough, we saw him, and we cheered at his good-luck gesture as we glided past him beneath the bridge. But as we entered the Pacific and I stood at a rail on deck, looking north toward the fast-receding coastline of my homeland, I thought amusingly that up there in that direction was Oregon, which I still had never seen and now probably never would.

The trip took twenty-four days, all of which were without sight of land. At first, I tried to figure the best place to stand in my gun tub so that in case of a torpedoing and explosion of the ammunition, I would not be blown inward into the inferno of the ship, but outward into the water. Then I decided it wouldn't matter where I was standing, and I relaxed and got to enjoying the trip, watching the heaving surface of the ocean carefully for a periscope but also delighting in the dolphins and flying fish and the fiery spectacle of the sunsets on the horizon and at night gazing at the gleaming phosphorus in the waves and at the position of the Big Dipper in the heavens and then, after we crossed the equator, of the Southern Cross, and in the lonely darkness of the deck listening to the rhythmic pounding and straining and creaking of the ship's running gear.

About two weeks out, we had an alarm. General quarters was sounded suddenly, and as we scrambled to our battle stations, the captain announced through the loudspeakers that our sonar equipment was picking up the pulsating noise of a submarine that was following in our wake. Although we stayed at general quarters for about twenty-four hours, tortured by the tension and exhaustion of standing watch for two hours at a time in our gun tubs, braced for an explosion, and then being relieved to sleep for only two hours before going on watch again, we saw no sign of a submarine but continued to pick up the warning signal. At length, in response to our captain's radio call to the Cook Islands, the nearest friendly location to where we were, a New Zealand military plane came into sight and, circling low several times around us, radioed that there was no sign of a submarine in our vicinity. Much chagrined, our captain finally had the sonar equipment pulled aboard and discovered that the "submarine" had been a shark, which had chewed the equipment and set off the alarm on the captain's bridge.

At Nouméa, after I disembarked with the other marines and with all my gear, I spent several days in Camp St. Louis, a large, muddy Marine Corps center on New Caledonia, run by a colonel known to the men as "Foxhole" Farrell, who was allegedly awaiting a court-martial because during the campaign for Guadalcanal he was supposed to have thrown an enlisted man out of his foxhole to use it for himself. The squalid camp was filled with casuals, mostly men who had been wounded and were waiting to be sent back to their outfits after having been treated in a navy hospital at Nouméa. I learned that the Third Division, to which many of the wounded men were returning, had completed its seizure of Bougainville from the Japanese and had gone back to a camp on Guadalcanal. While we waited for a ship to take us there, we were sent on daily twenty-mile hikes in New Caledonia's red-dirt hills and resplendent tropical vegetation.

Orders finally arrived to move on, and once again I boarded a ship, this time the flagship of a group of old transports that had already carried troops to and from a number of amphibious operations in the South Pacific. Again, I had to struggle with all the recording gear, as well as with my weapons and seabag and with my typewriter and typing gear, which I carried in the upper half of my transport pack. We were towed out from the shore to the transport on an unsteady barge, and a dozen times I almost fell into the frightening shark-filled waters of the harbor as I struggled to hang on to all my equipment.

Getting everything up to the deck of the transport was a daunting job. One of the casuals, whom I had met at Camp St. Louis and who had been wounded at Bougainville and was returning to the Third Division after a time in the hospital on New Caledonia, helped me. While he waited on the barge, I climbed hand over hand up the swaying cargo net that hung down the side of the transport, got a rope from some obliging sailors, and lowered one end of it to him. He tied it around my gear, and piece by piece I hauled it all up. Somehow, we then manhandled everything down four decks into the steaming humidity, heat, darkness, and stink of the depths of the ship's hold, where we were to bunk down during the voyage to

Guadalcanal. Fortunately, several of the navy petty officers aboard sized me up as a newspaperman or some special character who was worth being nice to, and they invited me and my equipment into their airy topside quarters. In that way, nursed and favored, with a clean, breezy bunk and plenty of good chow, I rode through the tropical seas to Guadalcanal, repaying my benefactors by writing feature stories about their war experiences, which, I learned later, when I again ran into some of the men, appeared in their hometown newspapers and made them heroes to their relatives and friends.

On Guadalcanal, the regiments of the Third Division, which had recently returned from their victory farther north at Bougainville, were encamped in a large grove of coconut trees and were already training for another operation when I arrived. Fighting on "the Canal," which was now considered a rear base, had long since ended, though there were still occasional die-hard Japanese stragglers to be flushed out of jungle hideouts.

I was assigned temporarily to the division's headquarters and service company and to a cot with mosquito netting in one of the company's large eight-man pyramidal tents that were set up in long rows among the coconut palms. In the sweltering climate, dry periods that filled the island's roads with hard ruts and clouds of dust alternated with sudden bursts of tropical downpours that drenched everything and in minutes turned roads and the grove into seas of mud. To the veterans of the division, who had lived and fought among the jungle swamps of Bougainville, the heavy rains were an expected fact of life, along with miserable, near-starvation-level meals. Even during the storms, the veterans, many of them hollow-eyed and emaciated-looking from their recent days of combat, slopped through the Guadalcanal gumbo and, draped in camouflaged ponchos, stood silently in the outdoor chow lines, receiving in their mess kits what the cooks could concoct from cartons of tasteless dehydrated foods, C rations, Spam, and other canned luncheon meats from the United States and New Zealand. Some of the men shook with malaria and were tormented by dysentery, and some had filariasis, which they had contracted during training on Samoa and which they called "mumu." Apparently, this was the first stage of elephantiasis, a dreaded South Seas sickness. One by one and in small groups, these men were being shipped back to a hospital in the States, where a cure, possibly the newly utilized penicillin, was reputed to have been found.

A few days after my arrival, Captain Henri reported in and took command of the dozen or so combat correspondents in the Third Division. To cope with all my recording gear, he got me a Jeep in which to get around and make recordings, and also a Seabee technician, Electrician's Mate

John Wheaton from West Virginia, who could run the equipment while I was interviewing someone or describing what was going on. At the same time, our combat training picked up, and in March word got around that we would soon be sailing farther north to Japanese-held New Ireland, where General Douglas MacArthur, of whose Southwest Pacific command we were a part, would use our division as expendable shock troops to seize the Japanese base of Kavieng in a flank attack against the much bigger enemy base of Rabaul. Largely because of his portentous communiqués and bombastic, strutting personality, most marines despised MacArthur, and the rumor that he considered us to be expendable in the New Ireland operation, earmarked to be wiped out if necessary while establishing a beachhead on which his army troops could then land with little or no opposition, did not add to his popularity. Nevertheless, we soon started to load ships, and all was grim and glum when one night the sexy-voiced English-speaking traitor Tokyo Rose, who was beamed to us regularly by the Japanese radio in an amateurish attempt to undermine our morale, revealed that our enemy knew just what we were doing and where we were going.

Then, suddenly, the operation was called off. Because of the seizure of Japanese bases farther north in the Admiralty Islands, the Marshall Islands, the Gilbert Islands, and other islands in the central Pacific by Marines striking westward under the command of Admiral Nimitz, Kavieng and Rabaul and their defending troops could be bypassed and left to wither harmlessly in the Allied rear. At the same time, it was announced that our division was being transferred from MacArthur's command to that of Admiral Nimitz. The word spread through the coconut grove like wildfire and set off an all-night celebration. Men got roaring drunk on hair tonic, sick-bay rubbing lotion, or anything that contained alcohol, and commandeered Jeeps and trucks to drive them among the regimental camps as they shouted the good news, singing derisively, "Give my regards to MacArthur, remember me to Dugout Doug," to the tune of George M. Cohan's "Give My Regards to Broadway."

The next day, we started unloading the ships, and gradually we returned to training. A few of our combat correspondents who had been at Bougainville were recalled to Washington for other assignments, and Captain Henri transferred me to the 12th Marines, our artillery regiment, to take the place of one of the CCs who had departed. My routine became a combination of crash training with the artillery batteries and their commanders and forward observers and writing newspaper stories and making interview and other recordings for hometown radio stations. The first of my records to be used widely on the networks in the States was a description of the Marine Corps cemetery on Guadalcanal, which I did for broadcast back home on Memorial Day.

In May, we began loading ships again, and this time it was for real. By coincidence, I ended up on the same ancient transport that had brought me to Guadalcanal from New Caledonia, and I renewed friendships among the petty officers, who by this time had received newspaper clippings from home of the stories I had written about them. Although we were not told where we were now going, we left Guadalcanal on June 4 in three long columns of transports and support ships, guarded by destroyer escorts and larger naval vessels, including an aircraft carrier, whose squat silhouette we could see on the horizon, moving along with us far off in the distance. We traveled north, and one day put into one of the big lagoons of the Marshall Islands and came to rest in a staging area among hundreds of other Allied ships of all types and sizes. While we took on fuel and supplies, we wrote last letters home, which our unit postal clerks collected and mailed at a navy post office on one of the atolls that ringed the lagoon. While we were still writing our letters, the exciting word came over our ships' loudspeakers that the Allies had landed on the Normandy beaches in France to open a second front against Hitler. The announcement was electrifying. We all whooped and cheered and agreed that now the Allies would quickly finish up with the Nazis in Europe and then come to the Pacific to help us knock out the Japanese and end the war.

I wrote this to my parents, but I knew that they, like I, would be thinking fearfully of Warren, who was sure to be among the invading forces in France, and when one of my friends among the marines suddenly exclaimed, "God, what casualties those poor guys must be having," there was an abrupt silence, for a number of those who had been whooping and cheering also had brothers or cousins in the "show" halfway around the world from us. That night, it was food for thought. Casualties were sacrifice. We on shipboard, waiting to go into combat ourselves, knew that. We had always known that a man dead in battle had died in an effort to make something else possible. But we rarely gave thought to what that "something else" was. Now we could see it clearly: The men who must be dying on the Normandy beaches were dying so that other men could get a foothold there, press inward, reach Germany, and vanquish the Nazis. Then they—the ones who survived—would come over to the Pacific and help us, thus shortening the time until we could get home. Perhaps this was a selfish way of looking at it, but it was realistic. Soon, I knew, my parents would also be worrying about me, and I wrote none of this in my letter home. But up on deck under the stars that night, I said a quiet prayer for Warren's safety.

A few days later, the ships in our convoy pulled up anchor and headed west out of the big lagoon. Our unit officers came down into the holds with relief maps and aerial photographs and told us at last where we were going. On June 15, two other marine divisions, supported by an army division, would invade Saipan in the Mariana Islands. We would stand by on our ships as floating reserve, and if we were not needed, we would attack Guam, which was also in the Marianas. The news about Guam excited us. It had been among the first American possessions seized by the Japanese after Pearl Harbor, and it would be the first to be retaken. We cleaned our weapons, studied maps, played cards, boasted of girlfriends and sexual adventures back home, and did everything but think of our personal fate in the combat ahead and that soon we might be dead or severely wounded.

On June 15, our convoy hovered near Saipan, out of sight of land, and for several days we listened to reports of the battle through the ships' loudspeakers. Things seemed to be going well, but just as we thought we could weigh anchor and start for Guam, we were told that a formidable Japanese fleet had been sighted steaming toward us from the Philippines. Turning about, our convoy of transports raced back toward the safety of the Marshall Islands and entered the protective lagoon of American-held Eniwetok. We stayed there for weeks until an American fleet under Vice Admiral Marc Mitscher intercepted the Japanese ships and turned them back with heavy losses in the Battle of the Philippine Sea.

While we waited at Eniwetok, we went through almost daily rehearsals of what we would have to do at Guam, going down cargo nets into little landing boats and riding the boats to shallow water, where the coxswains lowered their ramps to let us wade across the sharp coral reef to the beach. It happened that my assignments during the landing at Guam were to be ready to fight as a marine with my unit but also, as a combat correspondent, to make an eyewitness recording of the landing operation and of the fighting onshore, describing what the invasion of a Japanese-held island looked, felt, and sounded like, which the American networks could then broadcast to help make the war more real to those at home. The description of a ship-to-shore invasion by a fighting man participating in it had never been made. The idea at Guam was not to stay on a ship and describe it through binoculars, but to go along, talking into a handheld microphone all the way, from the moment I went over the side of our transport until I hit the beach with an assault wave.

In a way, for me, the practice landings at Eniwetok were rehearsals of what I would be doing on D day at Guam, and they revealed a flaw in my planning. Since my recording equipment was too much of a load to carry across the reef under fire, Wheaton and I had arranged to stow it on our

Jeep and go in to the beach with the Jeep. But I now learned that the Jeep was not scheduled to be unloaded from the transport until D day plus one, a day too late for the invasion description that I wanted to make. In our hold, however, were two half-track vehicles, mounting 75-mm cannons and machine guns and belonging to the Weapons Company of the 3d Marines, an infantry regiment. The half-tracks, which were going in with the first wave off our ship as support for the assault troops, had plenty of room in their wells to carry our recording equipment ashore, and in a last-minute change, Captain Henri agreed to my request to transfer from the artillery to the infantry regiment, and Wheaton and I moved all our gear into one of the half-tracks.

On July 21, we made the landing on Guam. At 6:00 a.m., speaking into a hand microphone covered with a condom to protect it from seawater and connected by forty feet of wire to the recording machine that Wheaton operated inside the well of our half-track, I began to make my recording, describing the scene as we went over the side of our transport and down into little landing boats. I continued to talk as we pulled away from the transports and headed for shore, passing cruisers, destroyers, and other ships that were firing on Japanese positions and filling the air with smoke. At length, as we neared the reef where we would have to get out of our landing boat, things began to get tense. Several waves of infantry, carried over the reef in amphibious tractors, were already ashore, and another wave, also in tractors, was alongside us. But the tractors could not carry our half-track, and along with that vehicle, which would have to drive across the reef under its own power, the thirty-two marines in our boat were going to be the first wave to wade ashore from the lip of the reef, a distance of about a quarter of a mile.

As we hit the reef with a thud and the ramp went down, we could see the red dots of Nambu machine guns and other Japanese weapons firing at us through the smoke from the hills behind the beach. In one way or another, we were all scared, but we tried to hide it from one another as we jumped into the water behind the half-track and started to wade. I just kept talking into the hand microphone, telling what I was doing, what I was seeing, and what I was thinking, and soon, amid the smoke and the noise of diving airplanes and the naval gunfire, I became so preoccupied with talking that I stopped being afraid and grew numb to the reality of what was happening.

It was a long, long walk across the reef, pushing my legs against the water, which at times on the slippery coral was knee-high and at other times reached my waist. Artillery and mortar shells began to burst around us, one of them setting fire to a nearby amphibious tractor that was full of men, and at one point I was aware that I was walking through a curtain of Japanese bullets that were kicking up the water in vicious little splashes around me. Our own men were beginning to get hit, and some of us stopped to put the wounded in a little rubber boat that we pulled. More and more men went down, and the sound track of my recording became a mixture of the desperate cries on the reef and my attempts to explain what was happening to us. As I finally reached the beach, I saw a friend of mine lying on his stomach at the edge of the sand. Blood was pouring from him into the water, and he was dead. But I was now totally beyond reality, beyond being shocked or made sick by the sight of death. More than twenty of the thirty-two men who had been in our boat had been hit crossing the reef.

On our section of the landing area, we were pinned down for the next two days, trying to drive the Japanese from cliffs and steep hills that overlooked the beach. Dug into foxholes with Wheaton, among broken coconut palms and shattered vegetation, I managed to continue making recordings and also to write stories describing the furious fighting that was costing us the lives of many brave men. On the third day, when the troops in our sector finally topped the heights and cleared the beachhead of most of the enemy's fire, I ran all my film recordings and stories along the beach—zigzagging in the sand as I ran so as not to provide an easy target to isolated Japanese snipers who were still holding out in caves and other hiding places in the hills—and delivered them to Captain Henri at the newly established division command post. Henri got the material to a ship, and eventually it reached Washington. Weeks later, I got a letter from General Denig, informing me that the record of the landing was unprecedented and was the best of the war so far and that all the networks had played it. When the battle was over, he promoted me to staff sergeant and awarded me a Bronze Star for making the 110-minute record, which since World War II has reposed in Dr. Spivacke's Music Division and its successor departments at the Library of Congress, and which fifty years after the war, when it was discovered and played on radio and television to a new generation, was said to be still the only description of a ship-to-shore landing under fire ever made by a participant.

During the D day fighting, the 9th Marines, another of the Third Division's three infantry regiments, had suffered the loss of both of its combat correspondents. One of them, a young journalist named Solomon Blechman, had been killed by a mortar shell on the beach, and the other CC had been seriously wounded and taken off the island to a hospital ship. The 3d Marines, with whom I had landed, was ably covered by a tough little correspondent named Cy O'Brien, who had been in on the struggle to get to

Battle-hardened sergeant
and combat correspondent
with the Third Marine
Division during the
fighting to retake Guam,
July 1944.

the top of the hills behind the beach. To give the 9th a combat correspondent, Captain Henri now transferred me to that regiment, and I began to cover it, only to be transferred again to the division's third infantry regiment, the 21st Marines, which was engaged in very heavy fighting in the center of our line and needed more coverage than it was getting.

If I wasn't already hardened to combat, I became so during my rapid transfers. Both the 9th and 21st Marines moved inland quickly, leaving behind scenes that should have stirred my emotions and nauseated me, but did not do so—harsh still lifes of our scattered ivory-colored dead not yet gathered for burial, lying alone and in groups, some twisted and contorted, some with outflung arms, resting in ghostly silence on the slopes of huge shell holes like young men fast asleep; and, near to them, scenes of masses of fast-bloating Japanese bodies and parts of bodies, severed limbs and heads with staring eyes, blown together in heaps of raw meat by our powerful naval gunfire, and everything now shrouded in carpets of buzzing blowflies and reeking with the putrid smell of death. Traveling along in the front lines, often with a new buddy, a blunt, fearless combat photographer named Walter Page, I saw, recorded, and wrote about it all—about a desperate Japanese night banzai attack that flowed over and into and past our foxholes and made the night hideous with drunken Japanese screams and with blinding bursts of grenades and bayonet and knife fights in the darkness, and about jungle ambushes and firefights, in one of which at a crossroads called Finegayan I aimed at and killed an enemy before he killed me. Unmoved by death, which seemed to come so easily and with such matter-of-fact finality, I was deadened myself, unfeeling about such scenes. Except one . . .

Throughout our fighting, we rarely saw a member of Guam's rather large civilian population, which prior to the war had been intensely loyal to the United States. Then one day, in the depths of the island's interior, we brushed aside a screen of Japanese troops and came on a large cesspoollike concentration camp in the jungle, crowded with sick, half-starved, and terrified Guamanian men, women, and children. Living in the mud in unsanitary conditions, denied medicines or adequate food, and beaten, raped, and bayoneted by their Japanese guards, they had been reduced to a subhuman level of existence, and many were dead or slowly dying. Previously, from time to time, some of my marine friends had wondered genuinely what the war was all about and why we were fighting in it. Now, with an understanding of what the Japanese might have had in store for us, they knew.

13   THE PRICE OF FREEDOM

On August 11, twenty-one days after our landing, Guam was declared secure, which meant that we had retaken every part of the island and that all organized resistance by the Japanese had ceased. But hidden among Guam's many areas of caves and matted jungle growth were still thousands of the enemy, disorganized and leaderless, holding out alone or in small bands and determined to continue to fight and attack us in guerrilla fashion. Most of them were concentrated in an extremely rugged fifty-square-mile area in the northern part of the island, where we had driven them in the final days of the campaign and where we were lying in bivouacs of muddy foxholes encircled by barbed wire, on which we hung tin cans that clattered when the wire was moved and alerted us at night to the presence of the enemy.

Behind us, to the south, the rest of the island over which we had fought was being rushed through a fantastic transformation. Seabees, engineers, and a host of army and navy units, along with heavy construction equipment and building materials, were pouring ashore to convert Guam into a giant American base, with ship-repair yards, airfields, submarine berths, four-lane highways, island-command office buildings, radio communication centers, large mess halls, barracks, hospitals, rest and recreation areas, supply depots and dumps, and, atop the ridge down which the Japanese had only recently launched a terrible night banzai attack against us, a new, advance headquarters for the commander in chief of the Pacific, Admiral Nimitz. To protect all this activity from the remaining Japanese, orders came down to us to stay where we were and get rid of the enemy stragglers.

It was a miserable assignment. The world was told that the battle for Guam was over, but we were still fighting it so that the rear elements could refashion the island without being harassed by surviving Japanese. Based in our jungle camps, living on a steady diet of rations, coming down with dengue fever, dysentery, jaundice, and malaria, sometimes two or three of them at the same time, going on patrols, setting ambushes, and losing men in sudden firefights or to snipers or booby traps in the jungle, we managed during the next two months to flush and kill some five thousand enemy survivors, many of them sick and starving. During those weeks, I made a number of recordings that conveyed the grimness of the guerrilla war in which we were engaged, though occasionally the situation proved too dangerous to worry about making a recording. One afternoon, for instance, Walter Page, my combat-photographer friend, and I joined a Japanese-hunting patrol and helped to set an ambush around an enemy food cache of rice and canned salmon that had been hidden in the jungle and that one of our scouts told us Japanese holdouts were visiting each night. Before it got dark, Page and I settled ourselves into a shallow foxhole in the middle of a circle of the foxholes of the patrol members and, turning on my recording machine and hugging a hand microphone close to my mouth, I prepared to describe the night ambushing of some unsuspecting Japanese.

It was a long and agonizing wait. In the blackness of the night, the jungle was alive with dozens of startling noises that sounded like those of cautiously approaching Japanese, but which were actually made by snorting pigs, scurrying banana rats, bats, gecko lizards, and falling coconuts. On our part, absolute stillness was required—no slapping at mosquitoes, scratching a jungle rash, or letting go with a cough or a sneeze. After a while, the moon came up, and in the intense new light we snuggled down close to the earth, trying to look like part of the thick vegetation. In time, the enemy came, four of them, swinging down a narrow trail toward the food cache, chattering away as they came. Suddenly, without waiting for a prearranged signal, one of our men with a Browning automatic rifle let go at them. In the blasts and confusion, the Japanese disappeared. After a moment, we heard what we imagined to be the singsong death chant of one of them, plaintive and sad. We couldn't see him, and we saw and heard nothing of the other three. The singing stopped, we heard a tapping noise, Page, who figured it was a grenade being hit against a helmet, hollered, "Duck!" and a blast went off, followed by a shower of pieces of metal and flesh and then absolute silence. A few minutes later, Page whispered, "Don't move. The other three must be around here somewhere, watching us. They got *us* ambushed now."

And so we believed that they did. The rest of the night was pure torture as we waited for a grenade to be tossed in upon us. But it never happened.

Recording front-line action: During a temporary Japanese holdup of our advance toward Guam's capital city, I interview Marine platoon leader Lieutenant Paul Smith, in prewar civilian life the editor of the San Francisco Chronicle.

As soon as it got light, we discovered that the one man who had been wounded had blown off the top of his head with a grenade, committing hara-kiri for his emperor. A fat toad was sitting among maggots on what was left of his face, feasting on flies. The other three men had gotten away; there was no sign of them. And in the fear of the night that demanded our silence, I had made no recording.

If there was anything good about this period of prolonged misery and tension in a kind of terrain that we marines called "the boondocks," it was that inadvertently I began for the first time in my life to feel a strangely close communion with nature. I hugged the earth repeatedly, dug my face into the dirt and the mud, and did not feel that I had to wash it off. Many a time, I also lay under a bush or some other vegetation in the rain, tired, hungry, and lonely, but soothed and comforted by listening to the slow drip of the raindrops that rolled free from the leaves onto my upturned face and seemed to assure me that somehow we were all bound closely together, the bush, the rain, and myself, and that the sense of unity was natural and good. I didn't think much about it at the time, but later on I would do so.

In early October, we finally gave up hunting Japanese stragglers and moved back out of the boondocks to a regimental campsite of pyramidal tents and to the luxury of cots and mattresses and camp loudspeakers that piped in the armed forces' shortwave radio station at San Francisco, broadcasting wonderfully warm recorded music from home like Jo Stafford's "I'll Walk Alone" and Marlene Dietrich singing "Lili Marlene," which increased our homesickness. We were settled near the location of the crossroads at Finegayan, where I had been in a firefight and had killed an enemy, but the site, like almost all of the central and southern parts of Guam, was unrecognizable. Everywhere, large tracts of brush and jungle had been bulldozed down and cleared away. Wide modern highways, policed by MPs, had replaced the narrow, twisting jungle roads for which we had fought. Native hamlets had given way to army, navy, and Seabee camps and barracks, and all kinds of new groups—quartermaster and service outfits, signal corps companies, construction, engineer, and stevedore units—seemed to be arriving on the island and adding to the new camps almost every day.

We had scarcely gotten settled in our new location when a typhoon roared in from the sea and struck us, blowing our tents down on top of us and exposing everything we owned to a tropical downpour. Among the people who hurried over to help pull us out from under the collapsed tents were two burly marine communications men, both of them Navajo Indians known as "code talkers," who during combat transmitted front-line radio and telephone messages in a code in their own language, which Japanese interceptors could not decipher. We had had very little to do with the Indians, who had seemed overly shy and had generally stayed by themselves. But now they laughed at our plight and stuck around to help us get resettled, and when we had the tents up again and had straightened up the mess, they joined us for a smoke. They turned out to be really friendly, telling a lot of jokes, mostly at our expense, and generally behaving like any other marines. But then they asked us our names, and when one fellow said that his name was Carson, they looked at him quizzically. "You a relation of Kit Carson?" one of them asked. The fellow shook his head, and the other Navajo grunted, "He was a shit."

When we asked why, they explained that in the time of their grandparents, the man we knew as a great western frontiersman had led an American army against the Navajos, killing many of them and driving the rest out of their homes in Arizona on a long march to a place of exile, where many of their women, children, and old people had died of starvation. None of us had ever heard any of this, and as the conversation continued, I remembered driving on washboard roads through parts of the Navajo reservation in Arizona with Billy Watters during my trip home from California in 1935 and seeing Indians still living there in hogans. I brought it up, and they said that the army had finally let their people go back home, but that in many ways they still felt like prisoners, because government agents still ran their lives and even then were causing the Navajos much hardship by making them kill their flocks of sheep because they claimed the animals were eating too much grass and causing erosion.

I suddenly wished I knew more about the Indians and their side of things, but some of the other men were beginning to get restless and cynical about the Navajos' griping, and one of them blurted out, "If the government's so bad to you people, what the hell are you fighting this war for?" One of the Navajos answered without a second's pause, "We're fighting for our country, too. The country of the Navajos." The conversation petered out, and although I continued to think for a while about these Indian marines, other fast-moving developments soon wiped the Navajos from my mind.

Near our camp, for one thing, the army was building a great new airfield with long runways, and it was rumored that B-29 Superfortresses, huge new planes that we had not yet seen, would be coming to Guam to use it as a base from which to bomb Japan. Shortly after we had gotten over the excitement of the typhoon, we were told that the army needed two more big airfields for the bombers and wanted to build them in the northern boondocks from which we had just come, but that despite our efforts, that area was still concealing numerous Japanese stragglers who could not be left at large as a constant danger and nuisance to the airfield builders. So back to the boondocks we were marched, on another try at the Jap holdouts—this time in a large-scale, organized campaign that was meant to rid the area for good of all the remaining enemy.

Lined up abreast from one side of the island to the other and returning to the tensions and discomforts of combat in the jungle, the three infantry regiments in our division were ordered to move north together, scouring caves and all manner of difficult terrain in a ten-day sweep to the cliffs, papaya groves, and reef-bound beaches that marked Guam's northern coast. It was a dangerous and tiring job, and although we killed another three hundred Japanese, others continued to slip through our lines at night or otherwise elude us. Nevertheless, time was running out for the army, the bombers were coming on schedule and the airfields had to be ready for them, and what enemy stragglers still remained were deemed too sick, hungry, or demoralized to constitute a serious menace. So we left them for the airfield builders to cope with and returned to our camp near the first airfield, where a few weeks later I recorded the exciting arrival on Guam of General Curtis LeMay and his Twentieth Air Force armada of gargantuan B-29s, which had left bases in Saipan, dropped bombs on Tokyo, and returned like big birds to roost in their new base at Guam.

The presence of the large planes that could reach Japan and bomb Tokyo made it seem like the war was almost over. But my experience with exhausting combat in the boondocks was not yet ended. Like others, I was wearing out and feeling like I was growing further and further away from everything in the outside world. Washington, my family, my home, my little daughter, Diane, everyone I knew and loved were the subjects of vivid dreams, night after night, as I slept and longed for them. But during the days, in the reality of the jungle, where I was unable to share anything with those back home, everything that normally would have united us was becoming not only far away but long ago, so very, very long ago.

Early in December, Captain Henri transferred me temporarily to the 6th Marines, an infantry regiment of the Second Marine Division on the neighboring Marianas island of Saipan, where bases had also been built for the B-29s and where a sweep similar to our own was planned to eliminate Japanese stragglers, who seemed more numerous and tenacious than they had been on Guam. On Saipan, I returned once again to life in the jungle, writing stories and making recordings of the sweep. The 6th Marines was something of an historic outfit. It had fought and distinguished itself in France in World War I, and almost every night as we probed onward through the island for hidden Japanese, an officer, reminding me of Chief Healy's stories at Camp Androscoggin about his marine brother who had been killed in France, would gather some of our men around him and instill pride in them by reading aloud from a book about their regiment's illustrious history in World War I.

The Saipan sweep came to an end atop a windswept seaside cliff, onto which hundreds of fleeing Japanese soldiers and civilians, men, women, and children who had lived on Saipan and had been trying to evade being captured or killed, had been pushed by our troops and from which they had all hurled themselves to the rocks and crashing surf below, choosing suicide rather than the disgrace of surrendering to our forces. It was a wild and sad place, and I was glad to get away from it. After a brief trip to other new B-29 airfields bulldozed from woods on the nearby island of Tinian, from which, the following August, a B-29 named the *Enola Gay* would fly with the first atom bomb to Hiroshima, I returned to Guam.

Soon after Christmas, we began to hear rumors of another move. Nothing definite was told us, but Guam was now a rear area, and we were assault troops with no reason for staying there longer. We went on conditioning hikes, stepped up our training, and had more classes, increasing our skills at taking caves, pillboxes, and bunkers. At the same time, we received replacements for the casualties we had suffered on Guam. Among the newcomers to my regiment were Lieutenant Angelo Bertelli, a Notre Dame all-American football player, who wore his celebrity status with good-natured modesty and became one of our most popular officers, and a slightly built, unassuming sergeant and prewar marine named Reid Chamberlain, who possessed a dramatic personal story.

An "old China hand" in the Corps, Chamberlain, along with his outfit, had been trapped on Bataan and Corregidor with General MacArthur early in the war. After the fall of Corregidor, he had escaped in a small boat to the Philippine island of Mindanao, where, receiving an officer's commission in the U.S. Army, he had helped organize and lead a Filipino guerrilla band behind the Japanese lines. Meanwhile, though the Marine Corps had insisted to his mother in California that he had been killed at Corregidor, she refused to believe it, maintaining stubbornly that one day he would be showing up at her front door.

After a year and a half, suffering from illness, he had been taken out to Australia in a submarine and had then returned to the United States, where he was accorded a hero's welcome, receiving the Distinguished Service Cross for "extraordinary heroism" and returning to his mother's home, as she had always known he would. But it was not the end of his story. Although he could have remained in the States, he felt alienated from the civilian population which had not experienced the war, and as long as the enemy was undefeated, he wanted to be back overseas among the men who were still fighting for victory. So he resigned his officer's commission in the army, told his mother once more that he would come back again safely, and reenlisted in the Marine Corps, which returned him to his original rank of sergeant and sent him to our division on Guam, where he ended up with the 21st Marines, living in our tent and becoming one of my closest friends. Eventually, there was going to be even more to his story.

Meanwhile, early in 1945, the rumors about our going into action again were confirmed, although we were not told where we were going. Once more, we boarded ships, and our officers informed us that on this operation, we would again be "floating reserve." Two other marine divisions would make the beachhead, and we might not have to land at all. If the others didn't need us, we could turn around and sail back to Guam without a fight, and then, perhaps, most of our men who had been overseas for a long time could be rotated home for a well-deserved furlough. At the same time, Captain Henri transferred me to the division headquarters company, explaining that if only one of our regiments did have to go ashore, our division commander, Major General Graves B. Erskine, would probably go in with it, and by being on the same ship with him, I would be able to land with whatever unit of our division went into action. My place in the 21st Marines, meanwhile, was assigned to a young line corporal named William Middlebrooks, who had been an infantry scout on Bougainville and Guam, but whose fine writing as a prewar newspaperman in Florida had come to Captain Henri's attention. With an ambition to become a well-known writer after the war, the twenty-three-year-old Middlebrooks was immensely excited by his field appointment as a combat correspondent and joined Dick Dashiell, the regiment's other correspondent.

Soon after our transports set sail, our officers broke out maps and overlays and revealed to us that we were going to Iwo Jima, a small, barren volcanic island only five miles long and two and one-half miles wide at its widest point. The tiny island lay within Japan's inner ring of defenses about 750 miles north of Guam, halfway between the Marianas and Tokyo. There was little on it but two airfields and a third one under construction, but it was stressed to us that there were a number of reasons why we had to take those fields for our B-29s that had been bombing Japan. First, Japanese planes based on Iwo had been raiding our airfields in the Marianas, damaging the big bombers. Second, the three-thousand-mile round-trip flight from the Marianas bases to Tokyo was too far for American fighter planes to fly, and without fighter escort, the B-29s were not only falling prey to Iwo-based Japanese fighters but had to fly so high over Japan to stay beyond reach of enemy planes that their bombing of Tokyo and other targets was not as effective as it would have been with fighter protection at a lower altitude. Finally, on the entire round-trip to Japan and back to the Marianas, any B-29 that had trouble caused by the enemy, the weather, or something else had no place to come down. They had either to make it back to their Marianas bases or fall into the sea. Seizing Iwo's airfields, we understood, would therefore help considerably to shorten the war, providing a haven for crippled B-29s and a base for fighter planes that could protect the Superfortresses as they brought the full fury of U.S. power at last to Japan's home islands.

As for Iwo, the aerial maps made the entire island from shore to shore look like an eight-square-mile section of the most strongly fortified line in the world. Every yard of its surface seemed covered by a multitude of weapons, including huge siege-type artillery pieces, mortars up to the tremendous caliber of 320 millimeters, antitank and antiaircraft guns, heavy rocket bombs, and machine guns and other flat-trajectory weapons that could catch us everywhere in devastating cross fire. But we were assured that for some seventy-two days our planes and warships had subjected the island to a murderous air and naval bombardment, which was presumed to have destroyed much of the island's defenses and killed many of the thirteen-thousand-man Japanese force that was estimated to be on Iwo. What we didn't know was that the island was honeycombed with interconnecting caves, concealed artillery and infantry firing positions, and underground tunnels and rooms protected by layers of steel, concrete, and volcanic rock in which the Japanese hid during our air and naval attacks; that our bombardments had done little but churn up again and again the island's ugly surface of black volcanic sand, rocky ridges, and stunted vegetation; and that the actual number of defenders was almost double the estimated thirteen thousand figure.

As we sailed north, it got colder, reminding us that it was winter and we were no longer in the tropics. One morning, to my consternation, I was told that the ship carrying the 21st Marines had left our convoy during the night, ordered to hurry on and reach Iwo ahead of the rest of us, ready to land the 21st at once, if needed. It was an ironic turn of events, and I felt both angry and guilty. I had left my outfit so that I would be sure of landing with the first regiment of our division that would go ashore, and now I was trapped with the division command, which was *not* going to accompany that unit—and the first unit, moreover, was going to be my own.

On D day, February 19, we were out of sight of Iwo, but we crowded around the radios of the signal companies aboard our ship and listened to the crackling reports coming from our air observers and from the units of the two divisions that were making the landings. For a while, opposition to our landing force was slight, and everything seemed fine. Then suddenly, all hell appeared to erupt on the island—part of the Japanese commander's strategy, we later learned, to let our troops get ashore and string themselves out in a line across the narrow waist of the island and then open up on them from both sides with everything that they had hidden, preventing our reinforcements from coming in and annihilating those who had gotten ashore. Our casualties were great, and they continued to mount that night and the next day, ranging in the various units from a shocking 25 to 35 percent of the men. By noon of the second day, we heard the ominous news that the 21st Marines were needed as reinforcements and were going in.

About the same time, someone aboard ship told us that, according to the shortwave radio transmission from San Francisco, President Roosevelt had been meeting with Churchill and Stalin at Yalta in the Soviet Union and they had decided to form a new United Nations organization to guarantee world peace forever after the war. It was a report I had first heard back on Guam, but now it was confirmed. Everybody around me greeted the news with cynicism. "Forever's a hell of a long time in the future," someone said. "Let's have it right now." I didn't say anything, but I felt both heartened and terrible. I believed that we were going to get that peace after we defeated the Axis powers, and that those three leaders at Yalta were going to give us a wonderful new world that would make the war worthwhile. But it was my regiment; they were my friends, who were going into the carnage and slaughter of Iwo to die for that new world. The promise of Yalta had to be true. Those three men could not let us down. That night, expecting that I also would soon be going ashore, I wrote with confused but deep feelings to my parents: "We didn't get much news of the FDR-Stalin-Churchill meeting, but the bare headlines sounded wonderful. The unity in wartime is certainly winning this war faster than any of us dared to hope. Unity in peace can really bring about all our hopes for a lasting peace, for good times all over the world, and for real security. Now that victory is in sight, we must do the things that will secure the peace we fought for. And that means unity in the U.S. and among the United Nations. It means international trade founded on goodwill and across-the-table settling of all problems."

On Iwo, meanwhile, the 21st Marines landed, and two of its battalions went immediately into the center of our line, relieving a worn-out Fourth Division regiment. In two days of nightmarish fighting, the two battalions of the 21st suffered huge casualties, trying unsuccessfully to drive north through an inferno of artillery, mortar, and rocket fire coming from a network of Japanese positions concealed in a desert of precipitous black sand dunes, scraggly bushes, and torn banyan trees. Behind their backs, on February 23, the 28th Marines of the Fifth Division lifted everyone's spirits by capturing Mount Suribachi, a 546-foot-high volcano at the southern tip of the island. Accompanied by Staff Sergeant Louis R. Lowery, a marine with *Leatherneck* magazine who photographed the event, the first patrol to reach the mountaintop raised an American flag on the summit. It was believed to be too small to be seen by those on the beach below, and a little later, a second patrol, accompanied by Joe Rosenthal, an Associated Press photographer whom many of us had gotten to know during the Guam campaign, raised a larger flag, which could be seen from all over the island. Joe's picture of the six men in the act of raising that flag became the most famous photograph of the war, although its composition was so powerful and perfect that some people at first thought that it was posed by Joe, which it was not.

Even though we had overrun the southern part of Iwo and everyone could now face north together in a single line that stretched from one side of the island to the other, our situation in the battle had grown critical. We had taken the first airfield but had been stopped cold trying to reach the second one. Time and again, our attacks had been halted without the gain of any ground, our two battalions of the 21st Marines had lost almost 50 percent of their men, and we were continuing to suffer casualties at a prohibitive rate. The day after the flag-raising, the 21st Marines' 3d Battalion, which had been held in reserve, went into the center of the line and, in one of the most dramatic charges in Marine Corps history, finally broke through the enemy's defenses and seized part of the second airfield. The ground over which the men had charged was littered with their dead and wounded, but now our whole line was at last able to move forward. Later, mopping-up parties discovered that the desperate ninety-minute charge with bayonets and hand grenades had carried the 3d Battalion past more than eight hundred individual, mutually supporting enemy pillboxes and blockhouses concentrated in an area one thousand yards long and two hundred yards deep.

On the same day, we who were still aboard the Third Division command ship miles from Iwo were told that at last we were going to land. The 9th Marines were also ordered ashore to relieve the 21st Marines, which needed a rest. We sailed through the night and at dawn were off of Iwo, and we felt a thrill when we made out the American flag flying atop Mount Suribachi. Our landing was held up for a day while we all helped to unload ammunition from our holds, filling a swarm of little boats and amphibious trucks, which we called "ducks," that circled around us in the water with crates and clover leaves of shells and high explosives to take ashore. That evening, I went down into one of the big holds in which we had carried some of our vehicles and got some things out of my Jeep, which was not going to be landed for another day or two. While I was in the hold, we had an air raid and were attacked by some kamikaze planes that had come down from Japan, penetrating a screen of carriers and warships that were guarding us from interference, sinking the escort carrier *Bismarck Sea* and causing a heavy loss of life, and severely damaging other ships, including the famous carrier the *Saratoga*.

Not wanting to be trapped in the hold below the waterline if we got hit, I went topside as fast as I could and found out on deck that our ships had put up a smoke screen that hid us in a thick fog from one another and from the Japanese suicide flyers. For a while, we heard planes over us and then ack-ack and explosions, and at one point something hissed through the fog. There was a crash, pieces of metal spattered against the hull of our ship, and a red flame burned in the water near us. Although the attack continued around us for another half hour, only one man on our ship was hurt, cut in the leg by a piece of flying metal. As it was, we didn't know whether he had been hit by fragments from a Japanese plane or from some of our own antiaircraft fire.

The next morning, we went in, ferried to shore by a coxswain with tired, watery eyes and an unshaven face. He had been taking men in since D day and had been sleeping at night on a cot in the well of his boat. He examined us with a bit of contempt. "What are you? The garrison?" he asked us. We didn't answer. A little later, a mortar shell landed with a crash near our boat, and we all ducked as a fountain of water sprayed us. "I thought the battle was over," one of our men said to the coxswain. "It is," he replied. "That's just some fanatic that won't give up." At about the same time, I realized that I had left my gas mask on the transport. Somebody in command seemed to have believed that gas masks might be necessary in this battle, and it was the first time that they had been issued to us. For a moment, I had a sinking feeling that I might die because of my oversight, but I got over the worry fast. I was damned if I was going to look the fool in front of the coxswain, and besides, if it was necessary, I was sure that on the island I could pick up a gas mask that had belonged to one of our dead. Fortunately, it was never necessary.

As our boat neared Iwo's shore, we could see a great confusion on the sand—mounds of supplies and equipment of all kinds, twisted, burned-out boats and vehicles, casualty evacuation stations, dugouts and foxholes, hulking tanks and artillery howitzers, and amphibious tractors and trucks. The entire slope of deep volcanic sand leading up in terraces toward the first airfield was covered with men and equipment, units so interspersed that it was almost impossible to distinguish any one particular outfit. Placards and signs waved in the breeze, indicating the code names for the various beaches, the location of message centers, and the directions to aid stations and command posts. From the midst of the confused mass, some of our artillery guns, dug into the sand, with only their muzzles pointing above ground, were being fired toward the north. Occasionally, a Japanese mortar shell burst somewhere on the slope, and everyone dived into the sand. Then we would see a team of litter bearers scrambling up the hill toward where the black smoke of the burst still billowed.

Close to the beach, the air over the water was filled with the familiar smell of blood and death. We passed pale white bodies still floating face-down, some of them bobbing among torn life jackets. Just as a command boat shouted instructions for us to land, a body without a head bumped lightly against the side of our ship, and we stared at it in sickened horror. The next instant, our coxswain gunned the motor and we shot up on the black sand.

It took me a long time to find the 21st Marines, which had been relieved by the newly landed 9th Regiment and was resting near the northern end of the first airfield. In a row of abandoned Japanese pillboxes and bombproofs, I found my company and most of my friends. Their faces were all familiar, yet unfamiliar. They were bearded and hunched over. Their dungarees and combat jackets were dirty and torn; their eyes distant and dazed; their hair matted; their lips puffed and black; and their mouths were open, as if they were having trouble breathing. Walter Page, the photographer, and Dick Dashiell, the regiment's other regular combat correspondent, were in one of the bombproofs and gave me the sad news that Bill Middlebrooks, whom Captain Henri had appointed a combat correspondent to take my place in the 21st Marines during the operation, had been killed, shot in the back by a Japanese sniper.

"He's not the only guy," Page said bitterly. "Bougainville and Guam were nothing compared to this. This is the worst." He began reeling off our casualties, naming some of the men we had all known and liked. "Captain Rockmore's dead. Captain Kirby's dead. Colonel Williams is wounded. Major Murray's wounded. Captain Cousins got a leg blown off. B Company's cut to pieces. All those guys who lived through the banzai attack on Guam are either dead or wounded. We've got only three company commanders left in the whole danged regiment."

I decided to visit the various companies and pick up stories to write, and both Page and Dashiell urged me to be careful, reminding me that there was really no front in this battle, that Japs were underground all around us, and that there was danger everywhere from their snipers and mortar and artillery shells. They didn't have to remind me. During my search for the 21st Marines, mortar shells had landed near me several times, and now, as I started on my rounds and made a first stop at the regiment's aid station, which was established against a wall of one of the first airfield's revetments, I was a witness to two tragedies: the instant obliteration by a Japanese shell of all the members of one of our artillery forward observer teams, who were on their way back to the beach for a rest, and the blowing up by a land mine of one of our half-tracks and the fiery deaths of all of its crew about fifty yards from the aid station. A little later, I crossed some open ground where several members of our division's band, carrying stretchers, were picking up dead marines to take them to the beach, and I ran into Reid Chamberlain, who was being used as a message runner for the commander of the 1st Battalion. After telling me that he had a two-man foxhole but that the other man had been killed the previous day, we agreed that I would start sharing it with him that night so that we could take turns staying on watch and sleeping.

The arrangement did not last long. During the next week, in the course of which my Jeep arrived, I spent the days with our infantry companies, writing on-the-scene stories for newspapers and magazines and making recordings that conveyed the intensity and violence of the battle. I got used to the snipers and mortar shells, and several times I got pinned down but stayed cool enough to record what was going on around me. After dark, I shared Reid's foxhole with him, staying awake on watch half the night, gazing at our illumination flares, which hung in the sky and cast weird shadows across the terrain, and at the occasional sheet lightning of artillery fire, then sleeping fitfully the rest of the time, hearing in my sleep the crash of mortar shells and dreaming that somebody was slamming doors, sometimes close to me and sometimes far away.

One morning, Reid had to deliver a message to Able Company of our 1st Battalion, which was again in our front lines, and I and several others decided to go along with him. We had left the area of the sand dunes behind us and were now fighting in a wild, barren stretch of hot, sulfuric-smelling earth and rocky ridges, cut into jagged crags, chasms, and gulleys and tunneled and undermined by the Japanese, who could fire at us from hundreds of small holes among the rocks. Rooting out the enemy required the use of everything we had, from artillery, naval, and air strikes to precision attacks on each hole by flame-throwing tanks and by fire teams employing, among other things, smoke bombs, phosphorus grenades, portable flamethrowers, automatic rifles, bazookas, and dynamite charges. It was a dangerous and laborious job, and even after our men were sure that they had cleaned out a ridge, the enemy would come back again through their tunnels and take us by surprise. With Reid that morning, we were making our way across a rocky amphitheater formed by the end of a ridge where there had been a lot of fighting and burning of enemy by flame-throwers and which we thought had been rid of Japanese sniper fire, when some shots rang out, and Reid fell dead, shot behind the ear. In an instant, the enemy had claimed one of our best men. Chamberlain's wonderful war record had ended abruptly. After so many heroic deeds, it seemed an added tragedy that he was killed while doing nothing but walking.

There was a final note to his story. When the Marine Corps again informed his mother of his death, this time on Iwo, she refused to believe it and was certain once more that he would come home safely to her. After the war, my wife and I visited Mrs. Chamberlain at her home in El Cajon, California, and although I told her the details of Reid's death, I could see that she still felt that he would eventually be coming back. A year or two later, when Congress authorized the return to their families for interment in the United States of the remains of servicemen buried overseas, Mrs. Chamberlain asked for the return of Reid's body. Shortly after his death during the battle, however, he had been buried near the Iwo beach in a long trench, along with other dead marines, and the Navy, unable to figure out which body was his, informed Mrs. Chamberlain that it had been unable to locate his remains. Although it infuriated me, I believed that Mrs. Chamberlain saw it for a number of years as proof of her conviction that he was still alive and one day would be returning home safely again.

After Reid's death, one day was like another, with the favorite subject on everybody's mind being "How do you stay alive on this island?" With Dashiell and several combat artists and photographers, I moved into a particularly luxurious captured pillbox that had served as an enemy sick bay. The fort had concrete and rock walls fourteen feet thick and was completely covered by volcanic sand that protected it from Japanese shells. To enter, one had to squeeze into a tiny opening below the level of the surrounding ground and push along a narrow passageway. Inside were cots, upholstered chairs, tables, and lanterns, which in the midst of the violence outside made it ideal working and sleeping quarters for us. One afternoon, a plane dropped sacks of our first mail to us, and although we got ours after dark, we were able to read it by the light of our lanterns in the pillbox. My mother, who had no idea where I was, enclosed a copy of Joe Rosenthal's flag-raising picture spread over the entire first page of the *New York Sun* and wrote, "Thank God you're not on Iwo Jima."* In a more lighthearted letter from Warren, sent, I figured, from somewhere in Germany, he wrote that soon his outfit would be coming over to the Pacific and end the "little popgun war" that I was in.

The day after I received the mail and read the two letters, I was blown through the air by the nearby explosion of one of the Japs' big 320-mm spigot mortar shells. I lay on the ground, stunned but unwounded, until friends got me on my feet and walked me to an aid station. There, I was told I had a concussion and was given two APC pills and directed to lie down for a couple of hours. Gradually, I felt better, and the next time the doctor looked at me, he told me that I was now okay and to get back to my outfit. Everyone seemed glad to see me again, and that night, in the heart-warming company of Walt Page, Dick Dashiell, and the others in our pill-box, I answered my mother's letter, revealing to her and my father that I *was* on Iwo Jima and trying to give them reasons why they should not worry about me. I wrote only for them, but somehow a copy of the letter, which they showed to a friend, got into the hands of the *New York Times Sunday Magazine*, which a few weeks later, unknown to me, printed extracts from it that reflected the emotional strain of Iwo and my gratitude at still being all right and included the following:

* At the time, Joe Rosenthal, who was in the pillbox with us, did not yet know which of the many pictures he had made atop Suribachi was being acclaimed back in the States. When I showed him the one my mother had sent me, he exclaimed to all, "That's the one!" In 1991, a professor at the University of Minnesota coauthored a garbled version of this story, assert-ing that Rosenthal only learned which of his pictures had become famous when he returned to Guam early in March and received a letter from *his* mother, who had enclosed a copy of the front page of the *New York Sun*. In explanation, the professor ascribed the error to Joe's memory.

There is great exhilaration at times like these in knowing that there are so many wonderful buddies around you, so many allies standing shoulder to shoulder with you, so much big equipment backing you up and so many brave guys in the trenches and foxholes up front. You may think that the person who is dear to you goes in there all alone, but to him it's actually different. At crises like this, whole groups of men rise to great heights, and when you're in there, you simply don't have the feeling that you're alone. You lie on the ground and you see planes come roaring over your head, and it's the greatest feeling in the world when you realize they're yours, manned by American guys from back home who are going after the guys who are trying to kill you. . . .

Even the fellows in your own outfit, lying all around you, suddenly become the closest and best friends you ever had, even if you hardly noticed them before. Because they're shooting at the people who are shooting at you, and you can see and feel it. Those who miss this experience miss one of the greatest moments of living, the moment of supreme companionship. You simply cannot imagine or appreciate it unless you go through it. It is one of the greatest thrills in life. . . .

People just don't get born and drift through life to die. They exist to find and secure happiness for themselves and their own. And that's what we're doing now. If what any of us do . . . contributes to the finding again of happiness, then we are achieving our mission. And we can feel proud of it, and happy about it, too. Confusion and sadness should come only to those who have no idea what they're doing and no pride in what's happened to them.

By early March, our advance units began to near the northern shore of Iwo, but still the terrible fighting continued. Almost every day, one or more of my friends were killed or wounded, and one day Walt Page was among the casualties, hit by a Japanese grenade and taken off the island on a stretcher to a hospital ship. With relief, we learned later that he would recover. Meanwhile, veteran officers were disappearing, sergeants with bandaged wounds were running companies, corporals and PFCs were leading platoons and squads, and newly arrived replacements were becoming casualties before they even knew what outfit they belonged to or who was giving them their orders. Finally, on March 8, some of the members of Able Company of the 21st Marines stumbled and slid down a rocky slope to Iwo's northern beach, where they stood along the water's edge, awed by the fact that they had cut the Japanese positions on the island in two. But out of more than two hundred men who had landed on Iwo with that outfit two and a half weeks before, only three were left. The rest were replacements.

There were still many pockets of Japanese resistance to overrun and a massive mopping-up job to do, and for weeks, units of all three divisions would continue to take heavy casualties as they turned back from the northern shore and searched among Iwo's sands and rocky ridges for bypassed Japanese who were still hiding in caves and underground rooms and tunnels. Meanwhile, in response to a radioed assignment from General Denig in Washington, four other combat correspondents and I wrote a joint account of the battle requested by *Collier's*, which that magazine rushed into print under our bylines. Then on March 16, five of us, including Captain Henri and three combat correspondents from the Fourth and Fifth Divisions, each received a sudden authorization for high-priority military air transportation to return to Washington for special duty in the United States. It took me less than an hour to gather my gear and say good-bye to those of my friends who were still on the island. At Third Division headquarters, our adjutant, Major Robert Kriendler, in civilian life one of four brothers who owned the famous "21" Club in New York City and who made out my orders to go, hollered after me, "Sergeant! When you get to Washington, get whoever you know to get me out of here too!" At the cemetery down by the beach, I walked for a few minutes among the crosses, stopping whenever I recognized a name and thinking to myself as I tried to hold back my tears, These guys gave everybody the right to live free.

Iwo's first airfield, from which the five of us left on different flights, was swarming with planes. While we had been fighting in the center of the island, Seabees and aviation engineers had pushed aside the Japanese wreckage and repaired the field. During the second week of battle, a crippled B-29 had made the first emergency landing on it, and we had seen the tangible fruit of our men's sacrifices. Later in the year, it would be announced that during the first hundred days after Iwo was secured, the staggering number of 851 B-29s, with more than nine thousand flyers on their way to or returning from raids over Japan, had found safety on Iwo. As we lifted from the dreadful island and I glimpsed the tiny flag flying over Mount Suribachi, my thoughts were more personal. I was filled with guilt over those I was leaving behind and felt that from now on, no matter how long I still lived, it would all be bonus.

14   ✠   A RUPTURED DUCK

The military transport plane from Iwo took me back to Guam, where I turned in my weapons to our rear-echelon quartermaster, arranged to have my seabag shipped back to Washington, and caught a navy plane loaded with stretcher cases from Iwo bound for hospitals in Hawaii and the States. Most of the bucket seats that lined the inner sides of the plane were filled with bandaged-up ambulatory cases, but I found an empty seat and sat down beside another hitchhiking passenger, the tall, lanky playwright and presidential speechwriter Robert Sherwood, who was returning from a mission to the Philippines for FDR and who pumped me for a few minutes about the fighting on Iwo. After we got going, Sherwood and everyone else on the plane became silent, and most of us slept all the way to Pearl Harbor, awakened only for brief stops at Kwajalein and Johnston islands, which from the air looked like tiny specks of coral and sand in the sparkling emptiness of the vast ocean. In contrast to the twenty-four days that it had taken me the previous year to cross the Pacific in the Liberty ship on my way to war, now two more quick plane changes at Hawaii and San Francisco got me back to Washington four days after leaving Iwo. Ringing the doorbell of our apartment, I was scared into a fit of trembling and nerves over what I was going to say to Roz and to our little daughter, Diane, who was now going on two.

I had called ahead from San Francisco to tell them I was coming, and they were ready for me, although seemingly as at a loss for what to say as I was. Roz, tall and slim, with a big smile on her face, sort of backed away, with Diane, about two feet tall, hanging on to her mother's leg for security and staring at me with great little-girl curiosity and modesty, while my ears rang with Roz's words to her: "This is your *Daddy*. Say hello to your *Daddy*. This is your *Daddy*." As Roz and I stood apart, beaming awkwardly at each other, I realized that we'd have to get to know one another again, and that it would take time. There was a lot that had happened to me, and I didn't want to discuss it. But there was a lot that had happened to her too. She had done a wonderful job on her own, maintaining our home and raising Diane. But she had also been independent again, living her own life, making new friends and meeting new people whom I did not know, and having experiences that I had not shared, and in many ways we were both bound to be new and changed persons.

Suddenly, Diane let go of Roz and came over to me with outstretched arms. I boosted her up and hugged her. After all the killing and evil of the war, my love had to go out to someone, and it went to this cute, innocent little black-haired squirt. As her arms tightened around me and she returned my hugging, I knew that we were going to be pals and that everything was going to be all right.

One by one, Captain Henri and the other three combat correspondents who had been recalled from Iwo arrived in Washington, and at Marine Corps headquarters, General Denig greeted us and told us what our abrupt return was all about. It seemed that the many casualties we had suffered at Iwo had resulted in a serious undercurrent of criticism of the Marine Corps in the United States and in a questioning by William Randolph Hearst and other anti-administration newspaper publishers and politicians of whether our bloody battle for the tiny island had been necessary. General Denig wanted us, as veterans of the struggle, to go on bond-selling tours and do some speaking and writing to help tell the nation why we had had to take Iwo Jima for the successful bombing of Japan and why the island's hidden defenses had cost us so many lives.

As a starter, three of us, promoted by General Denig to technical sergeant, addressed the members of the National Press Club in Washington, fielding questions in a large dining room packed with reporters and correspondents. Then all five of us collaborated in writing a book, entitled *The U.S. Marines on Iwo Jima*, about the battle and its causes, which Dial Press rushed into publication. In between stints of work on the book, we wrote magazine articles and went off on bond tours, telling large crowds in different cities about the battle and joining business and political leaders, sports and movie celebrities, and other combat veterans in urging the crowds to buy more war bonds.

Among those who had also been brought home from Iwo were the three survivors of the six men whom Joe Rosenthal had pictured raising the American flag in his photograph atop Mount Suribachi, and Keyes Beech, one of our returned combat-correspondent group, found himself assigned to shepherd the highly celebrated flag raisers on one of the bond

Back home at Marine headquarters after Iwo Jima, I receive the Bronze Star for "heroic achievement" at Guam from General Denig. I was glad to be alive, but filled with memories and guilt for buddies who would never come home.

tours. Everything went well except for one of the flag raisers, PFC Ira Hayes, a Pima Indian from Arizona, whose tragic post–Iwo Jima life— about which Keyes kept me informed—first aroused within me empathy for American Indians and a wish that I could do something to help bring justice to them. On the bond tour, Hayes met American hype and press-agent phoniness everywhere and recoiled from it. In his case, his conscience and feeling of self-worth were assaulted by a demoralizing combination of lionization as a hero, which he felt he was not, since all he had done was help to raise a flag; patronization as an Indian curio from dignitaries and crowds who knew nothing about Indians and who had no interest in their problems; and discrimination and prejudice from anti-Indian racists who insulted and hurt him even as they pretended to honor him. During the bond tour, with its many patriotic banquets, receptions, and events where beer and other alcoholic beverages were served, Hayes developed a drinking problem, fueled largely by his guilt at being hailed as a hero and by his desire to escape from the hypocrisies of the tour and get back to marine friends who he felt had done more heroic things than he and who were still overseas, unknown and unhonored.

His problems with alcohol became worse, and finally he was returned to his outfit, which by then was back in Hawaii, training for the invasion of Japan. At the end of the war, he was discharged, and Keyes stayed in touch with him until Hayes's death, trying to help him through his various jobs, bouts of drinking, and arrests for drunkenness. His end came from alcohol and exposure on his Arizona reservation in the darkness of a cold January night in 1955. Whether the hypocrisy of being called a hero—while at

home the expanding white population of Phoenix diverted water heart-
lessly from his reservation and treated him and his fellow Pimas as inferior
humans because they were Indians—had anything to do with it became a
subject of controversy. All that is known for certain is that Hayes fell on
his face on the ground, threw up, and drowned in his vomit, and that Joe
Rosenthal, the man who had taken the famous photograph, said after
Hayes's death that Ira "told me he was getting credit for a lot of things that
other men deserve."

After the simplistic, elemental thinking to which combat had accus-
tomed us in the Pacific, where almost everything was basically right or
wrong, good or bad, honest or dishonest, it was hard not to react as Ira
Hayes had done against the small, everyday shams and hypocrisies that
were practiced and accepted as a part of civilized life by people back in the
States, even among veterans. We who had returned craved the companionship of other combat veterans as the only people with whom we could
comfortably discuss our experiences and thoughts. But it was veterans
who first got me mad back in the States and made me want to return to the
Pacific. On Guam, a lot of us had joined the Veterans of Foreign Wars,
and one evening in Washington, I went with a group of marines to our
first VFW meeting. The hall was full of aging World War I veterans, some
of whom were sounding off to each other about gasoline ration stamps,
meat, and other things that they and members of their families had been
buying on the black market and about new automobiles that would be
coming off assembly lines again and that they intended to buy as soon as
the war ended. Soon we, who knew that there was still a lot of fighting and
dying to do and that sooner or later we would be sent back overseas to our
outfits for the invasion of Japan, which would end the war and allow these
old blowhards to buy new cars, decided that we had nothing in common
with them and left the meeting in a huff. When somebody said that a new
outfit called the American Veterans Committee, which was just for World
War II vets, was holding a meeting somewhere else that night, we went
there and, finding ourselves among a lot of kindred souls, including the
local chairman, Orville Freeman, a marine officer and a veteran of my own
Third Division who had been wounded on Bougainville, we signed up
with enthusiasm. It was the only veterans' meeting I went to in Washington, but years afterward, as I will relate later, Freeman, who went on to
become governor of Minnesota and President John F. Kennedy's secretary
of agriculture, was one of my traveling companions on an adventurous trip
in the red-rock canyons of the American Southwest.

In April 1945, the sudden death of President Roosevelt came to many of
us like a punch in the stomach. Like almost everyone else in the country,

political friend and foe alike, Roz and I grieved for this man whose more than twelve years in office had made him like a father figure to the nation. Millions of families credited him with saving their farms and homes during the Depression, and the whole country looked up to him as our firm, unflinching leader in the war. On the night of his death, although his body was in Georgia, something impelled me to walk down Connecticut Avenue to the crowd of dazed mourners in the streets outside the White House, where I said a silent thank-you to him. Then I thought of the sorrowful, haggard-looking pictures of him taken recently during his meeting with Churchill and Stalin at Yalta. I remembered the high hopes of a guarantee of a peaceful future for the world "forever" that the Yalta promise of a postwar United Nations unity had raised for me as I waited to go ashore at Iwo Jima and, suddenly likening FDR's successor, Vice President Harry Truman, to Andrew Johnson, the man who had succeeded Abraham Lincoln, I was filled with skepticism about whether Truman would be able to—or would even want to—implement the visionary but pragmatic promises that FDR had made at Yalta. In the days, weeks, and months that followed, as President Truman split with Secretary of the Interior Harold Ickes and other New Deal stalwarts, as the Cold War began and Truman set in motion the institutionalizing of loyalty oaths, which led inexorably to McCarthyism, my skepticism increased and my hope all but died that Diane and my generation's other children would never have to experience a Depression and war such as my generation had weathered.

Meanwhile, at the request of Colonel Joseph I. Greene, the editor of *The Infantry Journal*, which was published in Washington for ground combat troops around the world, General Denig assigned me temporarily to write articles especially for that magazine about Marine Corps actions in the Pacific. Colonel Greene, a soft-spoken, rather courtly man, had read some of my published military writings, and he set aside a small office for me in the magazine's building near the Mayflower Hotel, where, in the company of other busy writers, including Colonel S. L. A. Marshall, a well-known author of many books on infantry operations, and the diminutive E. J. Kahn, Jr., a *New Yorker* magazine writer and an old friend of mine from Horace Mann and Harvard who was now a chief warrant officer in the army and was collaborating on a book of brief histories of each of the army's divisions, I spent much of my time for several months.

During that period, the war in Europe ended amid the collapse of European fascism, the suicide of Hitler, the arrest of leading Nazis, and the exposure of the diabolically evil death camps. Although the barbarism of the Nazis and the existence of slave-labor concentration camps had been well known since the 1930s to a frightened world that had seemed unwilling or unable to do anything about them, there had been little or no publicity about the adoption by the Germans of Hitler's extermination policy and the deliberate mass murder of Jews and others in European death camps, which began early in 1942, after the United States was at war with Germany. On the whole, the American people knew nothing about the vast genocide that was under way in Europe, and public knowledge of it and of the depths of the Nazis' depravity came in 1945 as a last great, climactic shock, making clear to everyone I knew that we had been fighting a degenerate gang of inhuman murderers and thieves who had empowered and enriched themselves by frightening into submission one element after another of the world's population. For a while, again, we now thought we had learned our lesson about fascists—that is, to stand up to them, treat them as criminals, and fight them before they became too strong. But still, in our conversations, many of us wondered uneasily if we would eventually forget that hard-earned lesson.

By midsummer, it looked as if I would shortly be going back overseas, but first I had a thirty-day furlough coming, and Roz and I spent it in the sea breezes at Nags Head on the Outer Banks of North Carolina. The articles I had written at *The Infantry Journal* had meanwhile made me feel that I could write a personalized nonfiction book about a sergeant's-eye view of the battles of Guam and Iwo Jima, and I took along my portable typewriter and sat most of the time on the beach at Nags Head writing the book, which I titled *The Long and the Short and the Tall*, from the song "Bless 'Em All," which we sang overseas. Despite an unexpected attack of asthma, a condition that had never bothered me during all my time at Parris Island or in the Pacific, I wrote the book quickly and without difficulty. I went to the Naval Aid Station at Manteo, near Nags Head, got a shot of adrenaline, which eased the asthma, and managed almost to finish writing the book before we returned to Washington. Another Marine Corps public-relations assignment took me briefly to New York, and there, borrowing the empty apartment of Ian Ballantine, a publishing friend who before the war had introduced paperback books in the United States and was now away in the country for the summer, I stayed up almost all of one night and finished the book. The next morning, toward noon, the cries of newspaper boys hawking extras on the streets outside my opened bedroom window woke me up. The United States, the boys were crying, had dropped an atomic superbomb on Japan.

It sounded to me at first as if we had just used an extrabig regular-type bomb, but eventually the ominous meaning and ramifications of the word *atomic*—along with reports of a mushroom-shaped cloud, a huge fireball, a windstorm, a widespread fallout of lethal radiation, and an assumed enormous destruction and immense number of deaths that must have resulted both at Hiroshima and at Nagasaki—sank in, burying within a few days whatever qualms I might have had about the bomb's use beneath a relief that it was ending the war without our having to suffer great casualties of our own invading Japan. Although I was now spared from going back overseas, I was still in the Marine Corps, and I had to submit my book for censorship. It passed without difficulty, and when General A. A. Vandegrift, the commandant of the Marine Corps, read the manuscript and agreed to write an introduction for the book, General Denig made the selling of it to a publisher a Corps project. I told the general that the publisher Alfred Knopf was my uncle and that he might like a crack at it, but said that I would feel too awkward submitting it myself. In the end, the public-relations staff at our New York office handled its selling and started with Alfred, who snapped it up without trouble. In an appendix, it carried the complete transcript of the recording I had made of our ship-to-shore landing at Guam, and when it eventually came out, the book got gratifying reviews everywhere in the country, ranging from the *New York Herald Tribune*'s "Little in war literature is as stirring as Josephy's first-hand account," the *St. Louis Post-Dispatch*'s "Brilliantly done," and the Book-of-the-Month Club's "Has the excitement of battle itself" to the *Chicago Sun*'s "Every paragraph is powerful. . . . This book should be forced down the throats of all the smug, proud people who looked at their morning paper and said, 'Well, I see we took another island.' "

Meanwhile, with the end of the war, a period of many personal changes set in. Both of my grandmothers died late in that summer of 1945, S.K.'s widow simply falling peacefully asleep in a straight-backed chair in the lobby of a hotel where she was vacationing, and my iron-willed matriarchal grandmother Josephy dying in bed with the satisfaction of knowing that she had achieved her determination to outlive "that man Hitler." With the death of his mother, my father was finally able to make plans to retire from his business and, with my mother, move to Pacific Palisades, in Southern California, where they had bought a house.

That summer, too, Warren and our cousin Pat Knopf came home from Europe, and the three of us had a luncheon reunion in a midtown New York hotel. Warren was now an artillery major decorated with the Silver Star for gallantry in action in Germany, Pat was a flying officer in the Air Corps, and I, newly promoted to master technical sergeant in the Marine Corps, was by choice still only an enlisted man. But when Warren and Pat suddenly revived their lifelong feuding, this time over whether or not it had been Pat who had deliberately, as Warren claimed, dropped bombs on

Warren's outfit one day in France, I had to get between the two officers and stop the ruckus before all three of us got thrown out of the dining room. We then turned to what we were going to do when we got out of uniform. Warren was going back to work for his prewar employer in New York, and Pat was going to join his parents' publishing firm. As for myself, all I knew for certain was that I didn't want to go back to radio or to live or work in New York City again. I was tired of regimentation and discipline and of feeling fenced in, and if I could do so, and if Roz agreed, I wanted to go back west and start over again with a new life, perhaps as a freelance writer, in the peace and quiet and freedom of the open spaces of that section of the country that I remembered, partly through rose-colored glasses, from the mid-1930s.

I was already testing the waters of freelance writing and with the help of an agent had sold an article suggested to me by a friend who headed public relations for the Department of the Interior's Bureau of Reclamation. The article dealt with a giant dam and hydroelectric project that the bureau was planning to help Chiang Kai-shek's China, our wartime ally, build at the great gorge of the Yangtze River. As it turned out, political events in China would delay the project for many decades, but I didn't know it then, nor at the time was I in any sense an environmentalist who would have been concerned about the huge project's possible adverse impacts. The subject of the article—a vast development of natural resources for China's progress, much greater in scope than our own massive TVA development of the Tennessee Valley—inspired my imagination and excited me as an example of the ability of Americans to conquer nature in the same way that the General Motors' Futurama exhibit at the New York World's Fair had once done.

A few weeks before I was to be discharged from the Marine Corps, a tempting Satan in the form of Eddie Knopf, now a producer at MGM, reentered my life. With pride and the best of intentions for me, Eddie had passed around to various people at his studio copies of some of my war articles and recordings, including the one of the landing at Guam, which he had managed to have MGM sound engineers copy for him during one of its network airings. Now a sudden letter from Kenneth MacKenna, the head of MGM's Story Department, informed me that the studio wanted to take an option on one of my stories, this one about the death on Guam of an old veteran master gunnery sergeant, which *Look* magazine had published; in addition, he offered to hire me as a staff writer as soon as I got out of the Marine Corps. Of course, I could see that Eddie was behind this, and after my frustrating experience as a junior writer at MGM ten years before, I had little desire to go back and try again to be a successful screenwriter. L. B. Mayer was still at MGM, still ordering the making of unrealistic "escape" pictures and running the studio like a tyrant, and almost nothing had changed.

Still, there were counterarguments. Among those returning to the studios, I reasoned, there must be many veterans like myself who as a result of their war experiences would be unhappy with the usual screen hokum and would be feeling that the time had come for Hollywood to make pictures that dealt honestly with the realities of life. Maybe, despite Mr. Mayer, I could get a story produced that was based on real people and real events. So I delayed my response, writing and selling a short story about a returned veteran to see if I could tell a story rather than simply relate facts, and having proved to myself by the story's quick sale that I could do fiction, I began to waver before the devil. Gradually, I convinced myself, as well as Roz, that what really mattered was that we get out west and establish ourselves there so that eventually we could do whatever we wanted to do in a place where we wanted to live. And just maybe, I thought to myself, that place might end up being Oregon, which still had plenty of wide-open spaces. Although Roz was less enthusiastic than I about leaving the East, where she had family, friends, and a good job, the idea of becoming a part of the Hollywood scene and making new friends among movie people was appealing, and she agreed to the move.

In November 1945, a week after accepting Kenneth MacKenna's offer, I was discharged from the Marine Corps and given a Good Conduct Medal and a little lapel button that looked like some kind of a bird in agony—it was called "the Ruptured Duck" and it designated the wearer as a veteran. With my discharge money and some of what Lester Hofheimer had left me in his will, I bought a used Packard coupe, a huge black hunk of a car that seemed in good running order, and decided with Roz that I would go on ahead to California and find us a place to live while she stayed behind with Diane to sublet our apartment and ship our stuff west. One of my older cousins—an entertaining prewar Hollywood actors' agent named Billy Josephy, who had recently retired from the army, in which, as an officer, he had served principally as a stage manager for the Irving Berlin wartime show *This Is the Army*—joined me to drive across the country to return to his firm. So early in December, with both of us still wearing our uniforms, we set off for the West Coast.

From the beginning, it was a nightmarish trip. Within a hundred miles of leaving Washington, the Packard developed a series of strange groans and rattles, which no mechanic along the way could diagnose. The noises continued ominously but without interfering with the car's forward motion all the way to the Knopfs' house in Santa Monica, where I was going to stay until I found a place of my own and where I eventually got the car fixed at a large Packard place. Billy, who referred to my car caustically as "The Rock," didn't soothe my anticivilian feelings a bit by telling me that I was just another veteran anxious to buy something with my discharge pay who had been fleeced out of my money by a fast-talking used-car salesman. "Isn't it nice to be home?" he chided me.

To add to our troubles, we made the cross-country drive during a terrible cold wave that was made worse for us by our difficulties in finding a place to sleep each night. To try to avoid the arctic air, we drove south almost to the Mexican border, though the farther south we went, the colder it seemed to get. But we also learned that the whole postwar country seemed to be on the move and creating a critical shortage of housing and shelter, even for a night. Somewhere in Tennessee, it was almost midnight on the first night out before we found a single bed to share in an old farmhouse, and, only partly undressing, we shivered half that night under a skimpy quilt. The next night, it was worse. We drove around an oil-boom area at Midland and Odessa, in West Texas, searching unsuccessfully again for an auto-court vacancy. Finally, appropriating a big army walk-in deep-freeze unit that was sitting unused in an oil field near a place called Monahans, we passed another miserable night amid the roar and smell and eerie flames of gas being flared off in the field.

After reaching Santa Monica, I spent the better part of three months living as a guest of the Knopfs while I looked desperately for a place to which to bring Roz and Diane. Feeling estranged from nonveterans, I was exceedingly lonely, especially during the Christmas holidays, and gravitated to a large Santa Monica chapter of the American Veterans Committee, where I found many other veterans stewing in the same fix I was in, living with relatives in more or less cramped and tense situations and getting mighty mad and political about the housing shortage to which we had all come home. At one point, the frustrations and bitterness overflowed, and all the many AVC chapters in the Los Angeles area, together with some members of the VFW and the Amvets, another World War II organization, combined in a protest rally, digging foxholes and sleeping overnight in a public park in downtown Los Angeles. Among the five thousand or so veterans who showed up was the actor and future president of the United States Ronald Reagan, who was an FDR Democrat at the time and who strode past the foxholes in a long polo coat with fellow AVC members of the celebrity-filled Beverly Hills and Hollywood chapters.

One of the speakers at the rally was a man named Norton Long, who had come from Washington, D.C., and was assistant to Wilson Wyatt, administrator of the National Housing Agency. Spelling it all out in detail to us, Long blamed the whole housing mess on two of President Truman's poker-playing political pals, John Snyder, Truman's new secretary of the treasury, and George Allen, a high-powered Washington lobbyist and secretary of the Democratic National Committee. Under the pressure of influential construction and real estate interests and the persuasion of Allen, Snyder had, according to Long, ordered the premature ending of the smooth-working wartime system of priorities and allocations that had channeled lumber and other scarce building materials to where and when they were needed. The lifting of wartime controls had resulted in immediate chaos, with every builder scrambling for himself, in or out of the black market, to secure supplies for whatever he wanted to build, and with almost no one interested in constructing low-cost homes or rental units that veterans could afford. A number of congressmen had introduced legislation to reimpose the wartime system of priorities and allocations and start the building by the National Housing Agency of veterans' housing on a massive scale, but Snyder and Allen, still taking their cues from the building lobby, were working to defeat the bills.

The rally and Long's revelations made me an activist veteran. Long pleaded for our help in getting the bills passed, and I pitched in with enthusiasm, organizing a housing committee in our Santa Monica AVC chapter that helped win support for the bills from California's two senators, William Knowland and Sheridan Downey, and from our local Santa Monica congressman, Donald Jackson, an ex-marine and, although a turncoat New Deal Democrat who had embraced Republican conservatism, a young man of my age who became a warm and close friend of mine, as tolerant of my opinions as I was of his.

In the end, our AVC efforts accomplished little, and the scandalous housing crisis that followed World War II caused misery and hardship for several years until supplies finally became abundant and people like William Levitt mass-produced whole towns of new, affordable housing. In the meantime, veterans' problems multiplied, and I went on to become chairman of the Santa Monica AVC chapter, a member of the Executive Committee of the AVC's Los Angeles Area Council and, finally, vice chairman of the AVC in California. At the same time, I wrote a syndicated newspaper column on veterans' affairs called "We Won a War But . . ." and plunged into the writing of an autobiographical novel in which I let off a lot of steam and personal passion about getting readjusted to civilian life. When I had got the book half-finished, my agent, Curtis Brown, sent it to Knopf, where Alfred's wife and partner, Blanche, read it and got all excited about wanting to publish it. I knew she was sincere, because it was the first time she had ever noticed me, and when she came out to Los

Angeles on business, she had me to lunch and talked of big things for the book and for me as an exciting new writer "You're writing it at red-hot fever," she said. "Finish it as fast as you can."

But I never did. In Washington, Roz finally sublet our furnished apartment to one of our friends, a CBS radio news commentator who had returned from overseas, and she and Diane joined me in Santa Monica, where at last I found a small, pleasant house that I could afford. But it was too late. The separation and all we had been through were too much, and like the marriages of too many other veterans I knew, ours broke up. It seemed too personal and melodramatic to pour it all out in a book for others to read about, and I gave up the novel. Roz and I split amicably, and, taking Diane with her under a divorce-court order that crushed me by permitting me custody of Diane only in the summers, she went back east and settled in New York. For a while I kept as busy as I could with what I had meanwhile been doing at MGM and with my work in veterans' affairs.

As for the American Veterans Committee, ultimately a deadly fight between Communist and Socialist veterans over control of some of the AVC's big urban chapters, particularly in the East, spread through much of the organization, demoralizing and causing the wholesale resignation of members, including myself. By 1950, many of us, helped by the GI bill, were tackling problems for ourselves or finding comradeship and assistance in the VFW, the Disabled American Veterans, the American Legion, or in local groups like the Veterans' Service League in Santa Monica, for the AVC had practically vanished from the scene. Most of all, the GI bill was in full operation, helping veterans get a college education and afford their own homes and remaking America by lifting millions of former servicemen and -women out of a blue-collar background to create by far the largest and most stable middle class that any nation had ever known.

Meanwhile, at about the same time as the end of my marriage, some friends introduced me to a wise, well-educated, and dazzlingly beautiful young woman named Betty Peet, who was full of fun and laughter. She had come out to Hollywood from her home in Greenwich, Connecticut, to visit her uncle, a well-known director, and had stayed and gotten a job as a social secretary to the actor Dick Powell and his actress wife, June Allyson. As we began to see each other regularly, often on one of MGM's soundstages, where Betty stood attendance on June Allyson, who was making the musical film *Good News*, sunlight and meaning came back into my life. Betty, who overflowed with compassion for others, had inherited asthma from her father and had suffered greatly from it since she was a child, and during one of our first dates, she had a severe attack and had to use a small bronchial inhaler. It was the first time I had seen one of those relief-bearing gadgets, and when my own asthma began to bother me a little later, I borrowed her inhaler. Eventually, Betty and I were married in a Presbyterian church in Santa Monica, and at our reception she had immense fun telling all her friends that I had married her for her asthma inhaler. But it was the start of a wonderfully happy new life for me. Extraordinarily loving and caring, Betty became a second mother for Diane, having her fly out from New York to our home in Santa Monica to spend each summer with us and be treated then and through the ensuing years as one of Betty's own children, in equality with the three that we had together.

During all of this postwar period of stress and change, I had been working as a contract staff writer at MGM, and at the studio and at dinner parties with Betty at Eddie and Mildred's house, I met Spencer Tracy, Gregory Peck, Greer Garson, Deborah Kerr, and other of their movie friends. At first, I came to believe that an exciting new day of realistic pictures might, after all, be dawning at MGM. Although nothing came of the studio's interest in my *Look* magazine war story, I was introduced to a producer named Sam Marx and given the job of writing a newsreel-like documentary sequence of the history of the building of the atom bomb, based on a famous official government report by Professor Henry DeWolf Smyth of Princeton University, to include in an important new feature picture called *The Beginning or the End*, with Brian Donlevy and Robert Walker, about the development of the bomb and the dropping of it on Hiroshima. The film's script was being written by the Hearst newspaper columnist Bob Considine, and it looked like the studio was producing a drama at last that would deal honestly with a serious subject that was on people's minds everywhere. But the high hopes soon vanished. The material proved too daunting for Mr. Mayer and his committee of studio executives and old-time senior producers, which was known within the industry as MGM's "college of cardinals," and after many script revisions by additional writers, arguments with specially hired atomic-scientist consultants whose advice the studio sought and then refused to follow, and flounderings over what the picture would say about whether or not the bomb should have been dropped, the movie, when it was finally released quietly in 1947, was full of silly melodramatic fabrications and Hollywood hokum.

In the meantime, among my possessions that Roz had shipped to me from our Washington apartment, I discovered the book of excerpts from diaries of nineteenth-century emigrants on the Oregon Trail that the

Northwest journalist Dick Neuberger had sent me just before I had left for Parris Island in 1943. For some reason, the diarists' vivid descriptions and feelings of a century earlier about covered wagon trains, pioneer families, and daily life and scenes along the Oregon Trail had a big impact on me, as if in reading their eyewitness, real-life history of the American West, I was not only rediscovering a subject of intensely dramatic interest that had lain deep within me since I had been a child gazing across the Hudson River and listening to my father's stories but was now finding a therapy that by helping me identify with the people and places of the West would make life exciting again.

With my appetite aroused by the Oregon Trail book, I discovered others, most notably Bernard De Voto's wonderfully evocative *The Year of Decision* and *Across the Wide Missouri*, as well as a host of published nineteenth-century diaries, journals, and personal accounts of travels and adventures in the West, and through them I became familiar with the details of the Lewis and Clark expedition, the Rocky Mountain fur trade, the Donner Party, the California gold rush, and many other of the West's great stories. Somewhat under the spell of my reading, I wrote an outline for a novel about a group of veterans of the War of 1812 who took up military bounty lands in Missouri, and to my surprise MGM took an option on it and assigned me to write it as an original for a film. Unhappily, when it was finished, MGM, with a few exceptions, had again become a citadel of "escape" pictures, which mine was not, and the option was not exercised.

During the same time, while I was working on the Missouri story and courting Betty, a lot of Hollywood writers, directors, and other creative people fell victim to an infamous outburst of Cold War anti-Communist hysteria. One day, Howard Emmett Rogers and John Lee Mahin, two veteran MGM writers with whom I had been friendly, asked me into one of their offices, and after locking the door and looking conspiratorial, they invited me to join them and some other studio people, including Mr. Mayer himself, in "getting rid of all the Reds at MGM." They started to name people whom they were going after, and recognizing that the ones I knew all seemed to be peaceable New Deal Democrats like myself and by no stretch of the imagination a threat or danger to the country, I had to laugh, and stopped them. Both of them, reflecting some sort of bullying insecurity, were sounding exactly like Hitler, or, more charitably, like melodramatic, crackpot right-wing extremists, to me no different or better than left-wing extremists.

But it was no laughing matter. With the help of them and their allies at MGM and other studios, the House Committee on Un-American Activities—headed by a seedy, publicity-seeking New Jersey congressman who himself later went to jail for taking kickbacks and padding his government payroll—launched a boisterous, demagogic investigation of Reds in Hollywood. The committee pried into and condemned people's beliefs, flouted their rights and liberties, and ended by sending to jail ten persons who refused to answer the committee's questions and causing, in addition, the thoroughly contemptible and un-American blacklisting for many years of scores of others who had been accused of nothing but their suspected beliefs. Among those who went to jail in this dark throwback to the eighteenth-century Alien and Sedition Acts that Thomas Jefferson had ended was Lester Cole, an MGM writer with whom I often lunched at the writers' table in the studio commissary, and among those who were blacklisted by all the studios and deprived of their livelihood as screenwriters were Fred Rinaldo and several other writers with whom I had worked as a junior writer at MGM in the mid-1930s.

The following year, Mr. Mayer at last got his own comeuppance. He was paying more attention to his racehorses than to MGM's films, many of which, because of their continued syrupy avoidance of true portrayals of life, were doing badly at the box office, and the studio's financial powers in New York, led by Nicholas Schenck, an enemy of Mayer, forced him to give up his role as head of production at MGM. His place was taken by Dore Schary, a talented and experienced writer-producer whom Schenck brought over from RKO and who, to Mr. Mayer's disgust, not only was well known in the industry as a New Deal Democrat but was an outspoken champion of realistic films that dealt honestly with serious subjects.

I was one among many at MGM who hailed Schary's arrival, and I was ready for him with another original story proposal. This one, called *Red Clay*, sprang from an inspiring article I had read in the *New York Times* about the soil-conservation efforts of the black and white populations of a poor rural county in western Georgia who were working to restore their land, which had been ravaged by a century of cotton-growing. Dore was enthusiastic about the proposal, and, preparatory to my writing a script, he sent me on a research trip to Georgia, where I stayed in an old plantation house in a pecan-tree grove as the guest of Judge Robert Tisinger, a political and civic leader of Carroll County, located in the red-clay area of the Georgia-Alabama border, where the picture was going to be made. The countryside was a poor but proud and friendly region of sharecroppers, time merchants, mule barns, and meals of corn pone, greens, and squirrel stew, but it was in the process of getting its first electricity from the federal government's Rural Electrification Administration, and most people were pulling together to restore the worn-out land and lift the county to prosperity. Just before I arrived there, a white high school girl had been raped at night, and suspicion had fallen on a local black man. While I was there, the black man was cleared, and suspicion was shifted to a local white minister, who was also one of the leaders of the land-restoration movement. The real rapist, a white high school student, was eventually identified, but the tense episode added another potential element for use in my story.

When I got back to Culver City, Eddie Knopf had been assigned to produce the picture, and Jan Fortune, a Texas author, had been hired to collaborate with me in writing the script. For several months, we all worked hard on it together, improving the characters and story from one draft to another, buoyed constantly by Schary and others in the studio who read our drafts and predicted that we were turning out a sure Academy Award nominee. But I should have known better. Schary had begun having troubles with Mayer's old colleagues in the college of cardinals, who were not taking easily to the new kinds of pictures that Schary was accepting. They were forcing him to compromise and even reject stories that he had originally accepted with enthusiasm, and one day, to our horror, Eddie Knopf informed us unhappily that the two most powerful studio men under Mayer, Eddie Mannix and Benny Thau, had decided that *Red Clay* "wasn't commercial enough" and would be shelved. There was no appeal. Schary apparently put up no fight for it, and the project and all our work and dreams were dead.

After that, I was determined to leave MGM. I stayed on for a while with another collaborator, Sally Benson, the author of the Junior Miss stories and the original material for the Judy Garland film *Meet Me in St. Louis,* working on a story idea for Arthur Freed, the producer of many of MGM's really glorious Judy Garland, Gene Kelly, and Fred Astaire musical films of that period. Sally, however, was on a regimen of wake-up pills with her morning coffee and go-to-sleep pills with a stiff drink after dinner, and half the nights she was either deathly sick or ordering me unsuccessfully over the telephone in her hoarse, imperious voice, amid coughing spells, at three or four in the morning to get up, come over, and go to work on our script. Freed soon lost interest in Sally and in what we were working on, and I then went on to another assignment with a new collaborator. I now knew that I was spinning wheels once again in Hollywood, and I wanted to get out. It wasn't going to be easy. Betty had given birth to a handsome, sturdy little boy, Alvin Josephy III, and a second baby was on its way. One just didn't walk out on financial commitments to a house and family.

One of my closest movie friends was a fiery little freelance writer-director named Sammy Fuller, who was always chewing on a long cigar and who had fought as a combat infantryman with the First Army Division in North Africa and all across Europe during the war. It was our combat war experiences that drew us together, but we also shared the desire to make honest, realistic pictures. Sammy's great dream was to make a film called *The Big Red One*, meaning the First Division, about his experiences in the war, but although it would be almost thirty years before he would be able to raise the money for it—and then it would be acclaimed as one of the great war movies of all time—he had been successful in making other hard-boiled, realistic pictures. One night, we had dinner in a Chinese restaurant in Hollywood, and he started pounding my back playfully and jabbing his finger into my stomach. "Your problem is easy," he said. "Go freelance. Get the hell out of MGM, and make your agent get to work for you and your stories."

He was right. But before I could do anything about it, a promise of rescue came from another, wholly new direction. James Parton, an old friend from Harvard and chief of the Time-Life Los Angeles Bureau, had been assigned by Henry Luce, the head of Time, Inc., to start a new, innovative Time-owned daily newspaper for huge, sprawling Los Angeles County. Jim bought up thirty local papers in different parts of the county, each of which, under Time's scheme, would carry the same national and international news and advertising but would tailor the local news and advertising to their own areas. He invited me to come work with him; the only hitch was that until he got going, he couldn't pay me a living wage. But I jumped at the opportunity to join him and worked out a routine whereby I would continue to make my living by writing for the movies as long as necessary but would apportion my spare time to Jim as a consultant and a weekly columnist on California and national political affairs until he could afford to pay me full-time.

While it lasted, it was a nice arrangement. Accepting Sammy Fuller's advice, I got an agent, parted on a friendly basis from Eddie Knopf and a lot of well-wishers at MGM, and as a freelance writer at United Artists and Warner Bros. began to sell original stories and to work on movies with titles like *Operation Secret*, *Indictment*, and *Something for the Birds*, all of which got produced, although none of them was particularly distinguished or memorable. My contracts were written to allow me to work either at the studios or at home and deliver my movie scripts to my producers by certain dates, giving me a lot of free hours to devote to Jim's project, which for a time seemed on the road to success. It was working so well, in fact, that Hearst and the Chandlers, who owned the *Los Angeles Times*, finally panicked and threatened Luce and Time's directors with an

all-out newspaper war in Los Angeles that would also spill over into a costly, and perhaps violent, newsstand offensive against *Time, Life,* and other Luce magazines. All of a sudden, Luce's board decided to abandon the newspaper project, and Jim was ordered to liquidate everything and get rid of the thirty papers he had acquired as quickly as possible.

At a nighttime luau (an elaborate Hawaiian feast) on the beach at Santa Monica, Betty and I (center, me in profile) were among friends and staff members celebrating the first anniversary of Herb Chase's string of weekly newspapers.

The assets included seven local weekly papers in Santa Monica, Beverly Hills, and other communities on the west side of Los Angeles, and they were purchased by a friend of mine and a former marine, Herb Chase, who asked me to continue writing a weekly column and working with him as managing editor of the papers. It took little persuading and, continuing to support myself by my movie writing, I spent two days each week and almost every night meeting the stiff demands of the weekly newspapers. With Herb, it was great fun, but it soon became dangerous. Assisted by a private detective, who had come to us for help when his life was threatened because he had learned too much about a local bookmaking establishment, we launched an investigation of our own, discovering the presence in Santa Monica of some nationally known mobsters who were connected to the old Al Capone gang in Chicago and were running an illegal gambling operation that permeated all strata of the city's life and paid protection money to a "bagman" for the attorney general of California and to law-enforcement officials in Santa Monica and the city and county of Los Angeles.

During our investigation, and prior to our publishing what we had discovered, unsuccessful attempts were made to harass, intimidate, and bribe Herb, Betty, and me. A telephone company official who had supplied phones and wire-service facilities to the gambling parlors tapped our home telephone line; members of a notorious Mafia group known as the Detroit Purple Gang, who had driven over from Tucson, Arizona, and were identified by their license plates, sat menacingly in a car on our street, watching our house for several days; and an attempt was made in a backyard meeting at a home in Santa Monica to force a fat wad of bills into my hand as a "gift" for our second child, whose birth was expected shortly. Our great problem was that the corruption was so pervasive that we felt there was no law-enforcement official whom we could trust and who would protect us when we started running articles about our findings.

Betty and I in a Boston hotel during a publicity tour promoting The Captive City, *the 1952 film starring Joan Camden and John Forsythe based on our experiences with organized crime in Santa Monica.*

Fortunately, just when we were about ready to pull back the curtain and reveal to our readers the Santa Monica criminal organizations that were waxing fat on the "innocent" two-dollar bets that citizens made with neighborhood store owners, Senator Estes Kefauver, with his investigating committee on organized crime, arrived in Los Angeles to hold hearings on the situation in Southern California. Simultaneously with the start of the publishing of our articles, we gave an earful to the senator and the members of the press who were covering his hearings. Stories, resignations, arrests, and a movie that I wrote based on our experiences, *The Captive City*, followed. A lot of talented people made the movie, including the actor John Forsythe, the directors Robert Wise and Mark Robson, and the cinematographer Lee Garmes. But Betty and I didn't stick around to see the movie made.

At one of Jim Parton's dinner parties, I met Dana Tasker, the executive editor of *Time* magazine, who was on a visit from New York. We talked together much of the evening, and Tasker, a former English teacher at Amherst and a stickler for precision in writing, told me to call him the next time I was in the East. A month or so later, I let him know that I was coming east for a few days, and he telegraphed back almost immediately. "Call when you get here," he wired, "and we'll have lunch together. I have something for you to ponder."

15 ✛ INDIANS

Tasker, a tall, stimulating man in his early fifties, intellectually sharp and combative, was in charge of *Time*'s illustrations, weekly covers, and other special elements. Occupying about the same rank on the magazine as Roy Alexander, *Time*'s managing editor, he was close to Henry Luce and was known to the editorial staff as a hard-boiled perfectionist who frequently returned to chagrined editors interoffice memos that they had written to him and that he had pencil-edited for improved grammar, punctuation, sentence structure, or choice of words. At *Time*'s Rockefeller Center head-quarters in New York, I found out what he had in mind.

It was now 1951, and to mark the start of the second half of the twenti-eth century, Luce several months earlier had sent around a long memo-randum describing various important improvements and additions that he wanted *Time* to adopt, and he had put Tasker in charge of carrying out two of them. The first was the use of occasional color features in the magazine, which up to that time was printed entirely in black and white, and the sec-ond was the inclusion each week of a black-and-white spread of outstand-ing news photographs to be called "News in Pictures." Tasker needed somebody to get both projects under way, and Luce had told him not to raid the *Life* staff or use anybody from *Time*. ("They're writers, they won't know anything about pictures," he had told Tasker.) Instead, he directed Tasker to find somebody new who could write but who would also know a good picture when he saw one. Parton, who had once been an assistant to Luce, had apparently recommended me highly to Tasker, who, it seemed, had then done some checking of his own. "The job is yours if you want it," he said to me.

I wasn't sure that I wanted it, which would have meant going back to live in the East and work in New York. But Betty, who had given birth to a darling little girl, whom we named Allison, had been suffering terribly from her asthma, which was getting worse from an almost daily ocean fog that reached our Santa Monica home from one direction and from the increasingly bad smog and air pollution that had begun to extend toward us from the inland Los Angeles Basin. Time and again, her asthma had become so bad that we had dropped everything and, with Betty half-asleep in the car and pulling desperately for breath, had raced to a guest ranch run by a friend of ours two hours away out in the Mojave Desert near Victorville, where the high, dry air brought her miraculously rapid relief. We had even decided finally to buy a small desert ranch of our own for her health and had come close to doing so when we discovered that the exact sparsely inhabited Mojave Desert area where we were planning to buy was about to be converted by a syndicate of Long Beach investors into a huge, sprawling housing development and urban center named Apple Valley.

The deciding factor, however, was the job itself. As Tasker described it, I, as a *Time* contributing editor, would be responsible for the weekly "News in Pictures" feature but also, as head of my own new department, known as Color Projects, would produce approximately every other week a news feature of from two to sixteen pages. It would be printed in color within one or another of *Time*'s other departments, such as National Affairs, Medicine, Business, Art, and so forth, and would include photographs taken especially for this purpose, as well as captions and text story to run with them. In our conversation, moreover, Tasker realized my unhappiness that I would have to live again in the East, and we worked out an agreement that allowed me to travel extensively, doing whatever field research I felt was necessary to find subjects, gather information for the story, and write "shooting scripts" for the photographers.

Back in Santa Monica, Betty was delighted with the news that we would be leaving California, which she had come to equate with her physical suffering, and that I would try to find a house for us in Greenwich, Connecticut. An hour outside of New York City, Greenwich was where she had been raised and where she had many friends and knew tradesmen and doctors whose presence would give her security and comfort. While I packed up and returned to New York to start my new job, she stayed behind briefly with Alvin and Allison, getting everything packed and shipped and selling the Santa Monica house. Meanwhile, I located a new home in Greenwich, which was ready when she and the children arrived.

On my first day at *Time*, Tasker told me that Mr. Luce, whom he called Harry, wanted to meet me and that we were going to have lunch with him. I had visions of the great, internationally powerful publisher taking us to one of his clubs or to a pricey restaurant, where we would have a relaxed, interesting conversation, but he disappointed me by leading us instead into a downstairs coffee shop, where we perched on stools at a counter, hustling down a fast-food meal among swarms of noisy Rockefeller Center tourists. Nevertheless, as he discussed his hopes for the success of the color projects, suggesting fields like architecture, medical advances, and education to explore for newsworthy pictorial subjects, as well as what to stay away from, he awed me as a man of formidable likes and dislikes, of unique, unconventional thinking that buttressed and gave freshness and vitality to his views, and of contagious, almost naïve enthusiasms for whatever seemed to him new, exciting, and worth knowing about.

Time's editorial staff, with most of whose members I soon became friendly, included many unusual, self-confident characters, gathered, it seemed, from the ends of the earth. Among them were Eldon Griffiths, an arrogant young English writer on foreign affairs, who made a bet with some of us that one day he would be a minister in a Conservative British cabinet and then a few years later won his bet; Mark Vishniak, an elderly expert on Russian affairs with a mysterious Menshevik background; Irving Berlin's lovely daughter, Mary Ellin, a researcher who stashed her salary checks in her desk and never seemed to need to cash them; and *Time*'s picture editor, John McCullough, who hired the freelance photographers for our color projects, and with whom I started working almost immediately on experimental dummy layouts for both "News in Pictures" and the color stories. A stout, pudgy man with curly hair, McCullough, who also lived in Greenwich, was a belligerent anti-Communist and an ardent supporter of Alger Hiss's nemesis, Whittaker Chambers, a *Time* editor who had resigned from the magazine a few years earlier, leaving a staff that, when I arrived, was still divided bitterly between those who believed Chambers's testimony about Hiss, a former State Department official, being a Communist conspirator and those who did not. But McCullough had gone further. With his wife, he had recently caused an uproar by accusing two nationally known celebrities, Paul Draper, a dancer, and Larry Adler, a musician, of being Communists. When I arrived at *Time*, Draper and Adler were suing the McCulloughs, whom they had elevated into something like national figures themselves, making them temporarily penniless by tying up all their funds and bank accounts until the suit was finally settled to the McCulloughs' satisfaction. In the office, meanwhile, McCullough sometimes grinned about his predicament, but he frequently complained that the state of his finances was really no joke.

A year and a half after I began work with them, both Tasker and McCullough left *Time* to join *Look*, but, promoted to associate editor, I stayed happily at *Time* during the entire decade of the 1950s, presiding over the production of more than two hundred color projects on a wide range of subjects: from the newly completed St. Lawrence Seaway, industry's increasing use of automation, the state of cancer research, the growth of mechanized farming, the building of America's national interstate highway system, and new developments in oceanography to the wine-producing region of Burgundy, France, the proposed British Caribbean Federation in the West Indies, and the city of Los Angeles. But I had to get around and see things for myself, and a good many of the projects had me traveling, doing my own field research for the stories and writing detailed instruction scripts for the photographers and occasional signed editorial pieces for the magazine on significant broadscale trends that I had observed in my travels.

The projects that had the most appeal for me were those that reminded me of the theme of the General Motors Futurama at the 1939 New York World's Fair and told the reader how the American people were going through possibly the fastest transition in their history, conquering nature, developing their resources, and changing the face of the country. As an example, in preparing for an eight-page color spread on the many big dams and other flood-control, navigation, hydroelectric, and irrigation works with which the Army Corps of Engineers and the Interior Department's Bureau of Reclamation were remaking the vast basin of the Missouri River in the Middle American heartland, which had been ravaged by dust storms as well as by overflowing rivers, I toured the region just as a new catastrophic flood came roaring down the Missouri toward Omaha. My plane could get me no closer to Omaha than Des Moines, from where I took a taxi across half of Iowa, arriving at Omaha in time to pitch in and help pile sandbags along the banks of the raging mud-colored river. Afterward, I rode in little planes with Corps of Engineers personnel over the flooded Missouri Valley, writing excitedly of a proposed Missouri Valley Authority, like another TVA, and of the federal government's Pick-Sloan Plan (named for the head of the Army Corps of Engineers and a Bureau of Reclamation official) to build hundreds of miles of straitjacket levees and scores of large and small dams and reservoirs to "harness," as they put it, the Big Muddy and its tributaries and prevent future disastrous floods in the watershed.

Farther west, on the same project, I rode in other small planes over the eastern foothills of the Front Range of the Rockies with members of the Bureau of Reclamation, joining them in peering down through binoculars and shouting like an explorer above the noise of the plane's single engine, "There's another great place for a dam!" I must have been good at it, for each time any of us, including myself, sang out, we circled the spot, while the Bureau of Reclamation officials made maps and notations in the notebooks on their clipboards. In retrospect, they were proud at the time of their spectacular Colorado–Big Thompson Project, which would boost western-slope water backward over the Continental Divide and send it out to irrigate projects on the eastern Colorado plains, and they seemed rather overly eager to build more and more dams and other ambitious projects. To me, at the time, the junket was part of an admirable process of overcoming nature and developing America. To them, as time and changed perspectives eventually made clear to me, the trip's major motive was to find new projects to present to Congress to keep them and their colleagues employed and to justify the budget requests for their salaries and expenses—a motive as old as the federal bureaucracy.

The intensity of my prodevelopment feelings during the 1950s led me and our color projects trustingly down many wrong roads. At the Hanford plutonium-producing center in the state of Washington, where I did research for part of a color project on the expanding U.S. atomics industry, I swallowed hook, line and sinker the positive assurances of government and industry spokespersons that huge state-of-the-art single-walled tanks buried in vast earthen storage pits would safely hold the site's lethal radioactive wastes for thousands of years. Yet by the 1980s, the deadly wastes that they had buried in the pits were already leaking dangerously into the ground. In another of our projects, we illustrated modern tree farming of the timber industry in the Northwest, buying in ignorance from the Forest Service and logging company executives their arguments in praise of the mangy clear-cutting of mountainsides, total fire suppression, and other practices that were later shown to have been disastrous to the forests. At the same time, in color projects on dam building on the Snake River; on Americans, with the help of airconditioning, learning to live, work, and play in the deserts of the Southwest; and on the huge Columbia Basin irrigation project in the Big Bend country of Washington, my enthusiasm listening to engineers, developers, and other builders of the future blinded me to adverse impacts like falling water tables, urban sprawl, disruption of ecosystems, air and water pollution, the near demise of the Columbia River's great salmon runs, and the endangerment of other species.

Occasionally, Mr. Luce looked over my shoulder. Projects that I did on U.S. Air Force research and development, space medicine, continental air defense, rocketry, and other cutting-edge science and military subjects of the 1950s enthused him, and he was delighted in 1955 with something that had never been done before, an eight-page spread of color photographs of the Lewis and Clark trail that we ran to observe the 150th anniversary of the expedition. By the time I planned that project, I figured that I had already traveled some 225,000 miles by plane, train, car, marsh buggy and on horseback and afoot in the United States, Europe, and North Africa on stories for *Time* that had often taken me far from journalism's usual beaten paths. Now, armed with Lewis and Clark's journals, I traveled almost their entire route across the western half of the United States from St. Louis to the Pacific Ocean, finding among the rivers, mountain ranges, and forested wilderness many places where nothing had changed since the explorers had written their descriptions of what they had seen and experienced. In the shooting script that I prepared for Bradley Smith, our photographer on the project, I directed him to keep all signs of civilization out of his pictures and to take them as if he were standing next to the expedition's leaders, observing with them the wondrous sights of the West. He returned with an amazing number of magnificent transparencies of almost the whole route, and after we made our final selections, I ran beneath them excerpts from the explorers' journals, describing scenes that still looked exactly as they had in 1805. Although many writers, photographers, and publications later did what we did, our research and exciting photographic journeys made us feel like pioneers ourselves and made me feel personally that I had finally begun to experience the thrilling, real-life, adventurous West of my childhood fantasies.

From time to time, Luce, to my consternation, demonstrated his own powerful dislikes. For an Easter issue one year, I planned with our managing editor, Roy Alexander, and the editor of our Religion Department a spread of color photographs of European cathedrals that had been associated with the history of the Crusades in the Middle Ages. After months of work by several eminent photographers whose evocative "mood" pictures showed us such scenes as where Richard the Lion-Hearted had taken the cross and begun his journey to the Holy Land, Luce came on us while we were laying out our spreads, and after learning what the project was all about, he ordered it killed immediately. It seemed that at the time, Luce, whose family had been Christian missionaries in China and who occasionally seemed to be carrying the cross himself, was waging an editorial war against the anti-Western, oil-nationalizing Iranian prime minister Mohammed Mossadegh, and had broadened his hostility to include all of Islam in general. "The Crusades were Christendom's greatest defeat," he snapped. "There is no reason to remind the world about it today." So we dropped the project.

Luce directed even more anger against American Indians, and for a long while, until the 1970s, there was a ridiculous unspoken, but understood, blanket prohibition against running any story in *Time* about Indians. Luce simply did not like them and called them "phonies" because they refused to give up their reservations and live like everyone else, making their own way and paying taxes and stopping all their complaints and demands on the government. He had a simple and commonly held view about it. The whole history of the world was one of somebody conquering somebody else. Western Europeans had conquered the Indians. It was done. Accept it and get on with the modern world. Unhappily, in one way or another, his anti-Indian prejudice was accepted passively by *Time*'s editors. Though Luce might have killed it before it got very far, I had an unsuccessful time, for instance, trying to persuade Alexander Eliot, *Time*'s art editor, to agree to a color project on American Indian art, which was beginning to be collected and shown all over the world. "It's not art," he insisted. "It's all purple horses and beads and crafts and stuff for tourists."

At the same time, ironically, Luce played an unknowing role in bringing me together with a nation of Indians who influenced and changed the rest of my life. One September, I was in Los Angeles, about to go to Salt Lake City to begin research for a color project on the state of Utah when I got a call from New York with word that Luce's plane had had to make a forced landing at Boise, Idaho, that during his wait he had been shown around some of that state by the owner of the Boise newspaper and had been very impressed by what he had seen, and that he wanted me to "forget Utah and do Idaho." So I changed my plans and went to Idaho, which, along with its neighbor Oregon, was at the time one of the few states in which I had not yet been.

From the beginning, it was an unforgettable trip. On the way north, one of the two engines on our Western Airlines DC-3 airplane caught fire. Watching the flames anxiously, we circled around and around until we could set down safely on a small airfield near Delta in the western Utah desert. Another plane, sent from Salt Lake City to get us, had a hard time landing on the short runway among the sagebrush and an even more difficult time getting us back in the air again, and by the time I reached Pocatello, Idaho, in a roundabout way to Boise, I was far behind schedule. After that, our plane, following the historic Oregon Trail route across the Snake River plains of southern Idaho, flew above a succession of scenic wonders: huge black splotches on the desert floor, formed by fantastic flows and eruptions of lava thousands of years ago; deep sunken gorges of the river, which made the flat plains look like a tabletop that had been ripped apart; immense tawny buttes; thin streams of waterfalls that issued from the rocks of canyon walls; and "lost" rivers that disappeared in the sagebrush. With the Sawtooth and other majestic Idaho mountain ranges always in the background, we reached Boise, where Paul Nash, a tall, slender man in his seventies who was secretary of the Idaho Chamber of Commerce, bundled me into a small plane and for the next four days, without letup of sensational subjects to photograph, introduced me around the state.

Luce was right. Idaho was a stupendous, rugged country of colorful frontierlike towns and resourceful, fiercely independent-minded populations that were used to outdoor living and were still close to their pioneer heritage. Paul Nash had had in-laws, for example, who as children had come across the country with a Mormon handcart brigade in the middle of the nineteenth century, and there were many elderly persons still alive who could remember Idaho's Indian wars. People with such a heritage did not view it as history, but as a family affair and nobody else's business. They had had little need to worry about that. With few natural corridors through the state's maze of mountains for highways or railroads, it was one of the least-known and least-visited states, though I thought that it deserved to be better known, a realization that hit me with particular force in northern Idaho's warm "Banana Belt" town of Lewiston, nestled among towering hills at the intersection of the Snake and Clearwater rivers.

Nash and I had landed there after a long, spectacular flight through another of Idaho's great natural wonders, the awesome Hells Canyon stretch of the Snake River, the deepest gorge on the North American continent. Joined the next morning by Harry Hughes, the manager of the Lewiston Chamber of Commerce, and by the public-relations head of Potlatch Forest's paper and pulp plant, the town's largest industry, we toured around a bit and then stopped at the agency headquarters building on the nearby Nez Perce Indian reservation, where my three companions left me at the front counter while they did some business visiting with the agent. There was a tall, good-looking young Indian named Bill Stevens at the counter. He had heard that I was with *Time* magazine and he proceeded to tell me of some of the tribe's problems and complaints. Finally, he said to me, "You know, the way things are going these days, if we had half a chance, you'd see the damndest Indian uprising that ever took place."

It sounded very melodramatic to me, and when we got back in the car and drove off, I told the other three what the Indian had said. They kind of laughed, and Harry Hughes, who had come originally from Alabama before the war to command a Civilian Conservation Corps unit in the woods of Idaho and had then settled in Lewiston and later, during the war, had served as a colonel on General MacArthur's staff, asked if I knew anything about the tribe. I replied, "No," and he said with a serious expression, "Well, they once fought a war against the United States and beat four American armies."

Despite my interest in Ira Hayes, I still knew very little about most American Indian tribes and nothing at all about the Nez Perces, whose name did not ring dramatically for me like those of the Sioux, Arapaho, Comanche, or any of the other great historic tribes and whose best-known leader, Chief Joseph, sounded like an uninteresting, mission-controlled Indian. I had also never heard of the war that Hughes was talking about, although my companions were living with the idea that everybody in the world must be familiar with it because it had been such an unusual and fascinating conflict. Before I left Lewiston, they gave me some locally published books and pamphlets about the Nez Perces and their war, and after I began to read them, I could see what they meant.

During the nineteenth century, the Nez Perces (who received that name from French-Canadian fur trappers) had been familiar to many Americans. They had lived principally in northern Idaho, but also in what became southeastern Washington and northeastern Oregon, and, most importantly to the United States, they had helped to save the lives of members of the Lewis and Clark expedition, rescuing them from starvation in Idaho's mountains in 1805, assisting them to continue their journey to the Pacific Ocean, and for a long time playing host to them during their return trip to the East in 1806. In the explorers' colorful account of their journey, they wrote glowingly about the Nez Perce people, making the country aware of their honorable qualities, their warm and generous friendliness to Americans, and their many skills and talents, including their expertise in breeding horses.

For years, the Nez Perces got on in peace and friendship with American fur trappers, missionaries, miners, settlers, and military leaders who entered their country and wrote popular books of their adventures in the West that continued to praise the Nez Perces as a superior tribe of Indians. Then, in 1877, in an unconscionable act of treachery—tricking the leader of one of the Nez Perce bands into selling the lands of some of the other bands of the tribe—the federal government ordered the victimized groups to leave their homelands, on which they had lived for centuries and which the United States only a few years earlier had guaranteed by solemn treaty to protect for the Indians forever, and concentrate all of their people on a tiny, cramped reservation. The injustice of the government's action exploded into a war, in which the Nez Perces astounded the whites by resisting the American military in a "civilized" manner, devoid of scalping, torture, injuries to noncombatant tourists whom the Nez Perces captured during their flight through the newly created Yellowstone National Park, or other acts that white stereotypical thinking commonly associated with Indian conflicts.

The war's series of eighteen large and small battles, waged over several months and watched with growing wonder by the entire country, highlighted a desperate fifteen-hundred-mile fighting retreat by the tribe across much of the West toward hoped-for safety in Canada. Trying to evade capture and encumbered by their women, children, sick people, and elders, as well as by their horse herds and other possessions, the Nez Perces outmaneuvered and defeated one pursuing army after another, forces led by veteran officers of the Civil War. It was called by some people Chief Joseph's War, for the civil chief of one of the Nez Perce bands, a remarkable, statesmanlike Indian who had received his white man's name from missionaries and whom the government ousted cruelly with his people from their ancestral homeland in northeastern Oregon. Identifying him erroneously as their principal military opponent and unaware that councils of war, hunting, and civil chiefs from the different bands, and not Joseph alone, were directing the Indians' resistance, the army commanders covered the embarrassment of their defeats by publicizing Joseph as a "Red Napoléon," and when the war was over, they went on to teach what they supposed were his tactics in a class at West Point. Meanwhile, Joseph, one of the few Indian headmen who survived the war, gained added prestige from an eloquent speech of surrender that he delivered after about the fifth army to oppose the Nez Perces finally managed to surround them on the freezing plains of northern Montana, less than forty miles from the Canadian border.

Joseph and other Nez Perce prisoners were sent temporarily into exile in Oklahoma, then known as the Indian Territory, where many of them became sick and died. Their attempts to be allowed to return to their homeland gained for them a second round of national attention, but when at last they were permitted to go back to the Northwest, though not to their former homes, they and the courageous war they had fought drifted from the memories of non-Indians. By the early years of the twentieth century, both Chief Joseph and the great fighting retreat of the Nez Perces were almost forgotten by most of the American people.

Even related sparingly and unsatisfactorily in the chamber of commerce–like journalistic accounts, written with little passion or understanding for the Indians and given to me in Lewiston, it was, indeed, a great story, a deeply moving American epic. And if I had never heard it, I figured that millions of other Americans had never heard it, either. But there was a lot missing, notably the Indians' versions of all that had happened. Also, almost everything that I read dealt primarily with the war, and, save for references to the Nez Perces' meeting with Lewis and Clark, this material told me little or nothing about the prewar history of the tribe and its relations with whites and the federal government prior to the events that brought on the war. Moreover, so little was included about the details of the forced removal of the Indians from their lands that it was hard to understand what had possessed the government to commit such an injustice.

For a long time after my return to New York, the notion kept recurring to me that the history of the Nez Perces, a wonderful story with a grand theme, was just sitting there waiting to be written. Somebody, I thought, ought to write it, employing as much new material as possible, and bringing those Indians back into the knowledge and conscience of the American people. At first, I gave no serious thought to the idea that I might be the writer. I knew too little about Indians, and I would have had to devote too much time and attention, perhaps for years, to learn not only about the Nez Perces but about many other Indian tribes, as well as about Lewis and Clark, other explorers, fur trappers, miners, government officials, and everyone else who had had a significant impact on the Nez Perces at one time or another.

Soon afterward, however, Betty accompanied me on a summer-vacation drive across the country, back to the friends I had made in Idaho, where I thought she might incidentally like to look for that small western ranch with clean, dry air that we had talked about buying when we lived in California but that we had not found. At Caldwell, in southern Idaho, we stopped to visit Jim Gipson, the owner of the Caxton Press, one of the best regional book-publishing firms in the Northwest. Hearing of my interest in the Nez Perce story, he presented me with two marvelous books that he had published in small editions in recent years, *Yellow Wolf* and *Hear Me, My Chiefs*, both of them the dedicated work of a late great Washington State rancher friend of the Nez Perces named Lucullus McWhorter and both containing in voluminous detail and for the first time the Nez Perce version of many particulars of their tribal history and of the 1877 war. They were major finds for me, supplying not only massive cultural and historical corrections and additions to the white men's writings on the tribe that I had been reading but also Indian interpretations, points of view, and descriptions of people and events that made the Nez Perces come alive as three-dimensional, real persons, rather than faceless stereotypes.

After leaving Caldwell and establishing ourselves at Lewiston, I spent a day among McWhorter's yet-uncataloged papers in the library of what at that time was known as Washington State College at Pullman, acquiring a wealth of additional information about the Nez Perces. Betty then had to leave me and fly home, but with the help of Bill Johnston, the managing editor of the *Lewiston Tribune*, Marcus Ware, a prominent local attorney, and other Lewiston friends who knew and were trusted by the Nez Perces, I visited their reservation and began to meet and talk to many of the Indians. The Nez Perces were open and friendly to me, flattered that an editor of *Time* magazine from New York was showing an interest in them, and impressed that from my reading I already seemed to know accurately and sympathetically much about their history and about prominent Nez Perce individuals of the past and their qualities and exploits. Soon, I counted numerous helpful friends on the reservation, including Angus Wilson, the tribal chairman, Allen Slickpoo, the tribe's historian, the members of the tribe's governing executive committee, and the Nez Perces' three surviving veterans of the 1877 war, Albert Moore, Sam Tilden, and Josiah Red Wolf.

The scars of the war and its aftermath were still evident. The tribe was deeply split between what they called "Christians" and "heathens," the former being the descendants of missionary-influenced Nez Perces, numbering a majority of the tribe, who had accepted the small reservation, did not participate in the war, and regarded Joseph as a troublemaker whom the army, they had thought, would probably hang. When the war's survivors returned from Oklahoma, the "Christian" element wanted nothing to do with Chief Joseph, and I found his descendants and those of his followers still living among other tribes in exile on the Colville Indian reservation in the state of Washington, where Joseph had died in 1904 and was buried. Feelings between the two Nez Perce factions were still so strong that the "heathens" informed me with dismay that on Memorial Day, Nez Perce schoolchildren on the reservation decorated the graves of cavalrymen who had fought their people, and I had to visit the Colville reservation to find anyone who would admit openly to being related to Chief Joseph.

By the time I drove back east, I had changed my mind and was firmly committed to writing a narrative history that would make Chief Joseph and the injustice done to the Nez Perce Indians once again well known. But the scope of the work would be enormous. From the time of Lewis and Clark until the tribe lost its freedom in the 1877 war, it had been intimately associated with most of the historic events of the opening and development of the Northwest by whites, and to a large extent the Nez Perces' history was one of an interrelationship with the history of the non-Indians. What I had decided to do was to write an interracial book from the point of view of somebody standing on the moon, looking at a certain part of the earth, the American Northwest, seeing it become the homeland of the ancestors of the Nez Perces perhaps twenty thousand years

Our whole family, assembled in Greenwich for a formal picture in the 1950s. In front, from left, are Alvin III, Kathy, me, Betty, Allison, and our two dogs. Diane, the oldest, towers in the rear.

ago, then eventually seeing other people, whites from different parts of Europe and America, arrive in the area, gradually intermix with and surround the Nez Perce people, and finally overrun and take the area, as well as freedom, from the Indians.

So, as my research partner in this undertaking, Betty cleared a space in the corner of our bedroom (we had had another daughter, Kathy, and until we added a study to our house, we were out of rooms in which I could work), and there I set up my typewriter on a bridge table, and fashioned long boards and cinder blocks into shelves along a wall for my research books and papers. With Betty sleeping in the living room until I called it quits at two or three or four in the morning, I worked on the book at night and on weekends. Off and on, the history took me about twelve years to write. During that time, I read everything I could find on Indians that seemed relevant to the project. I became bleary-eyed wading through anthropological, archaeological, and ethnological journals, and I studied in exquisite detail the iconography and cartography of the West and pursued unpublished documentary materials from public and private sources ranging from the Hawaiian Mission Children's Society in Honolulu to the Hudson's Bay Company archives in London and the law offices of Wilkinson, Cragun & Barker and other attorneys for tribes in Washington, D.C.

Early on in my research, I was again in Washington State for *Time* and decided to make a quick visit to Chief Joseph's homeland in the northeastern corner of neighboring Oregon and see the country of present-day Wallowa County, from which the government had so unjustly driven Joseph's band of Nez Perces and started the 1877 war. It would be my first visit to the state about which I had dreamed for so many years, and I made my plans as if they merited some sort of special observance or celebration, calling ahead to Gwen Coffin, the publisher of the county's weekly newspaper, announcing my long interest in Oregon and welcoming his generous invitation to show me around his county and to have lunch at his home with his wife, Gladys.

Wallowa County was almost as large as Connecticut but had a population of only about six thousand. It lay in a remote and dead-end part of the state, bounded on the south and the west by majestic mountainous country and on the north and east, by an immense rugged area of steep, grassy basalt canyons that fingered down to the Snake River's Hells Canyon. Nestled inside the county amid a variety of largely uninhabited terrain— deep forests and lush alpine meadows, Kansas-like plains, a wilderness of snowcapped mountains, and the canyons—the bulk of the population, supported mostly by logging and cattle ranching, lived in four small towns along a river that issued from a spectacular moraine-hemmed glacial lake and wound beneath the mountains through three sparkling green valleys that gave the county the picture-postcard countenance of a Swiss landscape.

Driving along the walls of tall canyons on hairpin-turn gravel roads that still lacked guardrails to get into or out of the county was not exactly family motoring, but the adventure of the primitive roads, glimpses of elk and deer in the woods, and the occasional sight of old weather-beaten structures with frontier-style false fronts and strong-looking men in cowboy gear on horseback on the wide western streets of the little towns gave me a strange feeling that I was coming back to a long-familiar place. The Coffins were warm and friendly hosts with strong FDR-Democratic political views that matched many of my own, and after lunch, Gwen drove me around the county, showing me its many splendors. That night, I phoned Betty back in Connecticut, telling her that I had seen the most beautiful place in the world and that we should buy our ranch there.

It was several more years, however, before Betty could join me in another visit to Wallowa County, and then she agreed with me, feeling, in addition to her delighted reactions to the beauty and serenity of the region, that the high, dry mountain air would be good for her asthma. At first, I had guilt feelings about purchasing land from which the Nez Perces had been dispossessed, but that inhibition gradually evaporated as we discussed the matter with an increasing number of Nez Perce friends and after the tribe itself, because of government and intratribal technicalities, rejected an opportunity to acquire some county property offered to them. Eventually, we had a county realty firm look for a small residential ranch for us, and meanwhile we made frequent visits to the Wallowa country, sometimes staying with new-made friends and at other times renting places for extended stays while we familiarized ourselves with what we hoped would become our family's summer home and our ultimate place of retirement.

During my continuing research for my Nez Perce book, I occasionally discovered or corrected something that seemed to deserve an article of its own. In 1955, I paused long enough on the book to write an article entitled "The Naming of the Nez Perces" for the Montana Historical Society's magazine revealing the first recorded use of the name Nez Perce for members of the tribe by the French-speaking fur trappers, and seven years later contributed an article, "The Origins of the Nez Perce Indians," to the Idaho Historical Society's journal. But the greatest interruption occurred in 1958 when I wrote an article on Chief Joseph and the Nez Perce war for *American Heritage* magazine. The publication received a large mail response and many requests for rights to reprint the article, reflecting again how many people at the time were unfamiliar with the story. At the request of the National Park Service, I turned over all rights to the article to the Yellowstone Association, a nonprofit organization dedicated to service to some of the western national parks and their visitors, and the association has kept the article in print ever since as a small illustrated booklet, using income from its sales to purchase artifacts for a museum at the Big Hole National Battlefield of the Nez Perce War.

At the same time, Malcolm Cowley and editor Pascal "Pat" Covici at Viking Press asked me to interrupt my work on the Nez Perce book to do a volume immediately for Viking composed of chapters like the Chief Joseph article, each on a different great Indian leader of the past. I agreed to do so, and when that book, titled *The Patriot Chiefs*, came out in 1961, it received excellent reviews, largely I think because I had written the chapters like the *American Heritage* article, integrating biographies of Pontiac, Tecumseh, Crazy Horse, and other famous chiefs with the history and cultural background of their tribes so that, as in the Nez Perce book which I had temporarily put aside, I could convey my material with a maximum amount of contextual knowledge and understanding. In addition, Indians liked the book immensely. Soon after it came out, I received a telephone call from Edison Realbird, the chairman of the Crow tribe in Montana, and at the time a stranger to me, inviting Betty and me to a buffalo barbecue to be given in our honor on the Crow reservation. The book had reached them, and they especially liked the title. "This is the first time that anyone has ever referred to us Indians as patriots," he explained.

Initially, however, the book's sales were disappointing. My agent and friends tried to console me by telling me that, despite my interest in Indians, they were not "in" in mainstream America. Tucked away on their reservations, they were "vanishing Americans," "out of sight and out of mind," interesting only to missionaries, stuffy anthropologists, government agents, and museum directors who collected arrowheads and pieces of broken pottery. I walked up and down Fifth Avenue, stopping in at every bookstore along the way and discovering a lot of truth in what my agent and friends had said. In every store, books on Indians, including a copy or two of *The Patriot Chiefs*, were placed nowhere near sections on biographies or on histories of American, English, Jewish, or other humans, but were grouped among books on trees, butterflies, seashells, and other subjects of natural history. When I asked clerks, "How come?" they shrugged and said that that was always where Indian books were put. As I thought about it, I could see the logic. Indians, to most Americans, were people of the past, dead or dying people, who were studied by scientists, alongside dinosaurs and dodo birds, in museums of natural history, not human history. In New York, Chicago, Washington, Denver, Los Angeles, and other cities, Indians were sequestered in local museums of natural history in dull, lifeless displays. Thinking about it made me angry, and I vowed that someday, some way, I would do something about this ignorant insult.

The sales of *The Patriot Chiefs* slowly declined, and by the mid-sixties, the book was almost invisible. Then something startling happened. At a conference of academic historians, a Texas University professor told me that the volume had become enormously popular on his campus and was "the book of the quarter." What he wanted to know enviously was how had I been so smart as to write an "antiestablishment book" back in 1961. Sure enough, Viking told me that sales of the book were suddenly booming, that people believed that I was part of the flowering counterculture movement and had written *The Patriot Chiefs* to protest the side of America that had got us engulfed in the Vietnam War, and that Viking was bringing out a new edition. "Indians are in!" I was told. Of course, the writing of the book preceded America's involvement in Vietnam or the emergence of a counterculture movement, but the volume was launched on a new life of enduring popularity.

In the meantime, I had gone back to my work on the Nez Perce book, striking up cooperative working friendships with the remarkable Dale Morgan, who, though seriously handicapped in speech and hearing, was without peer as an authority on the Rocky Mountain fur trade; with Clifford Drury, who had devoted much of his life to editing the journals and letters of the Protestant missionaries in the Northwest; with Frederick Dockstader, the director of the Museum of the American Indian in New York; and with many others who generously gave me advice and shared their knowledge with me. At the same time, I took every opportunity during vacation or color-project travels to drive or hike along western trails and over mountain passes or visit battlefields and other sites associated with Nez Perce history and, with the assistance of Nez Perce friends, to attend intertribal gatherings and meet Cayuses, Yakamas, Salish, Umatillas, Walla Wallas, Coeur d'Alenes, and Indians of many other tribes, see their reservations, and listen to their accounts of their historic relationships with the Nez Perces as they had been passed down orally from generation to generation.

Soon after I had begun working on the book, Alfred Knopf, who had shown an interest in it and had indicated an expectation that I would submit it first to his firm, helped me greatly by introducing me to Peter Decker, one of the country's leading antiquarian book dealers, who specialized in buying and selling rare and out-of-print books on western American history. A feisty little man with enough eccentricities to make him a lovable character, Peter took me and my project under his wing and supplied me at bargain rates with books that he felt I should have for my research. Known as "South Pass Pete" because he once got lost overnight in the tall sagebrush that was higher than he was on the Oregon Trail at South Pass in Wyoming, Decker knew and loved the fast-disappearing Old West and, when out there, gloried in playing the role of an old codger. He got me to join the New York City "posse" of Westerners, a social group among whose active members were Mari Sandoz; Homer Croy; Sylvester Vigilante of the American History Room at the New York Public Library; Nick Eggenhofer, a noted western artist; and an aged gentleman who had been superintendent of a mine in Bolivia at the time of the death there of Butch Cassidy and the Sundance Kid. Monthly they gathered at a city armory for dinner and for professional arguing over such subjects as George Armstrong Custer, Billy the Kid, and which side of the river Lewis and Clark had gone up on. In time, Pete Decker became a fast friend of my family and spent his summers with us in the West, frequently taking long drives with me and introducing me to other old codgers, aged friends of his on ranches and in ghost mining towns. In the West, Peter claimed, he would never die—just dry up and blow away. And eventually, somewhere in his mid-nineties, that is just about what he did. Hale and hearty until the end, except for some gout in his hands from too much Canadian Club whiskey, he suddenly shriveled up and was gone, taking away with him, as far as I was concerned, a good part of both the myth and reality of the "Old" American West.

When in the early 1960s I finished writing the Nez Perce book, it presented a serious problem to Alfred, who had given me a contract for it in 1962. It ran to over one thousand typewritten pages, and Alfred and his salesmen said that at that size it could not make any money. "A thousand pages on a single Indian tribe," one of the salesmen chortled, "and a tribe that nobody ever heard of. Who's going to buy it?" Alfred's answer was that I would have to cut the book by a third. But my editor, Angus Cameron, agreed with me that the book simply could not be cut, and I finally repaid my advance to Alfred and went looking for a new publisher. The very next day I ran into Chester Kerr, the director of Yale University Press, who, when I told him what had happened, said simply, "Send the book to me." I did so, and less than a week later, Chester phoned to tell me that Yale would publish it.

Working with Yale's editor, I did manage to cut some material and present its substance in a thirty-two-page section of "Discussion Notes," mostly original research conveying information that had never been published before. Alfred, who watched from afar, was very bighearted and wrote me a touching letter that said that if I had any trouble with Yale, I should bring the book back to him. There was no need to do so. Yale brought the book out in October 1965, and to mark its publication, Yale and the Nez Perce tribe put on a big reception at the Lewis-Clark Hotel in Lewiston. Yale at the same time had published a book called *The Vinland Map*, purporting to show European knowledge of North America fifty years before Columbus's voyage. The book had aroused a lot of publicity and excitement in the media, and at the height of the formal program for our Nez Perce book, Chester Kerr was called to a hotel phone to talk to a newspaperman about the Vinland map book. When Chester returned, he apologized to the assembly and started to describe the widespread interest in the map, which seemed to show that Vikings had beaten all other Europeans to the "discovery" of America. Suddenly, Richard Halfmoon, the chairman of the Nez Perce tribe, politely but firmly cut him short, announcing to the crowd, "I am sorry, Mr. Kerr, but the subject is of no consequence to us Indians." It brought down the house and turned Chester's face red.

The Nez Perce book was taken by the History Book Club as a main selection and won many awards. Most satisfying to me were reviews and letters, many of them from leading American historians, praising the book as a pathbreaking one that showed the way in which Indian histories should be written. Hidden in the book, however, was an ingredient that had not been easy to acquire. By the time of publication, Betty and I over a period of ten years had become familiar with the many problems facing contemporary Indians. During that time, we had become more than historians of the American Indian. We had become actively engaged in Indian affairs and were now advocates for them.

V �902 WINDS OF CHANGE

In the 1950s, numerous Indian peoples were scandalously defenseless and put-upon. The only Americans without freedom, self-government, and the right to manage and control their own affairs, they were still beset by bullying government bosses, imperious missionaries, and thieving whites, and on their reservations were still victimized by grinding poverty and by political, social, and economic problems that appeared beyond the abilities of the government to solve. After the wars of the nineteenth century, the reservations had been all that the Indians had had left, however, and they still clung fiercely to them, bound spiritually to what remained of their ancestors' homelands, and in a world of still-alien and intimidating conquerors, they derived their only security from the family and community cohesion that the reservations afforded them.

During the decade of the 1950s, the federal government made things worse, adopting a cruel and fraudulent "termination" policy that pretended to "free the Indians" by ending the reservations and terminating all government relations with the tribes, including the observance of treaty-guaranteed trust responsibilities and the delivery of educational, health, and other services to the Indians. One by one, in the course of the decade, tribes were "terminated" against their will, losing their lands and natural resources to scavenging non-Indian ranchers, bankers, real estate speculators, timber companies, and other white interests and being forced to make their living competitively in the white man's world, whether they were prepared to do so or not. At the same time, Indians on many reservations were systematically "relocated" by the Interior Department to cities like Minneapolis, Chicago, Denver, and San Francisco, where, after initial government assistance, they were left to struggle for themselves to find jobs and homes and make a living in their strange new surroundings.

The implementation of the termination policy brought so much suffering and hardship to the affected tribal peoples and so many new social-justice and welfare problems to cities, counties, and states overwhelmed by the needs of the "freed" Indians that before the end of the decade, the policy was quietly abandoned by the Eisenhower administration. In time, some of the terminated tribes, with the help of sympathetic congressmen and others, were able to regain the recognition and rights that they had lost, but the termination period was a traumatic experience for an entire generation of Indians.

During those years, Betty and I observed many of the tragedies and injustices that the termination policy inflicted on the Klamaths of Oregon, the Menominees of Wisconsin, and other helpless tribes. Remembering with a surge of painful nostalgia and an ill conscience the shy, defensive Navajo code-talkers on Guam and the troubles of Ira Hayes, the guilt-ridden Pima Indian flag-raiser on Iwo Jima, I became dismayed and bitter at how little notice mainstream America, myself included, paid to what was happening to the Indians. In an attempt to try to do something about it, I revisited the terminated Menominees near Green Bay, Wisconsin, and began to collect research materials for a quickly written book about how, in attempting to adjust to the forced conversion of their homeland from an Indian reservation to a state county, they were fast losing their homes, lakes, valuable forests, and tribal bank accounts to slick white plunderers.

For a time, I pursued some information that rang with sensationalism. One of the principal proponents of termination and also the most rabid congressional leader in the assault on the Menominees was Arthur Watkins, a hardheaded Mormon senator from Utah, whose dogged advocacy of the policy and pronounced hostility to the Wisconsin Menominees, who lived nowhere near Utah, mystified many people. It appeared, however, that sometime in the recent past, though prior to the adoption of the termination policy, the Menominees had forcibly ejected from their reservation two proselytizing Mormon missionary elders who were alleged to have offended the Indians and caused a melee during a baseball game. Was there a connection between that ejection and Senator Watkins's hostility to Indians and particularly to the Menominees, or possibly even a connection with the very existence of the termination policy? It was a tantalizing question of possible revenge by the senator, but I got nowhere with it. I found the two elders, one in Canada and the other in Utah, but was unable to interview them. Other sources were evasive or unwilling to tell what they knew, and, absorbed also in finishing my Nez Perce history, I finally ran out of time and had to abandon the question, as well as the Menominee book project.

One other termination episode, however, changed my dismay to anger. In Washington State, rapacious white real estate interests helped to get the Colville reservation earmarked for termination, threatening the Chief Joseph band of Nez Perces who were still living there in quiet exile. That this final blow should be allowed to hit the valiant Nez Perce patriots seemed inhumane to me. Fortunately, under the determined leadership of Lucy Covington, a descendant of a powerful local chief named Moses and herself a popular figure on the Colville reservation, the Indian people put up such opposition that Congress never terminated them. Nevertheless, that and the frustrating Menominee experience fired me up to try to make non-Indians aware of the great communications gap that existed between themselves and the Indian part of our population, and I began to write and speak on the inability of the tribes to win the nation's attention to their modern-day difficulties.

As a journalist of the dominant culture, I seemed at the time to be somewhat alone in caring to speak out on the subject, and invitations to address gatherings began to come to me. At one of them, I changed my approach. Fred Dockstader at the Museum of the American Indian had invited me to speak to a meeting of ethnohistorians, mostly non-Indian academics who, in their studies and writings, were breathing life into a new discipline that combined history and ethnology. Instead of simply lamenting mainstream America's neglect of Indians that stemmed from ignorance, indifference, and even continued anti-Indian racism, I urged that the tribes be encouraged and assisted to learn the white men's modern-day skills and methods of communication and to go on the offensive in using all the media to tell the American people about themselves.

The proposal enthused one member of the audience in particular, an intense Oglala Lakota woman from South Dakota named Helen Peterson, who was executive director of the National Congress of American Indians (NCAI), a pan-Indian politically oriented organization of almost one hundred tribes founded in 1944. At her request, Betty and I went down a few weeks later to Phoenix, Arizona, where I delivered much the same address to an annual convention of the NCAI. Afterward, we stayed on at the convention, honored by the presentation of an eagle feather and a handsome Nez Perce corn-husk bag from Allen Slickpoo, the Nez Perce historian, receiving invitations from tribal leaders from different parts of the country to visit and write about the problems on their reservations, and attending a buffalo barbecue after witnessing a thrilling Wild West display of the prowess of some young Cheyenne hunters who chased and killed the animal destined for the barbecue.

Months later, back in Greenwich, Betty and I held a reception in our home for Helen and the NCAI's new president, Clarence Wesley, a chubby-faced Arizona Apache. In their entourage was the Reverend Clifford Samuelson, a loud, jolly non-Indian clergyman in his fifties, who lived on the grounds of the headquarters of the National Episcopal Church in Greenwich and directed, among other things, that denomination's work with Indians, which included helping to finance the NCAI. It turned out that Clifford, as he wanted us to call him, not only was a fellow resident of ours in Greenwich, Connecticut, but was thoroughly familiar with Oregon's Wallowa County, where he hunted for elk each fall and had many friends. In the weeks after the reception, our mutual interests kept bringing us together, and soon Clifford enlisted Betty to accompany him back to Wallowa County to participate with him in helping local parents establish a four-week nondenominational summer educational day camp for the children of ranchers, loggers, and others in that remote rural area where usual educational resources were severely limited.

The camp's first year, with classes held outdoors on a private ranch among huge ponderosa pine trees at the foot of the Wallowa Mountains, and with an invited faculty of inspiring college and prep school instructors and persons from industry and professions, was a great success. For the second year, Clifford and Betty proposed that the camp include several Nez Perce children from the reservation about one hundred miles away in Idaho. It was a daring idea. With the exception of a few individuals, the Nez Perces had never been allowed to return on a permanent basis to their prewar homeland. Sons, daughters, and other descendants of the original settlers who drove the Nez Perces from the Wallowa country some eighty years earlier were still alive, and the county, as Betty learned, was still riddled with anti-Indian fears and hostility, as well as a good measure of defensiveness and guilt. On the Indian side, plenty of bitterness against the people who had taken their Wallowa homeland from them still remained, and Nez Perce visitors to the county, come to fish for salmon or hunt elk in the canyons, usually held themselves contemptuously aloof from the whites. Nevertheless, Betty, with many friends on both sides, first broached the idea to those who ran the camp, and after promising to try it out as an experiment with three Indian boys and three girls whom she would feed, house, and take care of during the hours when they were not at the camp, she won their approval. An appearance before the Nez Perce Tribal Executive Committee followed, and there, too, she gained assent.

Again, the camp was a grand success. That summer, Betty housemothered six Nez Perce children who lived together in a rented house in the county with our four children and our two godchildren, who came up

Betty with some of the Nez Perce children who lived with us on our ranch while attending the summer educational day camp.

from Los Angeles. After a pillow fight the first night, which ended all inhibitions, the kids got on fabulously, not only delighting in such courses as one on shortcuts in mathematics taught by a General Electric atomic scientist from the Hanford Project in Washington State, who made the usually difficult classroom subject fun for them, but establishing wonderful new social relationships of trust and understanding between the Indians and white families in the county. Each summer for as many years as she was able to do so, Betty continued her association with the day camp and cared for an annual contingent of Indian children, which grew larger each year, finally reaching thirty in number and including Ute and Shoshoni-Bannock Indians, as well as Nez Perces.

The experience worked both ways, for through it Betty and I continued to learn from Indians and made many close friends among them. After the camp one summer, an especially bright and ambitious Nez Perce girl, the grand-niece of Josiah Red Wolf, the last survivor of the 1877 war, came east with the consent of her family and the tribe to live with us in the win-

ters and go to the Greenwich public schools. Eventually, she became secretary of her class and after graduating from Greenwich High School
went on to Skidmore College and then to a busy professional career in
Portland, Oregon. Another Indian, a Sioux boy from South Dakota,
joined us and also went to Greenwich High, graduating and going on to
college and then to a job with a television station in New York, and still
others made our Greenwich house their weekend and vacation headquarters while they attended Taft or other eastern boarding schools. To all of
them, in Wallowa County or Greenwich, our own children, Diane, Alvin,
Allison, and Kathy, now lively teenagers, became brother and sisters, playing hockey or the Indian stick game, reading J. R. R. Tolkien's *The Lord of
the Rings* or listening to the Indian version of Custer's Last Stand, and
Betty became "Mom," with no agenda of her own save to minister to the
kids' needs and see that they got love and every opportunity that life could
give them.

During the same period, Clifford Samuelson invited me to join him as a
representative of the Episcopal Church on the Council on Indian Affairs,
a powerful lobbying group of national church and other organizations
that worked on behalf of the tribes and whose members ranged from the
Daughters of the American Revolution and the General Federation of
Women's Clubs to Oliver La Farge's Association on American Indian
Affairs and the century-old Indian Rights Association of Philadelphia.
Joined by the NCAI and spokespersons from other Indian groups, the
council met periodically in a conference room in the Department of Interior Building in Washington with Secretary of the Interior Stewart Udall,
various congressmen and senators, and officials of the Bureau of Indian
Affairs to discuss Indian policies and programs, the status and condition of
tribes, and the many complaints that came from the reservations.

Udall, an Arizonan who knew many of the Indian leaders in that state,
had a genuine interest in the well-being of the tribes and, coming into
office with the Kennedy administration, hard on the heels of the Eisenhower administration's jettison of the termination policy, was anxious to
end the Indians' fears of the federal government, which termination had
fostered. At the same time, the policy-making powers in dealing with
Indians lay mostly with the Interior committee heads in Congress, Senator Henry "Scoop" Jackson of Washington and Congressman Wayne
Aspinall of Colorado, and there was only so much that Udall could do. He
and I had many talks and became warm personal friends, agreeing on
some of the basic conditions that would continue to make "the Indian
problem"—really "the white man's problem"—impossible to solve until
they were ended: White men spoke for Indians; white men made policies

and programs for Indians; white men governed every aspect of Indian life. In short, Indians, lacking the rights of self-determination and sovereignty, were like colonial subjects, ruled by other people's thinking and by decisions that were made for them. Furthermore, we recognized that the white men of these observations included Udall and myself. It was an uncomfortable feeling, but at the time it was the way things were, a fact that was made plain to me in another context.

In addition to my membership on the Council on Indian Affairs, I had accepted an invitation from Oliver La Farge, the anthropologist, Pulitzer Prize–winning author of *Laughing Boy*, and president of the Association on American Indian Affairs, to join the board of that organization, which at the time was made up of a considerable number of wealthy philanthropic people who, much like LaFarge, sympathized with the Indians and worked tirelessly to improve their lot but, believing that the Indians had to be assimilated, patronized them and treated them like children who needed white persons to direct them and handle their affairs. During the summer of 1963, when most of the officers of the Association were traveling on vacation, Oliver died, and I was delegated to represent the organization at his funeral in Santa Fe. In addition to many of his white friends and admirers, scores of Indians, including governors, officials, and chiefs of various southwestern tribes and pueblos, garbed in bright-colored traditional tribal dress, filed solemnly into the Santa Fe church to pay their respects to their departed white friend. I was sitting with an elderly woman, a well-known literary and social figure in Santa Fe and a longtime financial contributor to the Association, who whispered loudly to me, "Look at them. What will those poor people do now? They relied so on Oliver to do all their thinking for them."

The point needed no underscoring. Nevertheless, within the United States as well as abroad, the 1960s winds of change were already blowing and were beginning to affect the Indians. At a precedent-setting conference at the University of Chicago in June 1961, which I had attended with other members of the Council on Indian Affairs, more than four hundred leaders of sixty-seven tribes had for the first time appealed to the federal government for the right merely to participate in the making of policies, programs, and budgets for their tribes. They had been turned down, but rapid developments in the world, including the spread of nationalism and the emergence of newly independent Third World nations in Africa and Asia, the black and women's rights revolutions in the United States, the new attention being given to all American minorities, and the recognition of the values of cultural pluralism versus assimilation, conformity, and the old "melting pot" goal, influenced the Indians and kept the issue alive. By

Tribal leaders of the National Congress of American Indians and some of their non-Indian supporters, including myself (toward the back of the crowd), meet at the White House with President Kennedy in March 1963, to discuss Indian needs.

1964, they had expanded it into a campaign for additional rights, including that of self-determination.

In that year, Betty and I, as members of Clifford Samuelson's committee, were active participants in another large gathering of Indians and whites, this time sponsored by the Council on Indian Affairs and held in Washington, D.C., where Congress was debating passage of the Economic Opportunity Act, a key element in the Johnson administration's War on Poverty in the United States. Up to then, Congress, assuming wrongly that tribal needs were met adequately by the annual appropriation for the Bureau of Indian Affairs, had, with one or two exceptions, excluded Indians as beneficiaries of legislation intended to aid the general population. Focusing on the Indians' extreme poverty and the need to include them in the new act, those of us at the 1964 Capital Conference on Indian Poverty lobbied senators and congressmen, consulted with Vice President Hubert Humphrey and other administration leaders, and won our point. Under the act that established the Office of Economic Opportunity (OEO) and that included Indians as beneficiaries, tribes for the first time were permitted to devise programs to meet their needs, fashion budgets for them, and, if they were approved, carry out the programs themselves. It was a momentous breakthrough, and when the act proved a success and Indians demonstrated that they could run their own affairs, new programs and funds allowing Indian management came to the reservations from other government agencies, such as the Department of Labor and the Department of Health, Education, and Welfare, that assisted thousands of Indians in the following years to acquire higher education and gradually raised living standards among many of the tribes.

A notable addition to the ranks of Indian activists during this period was the National Indian Youth Council (NIYC), founded in 1961 by a group of dissident young college-educated Indians, some of whom Betty and I had gotten to know through their occasional attendance at meetings of the Council on Indian Affairs in Washington. Several of their leaders, including Melvin Thom, a Northern Paiute Indian from Nevada, and Clyde Warrior, a Ponca from Oklahoma, were charismatic speakers, and one of the unexpected highlights of the poverty conference had been an eloquent address by Thom, who was president of the NIYC and who had demanded and won the right to be heard by the older delegates. Earlier that day, with a group of tribal officers led by Robert Burnette, the former president of the Sicangu (Brulé, or "Burnt Thighs") Sioux tribe in South Dakota and currently Helen Peterson's successor as executive director of the NCAI, I had gone to the U.S. Capitol to lobby legislators and had been angered by a few senators who were still termination-minded and had used our visit to upbraid us for "wanting to keep the Indians on reservations like animals in a zoo." Back at the conference, however, Mel Thom was a stirring voice of reality and wiped the senators' ignorant strictures out of my mind. "As Indian youths we say to you today that the Indian cannot be pushed into the mainstream of American life," Thom declared, to rousing cheers from the poverty conference participants. "We do not want to destroy our culture, our life that brought us through the period in which the Indians were almost annihilated. . . . We are not going to disappear!" Continuing, he recalled to me the substance of my own address to the NCAI convention in Phoenix five years earlier, telling the enthusiastic Washington conference delegates, "We have got to educate the American public and also our leaders that we are here to stay. . . . We have a lot of communication to do. This communication has to come from the Indians themselves!"

As the product of an Indian voice at last, this, to me, was something new, something strong and stirring. As it turned out, it heralded the beginning of a period of widespread rebellious attacks by young nationalist-minded Indians in cities and on the reservations against the "Uncle Tomahawks" among tribal leaders—the "Apples, red on the outside, white inside"— who sold out the Indians by letting agents of the Bureau of Indian Affairs, as well as patronizing white do-gooders, decide what was best for the tribes. It was the start of a militant pan-Indian demand for "Red Power"— power of the Indian people over all their own affairs.

In the ensuing years, the goals of the NIYC won large support in the cities from relocated "urban" Indians and on reservations from spiritual leaders, full-bloods, and others who maintained the languages, beliefs, practices, and values of their ancestors and from many sympathetic mixed-bloods, like Bob Burnette, the Sicangu Sioux and NCAI executive director, who, although thoroughly assimilated into the white man's culture, frequently sought the curing rituals of traditionalist Sioux Yuwipi men and was supported politically on his South Dakota Rosebud reservation by traditional medicine men, full-bloods, and young Indians. Strong, tall, and powerfully built, Bob was combative and not universally loved, but he was scrupulously honest, and an uncompromising fighter for Indian rights, and he had ardent followers among numerous tribes besides his own, particularly on the northern plains and in the Southwest, where he had been a leader in organizing intertribal Indian councils in California and Arizona. He was a marine in World War II, which brought us together and made friends of our two families. Through the years, Bob often visited us in Greenwich, and, until his premature death from a heart attack in 1984, I traveled extensively with him through the West, visiting reservations, meeting many of his Indian associates and friends, attending social and religious ceremonies, and participating with him in Indian political meetings.

He and many others—among them, Oren Lyons, a traditional Onondaga chief and spokesman of the Hodenosaunee, Iroquois Six Nation Confederacy; Thomas Banyacya, interpreter for the traditional Hopi chiefs in the Southwest; and Franklin Fools Crow and Henry Crow Dog, Sioux medicine men in the Dakotas—taught me much and, by the beauty and integrity of their lives as well as by their words of instruction, made clear to me the pervasive ingredient of their cultures, the one that had helped American Indians survive five centuries of conquest, oppression, and corrosive Euro-American influences. This component, which was the unquenchable strength of the Indians' native religions, was conveyed to me outwardly many times in many forms by many individuals.

On one overcast day, for example, while accompanying Bob Burnette and some of his Sioux friends through a narrow gully surrounded by eroded multicolored buttes and amphitheaters of the Badlands of South Dakota, I observed a young member of our party, happy to have just returned to his home on the nearby Pine Ridge reservation after a year in Chicago, press himself emotionally against the base of a towering spire and caress its rough surface with his arms and body, as if he were supernaturally related to the rocks. At another time, I witnessed an elderly Devils Lake Sioux woman at a buffalo preserve near the Fort Totten reservation in North Dakota rub her small frame against the side of one of the animals, which made no move as she sought security and strength from the buffalo's spirit. How had such persons continued into the modern world as Indians? It was a question about which I had first wondered years earlier during my drive with Jimmy Loeb down to Mexico City in the summer of 1937 and then again in 1941 among the Mayas at Chichicastenango in Guatemala.

In the company of traditionals, in sweats and at sun dances, vision quests, and naming ceremonies, I learned to appreciate the depth of the full-time spirituality that permeated every aspect of their lives, made them group-oriented and cooperative, believing firmly that the well-being of the group came ahead of that of any individual, and endowed them with spirits of their own that long before the white man's recognition of an ecosystem linked the Indians harmoniously and in balance with the spirits of all creation in their universe. In time, I came to understand that in their religions and the values they taught lay the answer to the miraculous inner strength that had helped them survive. There was no secret about it; white men had simply ignored the Indians' religions or had denigrated them as the sorcery of inferior humans. But discovering much of comfort in them for myself, I found it easy to believe that in a future era of great problems for the American people, the group-oriented, traditional Indians, interrelated functionally with all of creation, would know how to survive better than the competitive, materialistic non-Indian population.

In the meantime, other changes and interests were also affecting my life. Toward the end of the 1950s, while I was in Mexico on a story for *Time*, my father died of heart failure in his Southern California home. I flew up, saw him lying in his open coffin in a funeral parlor, still with an endearing slight smile on his face, and recognized again, as I had at Guam and Iwo Jima, how frail and temporary life is. Four years later, my mother died in a restaurant in Rome during a trip abroad, and suddenly Warren and I were the senior generation of our families. Both our parents had died before doctors seemed to know much about cholesterol, low-fat diets, exercise, and operations for clogged arteries, and both of them, killing themselves innocently, in ignorance of the effects of sedentary living, pipe- and cigarette-smoking, and meals of atrociously rich and fatty foods, died young, my father at seventy-one and my mother at sixty-seven.

In the period between their deaths, my old Harvard friend Jim Parton, who had returned to New York after liquidating the daily newspaper he had tried to start in Los Angeles for Henry Luce, weaned me away from *Time* and over to his newest—and, this time, sensationally successful— venture, the American Heritage Publishing Company. Its major product, *American Heritage* magazine, dedicated to popularizing American history by good writing as well as sound scholarship, had been founded after the war by a group of eminent historians, led by the distinguished Columbia professor and Pulitzer Prize–winning author Allan Nevins, but had floun- dered financially until 1954, when Parton and two friends with whom he was running a custom publishing business—Joseph Thorndike, a former managing editor of *Life* magazine, whom I had known on the *Crimson* at Harvard, and Oliver Jensen, a former *Life* text editor—bought and restyled it. At first, Parton urged me to join the new undertaking, and although I decided not to leave *Time*, I became a steady contributor to *American Heritage*, writing mostly on Indian or western American history. From its first issue onward, the new version of the magazine, beautifully printed, with numerous color illustrations, a hard white cover that made it look like a slender book to treasure and keep, and an editorial staff that included the prominent Civil War historian Bruce Catton, acquired a large and loyal readership and made money. Within a few years, the mag- azine's success allowed the company to begin to publish books as well as a second strikingly handsome hardcover magazine, *Horizon*, which dealt with the histories and cultures of the rest of the world. In 1959, I wrote part of the text of one of the company's books, *The Pioneer Spirit*, and the next year finally acceded to Parton's continued urging and agreed to join Heritage's book division and produce a large illustrated history of Ameri- can Indians with a text by William Brandon, who had recently published an elegantly written book on the American West.

I had been extraordinarily happy at *Time*, working under Roy Alexan- der, a dream of a managing editor, and in a section that was pretty much my own, and when Roy gave me a farewell dinner at Brussels, one of our favorite midtown Manhattan restaurants, and announced to everyone that this was "just a leave of absence" I was taking and that I'd be back in a year, I half-believed him. But I was destined to stay at Heritage for almost twenty years and retire finally in 1979, long after Roy and most of those at the Brussels dinner had also left *Time*, taking with them, as I had done, wondrous memories of the golden days of editorial hegemony at that magazine.

One of my principal contributions to the Indian book at Heritage, in addition to helping Brandon outline his text and get it written and edited in time to meet our publication schedule, was acquiring pictures for the volume. We needed some 350 black-and-white and color illustrations to run with Brandon's narrative, and with a fifteen-thousand-dollar budget for their acquisition, which was extraordinarily generous for a single book in those days, I traveled westward by plane, train, and rental cars across the United States and then back eastward through the provinces of Canada, visiting museums, libraries, historical societies, and personal collections and viewing and buying permission for the onetime use of hundreds of pictures of Indians, enough to give us a large choice for our layouts.

I was very anxious to uncover old, contemporary drawings, sketches, watercolors, etchings, lithographs, photographs, and other documentary materials from the past that had never been published before, and time and again in the course of my research I was rewarded with finds that thrilled me. The most unexpected and exciting discovery was of the original sketches of the first-known views of Indians in large canoes and as slaves in Caribbean island gold mines, which an official Spanish chronicler, Fernandez de Oviedo, had drawn shortly after the voyages of Columbus.

After a disheartening six-months' search for the Oviedo originals, during which an American Heritage researcher had drawn a blank in every likely source in Europe and I had been advised in the Hispanic Section of the Library of Congress in Washington to give up the hunt because scholars had been searching for the pictures without success everywhere in the world for three centuries, I came unbelievingly on the very sketches I was seeking, drawn by Oviedo on the pages of his sixteenth-century manuscript, a valuable but little-noted possession hidden away in the collections of the Henry E. Huntington Library in San Marino, California. Like many other picture discoveries that we used to illuminate Brandon's beautifully written text, Oviedo's prized views, adding to our ethnographic knowledge of the Indian past, were reprinted in textbooks, research works, and other publications after their 1961 initial appearance in our volume. An immediate success with both Indians and non-Indians, and carrying an introduction specially written for us by President John F. Kennedy, *The American Heritage Book of Indians* stayed in print for many years, selling ultimately more than a million copies and helping to inspire new and more accurate writings on Indians.

Following the publication of the Indian volume, I cast my lot permanently with Heritage and assumed the senior role of editor in charge of a long string of annual Heritage and Horizon illustrated histories, beginning with one on flight and going on to others that ranged in subject from the United States presidency, vanishing primitive man, and World War I to Africa, the American West, and the law in America. The editorial staff at Heritage was an inspiring one. Some, like Oliver Jensen, William Harlan Hale, Eric Larrabee, Marshall Davidson, and Bruce Catton had reputations as established authors. Catton, indeed, was a national celebrity. A modest, unassuming former newspaper reporter, he had become one of the best-known writers in the country, showered with all manner of prizes and honorary college degrees for his highly acclaimed, best-selling histories of the Civil War, whose hundredth anniversary the nation began observing in 1961. During World War II, he had been director of information for the War Production Board in Washington, and I had become slightly acquainted with him at drowsy interagency meetings when I was with the Office of War Information. To some of us at Heritage who frequently lunched with him at his favorite table in the Algonquin Hotel, the most interesting things about him were, first, his prodigious thirst for ice-cold martinis, which kept us waiting for our food until he had slowly downed from three to five of the powerful cocktails and, second, his mysterious recuperative powers, which upon his return to his typewriter after lunch stoked his abilities to produce some of his clearest thoughts and most graceful prose.

Later on, another greatly talented historian, David McCullough, joined the company and, until he left to write his own prizewinning histories, worked with me as a friend and colleague in the book division, planning and editing a number of our volumes, including a magnificent illustrated history of World War II. In every sense of the terms, David was a gentleman and a scholar, kindly and generous to others, personable, full of enthusiasms, and in love with history.

In 1962, while working on a Heritage book devoted to the history of Yellowstone Park and other great natural wonders of the United States, I became aware of a strange, redemptive change that had come over me. The book's authors, whom I had specially enlisted, included Wallace Stegner, Peter Matthiessen, Supreme Court Justice William O. Douglas, and the poet Paul Engle, all of whom were well-known conservationists. Also, many of the images I had selected for the book were by Philip Hyde, Edward Weston, and other noted conservationists, including the demanding dean of all conservation photographers, Ansel Adams, who after sizing me up during a pleasant day at his seaside home in Carmel, California, gave me permission to include certain of his most celebrated photographs in our volume. Finally, in addition, a number of our book's spreads of pictures and text carried conservation messages, lambasting forces of greedy growth and development for their past or present sins of spoliation, pollution, and destruction, such as the extinction of the passenger pigeon, the wiping out of the vast white pine forests in the upper Midwest, and the desecration of the scenic beauty of Colorado's Garden of the Gods by real estate developers.

Somehow, and at some time, I had turned my back on the "bigger and better" and "more and more" vision of the unrestrained exploitation of the earth that the General Motors Futurama exhibit at the 1939 World's Fair had projected and which I had promoted enthusiastically in much of my writing for *Time* in the 1950s. Instead, as the natural wonders book reflected, I had become a "take a second look" conservationist and could see that unwary progress and growth could also mean mutilation and ruin.

In retrospect, my change had developed gradually from many roots, beginning with my love for the unspoiled parts of the West and my affection for Indians who regarded humans as stewards, rather than conquerors, of nature. At the same time, as early as 1954, while I was producing laudatory prodevelopment color stories for *Time*, Alfred Knopf, who had become a leading member of the National Parks Advisory Board, got me to join him in a nationwide campaign to prevent the Interior Department's Bureau of Reclamation from building two dams that would have destroyed much of the beauty, as well as the integrity, of the Dinosaur National Monument as a unit of the National Park Service in northern Utah and Colorado. During the course of that hard-fought campaign, which was ultimately successful in stopping the dams, I came to know and respect a number of dedicated conservationists, including the almost legendary Horace Albright, one of the founders and the second director of the National Park Service, and Sigurd Olson, the father of the Boundary Waters Canoe Area in northern Minnesota, both of whom became close friends and mentors of mine until their deaths.

Horace, however, and many of the country's leading conservationists, such as David Brower of the Sierra Club and, later, of Friends of the Earth, knew very little about Indians and were full of hostile, stereotypical thinking about them ("they were drunks; they were lazy and would not work; they could not be trusted to take care of their land and natural resources," etc., etc.), and when controversies arose over the building of two other big dams by the Army Corps of Engineers, each of which would drown the heart of an Indian reservation in the waters of a reservoir, the voice of the conservationists in defense of the Indians' lands was noticeably silent. Without potent opposition, the Corps of Engineers built the Garrison Dam, the largest rolled-earth dam in the world, across the Missouri River in North Dakota, ignoring the protests of Mandan, Hidatsa, and Arikara Indians and chopping up and flooding sacred sites and large parts of their reservation. Repeating their high-handedness, the Corps then broke the American government's oldest existing treaty, made in 1794 with the Seneca Indians of New York State, to build the Kinzua Dam, which flooded the center of the Senecas' reservation and the burial ground of their famous revolutionary-era chief, Cornplanter, and again forced a heartbreaking relocation of most of the Indians.

The conservationists' attitude in both of these cases, as well as in acrimonious conflicts between Indian peoples and the Sierra Club and other conservation organizations over issues at the Grand Canyon and in Alaska and elsewhere, troubled me greatly and, with the hope of gaining understanding and support for the Indians from the rest of the American people, moved me to write lengthy magazine articles about the Kinzua Dam affair and other injustices being visited on tribes by government agencies like the Corps of Engineers and even to address a plea to conservationists in an article on the Op-Ed page of the *New York Times*, pointing out why they and the American Indians should be natural allies, not enemies. At first, few conservationists agreed with me, but later, when Congress handed the Indians a victory and the conservationists an unexpected defeat over a fiercely fought issue affecting the Havasupai tribe's land claim near the Grand Canyon, David Brower, Alan Gussow, and other officers of the Friends of the Earth joined with tribal leaders in a friendly meeting I arranged in a New York hotel and eventually gave leadership to other conservation groups in a concerted effort to gain a better understanding of Indian points of view and to act with, and not against, the tribes.

At the same time, despite my attempts to work with conservationists, I still felt instinctive tugs to support certain practical growth and development projects. Among Idaho friends at Lewiston, where Betty and I made frequent visits, I joined Harry Hughes, the manager of the Lewiston Chamber of Commerce, and others in promoting and helping to win congressional support for the long-delayed completion of an east-west paved highway through the Bitterroot Range's pristine wilderness to connect Lewiston with Missoula, Montana, as well as backing for the establishment of a new national park headquartered near Lewiston that would tell the history of the Nez Perces and encourage the development of Hells Canyon to make it more accessible to sightseers and tourists.

These goals were all achieved, although Congressman Wayne Aspinall, the baronial-like little chairman of the House Interior Committee, suddenly and unexpectedly almost killed the park proposal because of an accidental mix-up in the time of his arrival at the Lewiston airport from Washington on an inspection tour of the proposed park sites. When no one was present to meet his plane, he flew away in a rage, leaving an aide to tell people that the park was dead. Thanks to the aide's reassurances that his boss would calm down, the tour went off successfully without Aspinall, but with Idaho state and local notables, Nez Perce Indians, and the press guiding Conrad Wirth, the director of the National Park Service, and a full complement of Park Service personnel from Washington to the different sites.

At one of them, overlooking the huge, scenic Whitebird battlefield, where the Nez Perces had defeated the U.S. Army at the start of the war in 1877, the absent chairman missed a most dramatic incident, one he might have remembered for the rest of his life. Wizened old Josiah Red Wolf, who during the Whitebird battle had been a boy taking care of his grandmother's horses and was now the last surviving participant in the war, was describing the fight that had taken place almost a century earlier, holding everyone spellbound as he told of Indian sentinels who had been stationed in hiding in the timber at the summit of Whitebird Hill to warn of the approach of the soldiers. Holding his cupped hand to his mouth, he lifted his head and, sending shivers down our spines, began giving the lonesome howl of a coyote, the long-ago signal that soldiers were coming. In the midst of the howl, one of the uniformed Park Service men, who had been standing apart with a small portable radio pressed against his ear, suddenly rushed at Josiah, waving to him to be quiet and telling everybody that Alan Shepard, the first American astronaut to fly in space, was coming back to earth through the atmosphere and that everyone should listen. Except for the blare of the announcer's voice on the radio, the place became absolutely silent. Josiah's coyote call of a remote and long-forgotten day had stopped dead, and the old man slunk off to a puzzled knot of the other Indians. When the radio description of Shepard's safe reentry ended, some of the Park Service people clapped. The rest of us returned quietly to our cars, awed by the marvel we had seen—a person whose life span went from the Indian wars to an astronaut's return from outer space. Soon afterward, Congress established the Nez Perce Historical Park, and a couple of years later, old Josiah Red Wolf died. Chairman Aspinall never knew what he had missed.

Meanwhile, Stewart Udall, whom I continued to see occasionally, invited me to join him and a large number of conservationists on trips to Rainbow Bridge and to the site of a proposed new Canyonlands National Park in the red-rock wilderness of southern Utah. Although he was an ardent conservationist, Secretary of the Interior Udall was also an able

Josiah Red Wolf, last surviving veteran of the Nez Perce War of 1877, recounting his memories of the Whitebird battle to a member of a government party from Washington which was considering the establishment of a Nez Perce National Historic Park in 1963. A moment after this picture was taken, Red Wolf's account of the fighting of almost a century earlier was interrupted for the party to listen on a small radio to the arrival of Alan Shepard, the first American astronaut, back from outer space.

politician and was trying to balance the demands of the conservation organizations with those of the proponents of growth and development and find middle-ground solutions that would satisfy both of them. At the time, he was having trouble with the conservationists, who were criticizing him harshly for supporting the building of the Glen Canyon Dam, whose reservoir would flood that beautiful canyon of the Colorado River and threaten Rainbow Bridge, one of the country's most inspiring natural wonders.

The first trip—by helicopter to the site of the bridge hidden in a deep side canyon—did nothing to reassure the conservationists. Both Congress and the Bureau of Reclamation, which was building the dam, had refused to support the cost or the practicality of a proposal by the conservationists to construct a protective dam to hold back the rising waters of the reservoir from the bridge, and a suggestion to them by Udall to solve the problem by including the bridge in a new national park was opposed by the Navajo Nation, on whose land the bridge was located and which regarded Rainbow Bridge as a sacred site and wanted it protected. The trip to view the awesome bridge, arching high enough beneath the desert sky to span the Capitol in Washington, D.C., provided an opportunity to air Udall's proposal, but nothing ever came of it. Glen Canyon Dam was completed, and although Udall failed to lead a fight to protect the bridge, it showed signs of being able to weather the waters that rose at its base and did not collapse, as some grim soothsayers had predicted it would.

The second trip—a reconnaissance of some of the most spectacular rocky wilderness remaining in the lower forty-eight states—lasted about a week and took us partway down the Colorado River from Moab, Utah, up the Green, and through an amazing region of majestic vistas, eroded canyons, and radiant buttes, mesas, and arches, all of them destined to become part of the nation's new Canyonlands Park. The trip was very much a holiday. Stewart had

Secretaries Stewart Udall of the Interior (left) and Orville Freeman of Agriculture on the Colorado River during our reconnaissance in 1964 that led to the establishment of the Canyonlands National Park in southern Utah.

his wife, Lee, and their children along, Orville Freeman, whom I had last seen at a veterans' meeting in Washington after I returned from the Pacific and who was now the secretary of agriculture, was along with his son, as were Senator Frank Moss of Utah and his son, and I had young Alvin with me. All the boys were about twelve or thirteen years old.

The most memorable thing about that trip for me, aside from the geologic wonders and beauty of the overpowering silent landscapes through which we traveled, was that it almost cost me my life. On calm stretches of the rivers, we sometimes jumped in the water and, encased in bulky life jackets, floated along in the current with our boats. Several times, we had to remind our sons sternly not to get in the middle of the river, where the current might be swift and able to whisk them away from us, but to stay close to the shore at all times, where there was less chance of getting into trouble. So what did I do? Just above the confluence of the Colorado and

Green rivers, another floater and I got so wrapped up in conversation that before we knew it, we were out in the middle of the Colorado, being swept by the swiftly moving current past the mouth of the Green and on toward the dangerous rapids of Cataract Canyon. Unable to swim against the current, we began to yell for help to those in the boats and to some of our people who were onshore, but for a couple of minutes, as we drifted faster and faster downstream, all we could make out was that our sons, who were playing in the mud on the riverbank, were laughing uproariously at us, as if our plight were a big joke. Then some blessed boatmen realized with a start what was happening to us and, gunning their motors, came racing after us. They did not dare stop in the roiling current to pull us aboard, so, grabbing our hands and wrists they dragged us through the water against the current, so violently that I thought my arms would come out of their sockets. We were finally deposited on the shore at the confluence, and all ended happily.

The following year, in the fall of 1963, I took a two-month leave of absence from American Heritage and went to work in Washington for Udall. The conservation organizations were still criticizing him for compromises and shortcomings, but the truth was that he had gone well past them, beginning to compile, with the help of New Mexico's senator Clinton Anderson and other powerful supporters in Congress, an astounding conservation legacy that would include the creation of five new national parks, six new national monuments, eight national seashores and lakeshores, nine national recreation areas, twenty historic sites, and fifty-six national wildlife refuges. In addition, the Wilderness bill, the Wild and Scenic Rivers bill, the National Trail bill, the Land and Water Conservation Fund, the Bureau of Outdoor Recreation, and the National Historic Preservation bill were all enacted during his eight years in office. Even more important for the future of the country, Udall had embarked on something of a personal crusade to get the American people to understand that conservation was only one aspect of what he and others were calling "environmentalism," or a concern for the safety and well-being of the entire environment and for the quality of life, which he considered were already in a state of crisis, facing such threats as water and air pollution and the increasing use of toxic materials.

Earlier, he had persuaded Wallace Stegner to join him for a few months as an adviser and sounding board for his ideas and to help him with his speeches and writings. To spread public awareness of Udall's environmental message, Stegner got him a contract for a book to be called *The Quiet Crisis* and helped him outline it and get it started. Udall, meanwhile, had enjoyed the notion of having a "writer in residence" with him, someone who was only temporarily a member of the government and from whom he could seek reactions and advice on all subjects and who could help him with the book and other writings. Wanting another writer, someone experienced in the publishing world, he lit upon me to succeed Stegner when Wally had to return to his teaching position at Stanford.

It was a fascinating assignment, for Udall kept me close to him all day, sitting in on most meetings and conferences in his office, accompanying him to many outside meetings, and participating in strategic discussions that he held with his chief aides, Orren Beaty, Jr., and Walter Pozen, or with the Interior Department's undersecretary, John Carver, or various assistant secretaries and commissioners like Floyd Dominy of the Bureau of Reclamation and Philleo Nash of the Bureau of Indian Affairs. On one occasion, Udall sent me to Big Bend National Park in Texas to represent him at a particularly sensitive meeting of the National Parks Advisory Board, during which a new director of the National Park Service was to succeed the popular Conrad Wirth. According to rumor, Wirth had run afoul of Congress and was being ousted, and there were many hard words and tears at the awkward Big Bend ceremonies of transfer, which both Wirth and his successor attended.

Toward the end of November, my term with Udall came to an abrupt and tragic end. He had chosen me to accompany him to Tokyo as his senior adviser at an annual meeting of American and Japanese cabinet members. Loaded down with fat briefing books and talking, position, and contingency papers on a score of subjects, ranging from the U.S. sale to Japan of Alaskan timber and methane gas to American cooperation in helping Japan establish its own system of national parks, we flew off from Andrews Air Force Base in Washington in one of the big U.S. 707 presidential planes, carrying Secretary of State Dean Rusk, the secretaries of the Treasury, Interior, Agriculture, Commerce, and Labor departments, President Kennedy's counsel and press chief, and various assistant secretaries, staff members, consultants, and wives. After an overnight stop in Hawaii, we departed the next morning, heading west over the Pacific Ocean. Two hours past Honolulu, I was sitting in an aisle seat opposite Stewart and his wife, Lee, busy writing a letter to Betty about our trip so far, when a State Department aide emerged from Dean Rusk's private compartment in the front of the plane and, hunching over toward the floor, made her way up the aisle, stopping at each row of seats to whisper something to their occupants. When she reached me, she whispered her dreadful information in my ear: "Word has just come over our ticker. President Kennedy has been shot." Then she moved on. I turned around to look at everybody, not wanting to believe what she had said but feeling that with her mention of the word *shot*, I had actually heard it ringing out sharply with the explosive whack of my old M1. Almost mechanically, I turned back to my letter and continued writing to Betty:

8:50 A.M. It is true. Terrific, stunned condition up here. No one knows how badly President is. Scty Rusk apparently has a news ticker up in his forward cabin. We are 2 hrs out of Honolulu. Gov Connolly has been shot too. [Assistant Secretary of State for Public Affairs] Bob Manning and Pierre Salinger [President Kennedy's press secretary] running back and forth to Rusk's cabin and to us. President shot in Dallas. Udall's jaw set and tight. He's holding Lee Udall's hand. [Secretary of Commerce] Hodges and wife look stunned. Report President still alive— being given transfusion. [Secretary of the Treasury] Dillon says we are postponing Tokyo conference—will go back.

9:00 A.M. Sudden sharp bank—we're turning. Word is we're going to Dallas—announcement from pilot—we'll refuel 1/2 hr at Honolulu—no one off plane, then stay together and go to Dallas—Mrs. Wirtz [wife of Secretary of Labor Willard Wirtz] praying—many women with eyes closed as if in prayer. No word—don't know if Pres dead or alive. Udall: "One of those goddamned madmen." All cabinet members in Rusk's forward compartment—then they come out and sit down and talk quietly to their wives—holding their hands. They go back in.

9:35. Rusk comes up forward again, takes intercom at pantry and says, "Ladies & gentlemen. It is official. We have had official word—the President has died. God save our nation." Pierre Salinger, in the aisle, grabs his wife. They cling in a terribly tragic embrace—Hodges, now seated across from me, buries his head in his hands and sobs, tears come down his cheek—others crying—Udall sits next to Lee, stares, tough-jawed, past her out the cabin window as he takes her hand—Manning sits opposite me—tears start in his eyes—Myer Feldman [Kennedy's counsel] crying—Wirtz mad—not a sound or movement in the cabin for 5 minutes.

After a brief stop at Honolulu to refuel, we headed nonstop back to Washington. In the rhythmic throb of the plane's engines, I, too, began to cry, feeling a sickly knot building up in my stomach and teardrops wetting my cheeks. At 12:30 that night, in the glare of batteries of television lights, we landed back at Andrews Air Force Base. In a brief farewell, Rusk, who had worried about the existence of a widespread conspiracy, snapped to some of us the hope that never again would so many leading members of the government be allowed to travel together on the same plane. The next day, with a new president in the White House, everyone seemed to be doing the correct thing and handing in their resignations. My two months were almost up, and I followed suit. Submitting my resignation to Udall, I said good-bye to him and, still dazed by the nightmarish event that had caused the trip to be aborted, returned to New York and American Heritage.

As it did to most Americans, the assassination of President Kennedy came as a frightful shock to Betty and our children, who sat in grim silence in front of our television set, watching the unfolding drama of the imposing funeral ceremonies, the astounding gunning down of Lee Harvey Oswald in front of the cameras, and the other unforgettable events that followed the president's death. On Thanksgiving Day, after I had rejoined them from Washington, I received a telephone call from Mims Thomason, an executive of United Press International, who lived near us in Greenwich. He wondered whether American Heritage could help his company produce as quickly as possible a memorial book on the assassination that UPI could offer to the readers of its many member newspapers throughout the country. I relayed the proposal to Parton, who jumped at the idea, and the next day I hurried into New York to help with the project.

As I ran through stacks of photographs of JFK and his family that UPI was gathering for our use in the book, I experienced again the private pain of a deep personal loss. The fun-loving, joking JFK had been the first president who had been younger than I (by two years). Given his charming, self-confident personality, his youthful but reassuring voice, his strong vision and idealism, and his seeming ability—like FDR's—to attract to government service some of the keenest minds from all walks of life, I had found it easy to relate to him politically. And now he was dead. But there was more. Strangely, the murder—whatever its motive— seemed to me something of a symbolic transitional event, announcing in the person of the twenty-four-year-old assassin, Lee Harvey Oswald, the ascendance of a brash, rebellious, "do whatever you want to do" generation that was already coming up to succeed my own.

A decade earlier, back in 1953, at the age of thirty-eight and with three preteenagers at the time and another one on the way for Betty and me to raise, a disquieting episode had first made me aware of how much of a middle-aged product of a disappearing era I was becoming. In Connecticut, I had been introduced to Abe Ribicoff, a very personable former two-term Democratic congressman and able vote-getter who planned to run for governor in 1954. During a private lunch with him at a West Hartford country club, I had been persuaded by his pragmatic, middle-of-the-road liberalism and bright, confident talk to join his campaign as a volunteer and do what I could to help him in the Greenwich area. At another meeting with him soon afterward to plan a fund-raising dinner, one of his aides played a sample recording of what was described as a local high school singing group that had been enlisted to provide entertainment at the dinner. It was music such as I had never heard—screams of pain, shrieks and yells, and repetitive wails of "Yeah, yeah, yeah," lacking any sign of beauty or of a recognizable melody. To my pained expression, as Ribicoff and the others laughed, the aide explained that this was rock and roll music, "the newest and hottest music among kids today."

It went that way throughout the decade of the 1950s and into the 1960s. In the presence of younger people I often felt behind the times, put off, puzzled, unable to understand, and sometimes offended by the frenzied popularity of the gyrating Elvis or the longhaired Beatles, by the foul language of Allen Ginsberg's poem "Howl," by Jack Kerouac's breathless *On the Road*, by my own Harvard classmate Bill Burroughs's vivid, drug-oriented *Naked Lunch*, which made me nauseous as I tried to read it, by the Beats and then by the counterculture, drug-ridden, "Don't trust anyone over thirty" hippies, and by whatever else seemed intended to shock and outrage people my age. In the end, none of these traumas of mine appeared to matter much. Ultimately, my own children understood whatever I did not and succeeded in explaining it all to me and in getting me to see the originality, genius, and honesty of Ginsberg and the other spokespeople of the nuclear-threatened generation behind me who were coping with the untruths and unbelievable obscenities of the Cold War era.

All through the storm of change, I could only do my thing, some of it in step with the prophets of the future, some not. I continued to assist Stewart Udall with pictures for his book, *The Quiet Crisis*, and it was finally published, giving support to the country's growing environmentalist movement. At about the same time, in Udall's office, I met one of the members of another movement, a slim, bright-eyed young photographer named Stewart Brand. He had come into Secretary Udall's office with an introduction from a mutual friend in the Southwest and, seemingly high on something or other, had made himself at home in the Department of the Interior Building. There he was trying to arouse interest in a proposed traveling exhibit, which he had titled "America Needs Indians," while at the same time demanding to know from anyone who would listen to him whether it wasn't strange that no one had ever seen the whole earth.

Udall asked me to take care of Brand, which I was delighted to do, because he was interesting, friendly, and utterly original. It turned out that he had come from San Francisco, where he had been a member of Ken Kesey's band of Merry Pranksters, and he said he had been a driver or doorman of the Kesey group's famous psychedelic bus. For a while, Brand, who was staying in the East with the LSD-boiled Timothy Leary, visited me in Greenwich, stirring Betty and me with scintillating conversation, a good part of which we barely understood. Later on, during a trip to California, I stayed with Brand at his apartment, a small cubicle with black-painted bare walls, and on another occasion, Betty and I joined him at a brain-rattling "sensorium" in San Francisco's North Beach, where still- and motion-picture projectors, Hopi Indian dancers and singers, the aroma of burning incense, whirling colored klieg lights, the music of flutes and drums, whistles, flapping banners, and other sources of madness simultaneously assaulted all of our senses. Eventually, we drifted away from Brand, who, finally seeing the world whole, settled down as a successful entrepreneur listed in *Who's Who in America* as the publisher of a brilliant, best-selling, National Book Award–winning *Whole Earth Catalog*, which gave access to ideas, practices, and tools that helped his generation change the world.

Meanwhile, my volunteer campaigning for Ribicoff's successful run for governor of Connecticut pulled me deeply into the waters of Democratic party politics. At the time, Greenwich was essentially a two-class, one-party town divided roughly between rich property owners and those who served them. By and large, many members of the latter group voted with the wealthy Republicans, and it was my hope to change a lot of them into Democrats. With the support of a few old-line Democratic district leaders who lived off of jobs and favors that the Republicans threw their way to keep them happy, a number of us formed an aggressive Young Democratic Club, which within weeks startled everyone in that overwhelmingly Republican town by enrolling more than three hundred members. Our birth and suddenly acquired strength drew the attention of Democratic party leaders in Hartford, including former governor Chester Bowles, Senators William Benton and Tom Dodd, and John Bailey, the chairman of the Democratic State Central Committee, who, accompanied by some of his state officials, came down to a banquet in Greenwich to present our charter to us.

I became the first president of the club, went on with Bailey's backing to become a vice president of the State Young Democrats, and two years later, when I reached my forties and could no longer qualify as a *Young Democrat*, was elected a member of the Greenwich Democratic Town Committee and one of Greenwich's two members of Bailey's Democratic State Central Committee. In 1956 and 1960, chewing long, dark cigars and doing dutifully whatever Bailey wanted me to do, I attended the National Democratic Convention as a member of the Connecticut delegation, voting happily in 1956 for Adlai Stevenson for president and working with other New England delegates to try to secure the vice presidential nomination for John F. Kennedy. We lost out on the vice presidency to the supporters of Tennessee's senator Estes Kefauver, who paraded around the convention hall clownishly in coonskin caps, but our efforts started the boom that in 1960 at Los Angeles won Kennedy the presidential nomination and Bailey the important chairmanship of the Democratic National Committee.

During the same period, in both 1958 and 1960, I took my lumps for the Greenwich party, running unsuccessfully for the Connecticut state legislature. In 1958, my opponent was the future United States senator Lowell Weicker, who told me with devilish good humor that, as a Republican in a Greenwich election, he could have vacationed on a Florida beach during the entire campaign and still have beaten me hands-down. The 1960 campaign also had an impediment, but of a different kind. As I went from house to house ringing doorbells for votes for Kennedy and the entire Democratic ticket, including myself, too many Greenwich neighbors slammed their doors angrily in my face, shouting that they would never vote for anybody on a ticket headed by a Catholic running for president. Although one day Lyndon Johnson, the Democratic vice presidential candidate, rode a commuter train with some of us from Grand Central Station to Greenwich, shaking hands and making a campaign speech to crowds at the Greenwich railroad station, we were unable to turn Greenwich into a Democratic-voting town that year. But we did cut into the size of the Republican vote and in 1964, with Greenwich finally voting Democratic for the first time in one hundred years, we carried the town for Lyndon Johnson. At last we did it, but in succeeding national elections, Greenwich went quickly back into the Republican fold, and it did not happen again.

Gradually, I dropped out of Connecticut politics, only to return temporarily in 1974 to try to win a Democratic nomination for Congress as the "favorite son" candidate of Greenwich and a lot of the smaller towns of our county. Again, I failed to win, but in our Democratic congressional convention at Bridgeport, it took seven raucous ballots and half the night for my opponent, the personal candidate of the Democratic boss of Bridgeport, to defeat me. As it turned out, my licking was all for the best, for I went back to my typewriter and, instead of serving in Congress, soon had a more satisfactory time writing a history of that institution, entitled *On the Hill*, which Simon and Schuster published. Carl Albert, the then Speaker of the House of Representatives, lauded it as "the most accurate and comprehensive account of the United States Congress under one cover," and in 1976, during the bicentennial anniversary celebration of the signing of the Declaration of Independence, he and Mike Mansfield, the majority leader of the Senate, gave copies of the book in the name of the Congress to the prime minister and other visiting members of the British government, declaring that they could think of "no more appropriate gift" to present to them.

In the meantime, my full platter of zestful interests and activities was topped off periodically by visits to Oregon's Wallowa County, where the dry climate and clear mountain air did wonders for Betty's asthma and increased our impatience to find a place to buy. For a while, the Realtor who was supposed to be looking for a property to sell us kept showing us everything *but* what we wanted—old Victorian houses with large porches but little or no land in one or another of the county's small towns; enormous working cattle ranches with government permits to lease additional public grazing lands (we had no intention of losing our shirt by going into a business about which we knew nothing and that would claim all of our time); and properties in every part of the county except in a very specific area with breathtaking views of the mountains where we had told the Realtor we wanted to live. Finally, at the end of one of our visits when I stopped at his office to say good-bye to him, he told me that some property in the area in which we were interested had just come on the market and that I ought to go around and see it on my way out of town. Betty had gone on ahead of me with a couple of our children to Lewiston, from where we were going to fly back east, but with the rest of our family and some of their friends, I made a brief stop at the newly listed property and knew at once with a thrill of excitement that it was exactly what we had been seeking.

It was what was known as a residential ranch, about one hundred acres of both high and low open country, lying by itself outside of the small town of Joseph (named by settlers for the famous chief after they had gotten him safely exiled elsewhere), with some remarkable 360-degree views of the valley and mountains, precisely in the part of the county where we had wanted to be. As we walked over the property, examining each part of it, the ranch seemed to all of us like something out of a storybook. It had a secluded six-acre lake full of rainbow trout jumping for flies; an ancient orchard of apple, pear, and plum trees; and two broad irrigation ditches with gravel bottoms and clear-running snow-melt from the mountains, bordered by banks of buttercups and fireweed and by stands of willows, cottonwoods, mountain ash, alders, and aspen that shaded the streams and made them look like natural rivers. It had a good deal of irrigated land for the raising of hay, and high, rolling pastures blanketed with the vivid colors of lupine, yarrow, Indian paintbrush, clumps of purple asters, cinquefoil, and other wildflowers that in the distance seemed to merge with the lid of the sky. It had horned owls in the trees along the ditches, blue heron, killdeer, and ducks about the lake, large-winged hawks and bald and golden eagles circling and screeching above us, and mule deer peering out at us from among the trees. It also had a collection of old tumbledown farm buildings and cheat grass, thistles, and weeds with thorns and sticky burrs growing galore everyplace where there should have been rich hip-high grass. But I figured we could take care of both of those problems, and the price of the place—which also suited Betty's needs for the three or four weeks of boarding the Indian day campers—was right.

In a burst of enthusiasm, I hurried the eighty-five miles to Lewiston and described the place to Betty. It sounded just wonderful, she said, and then asked, "Did you put some money down on it?" Of course, I hadn't. In a panic, I called the Realtor right away, but unbelievably, the worst had happened. In the short time since I had left the county, someone else had put down earnest money on the property, and we had lost it. My heart plummeted. Betty was a good sport about it, but I felt terribly guilty for having let slip away not only what was now assuming to me the status of being the best property in the county but a wonderful place for her asthma, and I was certain that nothing like it would ever appear again.

Fortunately, our gloom did not last long. A month or so later, all became suddenly well again. The Realtor informed us that the would-be buyer had been unable to go through with the purchase and that the property was back on the market. We swooped it up quickly and, enlisting the advice and help of friends in the county, including a local builder named Bill Dunn, prepared the place for our use the following summer. The aged house on the property had no foundation, and its uninsulated walls were full of bees and riddled with holes that were covered over or plugged up with newspapers, but while Bill worked with Betty on plans for a new house, he patched up the old one and, sleeping on cots and army-surplus stretchers and in sleeping bags in a cabin down by the lake, we and the Indian campers made it comfortably through the first summer.

There was also much to enjoy. We built a corral and repaired perimeter and cross fences on the property, bought horses and tack for each member of the family and for the use of the campers, and, guided by Don Miller, the local U.S. Forest Ranger, who became our friend, rode like veterans on steep sidewall trails past fallen pine trees and slides of shale into the heights of the Wallowa Mountains, whose glaciated peaks loomed above our place and, camping overnight, explored the wilderness lakes and passes. At our own lake, we built a dock and a fire ring and swam, fished, and watched muskrats swim across the water, then on occasional nights lingered on after flaming sunsets and darkness to have dinner by the fire and to sing and identify constellations before getting into our sleeping bags and drifting off under the stars. Sometimes, after the day camp was over and the students had left us, we took long trips up the Snake River on the weekly mail boat, staying overnight at the Copper Creek camp of Dick Rivers, the doughty mailman, deep inside the rugged walls of Hells Canyon. At other times, we took long drives from our place down dirt switchback roads to visit rancher friends in the canyons or to gather wild elderberries and blackberries for Betty to make into jams and jellies.

Our county friends were particularly wonderful to us, not only helping us get settled in but patiently and tolerantly allowing us to share in their own lives and to learn and adapt to the proud, independent, and resourceful culture of their remote western rural society. From ranching families and at social, sales, shipping, calving, branding, and other events that brought people together, we learned the annual rounds, practices, problems, and points of view of the county, many of which seemed to me to be as misunderstood or totally unknown to the urbanized eastern parts of the country as were aspects of Indian cultures. At the same time, our own work at our ranch demanded a considerable amount of self-education—knowing how to make do in a thousand and one daily crises, how to mend a fence and winch an errant vehicle out of an irrigation ditch, how not to ask a man how much land or how many head of cattle he owned, and, in our immediate case, how to restore our weed-choked land. With the advice of the county's soil-conservation agent, we devised and began to carry out a long-range irrigation plan for the property. We plowed and seeded the ground and put in mainline pipes with hydrants, and beginning that summer, Betty and I trudged over large parts of the property, setting and resetting heavy three- and four-inch pipes whose water, conveyed by pump and gravity from the ditches, began to get rid of most of the cheat grass, mullein, and undesirable stuff and to turn the ranch into a grassland paradise for wildlife and for the human soul. Finally, we named the prop-

Betty at the entrance to our Oregon ranch. Looming over us in the background, at times seemingly like a wall shutting out the tumults of the rest of the world, is the wilderness of the high Wallowa Mountains.

erty Palojami Ranch, which some visiting Nez Perce friends informed us was a word for "beautiful land," although one Indian teenage joker at the day camp provided great merriment to our son, Alvin, by telling him that it really meant "He has lots of women."

By the time we left to return to Connecticut for the winter, we all felt that we were no longer easterners, but, through the magic of our summer in Oregon, had truly become westerners. We were proud and happy about it, and back in Greenwich, we boasted knowingly about our new western home among the cowboys in Oregon. Meanwhile, during the winter and spring, Bill Dunn built our new house and by June had it ready for us. When we got out there, he met us and gave us a shock. He had just discovered that for some unexplained reason the man who had done the plumbing for the house had put a lien on our property even though he had not yet sent us his bill. In a sweat of panic and anger, I got in Bill's car, and we went searching unsuccessfully all over the county for the man. The next morning, the plumber showed up, saying that he had heard that we were looking for him. I asked him what he thought he was doing, putting a lien on our place. "Well, you're easterners," he snapped. "As likely as not, you could run off and never pay me for the work I did."

I paid his bill immediately, got the lien taken off the property, and never used the man again. But what he said was like a stab of truth. We were really not yet westerners, and Oregon's hold on us was very tentative. We still thought of Wallowa County as a summer vacation home and the place where we would eventually retire, but Greenwich was still our principal residence, I still had to make my living in New York, and our lives were still oriented around the East. Meanwhile, we continued to love the ranch and the people and the outdoor, friendly, and hardworking way of life in Wallowa County, and gradually, as we became increasingly integrated in the county's affairs and familiar part-time fixtures in its life, we felt that we could claim to be at least part westerners, especially in the summers, when we settled into an annual routine of cross-continent travel.

Each June, when school ended in Greenwich, Betty loaded our children into our station wagon and headed bravely for Oregon, driving them alone three thousand miles across the country, which was still without completed interstate highways, taking back roads or historic routes like that of the Oregon Trail, pausing on the way to visit friends, Indian reservations, and national parks and sites, and, with the help of a half dozen or so of the famous Depression-day WPA state guides that she took along, giving them a store of lasting knowledge about the western states of the United States. In August, when I could join them, I flew from New York, usually accompanied by "South Pass Pete" Decker, my pint-sized, elderly antiquarian bookman friend, complete in his cowboy hat and boots, first to some western city like Denver or Billings, Montana. There we would rent a car and then for ten days or so drive through the Rocky Mountain states toward the Wallowa ranch as Betty had done earlier, sightseeing at ghost towns and old forts and stopping to visit Indians, ranchers, and other friends before finally reaching Wallowa County and joining the family. Then, early in September, all of us would drive back together, arriving in Greenwich in time for the opening of school.

One year, I invited the historian David McCullough, who at the time was an editor at American Heritage, to join Peter and me at Sheridan, Wyoming, where we were attending the annual convention of the National Congress of American Indians, and then drive on with us to the Wallowa County ranch. David, who had never been in the West before, flew first to Denver and was ecstatic over the magnificent western landscapes through which he had then driven from Denver to Sheridan. But it was just the beginning. At Sheridan, for the first time, he was seeing Indians all about him and from almost every tribe in the country, drumming, dancing in traditional costumes, and politicking. The NCAI that year was in a crisis, strapped for funds and torn by bitter feuding between the followers of Bob Burnette and those of Helen Peterson over the election of the organization's next executive director. Clifford Samuelson was there as a self-appointed, well-meaning mediator, advancing his own compromise candidate for the position, a youthful Indian intellectual named Vine Deloria, Jr., the son of a prominent Sioux deacon in the Episcopal Church and the nephew of Ella Deloria, a much-respected Sioux anthropologist. Through Clifford, Betty and I had known young Vine and his father and aunt for a number of years, and after our arrival at Sheridan, Clifford had invited Peter, David, and me to call on Vine and him at Clifford's large motel room. In the room, Clifford was drumming up votes for Vine from a number of tribal delegates, promising to find money to help keep the NCAI alive if they elected Vine. "The NCAI is being torn apart," Clifford confided in me. "We've got to do everything possible to help save it. It's the only national voice the Indians have."

One way or another, Samuelson, whom Peter referred to approvingly as "the sporting parson" because of a supply of liquor that Clifford carried in his attaché case, was triumphant. Later that day, the delegates elected Vine, and, with Clifford's financial help, the NCAI weathered its crisis. In the following years, during his term in office, Vine spent a lot of his time writing brilliantly witty and perceptive articles for the NCAI publication, *The Sentinel*, that heaped scorn on non-Indian enemies and exploiters of the Indians, and in 1969 they formed the basis of Vine's first published book, *Custer Died for Your Sins*, a spectacular best-seller that established him as an exciting spokesperson for Indians.

Before we left Sheridan for Oregon, we attended a Miss Indian America contest, where I was startled by the introduction of a contestant from Greenwich, Connecticut, a handsome young Mohawk woman who lived in Greenwich and whom I sometimes saw riding on the morning commuter train to her job in New York City. I could scarcely believe my eyes, but there she was—sandwiched among Comanches, Navajos, Crows, Apaches, and others in feathers and beautiful beaded gowns, evidence of the modern-day ties that were bringing all Indians together. She did well in the contest, but not well enough, losing to a bright, lovely Arapaho contestant named Michelle Portwood from the Wind River reservation in Wyoming, whom Peter and I had met boning up for contest questions on the history of her tribe in the airport at Cheyenne on our way to Sheridan.

At length, we said our good-byes and took off from Sheridan, stopping first to visit friends on Tongue River ranches and then making our way to the Yellowstone country and the Jackson Lake Lodge, which was overlooked by the majestic peaks of the Teton Mountains. There, we were suddenly sobered by a national news development. In the lobby of the lodge, we saw a number of people clustered around a radio, listening to the news, and with dismay learned that, except for two of its members, the entire United States Senate had just voted for the alarming Gulf of Tonkin resolution, which would expand considerably our highly questionable military involvement in Vietnam. Step by step during recent months, the United States had been sucked into that conflict. Reminding me of the hollow promises and ineffectiveness of the preinvasion bombers at Iwo Jima, our involvement in Vietnam had first been sold to us by the Kennedy and Johnson administrations as an easy "push-button war" that would not require ground troops and could be won by the air force alone. Then ground "advisers" had been dispatched to aid the army of South Vietnam, and now, after all, U.S. ground troops would be sent to avenge something that maybe did and maybe did not happen in the Gulf of Tonkin.

I was too distracted by this new Cold War escalation and by what smacked of government lying to enjoy the Tetons, and, hurrying on toward Oregon and our ranch, we drove across the wilderness of the Bitterroot Range, following in Idaho the historic Lolo Trail, the rugged 120-mile-long ridge-top route of the Nez Perces, taken by Lewis and Clark and, years later, by Chief Joseph and the other Indians in their flight from the army. In Oregon, Peter and David remained with us at our ranch for a few days and then returned to the East.

In the following years, numerous other friends came to the ranch, among them the producer Stuart Millar, whom I helped as a consultant on his movie *Little Big Man*, the actress Barbara Bel Geddes, a longtime friend from our Santa Monica days, and the actor Vincent Price. At the time, Vincent was the chairman of the Indian Arts and Crafts Board of the Department of the Interior, which was charged, among other things, with helping Native American artists and craftspeople secure supplies, market their creations, and protect the integrity of their work from non-Indian forgers and exploiters. Stewart Udall had appointed me to the board in the mid-sixties, and soon afterward I invited its members to hold one of their periodic summer meetings in the dry mountain air at our ranch, rather than in the fierce heat and humidity of Washington. Vincent, a good-hearted, entertaining man, arrived, driving the largest and most ornately furnished motor home I had ever seen. We had one meeting of the board members, and then Vincent mysteriously disappeared. After frantic searching, we spotted his motor home in the distance and found him being taken around the county and shown properties by a Realtor. He was smitten by the area and had told the startled Realtor that he thought the county would make a good "hideout" for him, but though the Realtor, wondering from whom Vincent was trying to hide—a gangster, a bill collector, or perhaps his wife—worked hard for him, he made no sale, and Vincent departed without a sanctuary from whomever he was trying to dodge.

In the meantime, with the award of a Guggenheim Fellowship to help me with my research and travel to reservations and to national and international Indian meetings, I embarked on the writing of a new, tremendously ambitious book, *The Indian Heritage of America*, a unified, one-volume survey of the histories and cultures of all the native peoples of the western hemisphere from Alaska to the southern tip of South America and from twenty thousand years ago until the present day. The book, planned for the general public without footnotes or academic jargon, had several motives. First, I needed it as a reference book for my own use. There was nothing like it in existence—no single book written in a readable style, as devoid as possible of falsehoods, half-truths, and stereotypical thinking, and from which I, or anyone else, could derive succinct, up-to-date information on almost anything we might want to know about Indians.

Second, modern-day archaeologists had added considerably to our knowledge of the history of Native Americans prior to the time of Columbus, yet most historians and the world in general appeared ignorant of what had been learned and, using such clichés as "Indians had lived there since time immemorial," continued to give credence to the widely held assumptions that before the voyages of Columbus, there had been very few humans in the western hemisphere and they had had no history until the arrival of the Europeans. Not only was this wrong; it had a racist ring that continued on among many people until the end of the twentieth century, highlighted along the way by remarkable passages like the following from an influential textbook of the 1980s coauthored by three of the most distinguished historians in the United States, Alan Brinkley, Richard N. Current, and T. Harry Williams:

> For thousands of centuries in which human races were evolving, forming communities, and building the beginnings of national civilizations in Africa, Asia, and Europe—the continents we know as the Americas stood empty of mankind and its works. . . . The story of this new world . . . is a story of the creation of a civilization where none existed.

Drawing on the vast archaeological discoveries and the use of new dating methods since World War II, I wanted to bring an end to such thoughtless and insulting nonsense and pave the way for Indians to acquire knowledge and pride in their own, often very rich and complex backgrounds. My third aim, by showing the hemispheric unity of Indian history, was to counter Jacques Soustelle and other internationally respected writers who continued stubbornly but erroneously to claim that the Mayas, Aztecs, Incas, and other pre-Columbian empire builders of Mesoamerica and the Andean regions were not Indians, but some other highly advanced peoples who were totally unrelated to the "primitive" Indian tribes that dwelled in other parts of the Americas and who, because they were Indians, could not have possessed the talents and capabilities of people like the Mayas and Aztecs. Likening the civilizations and achievements of the empire builders of America to those of the ancient Greeks and Romans, they equated the "rude and violent" Indian tribes of North America with the barbarians of northern Europe.

I think I succeeded in all my aims. Angus Cameron, my then editor at Knopf, submitted my finished manuscript to John C. Ewers of the Smithsonian Institution and to a number of other ethnohistorians in North and South America. After getting over the shock of reading a book by someone who waded into the jealously guarded domains of so many different disciplines, they informed Angus that only a person not in the academic world would have dared to take on such an inclusive work, and they gave a green light to its publication. The results were exciting; warm reviews by both Indians and non-Indians, adoptions by book clubs and by high school and college classes, Colston Leigh lecture tours, a paperback edition and an English edition, excerpts in anthologies, radio and television appearances, and the nomination as a finalist for the National Book Award in history all followed.

At about the same time, the different rights movements and the cultural changes taking place in the United States in the 1960s and early 1970s were having a profound impact on Indians and their relations with the rest of the American people. The increasing assertiveness of members of the National Indian Youth Council, of the newly formed American Indian Movement (AIM), and of other activist Indian groups was making headlines, and interest in Native Americans and their causes was soaring. In New England, the impoverished Penobscot and Passamaquoddy tribes startled the country by laying claim to more than 50 percent of the state of Maine. Their case was a good one, and the Indians received a satisfying compromise settlement of land and money. In the Pacific Northwest, Indians fought pitched battles for legal recognition of their treaty fishing rights in the rivers of the Columbia Basin and around Puget Sound, and the U.S. Supreme Court ruled in their favor. Meanwhile, among non-Indians, old and new books on Indians, including *Black Elk Speaks,* John Neihardt's inspirational tome of the 1930s; Stan Steiner's *The New Indians,* on the young militants; Bob Burnette's *The Tortured Americans,* on the modern-day Indians' trials; Carlos Castaneda's teachings of a Yaqui Indian sorcerer; Dee Brown's *Bury My Heart at Wounded Knee;* Vine Deloria's book; and the first work of fiction by an Indian author to win the Pulitzer Prize, N. Scott Momaday's *House Made of Dawn,* became required reading.

During this period of turmoil and change, I was caught up in much of the new interest. Continuing to visit reservations, I wrote a stream of passionate but meticulously researched articles, aimed principally at non-Indian readers, for the *Atlantic Monthly, Life, American Heritage, Audubon,* and other publications on the history and the contemporary struggles of various tribes for such goals as sovereignty, freedom of religion and the safeguarding of their spiritual practices and sacred places, protection of their treaty land, water, and hunting and fishing rights, better housing, sanitation, health care, and educational and employment opportunities, and the truthful telling of their history. Some of these articles and the documents and research materials on which they were based, I was later able to include for wider audiences and a more enduring readership in two more books, *Red Power,* a documentary history of Indian affairs in the 1960s, which McGraw-Hill published, and *Now That the Buffalo's Gone,* seven narrative accounts of Indian-white relations, which Knopf brought out.

At the same time, I was enlisted frequently as a consultant on Indian matters by several U.S. House and Senate committees, the National Endowment for the Humanities, and the Ford and other foundations that began to give grants to Indian organizations, as well as by television and theatrical moviemakers, book and magazine publishers, and colleges and universities. The last were beginning to receive government money for Indian studies programs and, having no idea how to start, invited anyone they could think of, including myself, to come and discuss such questions as what courses should be given and what their content should be, who was qualified to teach them, what books and learning materials existed, whether they were reliable and sensitive enough to be used, and what department should be responsible for the courses—anthropology, history, political science, or what? At some Montana institutions, including the State University at Bozeman, good sense prevailed, and tribal elders and traditional teachers such as the Crow Indian historians of their nation, Barney Old Coyote and Joe Medicine Crow, and the Northern Cheyenne descendant of famous chiefs, John Woodenlegs, were invited to the campuses to get things started. But at other places, while college administrators and heads of departments wandered around trying to agree on what to teach and how to do it, young non-Indian professors who knew nothing about Indians seized the opportunity to make a name for themselves quickly in the new field and were soon winning attention as experts on Indians and publishing ill-informed regurgitations of someone else's defective, out-of-date work on the subject.

In January 1969, the newly elected president, Richard Nixon, requested that I prepare a study, with recommendations, on the status of Indian affairs that would help him formulate an Indian policy for his administration. Although he seemed genuinely friendly to Indians, he was the first Republican president since Dwight Eisenhower, whose termination policy had alienated almost the entire Indian population from the Republican party, and after eight years of Democratic administrations, he felt that the Republicans were out of touch with Indians and that he had a need to know what to do in order to regain their trust.

I agreed to do the study, and in mid-February, after three weeks of work on it, I presented it to the White House. Among its major recommendations, which reflected the opinions of tribes throughout the country, was that the president take immediate action to reassure the Indians that the termination policy was truly dead and that his administration now supported, instead, Indian self-determination and self-government. In addition, I suggested that for more visibility and importance, the Bureau of Indian Affairs be moved upstairs from the Department of the Interior to the Executive Office of the president and that it be restructured under an

Indian assistant secretary, with other Indians in top policy-making positions to serve, rather than boss, Indians; that a new independent government office be established, responsible to the Indians for the trust protection of their reservation lands and other assets; and that greater funding be made available to the tribes for jobs and economic development programs on the reservations.

Although the report received much publicity, nothing came of it for a while. Then, the following year, after widespread public sympathy and support had been aroused for a group of Indian men, women, and children who had occupied Alcatraz Island in San Francisco Bay to try to bring attention to the ill-treatment and broken treaty rights of Indians of all tribes, Nixon delivered an unprecedented message to Congress on Indian affairs that contained many of the recommendations I had made to him, as well as others from members of his administration. At the same time, the president sent to Congress a package of bills to implement the recommendations in the message and also signed legislation returning to the Taos Pueblo Indians of northern New Mexico 44,000 acres and their sacred Blue Lake, the fount of their religion, which had been taken from them and made part of a national forest in 1906. To many Indians, Nixon became known as the best president the Indians had ever had, and even to non-Indians who felt that Nixon presented them with little else to praise, his empathy for Indians—stemming perhaps from friendship given him in high school by a Cherokee football coach—was admirable. As for me, a liberal Democrat, three days after delivering his message, the President wrote me this much-appreciated note:

> Now that I have sent my message on Indian Affairs to the Congress, I want to take this occasion to express my personal appreciation for your effective contribution to the development of this policy.
>
> Your report on the relationship between American Indians and their government—begun at my staff's request, as I recall, before my inauguration—was a factor throughout. Thus, it particularly pleased me to see your favorable comment on the proposals that we ultimately made. I am grateful for your work at the beginning and for your words of support now.
> > Sincerely,
> > Richard Nixon

Unfortunately, the exhilaration over the administration's perceived commitment to Indians did not last long. Congress bottled up the bills; the White House, losing all interest, failed to push them; and the disillusionment, coupled with a rash of serious new Indian grievances, led to a series of dramatic confrontations between the government and angry, frustrated Indians, including a takeover of the Bureau of Indian Affairs Building in Washington, D.C., and a seventy-day siege by Sioux and other Indians who occupied the historic hamlet of Wounded Knee on the Pine Ridge reservation in South Dakota.

In the episode at the BIA Building, a terrible armed clash that could have resulted in numerous deaths of Indians and law-enforcement officers just blocks from the White House, was only narrowly averted. The Indians, men, women, youths, babies, and old people who had arrived peaceably by the hundreds in Washington from many parts of the country to draw attention to their problems, were led by Russell Means, Dennis Banks, and other urban AIM figures, as well as by present and former tribal reservation officers like my friend Bob Burnette and by other prominent non-AIM Indians. Assured ahead of time that the government would provide a place for them to stay in the capital, the Indians were enraged when they reached Washington and were shown, instead, a memo from an assistant secretary of the Interior Department ordering the Bureau of Indian Affairs "not to provide any assistance or funding, either directly or indirectly" to the Indians. In an angry scuffle that erupted at the BIA headquarters, the Indians, with no place else to go, swarmed into the building, occupying and barricading it against a ring of U.S. marshals and helmeted District of Columbia riot police.

The siege that developed went on for several days, drawing worldwide publicity while the government tried to figure out what to do and the Indians inside the building armed themselves for an expected assault by the marshals. On Monday, November 6, the day before the 1972 national elections, in which Nixon was running for a second term against his challenger, George McGovern, Bob Burnette phoned me in Greenwich and, telling me that the Indians had information that the government was going to storm the building that night, pleaded with me to come down to Washington right away and try to help convince the government that the Indians would fight back and many people, including women and children, would be killed. The specter of a bloodbath of Indians in the nation's capital on the eve of Election Day made me think that somebody had gone mad, and though I had no idea of what I could do, I flew down to Washington as fast as I could. Bob met me at the airport and drove me to the BIA Building, where he told me all the Indian leaders were about to have a meeting to prepare for the expected attack.

Inside, the building was a wreck. Desks, chairs, file cabinets, sofas, copying machines, and other office furniture had been piled in stairwells and corridors as barricades. Files, documents, and reams and reams of paper littered the floors and upended furniture. And among the chaos were Indian guards, all waiting anxiously and all ready and armed with one or more weapons that could kill—if not small arms, hunting rifles, as well as various types of gasoline-filled Molotov cocktails and knives and clubs of all kinds, many made from parts of furniture or from razor-sharp shards of porcelain smashed from sinks and toilet bowls in the building.

In the dimly lit upstairs office of Louis Bruce, the commissioner of Indian Affairs, which the Indians had taken over and made into their headquarters, the meeting had already started, and I recognized a number of Indian friends and acquaintances. But it was all business now, and one of them, Hank Adams, a slight, scholarly Indian whom I had known for years, told me that I was a white man and would have to wait outside— under guard—till the meeting was over. Bob Burnette tried to protest, but this was no time for an argument about me, and I went out and sat down on the corridor floor to wait. An unpleasant-looking guard with a wicked-looking knife attached to a pole like a short lance hovered over me. After a while, he asked me my name, and I told him. His face suddenly brightened, and he relaxed. "Are you the guy who wrote *The Patriot Chiefs*?" he asked excitedly. I told him I was, and when Bob Burnette finally came out, he found the two of us sitting on the floor together like old buddies.

There was really little that Bob and I could do. We went over to the Interior Department and had a meeting with three government solicitors, urging that they recognize the monumental blame that would come to the administration in the voting booths of the nation the next day if an attack were made that night on the Indians and people were killed. That seemed to give them pause, and they withdrew for a while to consult among themselves. While they were gone, Bob got a phone call, and suddenly things brightened. The White House had called off the marshals' attack and, instead, had set up a meeting with Hank Adams and other Indian leaders for 8:00 p.m. that evening. That settled it for me. The meeting came to terms, there was no fighting, the administration provided the Indians with funds to leave Washington, and I returned home.

Nothing positive resulted to give hope to the Indians, however. The government paid no serious attention to their problems, made no mention of the promises in Nixon's message, and offered no support for the Indian bills in Congress. In the months that followed, there were more confrontations, more occupations, and more Indian frustrations and bitterness, all reaching a climax in a revolt among some of the Oglala Lakota Sioux on the Pine Ridge reservation against the collusion between a corrupt, dictatorial chairman of the tribe and the BIA officials on the reservation and in the takeover of Wounded Knee on February 27, 1973, by a large number of armed AIM members and their supporters. This became a huge media event, because of where it took place—the site of a notorious army massacre of a band of cold and starving Sioux in the winter of 1890—and because it was a real, protracted battle, with people firing at one another and some of them being killed. For weeks, the government could not decide how to end it. In March, I wrote a long explanatory article for the *New York Times Sunday Magazine*, entitled "What the Indians Want," and on the day of its appearance, I received a call from an assistant secretary in the Interior Department, asking me to come to a meeting in Washington the next day.

Secretary of the Interior Rogers C. B. Morton was in California being treated for cancer, but an assistant, John Whittaker, ran the meeting, and a small squad of White House people, among them, Leonard Garment, special counsel to the president, and Bradley Patterson, Garment's able and well-liked specialist on Indian affairs, was there. I was the person who had written the study for the president, I, like everyone else, was supposed to be a Nixon team player, and I was on the griddle. *What* had gone wrong? somebody wanted to know. It was easy telling them, and I did so in a white heat. Why was nobody paying attention to the mounting grievances of the tribes? Why had the reforms promised by the president's message been forgotten? What had happened to the talk of self-determination, to changes in the Bureau of Indian Affairs, to legislation that would make tribal leaders accountable to their people and not to the BIA—which was mostly what the siege at Wounded Knee was all about?

I remember little after that. Somebody asked Leonard Garment if it was true that the administration had done nothing to help push the Indian bills through Congress, and Garment said yes, it was true. Then Whittaker asked me to go into another room with him. He had a confidential question for me, which I think he had discussed on the phone with Secretary Morton. He wanted to know whether I would be interested in being appointed an assistant secretary of the Interior Department. I was thoroughly startled, but I answered at once: "No, thank you." I treasured my independence in being able to write and say what I wanted.

When the siege at Wounded Knee finally ended, the government arrested more than five hundred people, charging them with various offenses. All but fifteen were acquitted or had the charges dismissed. One of the trials was put on hold while the court attempted to settle the question of whether the United States government had ever legally ended the sovereignty of the Sioux and acquired the right to prosecute the Indians. A number of us, including Vine Deloria, testified for the Sioux at the hearing in Lincoln, Nebraska, and although we persuaded the federal judge that history showed that the sovereignty of the Sioux Indians had been taken from them illegally, he ruled that there was nothing that a court could do about it now and that only an act of Congress could rectify the wrong.

During the next few years, something like a reign of terror existed on the Pine Ridge reservation, where Wounded Knee was located. The FBI and BIA officials, allied to the strong-armed tribal chairman and his personal "goon squad" of barroom toughs, harassed, beat up, and even killed Indians who had participated in or supported the takeover of Wounded Knee. In the fighting that went on, largely unnoticed by the rest of the country, two FBI agents also lost their lives. Finally, the Indians voted for a new chairman, and peace returned.

The siege at Wounded Knee was a watershed event in Indian history. The influence of the young militants who had taken over the hamlet spread throughout the Indian world and breathed new life into the Indians' fight for the right to manage and control their own affairs and rid themselves of venal leaders who made themselves accountable to the bosses of the Bureau of Indian Affairs rather than to their own people. Many of the tribal leaders got the message and changed.

In a postscript to Wounded Knee, when the siege was over, and it was not yet clear what it had achieved, a group of angry Sioux sent a message to Leonard Garment, Nixon's man in Washington, who had informed them that there was nothing for him to discuss with them. "In the coming years," they replied to Garment, "you will find greater resistance to the Government's unresponsive rules, regulations, and its so-called 'policies.' Our forefathers died protecting this land, and we would be cowards if we continue to allow the federal, state, and local governments to continue racial and cultural genocide against us and our Indian brothers and sisters across this continent. . . ."

The day of the "Uncle Tomahawks" and "Apples" on the reservations was over. A new generation was speaking.

The decades of the 1960s and 1970s were not always the easiest for parents like Betty and me. We had been raised in a time and environment that honored sentiments like that of Stephen Decatur, America's naval hero of the war with the Tripoli pirates, who had proclaimed, "Our country! In her intercourse with foreign nations may she always be in the right; but our country, right or wrong." As our children reached their late teens and early twenties, such words fell flat. The soul-destroying lies and immoralities of the Vietnam War rolled on, tearing apart our country, its traditions, and its culture and filling parents like Betty and me with fears, on the one hand, that our son would be sent to the terrible war and, on the other, that, in their revolt against perceived wrongs and evils of our government and society, one or more of the children would turn away from us for counterculture communes and "families" of their peers, who would agree with them more than we would.

They were right about Vietnam, and we knew it, and for many years we were torn by it, enduring in our efforts to hold on to our children such inanities of some of their desperate college-age friends as, "All history before 1960 is irrelevant"; or "Bobby Dylan will be popular long after Beethoven is totally forgotten"; or the somewhat painful pronouncement that we had had no business getting involved in World War II. Thanks largely to Betty's enormous love and patience, the family held together, and one by one, the three girls and Alvin went through their college years relatively unscathed.

On many occasions, my own anger rose at events in Southeast Asia, and, recalling with nostalgic sentiment the vigor and excitement of the peace parades of the 1930s, when I was very young, I felt with a twinge of conscience that I ought to join in the anti–Vietnam War demonstrations.

But I didn't. Then one day, Bob Burnette and a creaking busload of Lakota Sioux Indians, including many elderly men and women, Native American World War II veterans, and several medicine men, arrived unannounced at our home in Greenwich, having driven from their reservations on the plains of South Dakota to participate in a big peace parade being led by Martin Luther King, Jr., Stokely Carmichael, and others in New York City. Most of the Indians went on to overnight housing for them in Manhattan, but Burnette, the sprightly old Lakota medicine man Henry Crow Dog, his son, Leonard, and several others stayed on with us. Laying out on the floor a sort of altar of a small American flag and various medicine objects, Henry conducted a spiritual ceremony in our living room. The sound of the Indians' singing and the beating of their handheld drum carried over to the home of our suburbanite next-door neighbors, who were about to leave for a dinner party but who hurried over to our house in their formal evening attire, wondering whether we were in some kind of trouble. They had never seen an Indian before and stood transfixed for half an hour, scarcely able to believe their eyes as Henry Crow Dog led the others in a prayer ceremony of thanks in the Lakota language for his people's safe arrival in the East.

The journey of the Indians to New York finally shamed me into action. The next day, the Sioux, led by a short, bandy-legged Oglala war veteran carrying a huge American flag on a flagstaff pressed against his stomach and wearing a spectacular trailing headdress of eagle feathers and a deerskin vest hung with medals, marched in a place of honor at the head of the parade, along with Martin Luther King, Jr., and other notables, and our son, Alvin, and I walked with them, inspired by the Indians and feeling good at the storm of cheers that greeted them from the New York crowds that lined our route of march from Central Park to the United Nations Plaza where a rally with speeches occurred.

Several years later, with the war still raging and President Nixon presiding over new abominations, including the attack against Cambodia and the killings of protesting students at Kent State and Jackson State colleges, I flew to Washington and joined our daughter Allison and her date in an angrier and even bigger end-the-war demonstration. Hundreds of thousands of people poured into the capital from all parts of the country, filling the grounds between the Washington Monument and the Lincoln Memorial. Armed troops and police were everywhere, long columns of city buses barricaded access to the streets around the White House, and the capital looked like it was on the verge of a battle. The day, however, turned out more like that of a giant good-natured pep rally and picnic, featuring a rolling barrage of speeches, antiwar music, and, for some reason, sudden displays of nudity by deliriously happy individuals in the crowd. But this and the march with the Indians proved pretty much to be the extent of my activist role in helping to end the war.

During those years of bad conscience, meanwhile, I became a vice president of American Heritage, continuing with our book division and also doing some editing and writing on my own. Late in the 1960s, the shareholders of the company, of which I was one, agreed to sell American Heritage to the McGraw-Hill Publishing Company, and soon afterward my friend, Jim Parton, left the firm for other pursuits, including the writing of a book on his old war outfit, the Eighth Air Force. Somewhat later, Bruce Catton, another mainstay of the company, died near his boyhood home in Michigan. It seemed to me that in the 1960–65 period, the centenary years of the Civil War, Bruce, like a general during the actual years of the struggle, had been afire with vitality, turning out his magnificent histories of the war as if he were living through that conflict himself. Then in 1965, the centennial observance of the war had ended, and as it had been for many of the veterans one hundred years before, the excitement was over. And so, in a way, I felt it now was for Bruce. Although he continued for more than a decade to write beautifully on baseball, the Mayas, the founding of the United States, and a host of other subjects, including a final volume on the Civil War, he seemed then and until his death to be living a life of anticlimax, like a veteran of the actual war himself, missing his uniformed companions, the battles, the strategies, the color and the smoke and stench of the Civil War, a time that, with the anniversary of the coming of peace, had faded away, leaving him behind.

In the mid-1970s, American Heritage was sold again, this time to a private family. In the shuffle, I became editor of *American Heritage* magazine, then a director of the company and the editor in chief of all of our magazines. When market tests showed that *American Heritage* was losing its appeal to readers of the youthful baby boomer generation, I set about with a highly creative designer, Massimo Vignelli, to remake the twenty-year-old *American Heritage* into a livelier, more modern publication in look as well as content. With our other editors, I sought more articles that provided the historical background of contemporary newsworthy subjects such as the Arab oil boycott of 1973 or, following the Watergate scandal and the resignation of President Nixon, the secret, freewheeling activities of the Watergate burglars' "alma mater," the Central Intelligence Agency.

In the latter instance, I wanted *American Heritage* to carry an article that would shed light on how and when the CIA had become a loose cannon, lacking effective oversight or accountability to the American people or their representatives. For a while, the agency's spokespersons withheld their cooperation from us, but one day the new chairman of our board, Samuel Reed, introduced me to an old friend of his, George Bush, the future president, who was then the director of the CIA and had dropped in to see Reed. Our troubles were over. Bush was affable and eager to help, and with his intercession, doors opened, and we got two riveting articles. One, on the birth of the CIA by Tom Braden, a former OSS officer, revealed among other things how President Harry Truman had quietly granted the CIA unprecedented permission in 1948 to intervene secretly against the Communist party in the elections in Italy that year, thus setting a precedent for future covert operations by the agency in the internal affairs of Guatemala, Cuba, Iran, Vietnam, Chile, and other countries all over the world. The other story told in detail the behind-the-scenes role of the CIA in the Cuban missile crisis. Both articles were of the type that made the magazine more relevant to the changing times and interests of our readers, and helped *American Heritage* increase its circulation.

This period also proved to be one of the busiest of my life. In addition to my work at American Heritage, I was called on by Senator James Abourezk of South Dakota, the chairman of the Senate Committee on Indian Affairs, to assist him with some of his writing. I was also asked by feisty Congressman Wayne Aspinall to spend several months, off and on, editing a mammoth report to the president of the United States and the Congress by a commission he headed that reviewed the country's voluminous public land laws and recommended changes in them. In the same years, I wrote four long articles for *Audubon* magazine on environmental issues in the American West and several books, one of them a pictorial history of South Dakota's Black Hills for Times Books, another an updated revision of a 1950s Oliver La Farge history of Indians, and a third, done for the Amon Carter Museum in Fort Worth, Texas, a biography of Peter Rindisbacher, a little-known but greatly gifted young Swiss artist who had painted some of the earliest pictures of Plains Indians.

Indirectly, I had Ed Abbey, the author of *The Monkey Wrench Gang*, *Desert Solitaire*, and a string of other memorable books, to thank for the *Audubon* magazine assignments. Despite his fierce and often egregious hostility to the western cattle industry, dams, billboards, and other earmarks of man's despoiling presence on the planet, I found Abbey, who played the role of a curmudgeon and became something of a cult leader for an army of angry environmental activists throughout the country, an immensely likable person. He had been assigned by Les Line, the rotund, gourmandizing editor of *Audubon*, to write an article on the Hopi Indians of northern Arizona, whose land and water supply were being threatened by a Peabody Coal Company strip mine, but he had handed in what amounted to a diatribe against the Mormons, one of whom, a prominent Salt Lake City attorney who represented the Hopis, Abbey charged without proof, was at the same time on the payroll of the coal company and was selling out the Indians. Les Line felt he could not print the abusive anti-Mormon material, Ed Abbey would not change it, and, apparently because the story dealt with a conflict between Indians and whites, Line turned to me.

Abbey was content to have me take over the assignment, and although it required from me months of investigative reporting that failed to sustain Abbey's charges and my writing an entirely new article of more than ten thousand words that managed without invective to draw national support for the Hopis in their fight against the coal company, it had pleasant rewards for me. Abbey and I went on a camping trip or two together with others in the wilderness areas of the Southwest and became mutually respectful friends. In addition, I wrote three more articles for *Audubon*, one of which, in competition with others from such periodicals as *Time* and *Newsweek*, won a national magazine award in New York for excellence in reporting, apparently the first of such rarefied attention that the magazine had ever been accorded. Largely as a result of the impact the articles made, I also ended up being invited to join the boards of two of the country's major and most constructive environmental organizations, the Natural Resources Defense Council in New York and the Environmental Policy Institute (later called the Friends of the Earth) in Washington, D.C.

In 1979, on the eve of turning sixty-five, I finally retired from American Heritage and returned to a status that I had left long before, that of a self-employed freelancer. But times were different. In the busy sunset years that followed, my schedule was filled with invitations that involved me in such varied projects as teaching classes on western and American Indian history at the Buffalo Bill Memorial Center in Cody, Wyoming; lecturing to tourists on the Lewis and Clark Trail; writing for and helping to edit *American West* magazine in the warm winter bliss of Tucson, Arizona; sharing in the direction of annual four-day summer conferences of scholars and public figures on western issues and themes at the Institute of the American West in Idaho's Sun Valley; assisting in the establishment of a successful National Cowboy Poetry Gathering held each year at Elko, Nevada; and serving for sixteen years with Barbara Tuchman, Arthur Schlesinger, Jr., David McCullough, and other fellow historians on the executive board of the Society of American Historians and for one year as president of the professional Western History Association, most of whose members were academic historians on the faculties of American universities and colleges.

In a tit-for-tat encounter, Ed Abbey presents me with a bumper sticker after I had written an article reminding him that the successor to cattle ranches in the West would be more sprawl of housing developments and five-acre ranchettes.

At the same time, several of the invitations kept me at work on new books. For a series on the Civil War, I was asked by the book editors of Time-Life to write a volume on the war in the trans-Mississippi West. The notion excited me, for very little of a comprehensive nature had ever been published on the Civil War in the states and territories that stretched westward from the Mississippi River to the Pacific Ocean, fostering a false impression of an American West whose history, including that of the remorseless dispossession of Indians, stopped abruptly in 1861 and started up again in 1865 when the Civil War ended on battlefields in the East. The Time-Life editors required a text of only 35,000 words from me, but the subject proved so compelling (for instance, in the West during the four years of the war, more Indian tribes were destroyed and more land seized from them by whites in skirmishes, battles, and massacres than in any other four-year period in American history) that after the book's publication, I went on to write a greatly expanded version of my own, *The Civil War in the American West*, which Knopf published. Suggesting to reviewers and readers the need for including the far western theater more fully in future histories of the war, it became a selection of the Book of the Month Club and the History Book Club.

Knopf published two more of my books, one of which, *America in 1492*, I edited for Chicago's Newberry Library in connection with the observance of the quincentennial of the Columbus voyages and for which I did considerable planning and rewriting of individual chapters that were contributed to the publication by an international group of scholars. The other Knopf volume, entitled *500 Nations* and given great help by my Knopf editors, Ann Close and Ashbel Green, was a full-fledged, elegantly illustrated narrative history of Indians that accompanied a network television series of the same name produced by the actor Kevin Costner. Finally, the Ted Turner Publishing Company and the experienced publishing couple Ian and Betty Ballantine enlisted me to serve as a consultant on and to write the introduction for still another huge narrative history, *The Native Americans*, which complemented a Turner television series on the same subject. Indians were indeed "in."

The books and television series were only a part of a new, respectful attention that the Indians were receiving as a result of their nationalistic assertiveness and regained pride and self-esteem. In the new climate, a large part of my time was also drawn to the attainment of what had been one of my own dreams, one I had often discussed with Indian friends—the establishment in the United States of a national museum of the American Indian, where the tribes would be able to tell their own histories and interpret their own cultures and traditions. Much of my inspiration for such an institution came from the magnificent anthropological museum in Mexico City, which I had visited during journalistic trips to Mexico when I was with *Time* and *American Heritage*. There I had witnessed the pride that the museum's displays of the history and culture of the Olmecs, Mayas, Aztecs, and other native pre-Columbian civilizations inspired among modern-day families of Mexican Indians who brought their children to the museum to learn about the wondrous societies and achievements of their peoples. Why not such a museum in the United States, I kept wondering, one that would be run by Indians and would represent and affirm the native peoples of the hemisphere and their historic and contemporary contributions to the entire world?

New York City already had a Museum of the American Indian, opened to the public in 1922 by George Gustav Heye, a wealthy banker and collector who, assisted by numerous agents, had amassed the largest collection of Indian artifacts in the world and housed them in a museum in upper Manhattan and in a storage and research center in the Bronx. But Heye, who had deeded his collection to the people of New York, thus placing it under the guardianship of the state attorney general, died in 1957, leaving an endowment inadequate for the institution's needs. In the ensuing years, both the museum and the New York neighborhood in which it was located went steadily downhill, until the museum, grown old-fashioned and seedy, attracted barely forty thousand visitors a year, most of them classes of schoolchildren.

As I saw it, the museum also had another problem, greater than the others. Typical of its day, it was essentially a non-Indians' museum, with non-Indians running it, communicating non-Indian notions of Indian history and non-Indian interpretations—often distorted, untrue, half-true, misunderstood, or otherwise inadequate or deficient—of tribal cultures, values, and traditions. My friend Fred Dockstader, the museum's director, was aware of this and of the museum's other problems and tried to cope with them. But in the mid-1970s they apparently overwhelmed him, and the attorney general took over the affairs of the museum, forcing the resignation of Dockstader and most of the trustees and instituting a hurried search for a new group of trustees who, it was hoped, would be able to solve the institution's problems.

I was one of those who were invited to join the new board and, moved by the prospect of being able to help realize my own dream of an Indian-run museum, I committed myself to working with a task force of other trustees who accepted the challenge of trying to help save and make important to Indians and the world Heye's great collection. It took almost fifteen years to see the dream become a reality. During that time, first things had to come first. We raised working capital from foundations and other sympathetic sources, hired a new director, made an inventory of the collection, took numerous steps to protect and conserve the thousands of artifacts, added Indians to the board of trustees and to the staff, and searched and searched for a better location for the museum.

Our problems brought us more than our share of frustrations and humiliations. In New York City, our quest for funds put us in competition with a vast array of powerful cultural institutions, including other museums, and we were frequently brushed aside or given a token grant of one thousand dollars or less and told that we were "low man on the totem pole" and to apply again when we did something that would catch the interest of sophisticated New Yorkers, such as moving to a wonderful new building. With the help of my Harvard classmate David Rockefeller, who had become chairman of the Chase Manhattan Bank and was interested in our museum as well as in the development of the lower part of Manhattan Island, we found that "wonderful new building"—namely, two empty floors in the magnificent Cass Gilbert–designed U.S. Custom House facing Bowling Green, near the bottom of the island. But for a long time we ran afoul of New York politicians. In the run-down, drug-ridden area from which we were trying to move, the local state assemblyman and city council member understandably did not want to see us add to the desolation of their district by pulling out the museum, and they appealed for help to New York's loudmouthed mayor, Ed Koch, to keep us where we were. Koch obliged and in a meeting at City Hall we were told that we would have to stay where we were, and we would "have to like it."

The state attorney general and Bess Myerson, a former Miss America and commissioner of the city's department of cultural affairs, thought no kindlier of us. But the champion in the use of skullduggery against us turned out to be the state's Republican senator, Alphonse D'Amato, who, with his own publicity-seeking agenda, tried to force us to close our doors and give our collection to New York's American Museum of Natural History. Supporting that museum, which hungered for our collection, D'Amato showed no concern for the Indians' antipathy to being lumped in a museum with bugs and dinosaurs, and he managed to manipulate the editorial pages of the *New York Times* and other city newspapers into endorsing his ludicrous demand that the director and all the trustees of our museum be fired for incompetence because we would not give up our collection.

We overlooked his stridency and counterattacked, making public large financial offers we had received from Las Vegas, Indianapolis, Oklahoma City, and Dallas—in the last-named, specifically from the industrialist Ross Perot—to build us a world-class museum if we relocated there. Such a solution never got going, however, and in the long run, Senator Daniel Inouye of Hawaii, supported by New York's other senator, Daniel Patrick Moynihan, came to our rescue, directing the crafting of a complicated bill in Congress that transferred our collection to the Smithsonian Institution, which would house it in a new National Museum of the American Indian to be built on the Mall in Washington, D.C. Another provision of the bill required us to establish a smaller, permanent satellite museum in the Custom House for the people of New York, who would be giving up their ownership of Heye's collection. Still other provisos set the stage for Indian management and direction of the museum by ordering that the director as well as a majority of the members of the board of trustees be Indians. By the same and additional actions, Congress also initiated a strict repatriation policy for the return to Indians of human remains, funerary objects, communally owned native property, ceremonial and religious objects, and objects in the collection that had been acquired illegally by Heye or others from their original Indian owners.

In the course of the merger with the Smithsonian that finally took place, the retiring board of the New York museum elected me to membership on the new board of the national museum. Largely because I was known to almost all of the Indian members of that board, many of whom I had worked with on Indian affairs in past years, I was then elected the new museum's founding chairman, a role I filled for three years, at which time a prominent Oneida Indian educator, Norbert S. Hill, Jr., succeeded me. By then, the museum was well launched and, under the direction of W. Richard West, a Southern Cheyenne attorney with a master's degree in history from Harvard, was living up in every way to its promise.

The Indian peoples of the United States would at last possess the means to tell their own history and interpret their cultures and traditions, and the Mall museum, scheduled to open in 2003, with an enormous visibility that would come to it from its location close to the United States Capitol, would consti-

W. Richard West, the Southern Cheyenne director of the Smithsonian's National Museum of the American Indian, and I in 1992 at a ceremony marking the end of my three-year term as founding chairman of the museum's board of trustees.

tute a powerful reminder to the nation that Native Americans had survived all the years of oppression and adversity and were a part of the American future.

The years when I struggled with the museum's affairs were not without their stresses. One blustery wintry day before we had become part of the Smithsonian, I was hurrying from one appointment to another on Wall Street, trying to raise funds for our floundering New York museum, when I felt an uncomfortable heaviness in one of my shoulders. I already had a bad cold and, thinking I might be getting a case of walking pneumonia, I saw my doctor, who figured it was something else. He was right. After a visit to a cardiologist and tests, it turned out that I had angina. A few years later, I had a triple bypass. The operation occurred in July and was a success, but it delayed until late in the summer that year's cross-country drive to our Oregon ranch and set Betty and me to thinking seriously about our future.

We had built the ranch into what we felt was an earthly paradise, a place that through the years satisfied a hunger for the inculcation of the pride and self-esteem that comes from a sense of a personal and possessed past, as the author Wallace Stegner expressed it, of knowing who you are and how you are related to a place. We had raised our children there, and three of them had become westerners. Kathy, our youngest, lived with her two sons and a daughter full-time on the ranch, cultivating alpine wildflowers as a business and acting as caretaker of the place. Alvin and his two boys and a daughter lived in a rural part of Idaho and, along with Diane, our oldest, who was a writer and was married happily to an Idaho state senator and sheep and cattle rancher, visited our Wallowa Valley ranch frequently. Only Allison, our middle daughter, and her family, who lived near us in Connecticut, were eastern-urban-oriented; none of the rest, neither children nor any of our six western grandchildren, felt any attachment to the cities of the East or considered living there.

At the same time, Betty and I had been enriched by golden memories of our many years at the ranch—memories of working on the land, side by side, exhausted in the summer heat, when we were still young and strong, stripping hillsides of miserable cheat grass and weeds and seeding with soda wheat, rye, and other resplendent grasses that toward the end of some Junes now grew shoulder-high. We remembered riding over horse trails we had created along the banks of our sections of the ditches, through tangles of yellow clover, groves of rustling alders and aspen, and plantings of ash and apple trees that provided habitat for small animals and chattering birds and shade for the fish in the streams. Both of us recalled feeling nature's power in the ominous darkening of the clouds and the sudden roar of a wind that rushed toward us from the Wallowa peaks ahead of lightning, crackling thunder, and the first spitting raindrops of a mountain storm. We had walked together in radiant sunsets across the open foothills above the ranch, watching the ground intently for skunks and badger holes and listening to the screech of hawks that went suddenly silent as they swooped down on their quarry like torpedo bombers; had gazed at the nighttime spectacle of silhouetted clouds scudding across the face of a full moon whose glaring light illuminated the fences and pastures of the ranch; and had found solace many times in looking up toward the glacier-streaked rocky front of Mount Joseph, which, like a long, protecting wall, rearing nine thousand feet against the sky, seemed in our imaginations to be blocking out the threats and perils of the rest of the world from our secure Wallowa Valley.

From the beginning, Betty and I had assumed that one day we would retire to the ranch, but we both now knew that it would never happen. I had passed the time when I should have done so, and now it was too late. I had heart disease, and Betty, too, was not well. As she had aged, her asthma had grown very much worse. It no longer mattered now where she lived. It was bad everywhere, including Wallowa County. Aging people like us with increasing physical problems seek security, and security to us had come to mean Connecticut, where our family doctor and familiar medical facilities were located. In short, the triple bypass, if nothing else, brought us to accept the fact that now we could never leave Greenwich for full-time residence in Oregon.

It was a depressing conclusion, and I tried to cheer myself by remembering at first the western artist Frederic Remington despairing at the beginning of the twentieth century over what he had felt was the passing of an Old West that had inspired his work. "I knew the wild riders and the vacant land were about to vanish forever," he had written. "I saw the living, breathing end of three American centuries of smoke and dust and sweat, and I now see quite another thing where it all took place, but it does not appeal to me." I knew what Remington had meant, but as a historian of the American West, I also knew that, before and after Remington, each generation in the West had lamented in its own way the passing of its "old West." First the Indians and then the succeeding waves of others, the explorers with Lewis and Clark, the Jim Bridgers and other mountain men of the fur trade, the missionary preachers and priests, the California gold miners, the soldiers, the covered-wagon families of long-bearded settlers, the bad men and the sheriffs, and Charlie Russell's cowboys, each in their turn could have said, "It's all gone now, but you should have seen it when I first got here."

With whatever satisfaction I could muster, I realized suddenly that I, too, had had my "old West," which had begun with my drive with Lester Hofheimer to the Chicago World's Fair in 1933 and my bus trip to California the following year. My West hadn't been anything like the one of my father's stories or the one that I had dreamed about at the little red lighthouse in New York, for at the time, the West of that dream had been long gone and was only the stuff of movies and western pulp magazines. But the "old West" that I had experienced with Billy Watters, with Pete Decker, with Bob Burnette, and with so many others was now gone, too—changed by industrial and military centers, interstate highways, recreation developments, trophy ranches and urban sprawl, conformity, high-tech pop culture, television, and economically stressed cattle and lumber operations, struggling to survive against global competitors.

Even Wallowa County and the rugged little western town of Joseph had changed and now displayed the hallmarks of a new West, with a burgeoning population of artists and sculptors, along with sophisticated galleries and foundries to serve them, a Dairy Queen and other fast-food franchise restaurants, private homes converted into cozy bed-and-breakfast establishments, shopping malls and bookstores that served *caffè latte* and cappuccino to wandering goggle-eyed tourists from every part of the world, a golf course and a driving range, gift and health-food shops, a ski run, cell phones, a Best Western motel, annual literary conferences, a summer jazz festival, a costumed reenactment of a frontier bank robbery, and, with the popular American assumption that the fake can be better than the original, newly built main street false-front buildings evoking the look, if not the feeling, of the days of the pioneers. The wilderness of Hells Canyon, too, had all but disappeared, tamed by dam builders, water-skiers, rubber rafters, and roaring jet boats filled with tourists.

To me, the changes were regrettable but seemed also inevitable. In the future, they, too, I assumed, would be components of somebody else's "old West." Then one day, I drove up to a high point that overlooked a part of Hells Canyon, a remote spot that had once been the location of a fire lookout tower. Don Miller, our local Forest Ranger, had first taken me to this lonely site, but I thought back to another time when, several years before he had died at the age of ninety-one, Alfred Knopf, who had been visiting us at our ranch, had accompanied Don and me on another trip to the spot and had climbed the tower with us. As we three had gazed together at the wild draws and benches that led down to Snake River deep inside the canyon and then looked across to Idaho and the powerful ramparts of the Seven Devils Mountains, Alfred had been overcome by the silence and beauty of the scene. "We don't have anything like this back east," he had said. "Don't let anything happen to it." But something had happened, and now tourists could easily drive to the site over a hard-surfaced road that had a parking area and a turnaround where the fire tower had once stood. The wildness, in my mind a synonym for freedom and a losing bulwark against the changes that were overtaking not only Joseph and Wallowa County but all of the West, was gone, and remembering Alfred's words, it suddenly struck me that there would now be no more magical "old Wests" for future generations because the West today had become too much like an extension of the East, and with each year it would become more so. In other words, there was no more West. It had vanished. The whole country was becoming the same, and there was no more real wilderness in the West or the East and, for me at least, no more difference whether I lived in the East or in the new West.

Several months later, at a fall meeting of the Indian museum board in Washington, I got a phone message. Kathy had called from our ranch, and it was urgent. "She sounded a little hysterical," I was told.

I had to catch a plane back to New York, but I tried several times, in the museum office and at the airport, to call Kathy. I got no answer, and I was back home in Greenwich that evening before I finally reached her. *Hysterical* was an understatement. She was alternately sobbing out of control and screaming furiously a mile a minute over what had happened. It boiled down to something that was indeed terrible. That morning, after Kathy had gone into town, a man cleaning winter debris from irrigation ditches had driven a huge tractorlike backhoe across our land and into our principal ditch, which ran past our houses, tearing up our grassland, bulldozing some hundred or more trees, including apple and ash trees that Betty and I had carefully planted years earlier along a half-mile stretch of the ditch, and utterly destroying the beauty of our property. Two of our friends who hurried up to the ranch to see what had happened confirmed the devastation. "Your place looks like a battlefield," one of them reported to us on the phone.

When Betty and I finally got out there, my first horrified feeling was that we had been invaded and raped, that all the hard work that we had put into the place, all the peace and serenity and loveliness that we had achieved, were gone. The destruction, reminding me of the beach at Guam, chewed up and pitted by artillery shells during our wartime invasion, sickened me. Split and shattered stumps, large and small fallen trees, broken boughs, and ripped branches of dying leaves were everywhere, lying among huge clods of dirt and grass that had been scraped up by the backhoe. In the chaos, it was almost impossible to make out where the horse trail had been that we had built along the ditch. Torn junipers, wild roses, bulldozed apple trees, and masses of yellow clover, knocked down and left strewn together on the bank, hid the trail.

The explanation was that there had been poor communication between the ditch company and the backhoe operator, and the episode had been an accident. The backhoe operator had been ordered by the ditch company to clean the ditch where it ran through our land, and although the company had no easement on our property and should have sought Kathy's permission to carry out the cleaning, no one had informed her of the company's plans. When the backhoe operator drove his rig onto our place, Kathy was not there and, apparently with a go-ahead from the ditch company to cut down whatever trees interfered with his ability to get the backhoe into and out of the ditch, it looked like he had decided that everything was in his way and that he had permission to uproot, bulldoze, and scrape away grass, bushes, trees, and almost everything in sight.

In my mind, the dreadful ruination settled the future of our ranch. With so many of the trees gone, the birds and their voices were gone. With mounds of dirt replacing the stands of tall grass, the deer and the

AMJ, Jr., age 83, on our Oregon ranch.

smaller animals disappeared. I was convinced that Betty and I were too old to
bring the place back, too old to redo the
work we had put into it over the course of
many years, and I decided that we should now sell the ranch and leave its
fate to others. I was too pained by my decision, however, to discuss it yet
with Betty or with the rest of the family or to take it up with a Realtor, and
I put off doing so until we would leave for the East in the fall. As the summer progressed, I kept seeing Kathy, my grandsons, and other members of
the family continuing to swim and fish in the lake and enjoy the place as if
nothing had happened, but at the same time busy themselves picking up
the wreckage, repairing fences and gates, and helping to restore bits and
pieces of the property. Gradually, aware of how much the ranch had come
to mean to them, the decision I had made weakened, and by the end of the
summer I had replaced it instead with a determination to keep the property and, unlike the apocryphal story of my father's father, not turn our
backs on Oregon, but restore and save the ranch for our children and
grandchildren, who appeared so much to love it. They, too, would have an
"old West" of their own to look back upon, and it would include our Oregon home.

This revised decision was a good one. With the help of lots of people,
we brought back the ranch, planting new trees, restoring the grassland,
and eliminating the scars of broken stumps and chewed-up earth. By

1998, when Betty and I celebrated our fiftieth wedding anniversary at the ranch, the deer were back, the horned owls, the hawks, and the eagles had returned, as well as the songbirds along the ditch. Elsewhere in Wallowa County, it happened to be a memorable year for the Nez Perce Indians also. With the help of financial gifts and grants and the warmhearted support of a largely new generation of young, caring non-Indian families and business and civic leaders in the county, a coalition of Nez Perces and whites had purchased 160 acres in the county for a permanent Nez Perce Indian encampment and interpretive center. After 121 years of exile, the people of Chief Joseph had come back too. At their powwow that summer, the expressions on their faces were beautiful. They were home again at last. And in a way, I could share their feelings. So was I.

INDEX

Page numbers in *italics*
refer to illustrations.

PHOTO CREDITS

A NOTE ABOUT THE AUTHOR

ALVIN M. JOSEPHY, JR., is the author of many
award-winning books, including *The Patriot Chiefs*,
The Indian Heritage of America, *Now That the Buffalo's
Gone*, and *The Civil War in the American West*. He has
been a vice president and editor of *American Heritage*
magazine, the founding chairman of the board of
trustees of the Smithsonian's National Museum of
the American Indian, and president of the Western
History Association.

A NOTE ON THE TYPE

This book was set in Janson, a typeface long thought to have been made by the Dutchman Anton Janson, who was a practicing typefounder in Leipzig during the years 1668–1687. However, it has been conclusively demonstrated that these types are actually the work of Nicholas Kis (1650–1702), a Hungarian, who most probably learned his trade from the master Dutch typefounder Dirk Voskens. The type is an excellent example of the influential and sturdy Dutch types that prevailed in England up to the time William Caslon (1692–1766) developed his own incomparable designs from them.

Composed by North Market Street Graphics,
Lancaster, Pennsylvania
Printed and bound by Quebecor Printing,
Martinsburg, West Virginia
Designed by Anthea Lingeman